EXCUSE ME, MR. PRESIDENT

The Message of The Broken Eagle

Rick Paul Springer

Broken Eagle Press

P.O. Box 402

Arcata, California 95518

EXCUSE ME, MR. PRESIDENT

The Message of The Broken Eagle

"Rick Paul Springer's Excuse Me, Mr. President is a humorous, deadly serious, incisive look at the soft underbelly of the American System — its nuclear empire, its absurd leadership, its violence, racism and prisons. Moreover, Springer does more than provide perspective, he supplies examples; he has done something about official lying and crime."
     — Phil Berrigan - Spiritual Leader and 60's Plowshare Activist

"Like Nathan Hale and Thomas Paine, Rick Springer is an authentic American hero, and his book is an insistent wake-up call for peace activists everywhere."
     — Wavy Gravy - Woodstock MC & Rainbow Shaman

"Rick Springer has an important story to tell, more precisely, three interrelated stories. One is about the dangers of nuclear testing. Another deals with his varied attempts to alert the public and the obstacles he encountered. The third describes the realities of federal prisons to which he was committed for the crime of crying out a warning. Each of these stories deserves a broad hearing, as does Springer himself."
     — Bruce Lincoln - Professor History of Religions;
     University of Chicago; Author: *Death, War & Sacrifice;*
     Authority: Construction & Corrosion

"I support Rick Springer's stand in defense of our Mother Earth and against this nuclear nonsense that is poisoning all the life."
     — Corbin Harney - The Spiritual Leader of the
     Western Shoshone; Author of *"The Way It Is"*

About the Author

Rick Paul Springer is an advocate of nonviolent civil resistance for social change. He has been a wilderness survival guide for abused teens, an Emergency Medical Technician, an Alaskan salmon fisherman, a boat carpenter, a bicycle mechanic and an anti-nuclear organizer.

He has been a guest on CBS This Morning, NBC Crosstalk, and numerous television and radio shows. His articles have been published in The New Age Journal, Z Magazine, The Las Vegas Review Journal, and the Compendium Newsletter.

Cover Photograph by Jim Laurie.

Of 25,000 submissions, Las Vegas Review Journal photographer Jim Laurie, won the Award of Excellence in 1992 on the 50th annual Pictures of the Year competition for his still camera shot of Reagan and the author. The nuclear mushroom cloud inset is the 1970 supposed-to-be-underground, nuclear bomb test, Baneberry, at the Nevada Test Site that vented radiation some 18,000 feet into the atmosphere.

Book cover layout and design courtesy of Eric Brookey.

eric@iongrfx.com
www.iongrfx.com
707.822.7596

CONTENTS

Introduction

Part One:
The Hundredth Monkey and The Broken Eagle

Part Two:
The Degradation Ceremony

Part Three:
I Am Your Spy

Introduction

There is a Zen saying that goes, "I am the story of my life."

In the early '90s a group of archaeologists were employed to write the Environmental Impact Statement (EIS) for the Yucca Mountain Nuclear Waste Repository. They did a very commendable job researching this area of Nevada, adjoining the Nevada Test Site (NTS), by inviting the several local tribes to comment on the area in question. They solicited lore of all genre from the many responding elders of the several bands of Shoshone and Paiute.

With the elders' help, the researchers uncovered many details about the plant, animal, and historical aspects of this area being proposed for a style of decimation perhaps never before equaled: the United States main, high level nuclear waste dump.

But what these scientists were able to discern and, even more impressive, convey through their research, was the validity of the indigenous perspective of 'interconnectedness.' These scientists knew who would most likely be reading their report, government and corporate bureaucrats, who after a lifetime of bottom line figure shuffling were very unaware of this reality.

The native elders explained that when you disturb a hillside in this desert valley, the plants on the other side of the valley know it and are affected by it. Our inability to prove it, in scientific terms, is only an example of the present limits and frailties of science.

I did not walk the trail of tears with indigenous people as they watched their loved ones die from the bitter cold during the march to the reservation. My father has not been hung from a tree in Central America or burned by hooded men on a sticky southern night. I did not survive Hiroshima nor was I one of our many soldiers still suffering radiation poisoning from going in to clean it up. It was not my daughter suffering chemotherapy whose soft downy hair fell from her innocent head as she died in her mothers's arms.

US courts claim that I do not have 'standing' to empathize, but there is another piece of Zen wisdom that says, "You need climb a mountain only part way to know it is a mountain," and suffering is like that. You don't have to experience the nuclear holocaust, to be baked alive in a giant microwave oven, to know how painful it is, how wrong it is, and more important, that we must work to prevent it.

From whence comes this empathy? The same as love, it is taught from youth. My Mother taught me empathy, enough any way, to cry with the suffering, and to cry loud.

The segments of this story that depict the court scenes are taken verbatim from trial transcripts. They are a part of public record. They have been edited but I have attempted to include examples of my own failures as well as those of court bias and manipulation.

This book is about the myriad of prisons we create by the acceptance of violence as a means of conflict resolution and the victory and function of refusing that option. It is about the message of the Broken Eagle, because eagles have incredible perspective and vision. And that which is broken and heals is forever stronger in the broken places. We can't heal from a place of denial. Use your eagle eyes when reading.

For Life,
Rick Springer
1997

Grandfather,
look at our brokenness

We know that in all creation
Only the human family
Has strayed from the Sacred Way

We know that we are the ones
Who are divided
And we are the ones
Who must come back together
To walk in the Sacred Way

Grandfather,
Sacred One,
Teach us love, compassion, and honor
That we may heal the earth
And heal each other

— Ojibway Prayer —

Part One

The Hundredth Monkey and The Broken Eagle

Chapter One
CRUEL AND USUAL

* * * * *

LATE AUGUST 1993

BAM!!! BAM!!! BAM!!!

The hardened-steel hinge bolts held fast in the concrete wall anchors while the door rattled with an unforgiving shiver. It was not a nuclear bomb test, but it rattled my bolts in the same fashion.

BAM!!! BAM!!! BAM!!!

The red spot was now a splattered and running rivulet down the forehead of an old, toothless, dried-shrunken-apple of a face and with each BAM!!! the blood was beginning to spread on the four inch window slot. It began as a monk's sacred dab on the central upper forehead and became an evolving Rorschach inkblot test. The BAM!!! of human forehead on the cruel and usual plate of unforgiving glass became sand paper on raw nerves as the room full of pretrial inmates carried on, trying to ignore, slapping their dominoes louder on the Formica checkerboard tables. Some squirmed on their Rubbermaid Roughneck plastic stools, master-idiot-box-couch-potatoes with no couch, and the incessant circle jerks, walking lap after lap, trying to burn up some of the energy that was driving old Sparky insane.

Yeah, Sparky was playing with a short deck. But what do you expect in the Cuckoo's Nest of a federal prison, cell on cell, cage on cage, stacked like chicken boxes, lights blaring 24 hours a day, hatching daily the infertile eggs of stupor and exhaustion. Unit A of North Las Vegas Detention Center (NLVDC) resembled the rec area of a low-budget, steerage-class yacht cruiser. Door after blue door encircled the central tables and stools in a two-tiered horseshoe.

And there was poor Sparky, nothing more than the town Bo Jangles, harmless and rather endearing, engaged in a public escape attempt by beating himself senseless. His crime? Well, old Sparky ran his mouth in a Montana bar while on a thirty year drunk. The trouble was, he yelled the wrong thing about the wrong person. As Ronald Reagan's face appeared on the TV above the bar, he yelled, "I'm gonna go shoot that sonuvabitch." There you have it. "Threatening a former President" is a felony in America.

I had something in common with Sparky. I too was charged with threatening a former president, the same one in fact, Ronald Reagan. I now lived with Sparky and ninety others crammed into this lockdown facility, plopped along with the city of Lost Wages, smack in the middle of the Nevada desert.

With each lap of the rec area, we came by Sparky's cell window and there was his face, now a bloody auditioneer for Psycho 3D. "Sparky, come on! Stop that! It's okay," I pleaded, trying to command and soothe at the same time.

"Get away from that cell, Springer!" Officer Green ordered with a misplaced, bucktoothed grin connecting his ears.

"Get the nurse over here and get him some medication!" I ordered.

"Don't worry about it, Springer. He's okay."

I told officer Green, "I'm an Emergency Medical Technician," and made my best effort to convince him that the human skull was not designed to take that kind of abuse. I explained that the impact Sparky was exerting on his skull could cause a subdural hematoma, a bruise to the brain which is often fatal. Green's grin stayed on his face like he was gloating in his power while I was accenting head, hematoma, swelling, and fatal. "And what are you smiling about?"

"I always smile, Springer," but like a baby that just crapped his pants, his grin faded to a scowl.

"Well, then I suggest you get some therapy for that because this is not a situation to be smiling about."

"Move on, Springer," the scowl turned deeper and more hostile.

I continued my laps, circling the officer's desk, breathing deeply as Sergio, a portly, Hispanic inmate came along side. "I'm with you on this one, Springer. If you want to do a protest, let me know. I can't believe they stuck Sparky in with Ichabod again. He'd drive anyone nuts."

Sparky's cellmate, Ichabod, didn't talk enough for anyone to know just what his crime was. He was a tall, gaunt man, with hollow, bruised eye sockets and a ragged haircut. His silent glare at the floor, while pacing with his hands behind his back, gave him the aura of a worm-hunting chicken. And his vacancy sign, lights on but nobody home, was more than his cellce, old Sparky could stand, day after day, week after week. I noticed officer Green on the phone.

"C'mon Sparky! Give it a rest!" Sergio pleaded as the head banging became a cadence.

"Shut the fuck up!" Screamed a voice from another lockdown cell.

"It seems the guards thrive on creating these battles," I complained. "It breaks up the boredom of sitting at that desk doing nothing for ten hours. 'Hey we'll torment the inmates.' I'm not worried about my safety from 'the alleged' criminals. It's the guards, I'm worried about! I haven't seen a fight in here yet that couldn't have been avoided by common sense from the guards."

"Yeah, true, but not all of them are jerks, Ritzman's okay, O'Hare's not bad, --" Sergio reminded me.

"Hey, here comes Nurse Rachet!" Gilbert was the five foot tall male nurse that had tried to talk me out of my eighteen day fast when I first entered NLVDC.

"Hey Gilbert, I'm thinking of filing a malpractice suit for gross medical negligence. This guy's been smashing his head bloody for fifteen minutes and you're in the next building finishing your burger and fries. How'd you like to be a star on `Sixty Minutes' or `Donahue'... cuz it's coming up, Bud!" I was too disgusted to be nice.

"Go away, Springer," he ordered with a brush of his hand.

"I'd love to, but maybe you've forgotten the locked steel doors, the razor wire and the ten foot wall."

Sparky's cell door was popped open by the door monitor in the glass booth. Gilbert entered, and in three minutes Sparky was slumbering and slobbering off into the dreamless state of Thorazine, the government's version of 'never, never land'.

* * * * *

"Satan's Mama left him when he was only three
His Papa was a convict in the penitentiary
By the age of seven he survived by beg, borrow and steal
By nine he learned to sell a soul and close a drug deal
And still young Satan, yeah, Satan needs love too."
RP Springer Prison Poetry 1993

* * * * *

The plastic dog food tray came through a slot in the door. "Coffee or juice, Springer?" Queried Fat Thomas, the inmate trustee.

"Yeah, I'll have the brown water. Hey, what do we call this mystery meat, Thomas?"

"Road kill. But hey, if you want to trade we can arrange that." Fat Thomas did lots of trading as a unit orderly. Seemed he ate most of his trades himself.

"How `bout a banana?"

"We can work that out in the mornin'." Thomas' business was booming. At 6'2", 240 pounds, he resembled a sloppy, baby orca whale with a designer haircut. The blacks in prison had taken hair styling to the limits of art. Thomas' was very short cropped with an intricate Egyptian border running just over the ears and around the skull. Probably cost him three Snickers. Others spent the day creating a variety of corn row braids, therapy as effective and intricate as basket weaving.

In each of fifty cells sat two men, wolfing instant mashed potatoes, nearly brown green peas and piles of jello.

"Yumm, hospital food. Well, they wouldn't want to feed us too well for court. We might be able to think," I told John the Mormon, my present cell mate. John's big time federal crime?... drunk driving at Lake Mead, a National Recreation Area.

The cell door popped open and Officer Donelly, an over-stuffed pillow with a belt in the middle, filled the opening. "Pack it up, Springer." He announced with smug relish.

"Pack it up? Where am I going?"

"Lockdown," he goaded.

"What for? I haven't done anything."

"Just pack it up. I don't know. I was told to put you in lockdown."

Donelly leaned on the steel jamb as I gathered my blanket, toothbrush, comb, and papers. "Something about you refusing an officer's order."

"I didn't refuse any order." But it dawned on me. "Ahhh! This is about my insistence on decent treatment of mental inmates. Gilbert didn't like what I said about lawsuits and the media."

"Fine. Now get moving!"

I stepped out onto the catwalk and turned left, moving around the horseshoe to the corner of the unit and into the lockdown cell. The door slammed behind me. Donelly, like many guards, loved to accent the trappings of power in prison.

A rude voice beat under the cracks and through the food slot from the cell next door. In a mock Martin Luther King Jr. oration, the voice proclaimed, "I have a dream that someday little nigger boys will diddle little white girls and mulatto babies will rule the world."

My neighbor, Olson, was a demented genius. He could find and push buttons on anyone and he loved it. He was perhaps the freest man in prison, totally uncontrollable, unafraid of death or pain -- they were more than friends, they were mentors. At four years old he had become his Pop's best drinking buddy, sleeping in the car as the old man closed the bar. He had been beaten and left for dead too many times, as testified by the scars on his bald, Frankenesque skull and the two inch bony protrusions sticking grotesquely out of his elbows. His gaitered limping walk told of broken legs and bad healing. His rap sheet, which he passed around like a diploma, was proof that he had been jailed over 56 times, most recently for assault on a police officer. "Death, Death, give me Death" he loved to scream at 3:30 AM. "Just stick my feet in a bucket of cold water and turn on the juice," he taunted, alluding to the electric chair. "Any of you Mother Fuckers want to come along?"

"Springer, that you next door? Welcome, Neighbor. I'm the Welcome Wagon of lockdown".

"Shut up, Olson!" Yelled the guard.

I sucked a deep breath and knelt to pray. "I'm weak. I need you, God." My eyelids sagged. I held my headache in my hands as another day's gauntlet refused to come to an end. "Our Father, who art in heaven. Just how did I get here in hell?"

THE WONDER YEARS 1-35

It was March of 1951, the 23rd to be exact. My mother checked in at a small, local hospital. The Women's Hospital of Pasadena, California they called it. They razed that hospital since, but on that day, I remember, it was an especially bad day, it was my birth day. As fate would have it, they opened the Nevada Test Site that same year and began detonating nuclear bombs in our own backyard.

My mama was one of two twins, the lucky female in this case. Born to a German couple visiting the states, she was left behind, undesirable as fodder for the Nazi war machine. The good German patriots left her in the adoption center.

I say she was the lucky female because the Harpers who adopted her were good, salt of the earth people. Coming from Kansas to the grapes of wrath, they had in them just enough Cherokee to know that the Earth was God, and that everything, even the Rock people, were alive. Gramps was a 'health food nut,' as the nutritionally aware were called in the forties, and a hypnotist. He took baby Paula gold panning in the San Bernardino Mountains. I guess that's where my mother got her love of the outdoors.

Chuck Ewing, mama's beau and my sperm donor, loved his motorbike too much or was playin' around. Story goes, he wanted us brats in the sack by the time he got home from work. Mom decided her kids were not going to play second fiddle to a Harley nor she to another woman. Adios, Chuck E.

Mom was off for a job at the Cornet Five and Dime warehouse in Pasadena. Meanwhile, big brother John, my hero, and I were left to a variety of baby-sitters and often Gram 'n Gramps, none of which, though, were any match for John and me when we were 6 and 3.

Mom was a good looker, but more important, she had inherited a great heart. It wasn't in the blood or the genes. It was taught. She found another love in Jerry Springer. He married Mom, became our Dad and promptly trucked us off to the YMCA Indian Guides and then to the Mojave desert. Chuck E. was never to be seen again, and while I may be a little curious about the guy, I can't say I suffered any by his absence.

Gerald was a disciplinarian. I loved him, but he scared the crap out of me.

He seemed to have a clear grasp on justice though. Climbing on the school roof brought three swats on bare thighs with a wooden paddle, stealing candy from George's Jip Joint was five swats, and sassing Mom got you hit in the head and knocked off your feet. Some might call it child abuse but when offered the option of 3 swats or 3 months grounding, we invariably chose short term abuse over long term imprisonment. Don't get me wrong: that paddle stung like hell, but we liked confinement even less.

On Sunday mornings Gerald and Paula took a break by dressing us kids up in our munchkin suits and sending us off to the Altadena First Baptist church. I'll never forget a pale-brown, crushed-velvet dress my sister Roxanne wore. She was our Baby and we loved her. Four years later, Boo-Boo Bear took over as the family baby. Her real name was Sheree.

John was a jock with brains, which some may think is a contradiction in terms, but he got almost all A's in school and I never even saw him crack a book. He had so many sports ribbons that Mom had to make an album out of 'em. He gave me my first car, a turquoise 55 Chevy, for fifty bucks. Now he's a cop in LA, but I've always said that if there has to be cops, my brother's a good one. He was so good, it was enough to make you sick, so that's what I did.

I excelled in an entirely different direction. By six I mastered the petite mal seizure...day dreaming. By eight I learned to mix a concoction at home of scrambled eggs, canned dog food, and ketchup, to carry to school in a dixie cup and then chuck on the floor in class while making a vomiting sound. I did my own scientific experiments in the nurse's office by rubbing the thermometer in my fingers, creating enough heat to wrack that mercury to 99.8. I was sick a lot -- mostly from school. The downside was that Mom was into enemas as the panacea of all childhood ailments.

I like to blame it on my sugar addiction. It was serious. In the fourth grade I had my own paper route. The Dutch Oven Bakery gave us all their leftovers, and that box of sugar cubes by the coffee machine almost jumped into my pockets. They used to have coke machines at the car wash/gas station where the bottles lay on their sides. We learned that with a cup and a bottle opener you could drink about eight bottles of Orange Crush, Dr. Pepper, or Coke every Thursday mornin'.

In the seventh grade, I landed a job as candy man at George's Jip Joint and filled my own pockets before heading to class at Elliot Jr. High. It's hard to imagine how much candy I really ate but ten bars at one sitting was not unusual. You'd think a whole can of Betty Crocker's chocolate cake frosting would kill a skinny twelve year old outright, but I survived.

It was always a strange paradox I lived. While I won Bibles and pins for memorizing "For God so loved the world" and bringing the most kids to Bible school, it seemed God wanted to test me from the beginning.

I talked Roscoe Good into running away with me and since we were never comin' home, we needed some pictures of women with us so we could remember what they looked like. Before we ran off, I broke into Dad's garage to steal the 'girlie pictures' from the cupboard doors, the sweetest contraband of a youth's life.

Blame it on Hansel and Gretel, but the truth is, I was scared of witches. So I talked Roscoe into scrapping our life-in-the-wilderness plan after a night of terror. The cops busted us walking home. For the first of only two times I've ever heard, Dad swore: "You think you're so damn smart." Actually, I think that I was convinced, at eight, that I was thoroughly stupid.

Mom asked me the next day, "Did you get in your Father's garage and take anything?"

The execution I imagined for theft of girlie pictures was far too gruesome, "No, Mom," I chirped.

I wanted to scream 'foul' at her next tactic when she said, "Do you swear to God?"

I learned my first lesson of the double bind, damned if you do and damned if you don't. I knew from experience how hard Dad could swing that paddle and while I expected God could strike you dead, it had yet to be proven beyond hearsay.

"Yes, Mom, I swear to God" I spoke in my most confident voice. She bought it, or so it seemed, because I walked away from an age of innocence and entered my real escapades. Oh, I still got saved by Jesus every six months or so. It was strange how being saved wore off, but during the same era I was being saved, I took furloughs from my morning paper delivery to roll my pant legs up and wade in the Catholic grotto to dip out the silver. It was more profitable than paper delivery, and after all, they were Catholics, heathens of some sort, drinking blood and eating Jesus in wafer form.

I was the kid on the block who took in all the baby birds, and even though each one died, I kept eyedropping them milk sop. I did operate on one pigeon with my dissecting kit, pulling out a BB, and he healed and flew away. It was a victorious day when I chucked him up in the air with all the other pigeons at Elliot Junior High. They say pigeons are like flying rats, but to me it was damn near a calling to be become a healer, never mind those other fifteen dead chirpers. I graduated from aspiring entomologist to veterinarian.

John Muir High School was predominately black, but my mother had been adamant about people of color, any color. I was taught, besides singing in Sunday school, "Red and Yellow, Black and White, They're all precious in His sight", that people are all the same. As kids, our older black neighbors had John and me over for lunch so much, they seemed like an extra set of grandparents. While I remember they were black, it seems as unimportant as a good suntan.

I worked over 50 different jobs by age 35: from pizza delivery to auto mechanic, from Bank of America payment processor to restaurant cook, from boat carpenter in Mattapoisett, Massachusetts to bicycle salesman in Kirkland, Washington. I worked in the Merchant Marine on the Great Lakes and salmon fished in Alaska. I wrote for a small newspaper in Big Bear, California. I've worked in cabinet shops, built furniture, pounded nails with framers from Las Vegas to New Bedford, repaired plumbing, hung sheetrock and installed electric. I drove an English double decker bus in Traverse City, Michigan for two summers.

I worked with abused kids in a great program called Beartooth Wilderness Survival Schools in the Trinity Alps and the Marble Mountains of Northern California. I was a Youth Services Specialist with Redwood Community Action Agency and was on the Runaway Homeless Youth Hotline responding at 2 o'clock in the morning to cold and hungry runaways. I couldn't see any distinction between them and me. Seemed like just yesterday I was that troubled teen myself. I wrote a program for Child Welfare called Teens on the Trail, presenting wilderness experience as therapy for abused teens. I staffed and organized several backpacking trips for those teens.

Outdoor experience became my church. Rockclimbing, bicycle riding, sailing, running; there's something about the pumping of blood, dripping of sweat, air bolting in and out of your lungs like a bellows fanning a fire, cold biting cheeks or sun burning them, wind and clouds and colors... for me, that's religion beyond anything that can be performed in a building.

In Washington State, in my early twenties, I went to the Reverend Sun Myung Moon Christian Crusade. The Moonies impressed me about as much as the Krishna man at the market. After discovering that I was not going to give him a donation for his gift of a free book, he jerked it out of my arms and ran off. That spirituality stuff can be sticky, I learned.

After backpacking from the Olympics to the Adirondacks, I had developed my own spirituality. What amazed me was my discovery that as Columbus didn't discover America, an empty continent, I didn't discover a new spirituality, but an ancient one.

I realized what Everett Ruess described as "Beauty so awesome as almost kills a man just to look at it." I felt I could die at any moment and have been blessed beyond my due. I began to feel as though I owed some debt, that I had some obligation to see balance restored.

In my mid-thirties I married the Hundredth Monkey, a project to stop nuclear testing. While I tried to have other relationships during that organizing time, those women sensed they were only the mistress. They knew I was committed to the monkey on my back. And now, the monkey and I were both in prison.

An hour later the cell door buzzed open, and another inmate in gray smock and pants walked in.

"I'm your new roommate. The name's Lenny." He extended his hand.

"Whew, I was afraid they were gonna' put me in with some nappy-headed nigger," he spat.

I took the offered hand slowly, assessing my new cellmate. A cautious "Hey," was all I could offer.

"Do you mind if I draw on some of your paper here? If I can use some of your colored pencils, I can make a little commissary money selling artwork," Lenny claimed.

"Sure, go for it!"

"I don't know about you but I'm a member of the White Aryan brotherhood. I say we got to keep our people strong and pure. These jungle bunnies are takin' over Man, and that is not happening."

"Let's just lay it out right from the git-go," I offered. "I've heard every reason why I should hate every race and religion on earth since I've been in prison and I don't buy into any of it. If it's not the blacks, the spics, the Jews, the Mormons, or the Indians wrecking this country, then it's the damn feminist women out to castrate males or the sonofabitchin' Japs taking over the economy. It's just an excuse to hate, an excuse for nuclear bombs."

"Well, you got to admit, it's just a fact of life, Man. The niggers had one of the richest nations on earth, oil and diamonds and gold and what did they do with it. Nothing! They are a lazy, stupid people. Did one nigger invent a Chevrolet or even a toilet." Lenny's hate bubbled over as he rhymed Chevrolay and toilay.

Great, I thought, 24 hours a day in lockdown with a full tilt racist. I was compelled to stand up to racism, but I was too weak to be sweet about it. "Oh, right, because the blacks, the Indians, the indigenous people never felt the need to create technology, because they were content with the cultures they created that went from season to season in harmony with this earth, they're stupid. No, think again, my man." I fell into the LA ghetto slang I grew up with. "Native people, and those are the roots of the blacks, had cultures and ceremonies as complex as any on earth."

"But yaa," I was rolling now, "the smart honkies, in your mind, jump out of bed into their Chevrolet, sit on their toilet hemorrhoids for an hour in smog laden, rush-hour traffic and create more stress than being stalked by a jungle lion. Yaa, these same Aryan people invented smog alerts and MultiPure water filters. Tough luck for the poor people that can't afford the filter."

"Well, man, if you can't see it now, prison will teach you. I wasn't so prejudiced before I got here." Lenny was not convinced.

"To me, an asshole is an asshole. They come in all colors and so do human beings."

But Lenny wanted the last line. "Weeelll, just you wait till one of them colored human beings wants in your daughter's panties."

Chapter Two
BREAKDOWN:
THE ROOTS OF VIOLENCE

*"Nonviolent resistance avoids not only external physical vio-
lence but also internal violence of the spirit. The nonviolent
resister not only refuses to shoot an opponent but also refuses
to hate him or her. At the center of nonviolence stands the
principle of love." — Martin Luther King, Jr.*

The door opened and slammed shut behind me. I was home. Lockdown
with Lenny.

"So, have a good day in court with that cute attorney of yours? I hear she's
part black?" His sexism was stronger than his racism.

I sidestepped his interest in my attorney, "Not exactly. They basically refused my defense. No expert witnesses, no movie, no books on the testing
issue, but I do get to defend myself with assistance of counsel. That's good.
They're gonna let me talk, but they won't let me prove any of it."

"Yeah, sounds like they gonna get yo ass! Whaddya expect? Stroll up there
on stage and smash Ronnie Raygun's trophy. You're lucky they didn't drag you
outside and shoot you. So just what the hell happened with you and Reagan
anyway? I never did hear the story. You *are* the guy that attacked Reagan,
aren't you?"

"I never attacked anybody, but I'm not really in the mood for that story. It's
been a long day." I tried to escape by staring into the black fall night; through the
half barren branches I could see the silhouette of Red Rock Canyon and even
with the lights of Las Vegas, Venus was hanging just over that shaded line. The
petroglyphs I'd found in those rocks filled the walls of my mind. I couldn't
decide if I had come from the past or returned from the future but I remembered my lineage.

Somehow you had to get out of this building on a rec yard pass or a medical
excuse might do it. Next you had to get over or under the 8' chain-link fence
nailed down to the asphalt. I remembered the one U-nail that had pulled loose,
and thought I could shimmy under it rather than climb over the two rolls of

razor wire woven through the top. Then you had to have a partner to boost you or be one hell of a slam dunker to jump high enough to grab the top of that block wall, and there you were at the front entrance of the city library in prison clothes. But it could be done. It had been done already in NLVDC's first six months. Rumor was, the escapees half bled to death though. Prison guard rumor, I suspected. I knew I was here for the duration. I wanted to test the jury trial system despite rumors of a 97.3% federal conviction rate!

Lenny's bored voice droned in the background while I daydreamed. "Hey, I'm talkin to you, Dude. Anybody home? Hey, you havin' an out of body experience? Out there flyin around?" Lenny pried like he was taunting a mental patient.

"Yeah, Lenny, I'm here," my voice was short and impatient. The five by ten foot cell was getting smaller. Solitary lockdown was more appealing with each tick of my heart. I sucked a few deep breaths of the stale air coming through the air ducts of the twenty cells before mine. I knew I was getting the cold again. I remembered Melanie's song, "We were so close there was no room. We bled inside each others womb. We all had caught the same disease. It was a time for peace." "Yeah Lenny, let's give it a rest."

"Man, are you edgy!" Lenny kept on. "Hey, I'm supposed to have a hearing and get out of here, anyway." Lenny leaned on the door and started banging. He got the guard's attention, and through the glass motioned for the guard to pop his door.

The door opened, and Newson, a Bart Simpson look-a-like, stood impatiently, "What's up?"

Lenny seized his opportunity, "Hey Newson, I put in a kite to Director Brown about my release and expected an answer a couple of days ago. The Disciplinary Hearing lady said there was nothing keeping me in here. Could you check on it?"

"Hey Newson," I decided to ask a question myself. "Could you find out when my hearing is going to happen. I've already been in lockdown three days without a word."

"Yeah, I'll check, Springer," he concluded. The door banged closed.

Lenny turned to face me as I was lying on my bunk. "That was rude, man."

"What are talking about?"

"Well, I work for hours to get him up here to check on my release and you just interrupt and distract him."

"Newson is no wizard but I think he can handle two questions at the same time."

"No, you just butted in. I've been trying all day to get that jerk over here and you don't even have the respect to let me finish."

"I thought you were finished, Lenny. Let's drop it. We're not going anywhere."

But he couldn't let it go, and I was losing it, too. I felt the concrete walls struggling to contain the foul smelling energy swirling within the cell. As I jumped from my bunk my body was posturing, wanting to scream, "Fuck you, Asshole." The devil whispered in my ear, `Go for it. Beat his head in. Grab the few strands on his straggly, bald head and smash it against the floor until he shuts up.'

I pushed by him to the door and gave an open palm karate punch to the glass with enough intensity to impress Newson. I was not a door pounder. Newson knew I didn't cry 'wolf' unless there was a wolf.

"What do you want, Springer?" He half yelled as the door buzzed open.

I began slowly and deliberately, "You can take that asshole out of this cell," pointing over my shoulder, "Or you can take this asshole out of the cell," pointing to myself, "but if you leave both the assholes together, there is going to be a bloody asshole."

Newson motioned for me to come out of the door. "Com'on out," he ordered. He directed me to walk towards the end of the catwalk and signaled to the door monitor to pop 48, the last on the run. The door popped and he pushed me in.

Another five-by-ten cell, it smelled like rancid urine from the prior occupant who had peed all over just to piss off the guards. Some of these guys were sick animals, sick from a lifetime of abuse, and they had learned to abuse back. I was feeling sick myself.

I fell on my knees to the mattress crumpled on the floor, tears trickling down my cheeks. 'God, they're getting me.' I knew how close I was to beating his head in. With all my nonviolence training, all my speeches to the power of Satyagraha, soul force, I cried out loud, "My soul hurts!" 'Did you go through this, Gandhi? How did you do it?' My lips trembled, 'God, in just two months, is this a nervous breakdown?' A sense of utter failure consumed me. The days of immersion in the fight or flight response had worn me out. And flight was not an option. I had learned that emotional battles can beat you as thoroughly as a fist.

I commanded myself back to the cell and started to pick up the toilet paper scattered in wet mucous wads around the floor, wiping the smeared, caked shit from the toilet seat before flushing. The blaring TV outside provided the background racket, a constant symphony of the world's destruction as Van Damn, Seagull, or Bruce Flea shot up the bad guys with machine guns, grenades, bombs and even hands and feet. I felt immersed in a war, and I was a prisoner.

I found a stub of a pencil with broken lead and used the rough concrete floor to sand a point. Torn pages of a Readers Digest offered enough blank edge to write on. I let my depression speak.

Disgust in Prison

Toilet paper in my ears
To wipe the shitty ass of sound
Heated debates over TV shows
Ping pong balls worth $420.00

Daddy, Daddy, can I go to my room
Mommy, Mommy, can I come out now
I wave my towel through my food slot
Yes I shakin a stick boss, Really!

75 watts, two feet from my face
Piles of straw and broken camels
Three days lockdown goes the threat
Lockaway asshole, you win.

I fought the law and we both lost
Nonviolence—a good rap at convenient times
Yes, Robb, more like Malcolm X, Crazy Horse or ?
Oh don't flatter myself

Kool-aid, Snickers, greasy fries
But I don't need a defense
Here's the soft belly
You can scoop out yesterday's undigested bile

My woman waits in the shower stall
I got prison push-up biceps
She'll want me tonight
Cuz I can kick ass now

Nineteen years old starin at fifteen years
Credit card scammer booking Costa Rica next month
Red and yellow, black and white
They're all precious in his sight
But flush the toilet anyway

So Jesus, where's Jesus?
Must be somewhere in despair, self spity
But hey, thanks Gideons
Cuz we'd be lost sheep without you

From that tiny cell, I began to drift back to my own experiences with violence. As if in a guided meditation, I saw myself first as a little boy.

Spring 1957

The doors of the city bus fold open with a pssshhhh and present two huge steps. A small boy crawls up. John, the older brother follows, reaches into his pocket and produces the tokens Mom had given him earlier that morning. John drops them into a strange glass box and Rick, the younger brother stands mesmerized as the coins bounce back and forth before his face. The bus driver reaches out and pulls a lever that allows the coins to disappear into the box below.

The two young boys take their seats at the very front of the bus. Rick climbs up and slides back until only his shoes stick over the edge of the green naugahyde bench. He is quite small for six years old. They ride down Lake Avenue into Pasadena and then right on Colorado Blvd. At nine, John is tall enough to reach up and pull the wire. "Brrrnnnnn" sounds the buzzer and they climb off at Marengo Blvd. John takes his mission seriously. Rick could wander off in the blink of an eye so John holds his jacket while Rick acts like a little mule pulling the plow to the YMCA.

Once indoors, the YMCA is an adventure. The smells are so distinct, the disinfectant, the chlorine of the swimming pool filling the locker room, the sweaty, dripping musk of the weight room and basketball court.

With gym trunks hanging to their bony knees, they climb the stairs around and around to the third floor. The basketball court spreads before them, and on the other end, kids are gathering with the coach. Rick looks wistfully at the trampoline folded up in the corner. He hopes for another opportunity to bounce and bounce and bounce.

John slaps him on the arm to get his attention. Rick follows after the other kids. They enter a specialized room. Ropes cordon off a square with pads at the corners. Rick and another youngster his size are hustled up to the front, as a peculiar, exciting energy begins to build. The older boys are jumping around, punching one another and pushing, in some game the little ones have yet to grasp.

John grabs Rick's' arm and raises it into the air while a huge, padded brown glove is slid on and tied around his wrist. With both hands covered, he is pushed under the ropes and onto the mats of the square they called the ring. He is hemmed in by ropes, while the other boys gather around the perimeter and begin a taunting, cheering cacophony of yells and commands.

Rick stands somewhat dumbfounded as another half-pint enters from the other side of the ring. He too has the big brown gloves lashed onto his hands and arms. His face is covered ear to ear with a broad grin as he approaches.

They stand in the raucous din, each facing a mirror of innocence about to be shattered.

They smile at each other, and shyly giggle as hoots of "Hit him" and "Git your dukes up" bombard their rabbit ears. Something breaks through into Ricks' consciousness as he is prompted to approach the other boy. He raises his glove, cocks back and smashes the other boy cleanly in the face. The world stops as the glove falls from the young victim to reveal the horror of pain, confusion and betrayal in a red flushed face. In an instant, a smiling, laughing, trusting countenance is turned to the primal scream of human existence. WHY??????????

Rick vomits at the horror he created. He throws his arms to the floor in disgust, his monstrous gloves slapping the mats. He turns and tromps from the room, refusing to return.

But my thoughts returned to a room I couldn't leave. Was Lenny the result of some betrayal of childhood innocence? I saw myself again, this time as a young man.

Summer 1975

"If you don't back off and leave me alone, I'm gonna smash your fucking teeth so far down your throat, you're gonna have to sit on your dinner to chew it, you son of a bitch." Rick spewed with an unmistakable tone of commitment.

The two hundred ten pound wheelsman backed his nose away from Rick's middle finger and stared in disbelief. "Hey, no problem, I didn't mean anything."

"Yeah, sure, you have been pushin' me for no reason since I got on board this ship." Rick walked on, convinced that he had made his point. He walked the length of the freighter, all four hundred feet to the focsle, went into his berth and rolled up into his upper bunk. He let out a giddy laugh remembering the terrified expression of the wheelsman. He had called Rick names and verbally abused him since he shipped out on the SS Joe Young, a tired old Great Lakes freighter built in 1913.

Perhaps it was Rick's long hair and scruffy beard that caused some of the old farts to give him the cold shoulder. Perhaps it was because he refused to throw the trash overboard at 5:00 AM when they were at sea. Whatever, Rick was sick of being called a hippie bastard when they had to communicate and ignored the rest of the time.

Rick remembered scenes from high school and the aggressive behavior of some of the black youth. It was a lesson from a more animal world, a response not just to a life but a history of racism and oppression. It was a lesson in the feelings of being a minority, a lesson of deliberate intimidation, the way of the

Alpha male, the pack and gang mentality.

It was a street education in the power of bluff. He had seen it time and again. "You messin wit da wrong nigga, my man." Talk big, talk committed and people would back down 90% of the time.

'Why do these assholes have to keep messin' with me?' But he lay in his bunk impressed with the power of bluff. Is that what you have to do to get a little respect in this merchant marine world?

The walls of a Merchant Marine focsle faded back into the walls of a jail cell. I shook my head as the visions continued, remembering the confused roots of my social activism in Southern California.

Summer 1977

He sat there with his back slumped against the wall slurping ice-cream through his beard, while the SoCal summer heat lingered in the early evening shade. The asphalt gave back the heat stored through the day, invisible waves creating a city mirage.

He unconsciously heard the chatter of other ice-cream junkies at the front of the store. As he sat there out of view, a bundle of trash flew by his head from around the corner of the building.

What is it that gives one person the desire to keep a clean nest while others are quite comfortable messing in everyone's? Is it in the genes, in the family atmosphere? Society had coined an expression for the type of human that throws trash around, litterbugs, but neither bugs nor pigs make a mess remotely resembling what humans do.

Rick stood up and walked around the corner into the light in front of the Baskin Robbins, "Ya know, it's strange! You guys look like big boys but you must be babies. Here is a trash can three feet from you and you toss your trash out into the parking lot." There I was, an adult male, glaring at three men as big as me, early thirties, licking away at the melting goo in their hands.

"Look, buddy, don't worry about it," one of them responded, perturbed that Ranger Rick had crawled out of the dark.

"I am worried about it! If three adult males can't get their trash in the can next to them, then..."

"Hey look, we'll pick it up," he interrupted in a tone of bothered appeasement.

"Good!" Rick concluded, and headed off to his car. He sat and watched, warming the Karmann Ghia's already warm engine as the three stood conferring. No one was making any move to get the trash. It appeared to have turned into a challenge.

Rick backed out of his slot, pulled alongside the front of the store, and leaning out the window, yelled, "Hey, are you gonna pick that trash up?"

"I said, don't worry about it!" The three stood glaring as one man yelled back.

Rick jerked on the parking brake and jumped out of the car. As he approached the men, he glared directly at the one on his right and swung a full punch into the face of the one on the left. Rick watched the man's head take off, dragging the body after it in a flying spin towards the ground. The middle man was now backing off in shock as Rick moved towards him to give him the same treatment. The customers in the store ran to the front window for a better view.

As Rick was cocking for another punch he heard the third man yelling, "I picked it up, all right, I picked up the trash." He screamed into Rick's ear from the side, waving the trash as proof.

Rick glanced over at the pleading man whose belligerence had changed to conciliation. "You could have saved your buddy a punch in the face if you had just picked it up in the first place," Rick commented sadly.

He jumped in the blue and white Ghia and motored off. The adrenaline in his veins was sandpaper on raw nerves. He got back to his friend's empty house and collapsed in a chair. "What have I done?" He moaned with his head in his hands. "Not only did I probably give that guy neck trouble for life but they will also probably dump their trash secretly forever just to get back at me." He spent the evening feeling miserable. You can't throw your trash all over but you can't hit people to get them to stop. He remembered a strange quote from a Kentucky hitchhiker he had once picked up. "You can't kill people just because they don't want Jesus!"

In my mind I went from scene to scene reliving my life experiences with violence and nonviolence. And then I watched an incident close to home, after I was beginning to study and learn the lesson of nonviolence.

Spring 1982

The screaming noise of a two-stroke motorbike raced into my consciousness and up the narrow road in front of my farmhouse in Humboldt County. I knew the bike was headed off to the county park and the fragile sand dunes ecosystem at Mad River Beach. I envisioned the endangered Menses Wallflower, the foxes, and the beach grasses at the end of the road. Town meetings had made some progress towards enforcing the laws and protecting the area, but it was a slow and frustrating process of change. Many of the law enforcement officers were actually off road vehicle riders themselves and were sympathetic and lenient towards other riders.

I remembered the officer that had asked me what I had against the off-roaders. "They're illegal in the dunes, isn't that enough?" I responded, incredulous.

The whaaaaaaa, whawhaaaaaaaa, whawhaaaaaaaaaaaaaaa would not leave my ears as the dunes were only two hundred yards away. I thought of calling the sheriff again. I'd printed copies of the county laws prohibiting vehicles in the dunes and passed them out at the park to educate people. I remembered the many hostile encounters when I gave copies to ATVers about to unload for a day of screaming through the dunes.

At the house I tried to focus on work, but the sound of ATVers was like a fly in my ear. After an hour of sand-flinging, vegetation-destroying donuts in the dunes, I couldn't help but hear the noise returning..

I walked out into the street. I was going to see that this guy knew that children and dogs lived in these houses, and that he couldn't fly at forty-five miles an hour past our homes when the sign said fifteen.

I put up my hand in the stop sign fashion, but the RPM's increased instead of decreasing. Okay, so be it, I resigned! I decided the guy was at least going to have to run me down to get by. I made a gesture for him to 'come on'

As the rider zoomed up he attempted to swerve around, but I latched onto his arm. At 45 MPH, I was dragged backwards 60 feet before the bike crashed into the bushes. I was up on my feet while the young man was still floundering in the brush.

"I'm sorry, I'm sorry!" The young man was begging for mercy. He probably thought that anyone that was nuts enough to drag him off of his flying motorbike was going to beat him as well.

I looked into his crying face and somehow saw something familiar. I threw my gloves down and helped the guy up. "You can't ride that uncorked noise maker like a maniac in those protected dunes. We have children and dogs living on this road."

"I'm sorry, I won't do it again." He agreed, still in tears.

"Are you all right?"

"Yeah, I'm okay."

November, 1985

Another great barn-dance fund-raiser in the Arcata farmlands was coming to an end, with Clan Dyken still jamming and the barn floor vibrating with dancing bodies. It was a chill fall night. A couple of locals with too much whiskey in their guts cruised by the front gate yelling obscenities. They hated the environmentalist/peace groups, who they believed were stealing their jobs and ruining their way of life in Humboldt County.

I was at the front gate collecting the last of the evening funds and boxes of canned goods. The donations were for the Dine people of Big Mountain, a tribe known to white people as Navaho. Our benefit dance was to support them in their resistance against the oppression of coal and uranium mining on their lands.

I noticed a single woman heading back to her car to go home, and decided I should accompany her for safety. As we walked down Mad River Road towards her car, we began to hear a violent yelling. "You just keep on going straight to your car, and lock the doors when you get in," I told her.

As we passed the scene of the ruckus, a man turned and saw us. "Who's the asshole that locked his bicycle to my fence?" He screamed in a fit. "It's one of those mother fuckers in that party." He continued to try to rip the bicycle off of the barbed wire strands to which it had been locked. He picked it up and smashed it down, jerked it up and tried to tear it away to no avail. In a bizarre way it was almost hilarious to watch, but the unleashed hate was sad to experience.

I glanced to see the woman shutting her door and starting the engine.

"You're the asshole that brought all these people out here aren't you?" He yelled, panting.

"I'm Rick Springer. I rent this farm from Pete Bussman."

"These people have no right to be here. We were fine before they came. Get those fuckers outta here. My granddaddy cut down and cleared all the trees in this whole area. How do like that! You good-for-nothing son of a bitch," he screamed, taunting and jumping in my face.

I stood there, the smell of whiskey filling my nostrils, our faces two inches apart. I left my arms dangling, aware of the imminent threat of a punch to the face. "I live in a house built out of redwood".

"Yeah and so do all those worthless, welfare bums in there" the young rancher said, pointing to the barn.

"No, those people are here to help support some native Americans who were here when your granddaddy showed up," I reminded him.

"Well, I respect that. I have some Indian friends that are good people, but I still don't like these scum coming out here. We built this place, all these farms; we built 'em," he punctuated his words by picking up the bike and smashing it to the ground one more time. He seemed to be tiring out.

I looked at him as he came back still challenging, "Well, God bless you," I told him.

"Well, I hope God blesses you all too, cuz someone has got to help your lame asses!" He conceded as he walked away.

I walked back to the gate.

"Are you all right, Rick?" Tom asked.

"Yeah, I think I'm learning how powerful nonviolence can be."

October 1993

I sat slumped on the cold concrete prison floor, mulling over my misadventures in violence and the lessons of nonviolence, when the cell door buzzed and popped open.

"Let's go, Springer," Newson ordered leading me three doors back and into the same old cell. There stood Lenny, busy with his papers and trinkets.

'An hour break and they're stuffing me back in with him,' I thought in wonder as the door closed.

"I'm going home. They found my paperwork. I'm outta here tonight." Lenny beamed, apparently oblivious to the confrontation only an hour ago.

"Really?" I had learned to trust nothing, nothing I read or heard and only half of what I saw in this life behind the wall.

"I'm gone, Dude, 'Free Bird,'" Lenny mimicked Lynard Skynard, "I must be traveling on Babe, cuz there's too many places I got to see. Yeehaw!" He stuck his hand towards me, offering a handshake.

"Hey, I want to apologize for being such a jerk. You're a good man. You don't belong here. I know you're right!"

As we shook hands, I felt even more a failure. I failed at loving the racist, the bigot; and here in the end, Lenny, a man who hated men simply for the color of their skin, was apologizing and commending me. Twenty minutes later, Lenny disappeared from the cell, the unit and, I hoped, the prisons of racism and hate.

I heard a roar from the unit floor in some response to the TV news and then I heard my name, "That's Springer. He's up there in lockdown right now." A round of applause burst forth, accompanied by hooting and hollering.

A face appeared in my door window, "Hey, you're on TV, man. Good job!"

"Get away from that cell, Lewis," yelled Newson.

Although most of the inmates had some idea of why I was in prison, media slander and bits of the truth left the picture vague and distorted. But anyone willing to make a stand against a system they knew to be oppressive, was a good man. In some strange way I had earned my place and some honor among thieves and dissidents.

Chapter Three
THE HUNDREDTH MONKEY

"Springer, get up. You're getting a hearing," Officer Martine informed me. I was instructed to follow two black ladies, Mrs. Sanders and Mrs. Thompson, dressed in their Sunday best, into the corner room reserved for haircuts, bible study and disciplinary hearings.

"Mr. Springer, we're the disciplinary hearing officers, and this is your hearing regarding your refusal of officers orders on October 5th. We have determined that you will remain in lockdown for three days should you be found guilty of insubordination."

"Well, I've already been lockdowned three days; so let's just forget this trial and get me out of lockdown, since I've already done the time, guilty or innocent."

Sergeant Ellingston, standing at the side, gave me an 'I'd-like-to-slap-you' glare.

"Well, Mr. Springer, we get to these issues as fast as we can. We're sorry for the untimeliness, but we still must deal with this complaint." Mrs. Sanders insisted.

I was returned to my cell after my explanation of the Sparky incident, with assurances that the paper work for my release from lockdown would be submitted immediately. Somehow it was neglected for two more days. I used the time to review what I had been through and learned in the movement, the Peace movement, they called it.

THE MOVEMENT.....A JOKE FROM CHILDHOOD?
The honky guvmint official showed up on the res, claiming that the tribe had to move again. Coal or oil or uranium had been discovered and the Big Father in Washington needed it.

The chief of the tribe, Chief Bowels, listened to the official but was not impressed. Unfortunately the official got confused when Chief Bowels answered simply, "Bowels No Move."

Uncle Sam's man ran off to get a doctor thinking he had to solve the Chief's problem, constipation, before he could convince him to move. The doctor gave him his standard laxative but three days later the Chief still insisted, "Bowels No Move."

The doctor got more serious and moved from Ex-lax to the industrial strength Milk of Magnesia. The official got worried when that didn't work and Bowels still wouldn't move. Finally they administered the hospital brand. The following day they arrived to check on the Chief and asked again. "Well, Chief, will bowels move now."

The Chief responded, "Bowels gotta move: tipi full of shit."

I was hitching down the highway back in '69, the year I graduated high school, which had not been a high. I was up in South Dakota, east of those big carved rocks of white men, those famous presidents. They struck me as a bold and cruel statement. Conquer a people, take their land and then carve faces of your own people in their sacred mountains.

Still, the native people weren't destroyed. It's the home of the Lakota. Several of the states up there, as across the United States, are named after the native people, Minnesota, the Dakotas, Nebraska. It's really the Paha Sapa, the Black Hills.... Sacred lands. Some may argue that it's just a name but it's the difference between calling a place a church or a dump, a lady or a slut, a place you respect or something to rape. Miners rushed Rushmore for more gold but later they came back for the uranium, the yellow cake, not as shiny as gold but in our twisted system of power and capital, worth even more.

My thumb never failed. After a man picked me up in his beat-up Chevy van, he looked over at me and asked what I thought of Nixon and the whole Watergate thing.

I scrunched my nose as if I was about to check my shoes to see what I had stepped in, when I told him. "Man, I'm not really into politics."

He took his eyes off the road, looking at me with the eyes of age. His words sunk in like water splashed on a sponge. "Really? Well, politics is into you."

It took a dozen years for those words to ferment. They mixed with the sun of the Mohave, the salt water of Alaska's bays, the forests of Humboldt, the rocks of Mount Index, seasons of wandering in the desert, mountains and seashores of a continent. They made a bitter wine of that truth, . . . politics is into you! There was no use in denying it. I could love the earth all I wanted to, but everywhere, the pock marks and cesspools of industry and capitalism were, . . . how you say, . . . 'in yo face.' A cancer cluster here, cyanide in your water there, cesium, strontium, radionuclides in your bones, jet bombers screaming through your Idaho wilderness.

While I did my best to ignore the dysfunction of capitalist politics, it became obvious that it would not ignore me. Wherever I lived or traveled, there was a nuke power plant, a leach field mine, or a toxic dump polluting the water, land and air. These disasters, dubbed by congress as superfund clean-up sites, were not only approved and subsidized by the government, they were the government.

Birds, frogs, trees, fish and wildlife of all types were disappearing. It became clear that what I had learned to love most about life was not only at risk of extinction, but was daily being shoved off the brink. I wanted to keep the blinders on, relishing in that blissful ignorance, but the air smelled bad, the water was foul, and ignorance became a glaring stupidity even in the darkness.

I had seen too much of Earth's beauty, God in person, face to face, to ignore the demise any longer. I had no choice but to respond. The question was, 'where?' Where was the kingpin issue that would unlock the human mind, releasing us from that market morality of judging ourselves by our material possessions or bank accounts?

I asked what I could do? I prayed for guidance. I exposed myself to the issues. It's devastating to look at, but I did. Joanna Macy wrote a book about that process, Despair and Personal Empowerment in the Nuclear Age.

I watched the slaughter of the North American baby harp seals in a Greenpeace documentary film, and the Somalian mountain gorilla debacle in the movie Gorillas in the Mist. The apartheid dilemma portrayed on the big screen in Cry Freedom became intimately real for me in the story of Stephen Biko's life and death. I read of the decimation of the wild elephants while my own home county issued death warrants on the local and endangered mountain lions. In just twelve years in Humboldt County I no longer saw the sky get black with waves of birds moving down the coast on Mad River Beach. My love for animals pushed me toward the issues of species extinction. But fate had nothing so romantic in mind for me.

On a crisp and clear April morning in 1988, I met a Mr. Jim Smith at the Co-op parking lot. I jumped in his van, for my first trip to the Nevada Test Site (NTS), quite ignorant of nuclear weapons. After repairing two major breakdowns, a timing gear and a u-joint, we arrived just at the time hundreds of protesters were being arrested. Over a thousand of them were corralled in chain link pens, awaiting a bus ride and release in a neighboring town.

I jogged up a hill overlooking the Nevada Test Site, which the Shoshone call the most bombed place on earth. After over 900 nuclear detonations there, aerial photographs show it looking like the Swiss cheese of a lunar landscape.

While I gazed across the desert valley to the town of Mercury, employing up to 11,000 solely for the purpose of developing ever more lethal weapons of mass destruction, tears flooded my cheeks in the cry of a lifetime. It was strange how it hit me like a slap on the cheek. But like a Buddhist novitiate receiving a whack from the pole, I sat up straighter, and on a subconscious level, asked for another. It was bizarre to imagine that the path to heaven was through hell or at least by looking it in the face. Yeah, though ye walk through the valley of the shadow of death...!

No Dante, nor Kahlil Gibran, no Jesus, or Genghis Khan can describe hell more succinctly: Hell is nuclearism. We look at the ovens of Auschwitz as evil embodied, but as I sat there on that sunny desert day, my heart ached to see the testing grounds. I realized that nuclear bombs were portable Auschwitz ovens. Here in a modern technological madness we were creating giant microwaves that cook everything around the world to varying degrees from the inside out, from a tender roast where the meat just falls from the bones to a shadow of charred ash, from a partially cooked kidney to undetectable thyroid damage incubating in twenty years, from birth defects in fetuses to gene mutation. I found myself released from the societal admonitions that big boys don't cry.

I remembered a Karate teacher. Kung Foo San Soo was his style. His philosophy was that if anyone makes an aggressive act upon you, then their ensuing destruction is not your responsibility. It is their own karma. They brought the destruction on themselves. He therefore taught that if someone attempts to strike you, you must follow through with a series of moves that thoroughly and utterly destroys them.

Any attack produced this series of responses, ensuring that the attacker would be totally disabled. This seemed to be the same philosophy of nuclear weapons. I knew inherently that this method temporarily defeated an attacker but insured that if there was a next time, he would bring a gun. This philosophy does not solve problems, but creates permanent enemies.

Gandhi later corroborated that understanding. "Indeed, violence does not ever overcome evil; it suppresses it for the time being only to rise later with redoubled vigor."

At the time of that first trip to the test site, I had been working with Beartooth Wilderness Survival Schools and Youth Services Bureau. I had hands-on experience with seriously abused children. I met with them after school, if they attended, to discuss their problems. I met with their mothers coming home from the bar or mom's boyfriend coming home from prison.

While I learned that I couldn't reach all children, I had great successes. Some that were labeled 'developmentally disabled' proved to be the most advanced and loving. I saw a broad cross-section of America's youth.

People around me said I was a natural with kids. While the work was often depressing, I filled a niche that needed filling. The youth I reached grabbed hold, but the bureaucracy sucked back. I often spent more time filling out forms than working with the kids. The most important role I filled with these kids was that of an alternative model. Paper pusher was not the model I wanted to present.

Life had forced many of these kids to rebel, to rebel against mothers boyfriend who rubbed her 14 year old bottom and invited her into bed; to rebel against a drunk father slapping his mother around again; to rebel against money based authority or against their lack of that commodity; to rebel against an education system that rewarded for your ability to buy dogma and regurgitate it, claiming it a sign of intellect. I wanted to give these rebels a cause, a responsibility, a piece of this earth, and faith in their *own* ability to think.

But here I saw the test site, the government, the corporations, the American people, setting an international example of violence and destruction as a means of conflict resolution. I saw that same violence in the home. It became obvious to me that violence was no more a means of conflict resolution than rape was an act of love.

I saw the test site as the macro version of violence, and human abuse as the micro. I saw that as a religious society we have decided that murder and killing are not acceptable, but as political societies we practice and even glorify genocide.

It was my first antinuclear protest. After two hours of soul searching on that Nevada desert hilltop, I walked down with a burning question. How can we stop the violence? How can we stop nuclear weapons, the spearhead of that violence? How we can we stop nuclear testing, the poison tip of that spear?

I made it my question of the year. I asked every elder I came in contact with. Many responded that "if we knew, we'd have already done it". But the most viable answer and most consistent was `UNITE the PEOPLE'.

The age old adage, 'united we stand, divided we fall,' was the obvious answer. 'Divide and conquer' has been the maxim of any conquest. I left the test site, not feeling as though I had found my life's purpose, but sure I needed to study the issue more deeply.

I came to feel that no issue on earth stood a chance of long term success, be it deforestation, species extinction, resource depletion, pollution, abuse, crime, racism, sexism or any disease so long as we accept violence as a means of conflict resolution.

I left the test site with a question. That burning question launched me into periodic organizing with American Peace Test (APT). I witnessed a variety of civil resistance actions. American Peace Test events were easily stereotyped by the media as the tie-dyed Deadheads, the rainbow family, welfare bums or college students with nothing better to do. The fact that Grandmothers for Peace, Carl Sagan, Martin Sheen, doctors and professionals of almost every trade participated was generally ignored. While APT made efforts to reach out to minorities, they were relatively unsuccessful. Nukes to most minorities were just one aspect of an overall racist oppression.

At APT civil resistance actions, a few hundred protesters led by Shoshone elders crossed the cattle guard entrance onto test site property. The Shoshone issued permits for protesters to enter the test site because they believed it was rightfully their land. The 1863 Ruby Valley Treaty clearly deemed almost all of Nevada and portions of Idaho, Utah and California to the Shoshone who in turn granted privileges to the United States. But no interpretation of that treaty could be construed to allow the Nevada Test Site. The Department of Energy simply occupied an area larger than the state of Rhode Island, claiming Shoshone title had been extinguished. In other words, we no longer respect the treaty.

Private security forces, Wackenhut to be precise, were contracted by the Department of Energy to arrest trespassers. The arrests were coordinated by Nye County Sheriff Jim Merlino. Unfortunately, Wackenhut officers often treated protesters with unnecessary brutality. As private security, they were poorly trained and often visibly nervous. Sheriff Merlino allowed the brutality. While civil resistance was accepted as our right, brutality was a known risk.

Security paraded in paramilitary garb while maintaining threatening postures and expressions. They wore mirrored sunglasses and no name tags. They refused to identify themselves with names or numbers. The protesters were arrested, caged for the day at the site, and eventually bussed far enough away to insure they wouldn't do another protest the same weekend.

In contrast to APT, Nevada Desert Experience, a faith based organization, conducted protests with a calm, dignity and respect more in tune with Gandhi. Yet they seemed out of tune with the horror being opposed. Individuals walked over the line, often bowed in prayer, and were escorted, usually with no handcuffs, to the pens, where they were released within the hour and allowed to walk back across the line. The symbolism of the arrest escaped me.

My take on the situation was one of wonder. As I got more involved, I was astounded by the force already organized locally, nationally and internationally. Colorado SaneFreeze, a chapter of a national organization committed to freezing the nuclear industry, claimed to have over 300,000 members, in just one state. Hausman's Peace Diary listed over 1,100 peace organizations around the world, with organizations from Peru to India, Canada to New Zealand. It became clear that humanity was already in alignment as regards the absurdity of nuclearism, but the organizations were factionalized. From the accusatory, compensation-demanding Black Uhuru to the bowed and prayerful heads of the Franciscans, the movement covered almost every style of activism from radical to prayerful, demanding to begging, accusing to forgiving. We were divided and conquered from within, because each of these styles was exclusive in nature while claiming to be inclusive. The cliques of high school were now the cliques of adulthood and unfortunately, the movement.

It was 1988 when I first visited the Nevada Test Site. That visit began a period of soul searching. I asked the Creator, "Just what should I do?" The answer came after a couple of years. I awoke at 2:00 AM, bolt upright and sat for an hour of silent questioning. It was then that I noticed the little paperback, by Ken Keyes The Hundredth Monkey, that had sat on my bedstand for a year or more. The large print book took me about an hour to read. At the end, I had a clear vision of a huge gathering of half a million citizens followed by mass civil resistance at the gates of Mercury, Nevada.

It was not a new concept. CD at NTS. What was new was the number. Half a million, 500 thousand, seemed like it would do. A number that the government couldn't deal with in that desert without calling the National Guard or military. Such an event would make nuclear testing impossible for the media and the world to ignore. Only a hundred thousand committed resisters refusing to leave and insisting on returning indefinitely would expose the situation for what it is. It would also create the opportunity for a substantial shift in our thinking and, more important, our behavior.

Nuclear bombs themselves are ample proof that we could solve any problem facing humankind, from pollution to starvation, if we would just focus on the real problems.

As I sat in the dark bedroom of my old Arcata farmhouse, I was intimidated by the vision I had because I sensed that the answer to my question, "Just what do you want me to do?" was in that vision. "You want me to gather half a million people in the desert?" I even argued, "I think you got the wrong man." When I had asked in prayer, "Just what do you want from me," I hadn't considered the possibility that the answer would be, "Your life." I know now, there is no other answer.

I knew instinctively it would be a period of great spiritual growth because I felt there was no way it could happen otherwise. I was not enlightened, not a guru. I wallowed in power struggles in my relationships. I had no great organizing skills, no money, no contacts. I didn't even know what a venue was. But my love for this Earth is genuine and as strong an emotion as any I hold. It's the love of a parent for a child, the love of a child for it's parent, the love of mates, of beauty and song and more, and all these loves wrapped into the autumn leaves that carpet and nourish that circle of life.

I put this vision out there to the Western Shoshone National Council, to American Peace Test, to Nevada Desert Experience. My thought was to create a franchise event that every group would take on as their own. I called it The Hundredth Monkey Project after the book. The book promoted a concept of critical mass whereby each person was important and may be that hundredth monkey of consciousness that gives us the understanding to live in harmony.

Justine Cooper, a support activist of many years, told me she had the same vision. She had more experience and organizing skills than I did. We teamed up. She returned to Arcata with me after a presentation to the Western

Shoshone. She helped launch what turned into a two year project.

We set up headquarters in the farm house on Mad River Road in Humboldt County. I dubbed myself the Mad Man of the Mad River...seemed appropriate. Some troglodyte computer was loaned to us. We installed a phone line, jumped the county business hoops, and enlisted volunteers.

After three years of watching actions at the test site, I was not interested in repeating what had been done. But something termed *Reality* seemed determined to halt the Hundredth Monkey before it got going. How many porta-potties do half a million people need? How do you plan to feed these people? Some argued that half a million activists would trample that piece of desert for a thousand years. And of course, where's the money, the contacts? Have the Shoshone endorsed this project? What about sunburn, sound systems, medical, water?

The idea was slow to be accepted, and in some areas of the movement it was bitterly opposed. One young man with a family history in activism seemed determined to halt the project. He claimed I was 'not realistic.' I claimed he was stuck in the quagmire of reality. That I mentioned getting the Dalai Lama, the Pope, Thomas Banyacya of the Hopi, Dr. Helen Caldicott, Gorbachev, Nelson Mandela and others at this event made me an Icarus, attempting to fly to the sun with waxen wings. And I didn't even have feathers gathered yet.

I read a blurb in the LA Times about a gathering of over 300,000 bikers in South Dakota for a Harley rendezvous. Heck, if Harley scooter riders can gather well over a quarter million in South Dakota, then what was the problem to pull off this event just sixty miles from the world's largest convention center, I asked? Bob Dylan's prophetic words, "Get out of the way if you can't lend a hand," were not a part of the movement. American Peace Test had developed a reputation as the bottom line on Nevada Test Site actions. Without APT support, groups from around the world were skeptical of any new test site action, even though many of these groups had little, if any, personal involvement with ATP. APT wouldn't endorse without the Shoshone and the Shoshone were concerned why APT hadn't endorsed.

At the initial Hundredth Monkey proposal to the Shoshone council in Alamo, Nevada one of the council members told me, "Well, you kinda look like Jesus." I began to feel that humanity was duped into believing that nothing great can happen until Jesus returns. Any who make suggestions a Jesus might make are suspect. After all, Jesus was crucified as an imposter himself . . . The son of God, hah!

Another council member asked, "What will you do if the council doesn't endorse your project?"

"Well, I'll have to drop it. I respect that the test site is rightfully Shoshone land. I can't proceed without council approval." I meant it. While I felt committed to halt testing, I wasn't going to go very far with Shoshone opposition.

After waiting two months for a Shoshone reply to my presentation, I called Bill Rosse Sr., a Western Shoshone council member and ardent Hundredth Monkey supporter. He told me that the council gave it the thumbs down. "It's not really a hard `NO,'" he explained. He went on to say that the Western Shoshone National Council had never formally endorsed any event, had never been asked formally to do so. The Shoshone involvement with APT had always been a de facto relationship. Bill Rosse was also on the APT council, and approval of their events was just accepted de facto because Bill approved of APT events. Bill encouraged The Hundredth Monkey to continue regardless of council endorsement.

Still, a no was a no. I decided to cancel the project and hitch on down to the test site to fast till death. God, I was such a romantic!

As I was about to get on the road, Justine gave me a lecture I shall long remember. Justine grasped the hard and soft concept better than I did. As she was departing, she climbed on board a Greyhound like it was some Hollywood movie set and, leaning out the window, called me a quitter. "Before this is over they'll say you sleep with little boys." A lovely note to end on, I thought, but it later proved to be pretty much on the mark, at least in the degree of slander.

My young college roommate, Kristen, convinced me that I should at least attend the APT Body of the Whole meeting before totally scrapping the plan. It was there that Rick Gold, another dreamer from way back and long time, indefatigable, antinuclear activist, bumped me back into the project with an alternate plan. At the APT meeting in Oregon, it was Rick, with a glitter in his eyes, that turned the Hundredth Monkey Project into The Event, just outside of Vegas, The Walk, sixty miles to the test site, and The Action, CD, civil disobedience at the gates of Mercury. It was an even better plan. We gather half a million in the gorgeous desert just outside of Las Vegas, we inform, inspire and educate the masses to the issue of nuclearism, talk of nonviolence for social change, and then with U-2, Jackson Browne, Corbin Harney, and the Dalai Lama leading the tribe, we head off into the desert for five days of walking, praying, and preparing for a change in the consciousness of humanity. Each evening we set up a central stage to discuss nonviolence and the need for discipline. By the time we arrive for The Action, we're UNITED. That was the plan that we developed. It still makes me smile just to think about it.

We planned The Hundredth Monkey for April of 1991, but again fate had a different agenda. Greenpeace was investing in an action in Vegas, in January of that same year. I couldn't convince them to postpone until April to unite with The Hundredth Monkey. They were aligning with the United Nations conference on the Comprehensive Test Ban.

Strategy is a critical issue in movements. Gandhi spent months and years working to come up with the right campaign. The Greenpeace effort at the Las Vegas Sahara was beautifully orchestrated but ultimately cost twice as much as budgeted.

With Bill Rosse, Sr and Corbin Harney's blessing and encouragement, I went after organizational endorsements from the International Physicians for the Prevention of Nuclear War, (IPPNW) to my own home towns' City Council. August 15, 1990, was a beautiful local first step. It was titled Resolution NO 901-19 "A Resolution of the City Council of the City of Arcata in Support of The Hundredth Monkey". It began, "Whereas, the city of Arcata is a nuclear free zone in the nuclear free zone of Humboldt County" and succinctly pointed out, "The City of Arcata recognizes that nuclear testing, used to determine function and level of lethality in nuclear bombs is immoral and illegal in the highest laws of the universe."

Denis Hayes, the Earth Day International Chair, wrote a letter of support claiming that "nuclear testing must be stopped as a first step toward a sane future." In a lunch meeting he encouraged me by saying that "patience is not an appropriate virtue in organizing on this issue."

The California Green Party, Bay Area Action (BAA), Women Strike for Peace, Proposition One Committee, Rainforest Action Network (RAN), and a dozen other chapters of national organizations endorsed right away. The local chapter of Physicians for Social Responsibility (PSR), presided by dentist and activist Tom Lewis, agreed to be our nonprofit umbrella. We became a project of PSR.

We needed funding -- that was clear. With the help of an old friend we targeted roughly 50 foundations that we felt were appropriate to approach. While our original literature was pathetically amateurish, due mostly to my own lack of skills and, to some degree, rebellion against the concept that the medium is the message, we had adopted a professional aura by the time we submitted our grant proposals.

Our budget proposal was a mere $166,920. I say mere because it was bare bones for the project we were proposing. The Greenpeace event in Vegas cost almost $200,000, and they were not attempting anything close to what we proposed. Our budget included 'organizing only' with $62,000 in staff expenses (all staff being paid $5.00 an hour), $76,000 in office, phones, printing, etc. and $20,000 in travel for outreach. Porta-potties, water trucks, etc., would be covered by participant registration. Our proposal was to get the people there to the event and help prepare them for the ten days ahead.

It became obvious by the January 1991 Greenpeace action that our event needed more time. The middle east crisis, unfolding at the same time, demanded everyone's attention, and actions to halt nuclear testing were put on the back burner.

We postponed until April of 1992 and by doing so aligned not only with the Chinese year of the Monkey, but the 500 years of indigenous resistance. These signs, as well as the uniting of Easter and Passover on the same weekend, made us feel that all was unfolding as it should.

Allen Alfeldt was one of the key organizers for the Walk Across America and the main energy behind the Soviet Peace Walks, a very successful joining of Soviet and American citizens walking through the then Soviet Union. That walk called for an end to nuclearism. He told me, "You need three things, Rick. BIG money, BIG name artists, and a BIG venue. And with all of my contacts, I couldn't pull off what you're trying to do." I knew he couldn't, but with a hundred of us working together, I believed it was no problem.

My plan was to get the support from organizations, take that to the speakers, Helen Caldicott, Carl Sagan, Corbin Harney, the Dalai Lama, Martin Sheen, or Sally Fields, then off to the bands.

I am still convinced that the greatest uniting force on Earth is music. Focused politically aware music makes me stand up straighter. Everyone has experienced the rush, the goose bumps of a favorite hot tune with lyrics that makes you say as the Quakers do, "That Brother speaks my mind". Words put to music and sung with emotion and conviction, are capable of great inspiration. Music was a key component to our uniting strategy. Thirty years ago, Barry McGuire was singing the Eve of Destruction. "Think of all the hate there is in Red China, then take a look around to Selma, Alabama."

The challenge to create The Hundredth Monkey was best summarized by the ancient maxim of 'which comes first, the chicken or the egg.' Organizations wanted a commitment from big name bands, speakers, celebrities, or at a minimum, other organizations with substantial name recognition, before they would lend their name to The Hundredth Monkey. I found I had difficulty getting organizations without the celebrities. I couldn't get the celebrities without the organizations. I was told often to "come back when you have some big names signed up. Keep us posted."

I spent much of the first year trying to figure out how to overcome this dilemma. Friends promised to deliver letter packets personally to musicians that they would see at a concert or had personal addresses for. I researched and used the best management agency addresses I could find. I explained our project, but I found that there is a moat around the celebrity castle.

After several letters to Joan Baez, I began a fast in her Menlo Park office, Humanitas, to get her attention. The receptionist didn't appreciate my strategy, but in two short hours, Ed Lazar had Joan Baez on the phone and I spoke with her briefly. I was sorry to hear her perturbed tone as she conceded, "All right, let me hear your spiel." I felt like an appliance salesman with a customer who doesn't need an appliance. She explained honestly that she had spent her lifetime on projects such as The Hundredth Monkey, that she had just committed to take a year for herself. I respected her answer.

At one point I was given a rough description to Neil Young's ranch in the mountains outside Santa Cruz, on the California coast. Neither he nor his agents had responded to inquiries, so I drove into the hills until I hit a locked gate. I hiked by foot until I stumbled on his home, a fairy tale craftsman mansion overlooking a pond. I was impressed and heartened to see native American pipes peened in bronze on his front doors and native symbols etched in the glass. I delivered my letter of introduction from Shoshone elders Bill Rosse, Sr. and Corbin Harney to Neil Young's friend. He was kind enough to listen for a half hour. He assured me of Neil's agreement and probable interest in participating. He committed to deliver the letter. We never heard from Neil Young.

I contacted personally, wrote, faxed, or called many of the major promoters in America; Bill Graham Productions, Micheal Martin's Concerts for the Environment, Barry Fey Productions of Colorado, Micheal Sinclair of New York City, and Jackson Browne's promoter, Tom Campbell of Avocado Productions. While they were all encouraging, none were willing to help launch the Monkey or get us closer to artist commitments.

Artists, once they had reached international status, were commodities of an industry and almost impossible to contact. Tracking down even agent names and addresses was a research project. I had a justified cause, which made walking unannounced into an agent's office not only acceptable but necessary. As a disclaimer, the shrieking, indignant secretary followed me into the boss's office. So they bawled me out. The agents usually heard what I had to say. Still, they lied to me that their clients had received the information, claiming the artists had either declined or were undecided. The truth was that agents and managers weeded out proposals to appear at nonpaying events before proposals ever got to the artist. They were deluged with requests to do free fund-raisers for worthy nonprofit efforts. No doubt artists got plenty of requests from people who knew them personally. Rumor was that at times, Jackson Browne did so many fund-raisers that he couldn't even sell out a pay event due to saturation.

Eventually, I flew to Europe in an effort to secure band, speaker and organization commitment. After selling my woodworking tools and my windsurfer, I gave up my bedroom in the farmhouse on the Mad River. I got the tube schedule, London's version of the subway, and with a list of agents from Van Morrison to U-2, I made my way around from office to office. My hope, that as an American activist I would receive a better hearing, was disproved in reality. I was able to leave my packets, personalized 'for' each artist. The staff at Bob Geldoff's office, the man who had largely organized the <u>We Are The World</u> benefit concert, was pleasant and encouraging, but nothing came of it. At Paul McCartney's office I felt like the homeless activist I was. Speaking through an intercom, I was instructed to leave my packet under the door. I was able to meet with Campaign for Nuclear Disarmament (CND), Europe's largest anti-nuclear group. I formed ties with a young Quaker woman, working there on sabbatical, who agreed to be our London Hundredth Monkey.

I departed to the streets of London to sleep on a high-rise scaffolding. Shortly after dark I climbed, with my pack, up three tiers of scaffolding, where I was sheltered from the drizzle by the building's fourth floor overhang. I laid out my bag and read by candlelight thirty feet above the clamor of the London pavement. I slept like a rock. I awoke in the morning to find the workers inside on the third floor viewing me through the glass. I decided I'd better hustle off before the constable arrived. I've never packed my bag and gear so fast. It was only after I hit the ground and ran by the front entrance that I noticed the building sign: Northeast London Courthouse!

I felt some success when I was able to make a presentation at the T-BAG (Test Ban Action Group), a meeting of London activists held at the Greenpeace offices. Bruce Kent, a former-priest-gone-activist, was supportive and committed to attend The Hundredth Monkey himself if finances allowed. Rebecca Johnson, Greenpeace nuclear coordinator offered the party line, "Keep us posted," and a consolation prize of Greenpeace posters. Each of the five posters was an excellent landscape photo of the world's nuclear test sites with insets of it's location and details of each testing program.

I took a brief tour of England's own indigenous history by visiting Avesbury, a site of ancient pagan culture reputed to be 500 years older than Stonehenge. It remains a wonder to me that as I climbed Silbury Hill, perhaps the world's largest man-made hill, I heard singing on the top. As I crested the summit and the wind greeted me on a gray and green day common to that central England landscape, I saw a dozen people joining hands in circle. They were singing and dancing. As I approached, they opened the circle to accept my hands. I had traveled around the globe to sing a song on an ancient hilltop, a song we often sing in Arcata, California,

> Eh yanna, ho yanna, hey yan yan
> Eh yanna, ho yanna, hey yan yan
> The Earth is our Mother, we must take care of her
> The Earth is our Mother, we must take care of her

We became immediate friends. I discovered that they were a group of Dancers for Universal Peace. They put the world's most sacred prayers to song and dance and were touring the world's power spots doing these prayers.

In a series of encounters that bordered on spooky, I ran into this group two more times. We danced and prayed together in the rain amongst the rocks at Stonehenge, and again we met by chance at the Chalice Well in Glastonbury, the home of a festival as famous as Woodstock. The encounters reinforced my faith that the project was unfolding as it should despite the lack of any major commitments or money and that spiritual forces were alive and at work on behalf of The Hundredth Monkey. I finished my European outreach through

Belgium, Amsterdam and Germany, stopping at organizations en route. I left Europe feeling I had made a personal effort to connect with a larger world. A world also intimately affected by nuclear testing.

Some months later, our Arcata representative attended another American Peace Test meeting in the continued hopes of swaying that group to join us. Perhaps a month after that I became aware that our own representative, an Arcata board member, had spread a rumor that nearly brought our project to a halt.

The rumor was that the Western Shoshone were opposed to The Hundredth Monkey. Several successful activists and consequently organizations, quit working on The Hundredth Monkey without even notifying us. It was only when I contacted our London representative that I learned that Rebecca Johnson had announced that very rumor at a Test Ban Action Group (T-BAG) meeting.

I immediately contacted Bill Rosse, Sr. who assured me that such was not the case. The National Council was still unable to endorse, but he and Corbin, as well as several other of the most active Shoshone, were in support and would be at The Hundredth Monkey Event to speak.

But the damage was done. The momentum in London was halted. Did a government agent launch the rumor, or was it just jealous activists wanting control of certain issues? I found that our Arcata representative refused to share who had told her the rumor, but she had spread it locally without talking to me about it first. I learned how easy it is to divide and conquer the peace movement.

But we weren't quitting. We opened offices in Palo Alto, Oakland, Arcata, and Santa Monica, California, Boulder and Crested Butte, Colorado, and Portland and Eugene, Oregon. We had over 100 endorsements. Slowly speaker and band commitments were confirmed. The eco-rock band Clan Dyken took on The Hundredth Monkey as their own project. Groups from Grandmothers for Peace to the Jewish Peace Fellowship introduced us in their newsletters. Lois Nicolai on the East coast organized a Peace Train of Soviet citizens to cross the United States, doing press conferences in cities along the way and arriving at the Event in Nevada. We became the Earth Day International Action for 1992.

Peace Spokes organized over a hundred bicyclists to peddle to the Event from Oakland, California. Helen Caldicott, the Australian physician and author known as the Mother of the Nuclear Movement, committed to speak. John Robbins, the heir to the Baskin-Robbins ice cream fortune and founder of Earth Save, also committed. Casey Kasem, top forty DJ and activist in his own right, joined our effort, recording a Western Union Hotline message for us as well as being an MC for our event.

"Hi, this is Casey Kasem. Thanks for calling our 1-800-PEACE-92 hotline and sending your message to George Bush requesting the end of nuclear weapons testing."

In 1990, I heard Jesse Jackson speak to the Student Environmental Action Coalition (SEAC), "If we unite ourselves with the indigenous people, we will naturally be accomplishing our environmental goals." He was in tune with the times. Native American leaders, from Oren Lyons of the Six Nations of the Iroquois to Corbin Harney of the Shoshone, Thomas Banyacya of the Hopi to Mike Haney of the Cherokee, along with Tony Gonzales of the International Indian Treaty council, agreed to attend and speak out against nuclear testing on native lands. 1992 was a key year for native people in America. They worked hard to bring home the message that Columbus did not discover America. The continental United States alone was a land occupied for over 12,000 years by an estimated two and a half million indigenous people, whose culture was so varied and diverse that they spoke between one and two thousand different languages. The Hundredth Monkey joined in the effort to make that message known.

While there continued to be cause for hope that our event would come together, real money never arrived. Our continuous efforts for grants were unsuccessful until the very end.

Fate was almost cruel. In 1991 Ted Turner put out a call for a book to heal the planet, the Turner Tomorrow Awards. He was calling for a book describing how we could save the world. It was my belief that The Hundredth Monkey Project was the book. I wrote them of our project and said we were busy living the book. The winning award was $500,000, enough money to make the event an astounding success. The winner was a book called Ishmael, the story of human effects on Earth through the eyes of a gorillas.

Scheduled just after The Hundredth Monkey in 1992 was the Earth Summit in Rio de Janiero. At an event in LA, a group presented their film to be shown at theatres around the country. The film was about the earth's demise, again through the eyes of a monkey. The narrator, Edward Olmos, Jr., a Hollywood film star, put out the call for the President of the United States to attend and participate in the Earth Summit. Bush didn't.

Members of APT in the Santa Monica area continued to resist endorsement of The Hundredth Monkey and in fact, remained in firm opposition. The effect cannot be overstated. The tragedy was that the individuals most in opposition to the Project were also unwilling to hear or respond to efforts to assuage their concerns. People adamant about process were often willing to violate it. I found that the people who were the most opinionated and opposed invariably knew neither me nor the project team.

Regardless, our project did not lack in outreach. I went up and down the coast holding meetings and opening offices, bank accounts and phone lines. For six months I lived in a pickup truck. I flew to Illinois in 1990 and drove to Boulder in 1992 for the Student Environmental Action Conference. I flew to Washington DC. twice, London, Amsterdam, and Las Vegas. Just before the

Gulf war I flew to New York for the United Nations conference on the Comprehensive Test Ban which could eliminate nuclear testing forever. Then I flew to the Carter Center in Georgia in the hopes of getting a commitment from Jimmy Carter, and perhaps more important, CNN. Eventually Jimmy and Rosalyn Carter sent a letter of endorsement and a $200 check. CNN ultimately covered our event, but it took a little prodding. In fact, it took a broken eagle.

Photos by Linda Putman

Corbin Harney, the spiritual leader of the Western Shoshone. After a world of travels to indigenous lands, activist Bill Chisholm stated, "In the world of shamans, Corbin is as authentic as they get."

Photo by Linda Putman

Corbin using the eagle wings in a healing ceremony at the Nevada Test Site. The drum in the center is adorned with the design of the Nevada/SemiPalatinsk Movement: a Kazakh and American Indian sharing the peace pipe. Nuclear testing, uranium mining and nuclear waste dumping are done on indigenous lands around the world.

Photos by Linda Putman

Pauline Estevez is a Shoshone elder who speaks often at the test site and has toured the nation with women's groups to educate on the nuclear issue.

Photo by Linda Putman

Corbin Harney shares the pipe at the Nevada Test Site with Olzhas Suliemenov, a Soviet poet and dignitary, who helped launch the Nevada/SemiPalatinsk Movement.

Photo by Linda Putman

Vietnam veterans protesting and praying for a halt to nuclear weapons at the Nevada Test Site.

Photo by Linda Putman

World War II veteran reads and then destroys his honorable discharge in front of Jim Merlino, Nye County Sheriff, at the Nevada Test Site, 1988.

Photo by Linda Putman

Standoff - Hundredth Monkey protesters blockade Nevada State Highway 95 in an effort to get public attention to the atrocity of nuclear testing. Wackenhut thugs, employed by the Department of Energy, wearing no identification and using phony names, brutalized over 200 of the protesters.

This is just one example of the brutality supported by the DOE, the Nye County Sheriff's Department and the Nevada State Highway Patrol. Camera equipment was destroyed by officials to prevent the public from viewing the brutality.

Photo by Linda Putman

Wackenhut private security, the nation's largest illegal private army, sit in dune buggies, prepared to chase protesters across the desert.

Photo by Linda Putman

Mercury Highway, the entrance to the Nevada Test Site. In the early fifties, this was the largest, most pristine desert in the United States. Today, it is a national sacrifice area, polluted by well over 700 nuclear bombs and a myriad of toxic waste. Here are some of the men who protect the DOE's right to desecrate.

Please see following page for full text of the
Peoples' Comprehensive Test Ban Treaty, as shown in these two photos.

THE PEOPLES COMPREHENSIVE TEST BAN TREATY

EXECUTED ON MARCH 31, 1990 IN NEWE SEGOBIA
(WESTERN SHOSHONE NATION) NEVADA TEST SITE

WE THE PEOPLE DO AGREE:

Article I All nuclear states shall agree to end the conducting of or participation in any nuclear weapons tests or other nuclear explosions as the first step towards the elimination of all weapons of mass destruction. Any government that does not sign such an agreement shall be condemened as a criminal violator of existing international agreements prohibiting crimes against humanity.

Article II All nuclear testing facilities shall be closed and dismantled and control of the lands encompassing such facilities shall be returned to the indigenous peoples for peaceful purposes. Resources spent on testing shall be redirected to clean up and restore the land damaged by testing and to treat and compensate the people who have suffered health effects..

Article III All information about the environmental and health effects of nuclear weapons testing and production shall be made public. An international non-governmental comission shall be formed to investigate the impact of nuclear weapons testing and production on health and the environment, to monitor nuclear waste sites and to identify contaminated regions of the world.

Article IV All peoples are responsible for taking such nonviolent action necessary to enforce the terms and conditions of this treaty. All peoples are further urged to organize coordinated nonviolent actions and demonstrations against nuclear weapons testing prior to and during the scheduled June 10, 1990 US/USSR disarmament summit and January 1991 United Nations International Comprehensive Test Ban Treaty Conference.

Chapter Four
BLASPHEMY, BLASPHEMY

"To rid the world of the scourge of war..."
--- First and primary mandate of the United Nations Charter

✴ ✴ ✴ ✴ ✴

There I was, off the plane, my bags loaded with buttons and bumper stickers stretching my arms, riding the rails into New York City amidst the icy sidewalks, snow-covered garbage, and block after block of twelve story apartment buildings. I remember the urine smell of the subway tunnels, the clackety-clack of steel wheels on steel track, and the farting and belching of the brakes and the people.

I found my First St. exit and joined the other cattle moving through the turnstiles out into the evening air. I knew my way somewhat, about six blocks to the Catholic Worker House, where they were good enough to allow me to stay while I attended the UN Comprehensive Test Ban Conference. The Worker House was founded by Dorothy Day, a woman who was imprisoned for her social activism. She launched The Worker House for recovering street women. For me, it was a sanctuary in a jungle.

Alice, one of the long-time residents, let me in after the magic number of thumps on the front door. I went down to the kitchen, and after helping myself to the dinner remains, proceeded up the well-worn steps to find Jane or Cassie, the women in charge. I found Jane smiling in the little office off of the prayer room. I briefed her on my mission, the elusive grail, as ever, the pursuit of the Comprehensive Test Ban. She was kind enough to walk the five sets of stairs to show me my room on the top floor. I unrolled the Goodwill blankets, patched twenty times, and cranked the silver knob of the steam radiator wide open.

The next morning I dressed in my best shirt, a worn, handmade corduroy and my Woolrich winter backpacking pants. With my black bag swinging on my hip, I bounced down the stairs and into the hustle of a crisp January morning. Over a Budget Oatmeal Breakfast, a BOB, I scanned the paper for coverage of the United Nations conference. Not one word in the New York Times, even on the opening day of the conference.

The big seller for the Times was, as usual, not peacemaking but war-making, much more exciting and profitable. The imminent doom of Iraq was plastered front page, second page and in smaller clips throughout. There it was, Bush's challenge and threat,... Hussein, the madman monster,... and Kuwait, the poor, oppressed, and raped princess...the story had all the points of a classic fairy tale.

I found the U.N. building and was impressed with a sculpture of a huge bronze gun, the barrel twisted into a knot. I pondered just how one would go about tying that knot. The Comprehensive Test Ban was a good start, but we still have to melt the guns and the bombs. I envisioned another sculpture even more to my liking: a pile of guns, barely discernible, as they melted in a pot. Out of the tilted pot, they were being poured into a mold of plows and other farm tools.

I entered the north lobby and toured three floors of marble. The UN gift shop displayed peace buttons from across the nation and around the world. Having been a button maker myself, I realized that I may have stamped out these very buttons in Arcata. I recognized B4, Give Peace a Chance, B154, Martin Luther King Jr., "We must learn to live together as brothers and sisters or we will perish together as fools," and many others. I didn't see my favorite one though, "Wearing buttons is not enough."

I found the desk for the conference, and to my surprise a pass was necessary to get in. I was screwed. I had flown across the nation for this conference and had no pass. But like the street urchin of my youth, I scammed my way in through a Russian interpreter with Greenpeace. "He's with Greenpeace, but he must have been overlooked on the list. Would you please issue him a pass now," he explained diplomatically. I was in.

I took the elevator to the third floor, quite smug with my good fortune, and entered the balcony to hear the opening ceremonies of the conference. Secretary General of the United Nations, Javier Perez De Cuellar read a statement from Mikhail Gorbachev.

> *"I welcome your conference and take this opportunity to state once again the invariability of the Soviet Unions policy aimed at the speediest achievement of a Comprehensive Test Ban as a crucial step on the path to a nuclear free world."*

After three unilateral testing moratoriums, the Soviets were still pleading with the US to halt the arms race. The opening ceremonies were brief, and I left the auditorium to go back to the Worker House to write what I called the Common Man Paper on Nuclear Testing.

> *Gentle Women, Gentle Men of the United Nations,*
> *My name is Rick Springer. I am from Northern California. I work with abused teenagers in the wilderness as therapy. I have stopped this work because I saw no sense in*

healing these young people to a radioactive future or the threat
of death from a thermonuclear war. I am a common man
and I thank the Creator for my commonality. I feel if I can
understand something then all people can.

Nuclear testing is wrong. Wrong for four simple reasons.
It is wasteful, shamefully so! You already know the absurd
costs of nuclear testing. Former President Dwight D. Eisenhower
said, "Every gun that is made, every warship launched, every
rocket fired, signifies, in the final sense, a theft from those who
hunger and are not fed, those who are cold and not clothed.
This world in arms is not spending money alone. It is spend-
ing the sweat of it's laborers, the genius of its scientists, the
hopes of its children... This is not a way of life in any true
sense. Under the cloud of threatening war it is humanity
hanging from a cross of iron." We are stealing from our
children, we are thieves. What kind of sick culture is it that
will waste the birthright of its children to indulge it's own
pathetic fears and greed?

I listed three other reasons; it's polluting, illegal, and immoral. I closed
with a call for all nations to vote on the CTB and impose sanctions on any
nation, including the US, that would not comply.

After 27 years since the partial test ban treaty, the time
has come for strong words. The reality is that the United
States government is the leading warmonger of the world.
Let's face it. No nation on earth has the military might of the
US and the rest of the planet is only following that example.

I had to stretch it out to walk the eighty blocks uptown before the morning
UN sessions began. I wanted to hear all the delegates' statements. I arrived at
7:30 and found a copy shop uptown to plug in my word processor and make a
hundred copies of the Common Man.

Off to the U.N., I walked under a section of scaffolding, common in the Big
Apple, and found a village of homeless people living in cardboard boxes. I
could see the legs and ankles of sleeping bodies in boxes that once housed
refrigerators. They lay on other pieces of cardboard to insulate them against
the cold sidewalk. A few had blankets, but most just lay there in their tattered
clothes. My stomach turned, as I could see the front of the U.N. a block and a
half up the street.

At the west entrance of the U.N. building, I came upon a bronze bell about
four feet tall. The inscription told of how the bell was made from the melted

medals of war veterans from around the world.

Now, did the U.N. actually have the ability to accomplish anything? Although I was hopeful as I pushed the revolving door, I wondered if the words of the U.N. were like Lord McCauley's comment on the U.S. Constitution, "All sail and no anchor." I walked into the huge front lobby and entered the meeting room on the left. I made my way in, stopping at a literature table to lay some copies of my statement in a prominent position among the other propaganda.

The room was designed for a thousand people. The Secretary General sat high above the delegates like a kid on an oversized couch. The delegates' desks were arranged in a semicircle before the dais. On the armrest of my chair was a sort of hearing aid.

Although it was 9:10 AM, the room was still half empty. I began to think punctuality was an endangered concept. Finally, Secretary De Cuellar entered the room with the President of the Amendment Conference, Sri Lankas' Edmund Jayasinghe, and after whacking the gavel, De Cuellar proceeded to make a brief statement about being on time. 'All right, there's my man,' I thought. People scurried to their seats as others continued to file in.

They began immediately with statements, one powerful plea to end testing after another. I ran up to get a copy of each statement as the delegates dropped their extras on the public table. By the end of the day I had almost a dozen. The best summary of the opinions came from the Nigeria delegate.

> *This Amendment Conference is a culmination of...unfulfilled promises, failures and frustrations. Foremost it is the failure of the three Depository Powers to live up to their obligations under the PTBT, the Threshold Test Ban Treaty, and the Non-Proliferation Treaty. It is the failure of the vertical proliferation of nuclear arsenals by the three Depository Powers themselves....*

The three depository powers are England, the United States and the Soviet Union. It was encouraging to hear the truth spoken in an international forum of government delegates. The sentiment was endorsed in a variety of ways. The Pakistan delegate proclaimed:

> *It is ironical that those very countries which claim to be the champions of nuclear nonproliferation are creating obstacles in the way of a CTB.*

The Sri Lanka delegate reminded the Conference:

> *It is said that the total strength of present nuclear arse-*

*nals may be over one million Hiroshima bombs, that is over
some 13,000 million tons of TNT. It is often pointed out that
this is equivalent to more than three tons per every man,
woman and child on this Earth.*

*Mr. President, in this modern age it is against all civilized
standards and moral convictions to see that billions of people
are deprived of basic needs such as food, clothing , shelter,
health care, sanitation, education and other things that are
fundamental to live in dignity. Thousands of children die
from starvation and malnutrition every day while the international community is spending billions of dollars for destructive purposes. This waste of resources should end and
end without further delay. This time has come to search our
conscience.*

Delegate after delegate reiterated Eisenhower's message, New Zealand,
Japan, Brazil, Romania, Germany, Poland, Indonesia. I was inspired and hopeful. Armed with the proof that world governments agreed with the world
peace movement, it became obvious that the US military industrial complex
was cramming radiation, via testing and development, down the throats of the
worlds' citizens, despite our opposition.

During the lunch break I joined the Non-Governmental Organizations,
(NGOs) Pax Christi, Greenpeace, Sane/Freeze, Physicians for Social Responsibility and many more. I plied the trade of the activist net worker, sharing the
100th Monkey events and our year long postponement to 1992. I met with
organizers from around the world. I met a woman from France, Fernex Solange
and explained the three parts of the 100th Monkey to her. Solange told me of a
conference of world radiation victims taking place in France and suggested we
might pull those events together.

That afternoon back at the UN I heard more of the same support for the
completion of the 1963 Partial Test Ban Treaty "at the earliest date possible to
achieve the cessation of all nuclear weapons tests in all atmospheres for all
time." This mandate, although signed by 117 countries including the United
States, had been ignored by the US just as the 394 treaties made with indigenous people have been ignored. The US government is not good at keeping its
word.

The hearing aid device on the side of my chair turned out to be a language
converter. Channel one spoke in English, channel two in German, three in
French and on through nine. It was a wonderful tool to overcome the language
barrier. If only we could be so clever in solving our other differences. The
Brazilian Ambassador, Ronaldo Mota Sardenberg, stated,

The overwhelming majority of States has continued to express its unequivocal support for the cessation of all nuclear tests. These calls have so far remained unheeded. The reasons given are well known. The need to maintain a credible deterrent nuclear power—an argument in itself unacceptable— is supposed to justify the continuation of nuclear weapons testing.

Germany reaffirmed its *"solemn, unilateral pledge not to produce, possess or have control over nuclear, biological and chemical weapons,"* as did Japan. Iran reminded us again that:

A review of the nuclear power parties to the PTBT and the NPT, with respect to their obligations, distinctly demonstrates that they have ignored their commitments, and as a result have paved the way for the intensification of the nuclear arms race.

The main part of the afternoon was dedicated to the Non-Governmental Organizations, the NGOs. They were given the opportunity to speak to the delegates, but the delegates' presence was optional. Perhaps only half of the delegates attended, and those were already singing in our choir. The difficult challenge of the movement was always to preach beyond the converted.

Still, the voice of activists from around the world was empowering. Cora Weiss of Sane Freeze, the largest peace and justice organization in the U.S. called directly to the opposition:

It is to Mrs. Hoinkes, our United States delegate and I would like to include Mr. Kenyon of the United Kingdom, that we must address our remarks.
I would like to tell you that there is no public support for nuclear testing in our country. According to a series of United Nations resolutions and highly respected international lawyers the use of nuclear weapons is a crime against humanity.
Pushing nuclear testing underground may have put it out of sight, but lethal fallout continues to pollute the earth and water supply. You might want to take a trip 'downwind' of the nuclear test sites in this country so that you can meet the widows and widowers, the victims of thyroid cancer, the victims of leukemia, breast cancer and cancer of the prostate in abnormal numbers.
If you agree that nuclear war must never be fought and can

never be won, then why, pray tell, do you insist on having more nuclear weapons and more sophisticated nuclear testing? If you didn't want more, you would agree to stop testing. If governments don't behave morally, surely their citizens cannot be expected to behave morally.

She had hit on my micro and macro theory of violence. After working with abused teens, I came to see that as long as we accepted violence as a society, then of course we would have it in our homes and on our streets. Monkey see, monkey do, but this monkey had a different idea. This simple truth came from the Canadian Voice of Women for Peace.

> *If we had set out to destroy human life on this planet over a period of time, we could not have found a better way than the nuclear cycle.*

Sister Mary Beth Reissen, the Representative of Pax Christi, the International Catholic Peace Movement, said:

> *As Roman Catholics we are indeed mindful of the early and repeated calls of the Popes of this century for the cessation of weapons testing and production.*

It was the reminders of the mayors of Hiroshima and Nagasaki along with the indigenous people, Bill Rosse Sr. of the Western Shoshone and Topa Raphael of Polynesia, that hit me the most.

> *My name is Hitoshi Motoshima, the mayor of Nagasaki. On August 9, 1945 near the end of World War II, a single atomic bomb transformed Nagasaki into a city of death. Men and women, children and adults were burned, blown through the air, and died in excruciating pain. It was a scene straight from hell. Within five months more than 74,000 had died. Even today, the majority of survivors continue to suffer, plagued by blood disease, malignant tumors, and keloids.*

He ended on a positive note calling for the CTB and the NGOs to widen the grassroots peace movement. It seemed he was calling for the Hundredth Monkey.

> *There are 4,600 cities in 25 countries throughout the world which have declared themselves nuclear-free zones.*

Topa Merehau Rapael, a Maohi man from the Polynesian Liberation Front pointed an accusing finger at the French government:

> *Mountains of official declarations, missions, and false studies and all media operations, etceteras, were orchestrated and financed directly or indirectly by the French in order to abuse us. My people and the world have stopped counting the lies. We say, No More Nuclear Tests! Stop Hurting the MAOHI People!*
>
> *We have all heard President Mitterand condemning the occupation of Kuwait. I just want to remind you that New Caledonia and TE AO Maohi are also occupied by French army forces.*

The magnitude of impact on cultures around the world from nuclear testing was hard to grasp. My own exposure revealed that indigenous economies were manipulated or destroyed in the Koreas, Germany, Canada, China, Kazakhstan, Moruroa, Maohi, the Dakotas, Newe Segobia, and the Four Corners.

Bill Rosse, the Western Shoshone National Council's Environmental Protection Officer, came right to the point,

> *It is simply not possible to overlook the United States treaty making and breaking.*
>
> *The Western Shoshone Nation has classified the United States and Great Britain tests as bombs. The purpose of a bomb is to destroy; if the tests were not destructive, they would be performed in the Americas or British territories.*
>
> *Although the Western Shoshone people wish to emphasize the fact of our nation's unextinguished land title, our opposition to nuclear testing is not based on legal or nationalistic self-interest. All unlawful violations of the Treaty of Ruby Valley concern the Western Shoshone National Council, but the acts of greatest concern are those that threaten the world and affect all forms of life.*
>
> *I want you to know that I also speak for the water, land, plants, and animals that are suffering, and cannot speak for themselves. We are responsible for these things, and the Western Shoshone Nation will not give up this responsibility.*
>
> *In 1988 the WSNC began to issue permits to anti nuclear activists on Western Shoshone land at the Nevada Test Site gates. The strategy was to use arrests for trespass as a means*

*of demonstrating that the United States cannot accuse some-
one of trespass on land it does not own. Indeed this strategy
worked. Since permit issuance began in 1988, approximately
15,000 permits have been issued and charges of trespass carrying six months in jail and $1000 fine maximum penalty
have been consistently dropped. This is implicit recognition
of Western Shoshone title.*

With the day's session ended, I joined a vigil across the street at the Isaiah
Wall. There etched into the sixty foot marble wall was the quote from Isaiah,
Chapter 2, verse 4, "They shall beat their swords into plowshares, and their
spears into pruning hooks: nation shall not lift up sword against nation, neither
shall they learn war anymore." A twisted gun barrel, a bell of heroes medals
and a biblical mandate to beat swords to plows... it seemed I was in sync with
the U.N. The question was, how to get the U.S. in sync with the U.N.?

*"By what right do they decide the fate of all humanity? From
Scandinavia to Latin America, from Europe and Africa to the
Far East, the destiny of every man and woman is affected by
their actions." Juan Perez de Cuellar, addressing the UN
assembly on the arms buildup by the super powers, Dec. 1994*

* * * * *

Wednesday morn, I decided to take a day to do my handyman duty for the
Worker House, the least I could do for their hospitality. Downstairs, I lucked
out to pancakes for breakfast with the women, but the stench of cigarette
smoke drooling over my cakes made syrup almost redundant. I guess it was
just too many family vacations as a child, stuck in the car with a Mom and Pop
cigarette smoking team. Did it contribute to my sickly childhood and bronchial
pneumonia? At seven, I knew I felt like I was suffocating. But watching gramps
die from his smoking was the hardest thing. The stench smelled like death to
me, more government subsidized death.

In the afternoon, I joined the Catholic Workers in prayers I didn't know,
but I mumbled the meaning clearly. "Please Creator, God, Buddha, Allah, halt
the increasing threat of a Middle East war with Iraq." I felt I was a Catholic as
much as a Buddhist, a Shoshone as much as Jew.

A look at the Tuesday Times put me in a state of disgust. How convenient,

I thought, that the war was escalating right during the CTB conference.

The next morning I took a brisk walk uptown and entered the UN building. The delegate from India approached me in the lobby and introduced himself. "I was impressed by your Common Man paper. It was very good. Thank you."

He asked me if I'd heard the U.S. statement yesterday.

"No, did I miss it?"

"Well, you certainly didn't miss anything worth hearing," he summarized the US delegate's delivery. "'The US still views nuclear weapons as a deterrent to war and must continue testing for that purpose.' The sad part was her closing remarks, 'The United States will not participate in, or provide any financial support to, or any continuation of this conference in any manner beyond the scheduled two week session. We urge other parties to join in bringing this process to a close.'"

"That's disgusting! When will they ever learn?"

"Yes, but we must keep trying. Thank you again." He bowed and parted.

I entered the main chamber and threaded my way through the tables and chairs to the desk placard displaying "United States of America." I had heard of the US delegate Mary Elizabeth Hoinkes, but as yet had no face for her. A tall, balding man with glasses stood shuffling through his briefcase. I got his attention and introduced myself.

"I understand that you are in favor of continued nuclear weapons testing," I began.

"That is the U.S. position. Yes," he responded curtly.

"No, that's not true. The majority of Americans are in favor of stopping nuclear testing and have been for many years. You are misrepresenting the American public here at this conference."

"Well, you should talk to the delegate about that. I take notes and help her."

"Well, then you're an accomplice to this crime of poisoning our planet." He only glared at me.

I continued, "My position is that we must follow through with the mandate of the 1963 Partial Test Ban Treaty and stop testing NOW! That is the position of the United States and that is your job; to represent the people, not some narrow special interests making a fortune on weapons production and testing. Remember the Nuremburg Trials. You can be held accountable." He listened because he had no option. I was in his face.

I walked away, certain at least that he knew my position. I took my seat, and again I was witness to testimony after testimony supporting the CTB. Some nations were not so bold in swiping at the depository powers, specifically the US and Great Britain, but all knew the time was ripe for a CTB. I suspect some nations were reluctant to risk their US foreign aid for an opportunity to reiterate the truth.

Outside, the weather had turned, and snow was falling in waves and flurries. The streets were covered with four inches; cars were swerving and sliding as they tested their tires and skills. The U.N. snowblowers were already on the sidewalks, spitting snow off into the blanketed shrubbery.

During lunch break, the members of the Non-Governmental Organizations (NGOs) moved across the street for lunch and conference. I was happy to see Bill Rosse, Sr. and Corbin Harney there at lunch. They were accompanied by two women I recognized from test site actions. In the year following, Linda Putman became a dear friend and Sue Navy became an intimate partner.

I squeezed in at the table of the Campaign for Nuclear Disarmament (CND), Europe's largest antinuclear group based in London. It turned out that a full dozen of these committed activists had flown the Atlantic Ocean to lobby the British delegates to stop testing.

I arrived back at the UN just after the start of the British delegate's statement. I took a deep breath, knowing full well Mr. Kenyons' statement would echo the US position. I felt a funeral atmosphere in the hall.

I heard him say,

> *The world agonizes over an age-old problem, namely the painful necessity of deterring aggression. How are governments to respond to this new mosaic of circumstances in ways that enhance, rather than undermine their security? Perceptions differ, depending on one's vantage point.*

Yeah, I thought, those that get rich off the arms race have one vantage point...the buck. Those that are oppressed by it have another...death and suffering.

I looked over to the seating on the right front to see the British CND people in the front row. Just as I noticed them, they rose to their feet, and as the British delegate spoke, they turned their backs to him. It seemed a fitting protest and I wanted to join them.

> *I would draw attention to the second paragraph of the Partial Test Ban Treaty which places the objective in its proper context, namely 'an agreement on general and complete disarmament...which would put an end to the armaments race and eliminate the incentive to the production and testing of all kinds of weapons, including nuclear weapons.' In other words, the Treaty itself implies that a nuclear test ban should be seen in the context of wider disarmament.*

'Bullshit!' I muttered to myself. 'Absurd!' His rationale stated that since we cannot reach our ultimate goal now, then why take the first step. The key words he left out of the first sentence were, "the speediest possible achievement."

My emotions started to get intense as I moved into a corner, behind the Brits. I was overwhelmed with the reality of what was taking place. The vast majority of the world wanted to move away from nuclear weapons and immediately away from testing them; yet here, embodied in this British colonialist voice, was the fact that this small oligarchic faction, under the guise of democracy, was insisting on the continuation of nuclear testing. It was forcing the world to smoke two packs of radioactive cigarettes a day, everyone: fetuses, pregnant women, children, old folks, ministers, dogs, and the rest.

> *Again I sense the reaction of some delegates, this time one of frustration that a prized objective must remain a long-term goal.*

Now there's some creative interpretation, "speediest possible" equals "long-term goal?" I stood there in the wing, hearing the voice of pomposity telling me there was nothing we could do about it. I prayed for guidance, "Show me what to do, Creator." My body began to tremble as if an earthquake or a nuclear test were about to let go, pre tremors running through me. I felt like I was about to have a seizure, the emotion was so intense.

> *I should like to answer a point raised by some delegations about the environmental effects of testing. A 1989 report from the US Congress Office of Technology Assessment concluded that the sum total of all radioactive releases since 1970 could not have posed a threat to public health, even on the immediate boundaries of the Nevada Test Site.*

These words knifed into my soul like a blunt crow bar. A red light began flashing in my mind. I remembered the Mighty Oak nuclear test disaster of 1986 at the Nevada Test Site, which released 2000 times more radiation than Three Mile Island. My head tilted back and my throat opened to a flow of power bursting through a crack somewhere in the earth.

"Blasphemy! Blasphemy!" It bellowed from deep within. The volume reached through the entire hall. The delegate stopped speaking. I turned and rushed to the front of the room and stood wide-eyed before the delegates. I needed no microphone. "How long will you sacrifice present and future generations for your confused concept of security?" I demanded. I stared out into the audience, no longer seeing, overcome with emotion, drained in an instant.

I walked back into the corner and half kneeled, half fell to the floor. I began to pray, already questioning my actions. The room was silent until there began a single clap, clap, clap, echoing hollow against the walls. A lone, slow, unhurried sound hanging on its own until another clap joined and another and another until the room was consumed in applause, in agreement. The sound was deafening, and when I turned, the whole room was standing. I was weak and overwhelmed, but I began clapping with the crowd.

I moved from the corner and looked down towards the main bench to see the Secretary General of the United Nations, Javier De Cuellar, walking my way, followed by the assistant general. He strode directly up to me, offering his hand, looking deep into my eyes, and said, "I know just how you feel and I feel the same way." In an instant I recognized the integrity of this man, not just because of his words, but his eye contact. We shared a brotherhood lasting only an instant, and yet an eternity.

The clapping continued and had evolved into the rhythmic clapping of an encore demand. Clap, clap, clap, clap, clap, everyone together. It had become its own spontaneous action.

De Cuellar continued loudly, "But you know, the Non-Governmental Organizations had their chance to speak and nobody interrupted them."

"Yes, but they weren't lying," I pointed out.

His face betrayed his frustration with my answer, knowing that you can't argue with the blunt truth. "Well, can we stop this demonstration and continue our session?" He asked, as if I had some control over it.

I looked out into the crowd, listening to the deafening clap, and told him, "They can stop whenever they want." I tried to let him know I was not in control, but with a vague bow he departed back to the podium. The wonder and awe stayed with me as well as feelings of exhaustion. Those two short bellows took something out of me. As I stood there, dumbfounded, about to slump to the floor, I felt an arm wrap into mine on the right and then another on the left. I looked to see Dr. Carolyn Cottom's face, her arm holding mine tightly. Another body linked onto hers and on each side a chain of four or five people formed. "What's going on, Carolyn?" I asked.

"If they take you, they'll have to take us all," she informed me.

"Oh, they're not going to take anyone anywhere," I hadn't even considered getting arrested, but it was for certain I wouldn't be going alone. Through my arms I felt a flow of invincible energy starting to rejuvenate my being. I looked into the determined eyes of the women linking arms and I was near to tears. The President of the Boston Physicians for Social Responsibility came up and shook my hand. "You're like my son, all mild mannered and quiet, and then roaring the truth in their faces." He patted my shoulders and hugged me. The clapping was still thunderous.

There was a commotion at the doorways as half a dozen security police ran into the room. They looked in all directions, apparently searching for something, but not quite knowing what it was. In a stop-and-go fashion, they ran down to the other end of the room, heads bobbing, eyes scanning, and returned to the front entrance to depart for further orders.

I decided it was time to move on, and thanked Carolyn and the others for their support. I needed to sit down. I moved out into the lobby to find a couch, but before I got there a woman approached me with questions.

"Are you the one that just disrupted the U.N. session?"

"Yes, but let's go sit down on the couch," I pointed to one in the lobby.

"How did you get into this conference, who are you with?" I suspected she was a U.N. official.

I didn't want to jeopardize Greenpeace or the fellow that was good enough to get me in, but it was there in the records if she wanted to look.

"Check your books. I'm an independent, but I work with a group called The Hundredth Monkey."

"The Hundredth What?"

"Now I am obliged to report to governments and to the public that progress has slowed. Agreements have been entered into freely, but the will to enforce them has often been lacking...The pace of government action has faltered...It is not with any satisfaction that I am forced to report this failure of political will."
— *Mustafa Tolba United Nation's Environment Programme*

As I crossed the street to the Isaiah Wall I was pleased to see that our vigil against the impending war had grown to about thirty. The cold kept us moving, white fluff gathering on our shoulders. The delegate from Sri Lanka joined us briefly, a token well appreciated.

During our vigil I heard bits of the controversy over my action. Sister Mary of Pax Christi was not happy at all. Nothing like this had ever happened at a U.N. meeting. She was very concerned about future involvement of NGOs being curtailed.

I remembered Gandhi's quote, "God never came to me in person, only in action." Was that God's voice that had come through me? The resulting clapping had certainly substantiated agreement.

Upon returning to the Catholic Worker House, I was granted a reprieve from the blues by a new room mate. Kevin was studying to be a brother in the Paulist order. After the 'Blasphemy' story, we became good friends immediately.

I awoke at 5:00 AM to the sound of water splattering in the shower. Kevin was up. I was excited to write a letter to try to alleviate the NGOs of responsibility for yesterday's interruption. I wrote,

> *An APOLOGY to all participants of the United Nations Amendment Conference. My name is Rick Springer. I am an independent citizen representing, as the Yugoslavian delegation put it, 'the man in the street'. I would like to formally apologize for the manner in which I disrupted the Thursday session. My intent was not to alienate participants or disrupt the process.*
>
> *Let this apology not be remotely misconstrued as a retraction of or an apology as to the content of my statements regarding the United Kingdoms address. His statements were indeed blasphemous. He is either lying or incredibly naive. Underground nuclear testing is poisoning our environment and killing the very people it is purported to protect.*

I approached the revolving doors of the UN once again, the snow blower howling, removing the stark white remnants of yesterday's blasphemous day. I was partly expecting to be accosted, my pass revoked, my person not welcome, but it was not so. If the guards recognized me, it didn't show, and I wheeled through the doors. I carried my new statements to the information table.

I gave up early on Friday, somehow having lost my heart for it. I had a feeling that no matter what the rest of the world said, these immoral tyrants, the U.S. and Great Britain, were going to prevail in preventing the signing of the CTB Treaty. Were these people beaten constantly as children, were they left unloved to hide in the garage to see if anyone missed them? Were they witness to Nazi terrorism, responding to those horrors and unwittingly recreating them? How could I forgive these ill and ailing people? Gandhi's words came to me again, "Before we dare think of peace, we must be brave enough to love one another." To love the perpetrators, the proponents of nuclear testing, was a challenge of which I was still falling short.

That Friday a rally of about 5,000 African Americans gathered at the Isaiah Wall, proclaiming their outrage that the White House was planning to launch a war on Martin Luther King Jr's birthday. As I worked the crowd from inside I found that almost no one was aware of the CTB, let alone the conference.

I was sad to feel more of the Malcolm X militancy than the Martin Luther King Jr wisdom. Still, as a white activist surrounded by angry New York blacks, I felt safer than an environmentalist at a Humboldt County timber worker picnic.

The crowd continued to grow, swelling until it nearly choked off the four-lane boulevard in front of the United Nations. A loudspeaker from behind ordered the group to disperse.

I had moved to the outer edge so I could see the mounted police moving their horses in to disperse the crowd. I attempted to leave northward, as that was the path of least resistance, but the officer before me insisted I move south only. The crowd to the south of me was packed and impenetrable.

The frothy mouths and wide shiny eyes of several nervous horses stood before me. The officers were beginning to push the crowd by turning the horses sideways and leaning into the people on the periphery. The inner crowd couldn't hear the police or even see them.

This was a first for me, seeing horses used in crowd control. I tried to convince the officer on the horse with logic, "Well, you're gonna' have to move the crowd on the other side to get this side to move."

"Just get movin' and they'll move." Each officer was brandishing a billy club, waving it like a cowboy hustling cattle.

I resented the use of horses, feeling their sense of abuse as the energy stretched like a tight wire. The policeman began leaning his horse against my shoulders as the horse's hooves danced over my feet. I glanced at the horse's front legs, thinking that I could tackle them and bring him down if I had to.

I yelled at the officer, "Hey you idiot, you're gonna break my feet. Can't you see, I can't go anywhere?" I pushed back into the horse's brown, sweating belly, trying to make some space. I considered dragging the officer off the horse; that's how threatened I felt.

Finally, the police changed strategy and moved to push from behind the crowd, allowing people to move out of the street, both north and south. I left the event awestruck and wandered to Dag Hammerskold Park, a couple blocks north.

I saw that the war protest was bursting out all over the city in rallies, street blockades and police confrontations. Paddy wagons were being filled with protesters. The war had already begun, as far as I could see. I marveled at the strange twists of fate that send one young man off to die or kill in Iraq and another to be beaten over the head ten blocks from home for protesting the death and killing. I moved north on First Avenue, wondering how the world got sucked up into these political fights. Poor young brainwashed men running off to die for some old fart's business decisions.

I saw myself standing in the Marine Corps recruiting office. Eighteen years old, fresh out of high school, a pacifist by birthright; but there I was, wondering what to do with my life now that school was completed. The Marine Corps claimed "We build men." At eighteen with twenty blond whiskers on my chin, that thought held more subconscious appeal than I knew. Nobody else offered any rites of passage so blatantly.

They even had all the necessary components of the rites; jerk you from the women, hazing for days, belittling your masculinity, "fifty push-ups, pussy," pushing, pushing, till you learned that you could endure more than you ever thought. Entering a new world, a world of death, that should you come out the other side, you would be different, never able to go back to boyhood, the shelter of a mother. The boy died and a man was born....sometimes.

The terrible sadness was not only that the rites had become institutionalized, but that real, as well as symbolic death had become a part of it. When you killed another human you were certain you had passed. You had dealt with the ultimate horror, taken life into your own hands, and proclaimed that even the ten commandments were a judgment call.

There I was at eighteen, my life spread before me, not knowing what I was going to do with it. My girlfriend's sister, Colleen, had somehow figured it out long before me.

"Rick, do you have any idea what the Marines are gonna do to your head?" She didn't have to wait for an answer, since here I was at the recruiting office. "They are gonna brainwash your already feeble mind 'til it is so bleached white that you don't have an original thought left. Yess Sihr" she taunted me with disgust. "Do you know what they're gonna teach you how to do?" She jumped into my face for effect, "Kill people, Rick. That's what they do in the Marines. And then you get to come home and feel bad about it for the rest of your life!"

"OK, Colleen, back off just a little bit," I said sarcastically. She was getting to me. The fact was, hard as it is to believe, I had never really considered that I might have to kill anybody for any reason. The political aspect of becoming a man for Uncle Sam was way beyond me. I didn't understand, and didn't want to understand. The Marines was just a job, a paycheck, a rite of passage, although I didn't know what that was at the time. It was a direction for my life until I came up with my own plan. Besides, my big brother was in the Marines, and I really respected him. My dad had been in the Navy. It was something males had to do, or so I thought.

I listened to the recruiter rap, but halfway out the door decided to put some more thought into it. There was something convincing about Colleen's disgust with this whole military idea.

And here I was in New York City, 39 years old, knowing exactly how lucky I was to have had Colleen there in my life. Actually, it was a series of lucky events. First Colleen, then my number 74 lottery ticket with the military, then my motorcycle wreck while riding like a wild kamikaze in the Mojave desert, my broken jaw, my six-month draft deferment, and finally my erroneous reclassification as 1-Y, not eligible for military service.

Yes, here I was in New York. In this chaotic crowd of thousands, I ran into my new roommate from the Catholic Worker House, the Paulist, Kevin.

"This is bizarre," he commented. We stared in disbelief as police horses stomped on fallen screaming bodies. "See that older woman in the business suit? She's the councilwoman for this borough and very well liked. She will probably get into the paddy wagon with the people to make sure they are treated fairly. I'm sure she's opposed to the war also."

"Well, that makes everybody except the government and the police. Makes you wonder why anybody pays their taxes." A couple of heads in the crowd turned and nodded approval to me. "So what's the church doing about this?"

"Not a lot really. They have issued an opposition statement, but other than that they watch and keep their nose out of it."

We watched another screaming woman break from a policeman's grip and run back to the road blockade. For her commitment, she was clubbed brutally in the kidneys and dragged back to the paddy wagon. Kent State began to come alive for me, and the term 'police state' took on new meaning. I was impressed that in this entire unruly crowd, I had not seen one act of violence from the people. The police were disgusting; the protesters were inspiring. It made a bald-faced lie of every childhood picture book of the kindly policeman helping the citizens. Today they were the henchmen of the rich. We're going to war for a paycheck, and don't you try to stop us. I was damn near one of 'em. How many wake up calls do we get? I woke up a bit more.

I left the emotionally burning city to take advantage of New York for The Hundredth Monkey. I took an hour, beat feet across town, and explained the Hundredth Monkey Project to Little Steven Van Zandt's promoter Mike Sinclair. He was good enough to hear me out and, even more, offer some positive suggestions. He felt a coalition of promoters was a possibility worth following up. He was also well connected with Native people and shared his office with a new publication called Indian Voices.

I left Sinclair's office and began the journey back across town. New York was not happy about the possible war; I don't care what the polls indicated. I encountered what I estimated to be about 20,000 people marching in the streets that night. At some areas they seemed to be pouring out of the buildings like ants out of a stirred nest.

When I made it back to the U.N. headquarters it was almost 7:00, dark and nippy. There in the U.N. driveway, the Native Americans had gathered another thousand protesters. With drums and songs, they burned sage and prayed that violence aimed at Iraq would not begin.

On my way to the subway, I noticed the cardboard village again, hoping those villagers would make it through the night, and that tomorrow some refuge would arrive. I sat in the subway train on the way home to my own refuge of the Mary House, my legs tingling from miles of pounding in the concrete jungle. I was thankful but it was becoming more clear all the time that "when any are imprisoned, none are free." Prison could be a cardboard box, a steel cage or an arsenal of threats, sometimes even a glass house.

It's a strange phenomenon, or perhaps a methodical strategy that has forced us to live under the shadow of death known as nuclearism. Now *that* is a prison!

✳ ✳ ✳ ✳ ✳

I returned the following morning to the Isaiah Wall. I marveled at how just the night before, the streets had swarmed with protesters, and now perhaps only two hundred stood watching a parade of people dressed as bombs, detailing the history of America's corporate incest with the nuclear industry. Perhaps thirty activists paraded by, each portraying a particular nuclear bomb. "My name is Trinity" a woman announced, "'the destroyer of worlds.' So claimed Oppenheimer when he saw my power unleashed. I was the first US nuclear test in Alamagordo, New Mexico."

"My name is Fat Man." "I'm Little Boy." "My name is Baneberry." "My name is Mighty Oak." Each person told the history of the bomb they represented, their kilotonnage, their power, the damage they caused, the public response or lack of, their costs in dollars, in deaths. It was a parade worthy of a film, but only a handful heard the presentation.

My action at the U.N. on Thursday remained a topic of discussion. Author and activist Terry Tempest Williams, whose work, <u>The Clan of the One Breasted Women</u>, had dramatically affected me, introduced herself at the rally. She shared what she had heard, telling me that many others had felt just as I had felt during the British statement and were so inspired by my interruption that they would never be silent again. She felt it was important for me to know that the action was positive.

Aaron Tovish, the head of the Global Parliamentarians, explained to me that the British delegate was not so cocky after the session reopened. "It was obvious he had been humbled a bit." He shook my hand, congratulating me on a good job.

In the afternoon at a church rally, I set up a table of buttons and bumper stickers to spread the word and raise money for The Hundredth Monkey. A woman approached to tell me that God had a mission for me. "Do not be afraid of it." While I was quite aware of the mission, the fear didn't just disappear because she said so.

From my table in the lobby, I could hear Corbin Harney beginning his prayers in the language of his ancestors, the Newe of Newe Segobia. I had heard Corbin so many times at the Nevada Test Site that I could say many of the prayer words along with him.

"Shundihai... There," he concluded

With sparkling eyes-of-age, Bill Rosse, Sr. stepped up to the mic and introduced himself as the Environmental Protection Officer of the Western Shoshone National Council.   Now, if we could boot the James Watts of America and install a Bill Rosse, this earth would have a chance.

> *The US Government says they own the Nevada Test Site. Now that can't be true 'cause they give it to us in the 1863 Ruby Valley Treaty. Now we know you can't give someone what they already own, but we figured we had ta humor 'em cause they were a wild bunch.*
>
> *We give 'em the right to come and go and build towns and telegraphs and we kept our part of the bargain, but we never give 'em our land.   That land belongs to the Creator and we are the rightful caretakers of that land.*

A roar of applause gave support to his claim.

> *In 1951 the US government came in and took over a piece of our land and called it the Nevada Test Site, and they have been out there polluting it ever since with radioactive bombs. We have been to Washington many times fighting this illegal use of land, but what they really done was take the money from one pocket and put it into the other. We never took a nickel, so they appointed some Bureau of Indian Affairs person to accept it for us, and today it sits in some bank account somewhere. Well, we are never going to take it.*
>
> *Our chief, Raymond Yowell, has issued a statement demanding that the US government immediately stop testing nuclear bombs on our lands and clean up the mess. Thank you all. It's gonna take us all to wrap up this job. The US government doesn't know what's good for 'em, so we are gonna have to work together to help them understand. Thank you!*

The audience raged with applause.

I decided to get aggressive with my sales tactics, and pinned twenty buttons on for the subway ride home. "Anti-war buttons, only one buck, or three for two bucks. Come on folks, help put an antinuclear activist through Washington, DC."

This was my last night in the Mary House. I was happy and sad at the same time. I counted up the day's take, and was sorry I could only spare a twenty for the hospitality and generosity of the Catholic Worker. The BIG money that Allen Alfeldt said I'd need to organize the Monkey was not jumping in my lap.

Chapter Five
WAR AT THE WHITEHOUSE

IRAQ Saddam Hussein believes he is the son of Nebuchad-nezzar, and the Prophet Muhammed. Iraq bought a small French nuclear reactor called Osiris (the Egyptian version of Pluto, the Greek God of the underworld), capable of quickly generating enough bomb-grade material for three Hiroshima-size bombs. On Sunday June 7, 1981, the Israeli Air Force blew it to smithereens. "Peace-loving nations," said Hussein afterwards, "should now help the Arabs to acquire atomic bombs as a counter balance to those already possessed by Israel."

— Marc Ian Barasch, The Little Black Book of Atomic War 1983

* * * * *

Plane flights had become an evil necessity. They cost big money and made me nauseated. Jet lag was the time it took me to overcome the sense that I'd like to vomit. Sometimes, I'd lay down in the airport, under a row of chairs, a bum in transit, until I recovered enough to head out into the streets of... and yes, here I was again in Washington, DC.

The deal was that I would get my plane ticket covered to the United Nations conference if I would be in DC for the White House war protest. My job was to sell buttons, bumper stickers and T-shirts, all with an anti-war message. It fit into my plans perfectly and gave me another opportunity to meet with Women Strike for Peace, Greenpeace, Sane Freeze, and the Center for Defense Information (CDI), the DC biggies in the anti-nuke movement.

On prior trips to the US capitol, I had developed friends. Life was good this round though I had slept several nights in the past by hopping over church fences to crash in their bushes. There had been no budget for lodging, and if the meek were to inherit the earth, then maybe the occasionally homeless would qualify.

When I visited Women Strike for Peace it became clear that efforts other than war resistance were a waste of time. Some of their staff were busy with nurse friends draining pints of their own blood to pour on the steps of the White House. I put the Monkey on hold. It's odd to think that I never took the war idea all that seriously---until they started dropping the bombs.

I took the bus and then walked back to Richie's, where I was staying. No sooner had I got in the door than the phone rang and Richie was screaming. "We're at war, man. The old asshole did it. They're bombing the hell out of 'em right now. Why don't you come on over to my folk's so we can watch it all on the big screen. Jose is comin over here. I think we'll head down to the White House later on. C'mon over!" He sounded like a runaway train, choo, chooooo!!!

'Nooooo,' I thought to myself. 'This is sick! Watch it on the big screen?' Somehow the idea of war on TV smacked of a society of ambulance chasers and fire fiends. I felt like we were watching the neighbors abuse their children, offering commentary on the strategical strike to the child's head while we ignored the screaming.   Still I hoisted my loaner bike on my shoulder and thumped on down the stairs to pedal over to join Richie and Jose in the latest reports.

The United Nations conference, convened after 27 years of ignoring the mandate of the 1963 Partial Test Ban Treaty, was now nothing more than another broken dream. The war didn't just overshadow the historic CTB effort, it blacked it out, a total eclipse of the nuclear sun. The boogie man, Hussein, was justification for more and better nukes, more jobs and more profit. While pedaling across D.C., I sang the words from John Fogerty of Credence Clearwater Revival,

Violence is Golden
Pass another fleet of B-1 bombers. Grab an M-16.
Buildin Chevies was never the fun as buildin up the war machine.
Got a rocket in my pocket. Do you think we can deal?
Got a year-end sale goin on. You can see the appeal.
Cuz I'm sellin both sides of the fence. That be the name of the game.
I don't care bout your silly little struggle. Money's colored all the same.
Take a handful of star war missiles. Maybe super laser gun.
Gotta keep stuff movin out the door. Got a business to run.
Violence is golden! Violence is golden!

I climbed the porch steps and brought my bike into the house so it wouldn't ride off on its own. It was already dark, and Richie was glued to the screen. "Check it out, man," he stated in a fervor of disbelief. "Man, dese guys are goin' for it. It's unreal."

I found a chair in front of the screen. The psychic numbing moved into full swing as my emotions seemed half dead just from Richie's announcements. The TV broadcasters were showing maps of Iraq and the places where US bombers were working. They were dropping conventional bombs on what they were calling military installations, trying to assure us that this was so very humane, indeed, that they were 'surgical strikes.' The word 'sortie' entered my vocabulary as each bomber flew a flight pattern to the target and, as the crosshairs lined up on his screen and ours, pushed the button to release the bombs.

I thought of the poor soldiers of Iraq, that in ignorance and in need of a job had enlisted into Hussein's army. Well, here they go, Hussein's fodder. I heard the Neville Brothers from their <u>Brother's Keeper</u> album,

> "Now they've got us hypnotized and hysterical
> Screaming for blood and justice
> Now they've got us hypnotized and hysterical"

The TV screen differed very little from the myriad of computer games, arcade machines, and movies so many Americans played or watched as entertainment. The fact that people were 'really' dying was incidental. It was almost the big payoff for all of our practice in violence as a means of conflict resolution, violence as a means of manhood, of proving righteousness, of livelihood, of might makes right, and worse, of entertainment.

I opened some of the Peace Resource Project boxes that had arrived via UPS that day, and looked through the piles of buttons and stickers: No Blood For Oil; War Is Not An Energy Policy; Support Our Troops...Bring Em Home Alive; US Out Of The Gulf. Feeling like a soldier of fortune, a stateside mercenary, I threw the stock back in the boxes. Richie and Jose were discussing strategies for the evening at the White House. I felt as though I should be trying to sell also, but I couldn't get my heart into it. I tried to rationalize, 'Hey, these people that buy these buttons and stickers are happy to get them. We're giving them the opportunity to express their opinion of the war and maybe help change the policy faster. Not to mention that The Hundredth Monkey was hungry.

It didn't matter; the thought of changing American currency on this evening when Iraqi citizens, desperate for a paycheck, were being bombed with US tax dollars, was more than I could overcome.

We got into Jose's 'stallion,' the old Ford Mercury Thunderbird. It was a safe car for DC. Old enough to be built of steel and ugly enough to be ignored by thieves. They schlopped their merchandise into the trunk and we drove on downtown. After arriving at Lafayette Park across from the Whitehouse, we separated with plans to meet in an hour at the Proposition One sign.

Here it was in real life: 'If you kill one person, it's murder, but if you kill ten thousand, it's foreign policy.' I said some prayers as I walked across the park towards the blaring lights of the White House and wished I had some sage to burn. The thought came back to me of Corbin's prayers in New York for the Comprehensive Test Ban and for peace in the face of this war . I guess there were just not enough of us praying. We were still a few monks (or monkeys) short.

* * * * *

"Professor Howard R. Raiffa of the Harvard Business School calls the new public relations style, 'strategic misrepresentation.' A massive public relations industry is designed to 'sell' government and industry decisions to the public, spawning public distrust, but also political paralysis and ineffectiveness. Unemployment is blamed on `cheap foreign competition,' while businesses deliberately move jobs to ghetto-like cheap labor pools in the third world. Labor is pitted against environmentalists, men against women, the middle class against the poor, the guerrillas against the para-military, right against the left, the first world against the third."
— Dr. Rosalie Bertell <u>No Immediate Danger</u>

* * * * *

The crowd had gathered, probably about three thousand people already. Banners were waving, drums beating, chants raging. "One, two, three, four. We don't want your fucking war!"

I had only just arrived when a major commotion was happening to the left of the front gate at the White House. I ran down the sidewalk to check it out. In front of my face, I could see the horses highstepping towards a line of people sitting in the road. The protestors were trying to block traffic and stop business-as-usual. The police had another plan. The people sitting in the road were linked arm in arm, but they freaked out at the sight of prancing horses, hooves flying, descending upon them. People began screaming and running in all directions. I watched as the blockade broke up and the protestors scrambled to get to their feet, desperate to escape horses' hooves on human bones.

My EMT mothering instinct emerged as I watched with trepidation. The lead mounted horseman had come unglued. He was chasing after people, and from the vantage of his horses height, was smashing down on their skulls with his billy club. I was astounded, feeling as though I was witnessing murder, first hand, by the very force that was supposedly hired to prevent that act.

One man reeled from the blow but was able to keep running, staggering, while the horseman focused on another target, running my way. I stepped into the street, screaming at the horseman. "NOOOOO, You're PEACEKEEPERS, REMEMBER, YOU'RE PEACEKEEPERS!!!"

His billy club was raised high over his head, like an ancient samurai about to behead a fleeing opponent. He brought it down on the unsuspecting refugee, his hate-grimaced face, teeth clenched, shining through his riot shield.

I moved inward another step and screamed again as if commanding a child to back away from a cliff, "You're peace---" My words were stopped in my throat. My ribcage flexed in and pushed on my heart as if I were receiving a jumpstart from a defibrillator. I flew backwards through the air about four feet and almost fell back on the sidewalk. I hadn't seen the muscular black policeman coming from the side or his billy club clenched between both fists as he slammed it into the center of my chest.

"Get back on that sidewalk, NOOOW!".. He yelled in my face. He kept showing his teeth like a wild animal, his nose scrunched up to allow more air flow. My pleading reminder to them that they were peacekeepers had been wrong. I had bought the Orwellian doublespeak myself. They were war officers defending Dictator Bush, the Duke of Exxon and Count Rockwell. Peacekeepers do not use violence to halt a nonviolent protest.

He stood just six inches from my face making a wall of his body. I recovered with a deep breath, and a foul calm came over me, much as the reprieve between the vomiting and retching sessions of a sick man. I looked directly into his unseeing eyes, his lips now pursed tight, his body in at-ease position but ready for action, baton gripped to strike at the slightest provocation.

"I'm sorry you were so abused as a child that you have all this hate in you, that you're willing to beat on your own people. I'll say some prayers for you tonight." He gave no indication of acknowledgment, but I could see into his eyes. He heard me.

I turned into the crowd behind me and went in search of the injured. I didn't look far before finding a man with trails of blood running down his forehead, behind his ear and into his shirt. The bombing had hit home already I prayed another marble wall with little names carved on it wouldn't be erected again, not here in DC or in Iraq.

I introduced myself as an EMT to the stunned man and asked if I could help. He agreed, with a vague nod. I parted the sticky wet hair to see the injury and promptly found the protruding goose egg. It seemed to be clotting up as the hair aided in forming a sticky scab.

"Now look, you're probably fine, but you are going to need to get checked out further at the emergency." I looked into his ears for cerebro spinal fluid (CSF) and they were dry. I looked into his glazed eyes and demanded that he come back to me and look at me. "Now look at my finger," I told him. His eyes followed my finger back and forth, both eyes working in unison.

"That's good. There is a thing called a subdural hematoma that can be caused by a whack on the head like you just got. What it is is a bruise under the skull, and the bruise can cause pressure on your brain. It is very important to get this checked out further," I told him. "Do you understand me?" I spoke loud and clear in the midst of the crowd. He nodded. "Are you with anyone?" I asked. He pointed to a woman by his side. "Do you understand?" I asked her.

"Yeah, we'll get him checked out," she responded.

I gave him a quick hug, to which he barely responded. He was in a state of shock, still not believing that the police had beat him. I couldn't believe it either. I was a bit shaky myself. I took another deep breath to check my ribcage, and went in search of the second man, but I was disoriented.

I wandered back towards the front of the White House and became distracted by the pro-war-testers. There were about fifty of them milling around in the midst of the much larger peaceful masses. I hoped the pro-war faction wasn't another team of head busters in civilian clothing. They were quite vocal, yelling, 'Down with Iraq!' 'Bomb Hussein!'

I actually found myself talking with one of the leaders, and I felt like we maybe made some ground. His buddies seemed ready to bust a head or two, but he was smarter, willing to hear another opinion. His argument about Hussein and Iraq was the old standby, "Who's gonna stop them when they get more powerful? Let them control and cut off our oil, cripple us, and then we'll be in real trouble. This guy's a madman. Don't forget Hitler."

To which I responded, "Don't forget Bush," and that ended that.

That night began perhaps the oddest week of my life, television portrayals and government betrayals. I knew for certain we were not getting the big picture in America. The TV stations vied for coverage and ratings as if we were watching the Olympics. Specials on battle strategies, heroisms, and bomb dynamics, team captains dressed in military attire giving press conferences at the capitol. Polls were run as regularly as Santa Anita horse track took bets on T-Biscuit. Just how popular was the war? I stuck with Orwell and figured it was all conjured by Minitrue, the Ministry of Truth.

I struggled through the weekend rally, trying to be an aggressive button and t-shirt salesman, but I couldn't shake the hypocrite feeling, regardless of what good the money would do.

Finally, my time in the east ended. I sat in the plane, flying back to another planet called California. Flying up the coast, I marvelled at the phenomenal destruction of the timber wars in my own backyard. The hills and mountain tops were a patchwork of clearcuts, second growth and struggling seedlings in fields of erosion. From the plane it was a battlefield that the trees had obviously lost. And it wasn't just the trees but with them went the salmon, the spotted owls, murelets and who knows how many species we never even named. It was strange what a war could do to ones psyche from 6,000 miles away.

Upon arrival in Arcata, I learned that the war was worldwide. The City Council of Arcata, considered a progressive community, had passed what was called the Sanctuary Resolution. The resolution allowed that military objectors to the middle east crisis could find sanctuary in the City of Arcata. It was a bold move, one I remain proud of. The tragedy was the response from local war supporters, mostly from the surrounding communities. The city council all received death threats for the resolution. Demands were made that it be rescinded. A parade of logging trucks waving flags toured the downtown Arcata plaza. A local civil war seemed imminent.

At a city townhouse meeting, citizens were allowed to air their views of the resolution. War supporters called it traitorous, cowardly, and out of order for a city government to mess with federal policy. Although those in favor of the resolution outnumbered the war mongers two to one, the threat of violence suceeded in bringing about the dissolution of the resolution. It was true that the resolution had passed in one night in contradiction to process. It was also true that the bombing of Iraq necessitated a more timely process on that occasion.

Three months later, the HOPE Coalition, Humboldt Organized for People and the Environment, brought Dr. Helen Caldicott, a world renowned anti-nuclear activist, to Arcata to speak at Humboldt State University. The Mayor of Arcata, Victor Schaub, introduced her by reminding the crowd that Arcata will always be a sanctuary and a nuclear free zone. The words sounded good, but we had learned that war doesn't stop at the edge of the sanctuary and radiation doesn't stop at the border of a nuclear free zone.

Chapter Six
THE EVENT,
THE WALK AND THE ACTION

After two years of organizing, we still had not confirmed the location of our event, our venue. It was hard to believe we had come this far and had been unable to confirm a venue. It had not been for lack of effort. We made several trips to Las Vegas, met with the Paiute tribe, which owns an ideal parcel just outside of town, began negotiations for the Thomas and Mack Center at University of Nevada, Las Vegas (UNLV), worked with the Jr. College in North Vegas to use their campus, and scoured the surrounding desert, but still nothing was confirmed. We couldn't announce our event without a location. Where can half a million outraged citizens gather in the Las Vegas Area?

We finally found it out in the open desert. The Red Rock Wash Detention Basin was perfect in many respects. The panorama of Red Rock Park was inspirational beyond our hopes. The wash detention basin created a rock bowl to protect us from wind and help with the acoustics of a sound system. It was easy to find, just fifteen miles from central Vegas, straight out Charleston. The surrounding desert offered unlimited camping space. The bowl had been scrafed with graders, so desert tortoise habitat was not a concern.

We went up there one month before our half a million attendees were due to arrive, and more than anything else, felt the spirit of the place. With Mark Dyken, the drummer from Clan Dyken, Matteo and a group of us drumming and singing, we decided for better or worse that the Red Rock Wash Detention Basin was the home of The Hundredth Monkey Event.

Then came the real work. The City of Las Vegas had passed laws years back to be able to hold the reins on any event that might happen around Vegas. They didn't want competition without their approval. The Grateful Dead had just had their first Vegas show the year before, an event that prompted a BLM/DOE effort to prohibit camping on BLM lands around Las Vegas.

Just two weeks before our big event, a band known as Mary's Danish contacted us and wanted to play at our Earth Day event. We were happy to have them. But a local entrepreneur with a history in Vegas entertainment was disgruntled that they canceled out on his pay event to play ours for free. In a foreboding phone call, he claimed he was, the Godfather of Las Vegas. I suspect he was behind the city effort to halt us. But they just didn't know how high or how many hoops a monkey could jump.

The Hundredth Monkey had rented a house, our central office and staging area in North Las Vegas, right in the middle of the smack and crack neighborhoods of North Las Vegas. The price was right, and it had a huge backyard with access for support buses and tents. We built desks out of dumpstered pallets and lined the bedrooms with wall to wall sleeping bags.

It began to look like we might pull the rabbit, or the monkey in this case, out of the hat. Greenpeace endorsed us three weeks before the event. Ben and Jerrys, while they wouldn't change the name of their Chunky Monkey ice cream to The Hundredth Monkey, did confirm they were sending the free ice cream truck. Jefferson Starship was willing to come, if we could fly them in from Hawaii. U-2 was on tour in Arizona the Friday our event began and in LA on Sunday. With our Earth Day contact in British Columbia, Canada, it appeared possible to get U-2. We sent them an invitation from Corbin and Bill of the Western Shoshone to please lend their voice to ours.

The innumerable facets of how it all came together is a book in itself. We were as driven as any paid political campaign, but we ate out of dumpsters, slept on the floor or in cars, and begged from every person we knew to cover our phones and rents. Our offices in Bellingham, Washington; Portland and Eugene, Oregon; Arcata, Oakland, Palo Alto, and Los Angeles, California; Boulder, Denver, and Crested Butte, Colorado; Dayton, Ohio; and Austin, Texas were communicating their successes, newspaper coverage, new offices, fundraisers.

A Peace Train of 35 Soviet citizens flew in to the east coast. Travelling in a caravan they stopped for media interviews in cities along the way to the Hundredth Monkey. Even those who were stuck in the quagmire of reality jumped in to help, because they realized it was happening in spite of reality. In spite of the fact that the new kids had no experience, something was happening.

The event was confirmed to be totally solar powered, with over a hundred solar panels coming from David Katz of Alternative Energy Engineering in Humboldt. The Hundredth Monkey may have been the largest solar powered event in world history. The power of the team who put the system together was perhaps a greater electricity than that of the solar cells themselves. They were determined to power our entire event off the sun, and they did.

A team comprised of Sara Seeds, Matteo Ferriera and I proved the value of diversity. Sara had years of organizing experience with the Great Peace March and Seeds of Peace, one of the most anarchistic, hard-working groups of rebel activists in the nation. She looked like she might be the president of Associated Press or a partner in Spence, Kuntzler and Seed Law Firm, Inc.

Matteo looked like a young, long-haired Rudolph Valentino. He consistently wore the tie-dye uniform of the Rainbow family for which he was a vocalizer. He seemed like he could have just returned from the revolution in Niacaragua, but had actually spent time in Brazil.

I tried to fulfill the role of a no-nonsense businessman in a casual sports coat and Levis. My position was, "We can work it out and make a good thing happen." As a trio we were accepted where we would have received little credence as individuals.

We began the permit process with the City of Las Vegas and Clark County. We jumped every hoop they asked, and then they made more hoops, and if we couldn't jump them we did the hoola.

Sara was just sexy enough to distract them and sharp enough to intimidate them. Matteo insisted it was our land, refused the notion that we would pay fees or sign bonds and convinced them we would leave the Red Rock Bowl, as we called it, cleaner than we found it. And me, well, I attempted the voice of reason, but agreed Sara and Matteo were right. Somehow, as a team, it worked. I say it worked, while at the same time the city threatened to throw my ass in jail if the event came off. We called their bluff!

BLM met with us several times. The event happened ultimately without permits, and none of us were jailed for that event. Las Vegas Metro Police provided us with security in spite of our confirmation that we had competent peace keepers available. We were supposed to pay police wages for them to stand around for two days.

Because it was public land, we couldn't charge admission, and due to that we lost our pants. Thank the Creator that the REX foundation donated $5,000 just before the event, which covered our porta-potties. Thanks also to the Vanguard Foundation, which kicked in at the end.

Matteo and I continued to argue about band and speaker expenses. I said, "If a broke carpenter from Humboldt County can get his lame butt to the test site, then certainly U-2 can figure out some way. We'll feed them out of the dumpster like everyone else." Matteo drew the line on that one. He insisted we would have to pay their plane fare, lodging, and meals and be damn thankful if they played for free.

He was right. After the event, I owed American Express, Bank Americard, Visa, and Chevron for Richie Haven's plane ticket, motel room, and lunch, along with Dan Elsberg, Oren Lyons, Tony Gonzales, and two dozen other performers and speakers from around the nation. I used credit cards to charge the 40' flatbed rental truck we used to bring the rented stage from LA to Vegas.

The event itself was something incredible. In terms of attendance, it was a major failure. But three thousand organizers, representatives from seventeen nations and eleven American Indian tribes created a force beyond the numbers. It was that force I plugged into the following day.

* * * * *

"Science has brought forth this danger, but the real problem is in the minds and hearts of men. We will not change the hearts of other men by mechanism, but by changing our own hearts and speaking bravely." Albert Einstein, 1946

* * * * *

April 13, 1992

God, I couldn't believe it: the event was over after two years of intense organizing. It was 5:30 am already! My body was whipped, and the day hadn't even started. My eyeballs had fallen into my skull and struggled to peer over the edge of my drooping, sagging lower lids to see what light might be shed on day. Still, there was more to be done than was humanly possible.

The prior evening's events began to flood back into my mind. The final number of The Event, the first of the three parts of The Hundredth Monkey, was led by Robbie Romero, an Indian man who played with a band called Red Thunder. The stage was packed with musicians, including Richie Havens, Clan Dyken, Jim Berenholtz, Matzl Galindo, and others. It was a powerful ending.

I wandered the site that morning, the Red Rock Wash Detention Basin, and assessed the situation. The stage still had to come down, get loaded on the rental truck and hauled off to L.A. Tents, buses, parking equipment, and fencing all had to come down. Yet almost all of us were running off to the DOE for a protest rally before the 60 mile march to the Test Site began, and in a week...Easter weekend, Passover, and the Earth Day Action. I wondered how we could get The Walk to pass by the Las Vegas Hilton where the National Association of Broadcasters' (NAB), opening ceremonies were happening. The potential for media exposure at the NAB opening luncheon seemed great.

No cohesive plan had formed for the Monday morning action other than to gather, against the advice of Metro police, at the DOE, and then begin The Walk.

I left the breakdown till afternoon and headed for the DOE. I pulled up the little hill out of the flood control bowl just before 6:00 AM. I'll never forget Peace Spokes, the group of people that had ridden bicycles from San Francisco Bay to the test site to join in these actions. They were rolling the eleven miles down Charleston to the DOE, a tribe of rainbow shirts passing Rainbow Blvd. I

Karabek was born with no arms on the perimeter of the Soviet test site, Polygon, in Kazakhstan. Birth defects are common in that area but he holds the brush in his mouth to paint the nuclear mushroom cloud in the picture on his right.

Photo by Lisa Law

Photo by Lisa Law

Vladimir Iakamets, far right, shares his message from the Soviet Union at The Hundredth Monkey. Next to him are Jackie Cabasso of Western States Legal Foundation, Lois Nicolai and members of the Peace Train, a group of over 30 Soviet citizens that traveled across the nation stopping at newspapers calling for the words of their banner.

The Event Site— With a lot of hard work from an all-volunteer staff, we were able to gather the support for a huge event. Thanks to a last-minute grant from the REX Foundation, we even had enough porta-potties.

The Red Rock Bowl, eleven miles west of downtown Vegas, was the perfect desert location for the Event.

Photos by Lisa Law

Wavy Gravy - Woodstock MC, Camp Winnarainbow Director, author, and sha-man from the sixties through the nineties, inspires the Las Vegas Metro police to clown around a bit at the Hundredth Monkey. Dressed as the Easter bunny, he was accused by local media of being a cult leader because he joked that he carried a lucky human's foot.

Photo by Lisa Law

Thanks to David Katz of Alternative Energy Engineering, Joseph Marino of Batteries Inc., Clan Dyken, and others, the Hundredth Monkey was perhaps the largest solar powered event in history. Over 100 solar panels and one ton of batteries provided power for the stage and massive sound system. We not only opposed nuclearism, we offered a viable alternative.

Musical artist and leader Richie Havens with Lakota elder and Hollywood celebrity Floyd Westerman join the call to halt nuclear testing.

Winterhawk - An Apache man with very disciplined ideals, his voice and music were an inspirational force beyond sound.

Oren Lyons - Faithkeeper of the Turtle Clan of the Onondaga Nation. In the 500th year of Resistance since the invasion of Columbus, he joined in the Shoshone and Paiute desert to call for a halt to the latest form of colonialist oppression: nuclearism.

Photo by Lisa Law

Photo by Lisa Law

Norb Drouhard - a farmer and a grandfather from Washington State, he was on the tracks when the arms train ran over Brian Willson's legs. As a WWII veteran, Norb marched arm in arm with Soviet vets on the Soviet Peace Walks. He was one of the Hundred Monkeys.

Father Louis Vitale of Nevada Desert Experience and Pace e Bene (a service in nonviolence), just released from jail on April 13, 1992 for protesting at the Department of Energy. This Franciscan has been arrested repeatedly for his nonviolent protests of nuclear weapons.

Photo by Lisa Law

Photo by Lisa Law

Bill Rosse, Sr. is a legend in his own time. He is a Shoshone elder, the environmental protection officer of the Western Shoshone National Council (WSNC), an active board member of APT, NDE, WAAME and Citizens Alert, most importantly a human being. He traveled the world to halt nuclearism. Shot by friendly fire in WWII, a diabetic with triple bypass heart surgery: strokes, heart attacks, blown head gaskets or falling off mufflers; nothing can stop him.

Photos by Lisa Law

Raymond Yowell, (on left) the chief of the Western Shoshone, with Max Gail, TV celebrity, in the background. Both have worked extensively to halt nuclear testing.

Photo by Lisa Law

Floyd Westerman, (activist, flim actor), Tony Gonzales, International Indian Treaty Council (IITC), and Mike Haney of Native Americans for a Clean Environment (NACE).

Photo by Lisa Law

Daniel Elsberg, author of the Pentagon Papers and one of the first activists to do back country action at the Nevada Test Site.

Photo by Lisa Law

Gatewood Galbraith, ran a Kentucky gubernatorial campaign based on hemp, a plant that is not only a powerful medicinal/spiritual herb, but also one of the most versatile fibers on Earth. He was a dynamic speaker at the Hundredth Monkey.

Casey Kasem, the world famous voice of the Top Forty Countdown, has been an active supporter of ending nuclear weapons for many years. Casey does not just write a check; he participates on the boards of many excellent groups, including Fairness and Accuracy in Reporting (FAIR). He recorded the 1-800-PEACE92 hot-line calling for an end to testing and emceed Hundredth Monkey events in Santa Monica and in Las Vegas.

Photos by Lisa Law

Photo by Lisa Law

Vivienne Verdon Roe - founder of the Video Project, she has promoted a halt to nuclear weapons internationally through speech and video.

Photos by Lisa Law

Clan Dyken - this eco-rock band travels around the globe inspiring activists with music as dynamic as U2, Sting or Bob Marley. They have toured with Corbin Harney and Wavy Gravy, calling for people to "Stand By Your Watch." They were instrumental in organizing The Hundredth Monkey and many other events to create a peaceful world.

Photo by Lisa Law

Backstage at the event, Corbin Harney, Justine Cooper, the author, and Matteo Ferreira.

Photo by Lisa Law

Michelle Shocked committed early to perform at the Hundredth Monkey. She stayed committed.

Photo by Lisa Law

Yamato, a Buddhist monk, often leads prayers and chants at Nevada Test Site actions.

waved, they screamed. "No more testing!"

Our hope was to arrive by 7:00 AM, in time to confront Department of Energy workers with signs and songs. It was no surprise to the DOE. We had announced that we were coming. The Wackenhut private security was beefed up; metro police were on call. I approached the front doors of the DOE, only to be informed that it was closed for the day. No public access would be allowed during our rally. I walked around back and found that employees had been told to enter from the rear of the building. We held signs and talked to the employees as they entered the back gates. Security officers checked their badges before they drove into the parking lot. We were held back.

Cars and bikes of protesters arrived, and the crowd began to grow. It was shaping up into a healthy rally. The only problem was the appearance of the crowd. Overall, it was still predominately that rainbow, bliss bunny, hippie appearance. The Ewoks of the twentieth century. It all seemed like a contradiction somehow. Here we were, another day, another action, more arrests, more walkers. The idea was right, but we still didn't have The Hundredth Monkey, the critical mass necessary to end this stupidity. Or did we? I was outraged at some news I had just received that morning. The test site was planning a nuclear bomb test tomorrow.

Part of the group were holding signs on the boulevard. The Monday morning traffic honked approval and waved fingers of disgust. Some of the crowd were handing out Hundredth Monkey books to those passing by. I was drawn to the street and found myself blocking traffic, trying in some way to draw attention to this nuclear horror disguised as national security. Several others joined and we stood in front of a diesel truck. He was so pissed off, he was debating if he should roll right on over us as we leaned against his chrome grill. He yelled, "Get the fuck outta my way, before I run over you." We could feel the clutch slowly engaging as the bumper pushed into our backs. A woman looking up at the driver yelled, "Hey, you stop that thing or you'll end up in jail for manslaughter." She commanded so forcefully, that he pushed the clutch back to the floor and sat still as our parade took over the pavement. There was not enough law enforcement to stop us. Stilts, puppets, drummers, and citizens took the road, and we walked south to circle the building. Boomp baa baa bump bump---boomp baa baa bump bump. As always, the primitive beat of congas drove the crowd, overcoming conversation with the rhythm of a war party. We made our way back to the front entrance, where people were blocking the doors and demanding entry.

"This is our public building. We pay our tax dollars for this. You're a public servant, we want in to our library." There is a public reading room in the DOE building that is usually open to the public.

The security officers pushed their way in front of the doors to protect them, and the crowd thickened. With the drums, the energy was intense. The crowd was making demands. Eventually, DOE spokesperson Derek Scammel appeared and squeezed through the doors. The crowd made an effort to enter the lobby, but torn between the nonviolent ethic and the desire to make a bold statement, they let the doors be locked back up.

It was a strange scene. There he was, a thin, cowardly looking man with a ruddy complexion and an English accent, smashed against the doors with six Wackenhut Security pushed tight in front of him. The crowd perspired. Scammel's head popped through between the expressionless, cold, ungiving faces of Wackenhut employees. Someone asked the female Wackenhut about her motherhood and her responsibility to her offspring. The guard was asked, "How can you sell out your grandchildren?"

"Well, you know I am not an expert, I'm only a spokesperson. I'm not a scientist, but I can answer questions as best I can." Scammel began with the standard DOE disclaimer. He could just as well have said, `nothing I say means anything. I'm only here to placate.' Microphones on poles stuck in his face. Several filmmakers were present, including David Brown, who had created perhaps the most succinct film on the worldwide human damages of the nuclear testing industry, "Bound By The Wind."

I glanced over to see four faces more powerful than any Mount Rushmore. Mike Haney of the American Indian Movement, Daniel Elsberg, author of the Pentagon Papers and a great leader in the antinuclear movement, Vladimir Iakamets of the Nevada Semipalatinsk Movement of the Soviet Republics, and Corbin Harney, the spiritual leader of the Western Shoshone Nation were standing side by side. I felt a brief flash of history in the making. They represented a more Earth based patriotism, a patriotism of survival.

The press was ready to go, cameras set-up. Dan Ellsberg, Norman Solomon, Mike Haney, and Corbin Harney were ready to explain why they were there.

Sue Navy, a key Colorado Hundredth Monkey organizer and intimate friend by that time, reminded me that I still had to get a rental car for one of the Native American women. I hoped they were waiting patiently in the motel, but I knew they were wondering where I was with the transportation. I asked Sue if she knew what motel the Indian people were staying in. She didn't know either, 'dog gonnit'. After a carnival act at Budget car rental, we drove away with a Lincoln Towncar. We headed back to the Monkey House, our Vegas headquarters, to find Elizabeth, our nineteen-year old, motel booking wizardess, for further directions.

At nineteen, Elizabeth was the classic example of what naive optimism can accomplish. Like a young boxer, they've never been whipped. The military knows this fact, but it sometimes seems the peace movement has yet to discover it. With no experience at all, she handled all the motel and booking arrangements for celebrities from Casey Kasem to Dan Elsberg, Richie Havens to Mary's Danish. She arrived on a phone call from the Las Vegas youth hostel, a gift from heaven, two weeks before the event. I dumped the rental car keys in her hands and told her to give them to the native women when they arrived.

I remembered the National Association of Broadcasters convention and felt a fleeting sense of frustration. The protest at the DOE had ended and the 500 walkers were heading out of town, without a tour by the Hilton convention center. Broadcasters from around the nation were there, just looking for a story, and we missed 'em.

I couldn't let that NAB press pass go to waste, but at a quarter to twelve I knew my chances were ticking away. My media friend, Rose, had heard my call for a press pass, and going through the standard NAB channels, she had applied for a pass for me under the auspices of her local paper, Indian Voices. She got the press packet to me only the Friday night before The Hundredth Monkey Event began. I stuffed it in my black bag to check out later.

Before Sue and I left the Monkey House, I noticed my dog, Hobo, the president of Pitbulls for Peace. Two flops of the tail, flap, flap. Life as a peace activist had made a gas-station dog out of Hobo. She couldn't type, fax or answer a phone, and gophers, seals, and fish were a rare commodity in an activist office. She licked the activists, endured constant hugs and kisses, and begged unabashed at mealtime. She joined the evening prayer circle, thankful for the dumpster divers that brought her torn bags of Purina, outdated turkey sandwiches, and buckets of unsold fried chicken. She had her niche in the movement.

In the car, I pulled the manila envelope out of my black bag and for the first time looked at the program agenda of the NAB convention. "So what are you gonna do in there?" Sue inquired.

I knew I may have a unique opportunity to address an influential crowd. I remembered the Robin Williams movie, Dead Poet's Society, about the teacher who pushed his students to 'carpe diem,' or 'seize the day.' If the opportunity arrived, I hoped I would be able to seize it, because as the film reminded, we would all be worm fodder tomorrow.

"Well, I don't really know. Maybe I'll try to make an announcement about tomorrow's bomb test." Just the memory raised my hackles and brought me back to life. It was becoming rather common for nuclear tests to be conducted during protest rallies. Coincidence? Remembering the test renewed my strength. I started waking up some more, overcoming exhaustion.

The event at the NAB was reputed to draw upwards of 70,000. The National Association of Broadcasters has some 17 million members and a professional staff of 165. It publishes two annuals and two weeklies, maintains 28 standing committees, and has an annual budget of $17 million. In the broadcasting world, they don't get any bigger.

I started thumbing through the glossy pink and green agenda catalog. I got into the program section and found Monday, opening ceremonies. I looked at the press badge, a plastic laminated card with, hey, Rick Springer, my own name on it. Perfect!! I pinned it on.

My eyes were back on the program, and there it was, the Opening Ceremony Luncheon Banquet. Guest speaker, NAB president Edward Fritz; next line—NAB award recipient: Ronald Reagan. "Hey, guess whose name is on the agenda?" I quizzed Sue.

"Who?" She responded like an owl, up for any game at this point.

"Ronald Reagan! I don't suppose he's gonna be there in person. He'll probably receive it, uh what's that word, not incognito but, uh. Anyway, they'll probably just announce they're giving it to him and mail it."

"Really! Who knows?" Sue responded.

The thought of Reagan slipped out of my mind. At best, he was a man I thought little about during his presidency, and even less in retirement. The Hundredth Monkey philosophy was one of personal empowerment, not one of blame on the politicians.

"So what are you gonna do, Sue? I think you should drop me off and go check on the walk. It might be better if there is no car around. That way I can just walk over to the truck when I get done. It's only about twenty blocks." My truck was parked at DOE with a bunch of walker's packs in the camper.

"Well, let's see what happens." She seemed to be enjoying this wee bit of domestic espionage. "I'll send you sandwiches. Don't expect pies or cake, but sandwiches." She scrunched her face and bobbed her head to confirm the commitment.

"And files in the sandwich, yeah! So here we go, off to a life of crime, Bonnie, in our Dodge Dart getaway car. Well, I always said that the slant six was a great engine. I hope you're up to some fancy driving."

Sue joked, "Oh officers, he made me do it. He kidnapped me and made me his sex slave for months and then made me perform these crimes. I was just an innocent girl before I met him."

Sex slave, hmmmm, didn't sound like a bad idea. But, of course, I had another job at the moment. We pulled into the Hilton Convention Center.

"Well, I know you'll do something worthwhile. Go for it," Sue encouraged.

"Thank you, Miss Bonnie." I hopped out. "See ya, kid," I dropped in my best Bogart. She reached for and squeezed my hand. I double-stepped to the doors in front of me. One o'clock, I was late. My chance may have already gone by.

Chapter Seven
THE BROKEN EAGLE INCIDENT

*Iconoclast n. 1) One who destroys or opposes the use of
sacred images. — Webster's II*

✴ ✴ ✴ ✴ ✴

I entered the multiple glass doors and walked directly to "INFORMATION."
"So how do I get to the banquet hall?" I asked the lady at the counter.

"Oh, you should know that if you're press." The information lady noticed
the NAB badge clipped to my shirt, but gave me some vague directions that
made no sense at all. I wandered in the direction she had pointed, and eventually a security guard stood in front of me, blocking my entrance. "Go to those
doors down there," he commanded, already angry about something.

I found a set of doors still swung open, and I entered into a huge room, the
size of a football field. The lights were already dim, but a row of tiny lights on
the floor still lit both sides of the center aisle, cutting a swath fifteen feet wide
across the fifty-yard line. A guard put his hand out to stop me, saw my press
pass and said, "Oh, you're press. Okay, go ahead."

I had managed to hold onto my envelope containing my program agenda
and convention information packet. I walked through the center of the room
to the east side. As a pressman with a mission, I made my way aggressively to
the front left of the room. I couldn't get over the size of the room. It was twice
the size of the Rose Palace of my Pasadena youth, where they build Rose Parade
floats. Hanging from the ceiling, running the length of the room, were eight
two-sided 10 by 20 foot television screens. With a screen on both sides, they
were positioned: two at the twenty yard line, two at the forty, sixty and eighty.

I arrived just in time, as Eddie Fritz, the president of the NAB, was beginning his opening remarks. His round, chubby face appeared on both sides of
each screen, six-feet tall, with foot-tall eye glasses.

I soaked up the scene while the dim lights still held. The entire football field
was filled with round dining tables. Ornate silver bowls centerpieced each
table, full of crushed ice and adorned with canned Budweiser. Were the attendees half crocked by now or just a beer or two to round their bellies after the
luncheon? The room seemed sold out. As far as I could see, there wasn't an
empty table or chair. I was glad I had missed lunch. Surely, I would have stood
out like the sore thumb I am.

I remembered Casey Kasem mentioning Eddie Fritz and recommending I make contact with him to try to get a speaker on our topic before this very luncheon. Overwhelmed with work, I had tried to delegate the job, but it didn't go far. Norman Solomon, author of <u>Unreliable Sources</u>, a critique of the media or Jeff Cohen of Fairness and Accuracy In Reporting, (FAIR), were my first choices to address this convention. Norman Solomon expressed an interest in such a possibility. I knew now how unlikely that possibility had been.

I held my agenda like a clipboard and pretended to take notes, assuming the role of a reporter. The lack of a pen didn't bother my pretending; I just scribbled away, practicing mime.

My original plan of a hundred protesters was another of the dozen ideas I had that just didn't come together for lack of time, money and staff. It was a great idea, I thought. Our project was named after the Hundredth Monkey book, and I had envisioned a hundred protesters dressed in monkey suits carrying signs like in the book: "Nuclear War is bad for ovaries," "Nuclear war is bad for butterflies," "Nuclear war is bad for the water supply." I hoped with a press pass I could get into the convention and open a side door and all the monkeys could run around the convention to get the nuclear testing message out. But monkey suits were not cheap to rent, and getting a hundred of them was a project in itself.

The walkers were already heading out of town towards the test site. The message I received late the night before our event finale came from our local expert, who listened to the scanner channels of the Nevada Test Site. From years of listening to dry run countdowns, he could predict when they would detonate a bomb test more accurately than Washington, DC. He expected the next test, Hunter's Trophy, to go off on Tuesday morning, tomorrow. With what I know of radiation, any detonation of a nuclear bomb is war on Earth.

Here I was at the NAB opening luncheon. I moved up towards the front of the stage, careful not to block the view of those I passed. I noticed, only 50 feet away, a row of tables in front of the backdrop curtain. Mucky-mucks of the broadcasting world, and there on the left sat, sure enough, former President of the United States, Ronald Reagan.

I noticed the half round stage, only three feet high. The filming cameras projecting onto the screens made the scene viewable to the entire room. A set of three steps was located on each side of the stage. The steps on my side had two football players, stuffed into business suits, standing in front of them. Secret Service, I decided. I wanted nothing to do with a mobile brick wall disguised as a human. I looked around to the steps on the other side. Nobody over there. I liked that side better. I turned and made my way, in the now black room, back the way I had come. I was thankful for the darkness as I crossed again at the wide path in the 50 yard line.

I walked down the west side towards the stage again. It seemed obvious there was only one way to effectively address this crowd, and that was to stand at the podium and speak into the microphone. Walking towards the stage, I paused at a side stage set up for another cameraman. On his perch, he sat on a stool behind his camera, a huge camera, probably state of the art for the broadcaster's convention. I tried to get comfortable and casually put my foot up on the edge of the stage, just six feet from the film machine. I must have caused enough vibration for him to feel, because he turned to me and with a wave of hand and grimace of face told me in no uncertain Monkey talk, "Get your foot offa my stage."

I put my leg down and took the opportunity to move in closer to the front stage. There I was, trying to look like a mainstream reporter, while my worn gray corduroy trousers, soiled cheap deck shoes (recently spruced up by Justine with Wesson cooking oil), and faded, old, handmade shirt, portrayed a stage hand more than an invited member of the NAB talking heads. A business suit had never been a part of my wardrobe, and the last minute arrival of my press pass hadn't left time for a trip to Saint Vinnies or the Salvation Army.

Eddie Fritz delivered such a droning speech cadence, I couldn't believe the crowd was applauding at the end. The speech could be summarized in "We're the media. Aren't we great?" and "Of course, we're great!"

Ronald Reagan made his way to the podium amid cheers. "I'd like to present this award to Ronald Reagan for distinguished service to the broadcasting industry."

Here he was, in the flesh, the GE/NBC PR man himself, the 1950s host of the popular General Electric Theater. He had toured the country giving stump speeches to all 135 General Electric plants addressing over 250,000 employees. He often compared GE to "the cavalry riding to the rescue."

But as the nation's second largest military contractor, General Electric seemed more like the crucifiers at Calvary than a cavalry to the rescue. Bringing good things to life, they built Stealth bombers and nuclear bomb triggers. In 1985, General Electric became the first weapons contractor to be found guilty of defrauding the US government by overcharging on military contracts. GE had also acquired RCA, the parent company of NBC. I had worked with the GE boycott movement, INFACT, as a key component of The Hundredth Monkey.

Mr. Fritz shook Mr. Reagan's hand, while the camera panned to a crystal eagle sitting on a Formica pedestal about fifteen feet from the podium. My own eyes panned from the crystal on the stage to the screen where it was bigger than life, all sixteen times, up and down the hall. It appeared on screen after screen, as in a house of mirrors, a gorgeous, crystal eagle with wings spread in flight, probably the most familiar and bastardized symbol of freedom in America. And tomorrow the DOE was gonna shoot down the real eagle with a nuclear bomb test named Hunter's Trophy.

I felt as though I was in a Fellini film, not fully able to grasp the meaning of details, the story somehow distorted, demented. Just what was the message? My own mind's eye became a camera and ran another movie, meshed and interwoven with the dream before me. I was back in the desert, across from the test site, and there was Corbin Harney, the spiritual leader of the Western Shoshone, singing and praying. I smelled the burning sage in my nostrils. Corbin's song was real in my ears. "Eh Na na na nay, Eh na na na nay, eh na na na nay." He raised two whole eagle wings over his head as the song came, mournful, yet hopeful, from his barely moving lips. His native tongue made ancient sounds in the here and now. Corbin fanned the wisps of rising sage smoke from the abalone shell, using the eagle wings, the sacred symbol. Now a bird on our endangered species list, like the symbol of a buffalo, it's a commodity sold to us in every month's issue of Parade magazine as a collector's edition china plate or mantelpiece knick-knack. Rachel Carson's "<u>Silent Spring</u>" was too close to silence for me.

In my mind the nuclear test site sat stubbornly across the valley as an eagle flew overhead and screeched. It was so real, it almost terrified me. I felt my soul splitting and being torn into two fragments, two places at the same time. Was Corbin somewhere praying for me now, talking to me? I felt I had just been purified for the Sundance, while at the same time I felt I would fail.

I came back to laughter in the convention, my palms sweating, confused, looking at the faces of the waxen mannequins surrounding each table. Their foreheads were glistening in the turned up lights, hands outstretched towards another Bud, they snatched it from the silver-iced bowl.

I saw the dead, emaciated, fly-covered body of a child pass before my eyes, one of the 13 million destined to starve to death this year, fifteen hundred per hour, 25 per minute, somewhere on earth...right now! Her mother absently passed her bony hand back and forth, vacantly staring into the needless space of hell. Why did I torment myself so, sleeping like an exhausted babe in the night and having my dreams and nightmares in the day?

"This is a beautiful award and a very special honor. All the more so because it involves a business that has been my heart and soul for so many years."

Reagan paid homage to the media industry and in essence backed up Eddie Fritz, "Aren't we great?"

He had left the presidency behind, the role of a lifetime, and was now enjoying his last years as a comedian, still the Joker in Chief of the United States.

"It's a pleasure to be in Las Vegas, the city that never sleeps. I was telling Eddie, I used to work in a city that never wakes. But I didn't have to tell him which one, because he worked

there with me. And of course, Washington is in the throes of a political season, angry rhetoric, intricate parliamentary maneuvers, treacherous backstabbing. And that's just the debate over new broadcast licenses.
    Sounds like a good pilot for the new TV season."

In his opening lines, he had confessed the sale of his heart and soul to a business rather than a God, his political incest with the media, and the truth of a sleepwalking, world-manipulating bureaucracy, while shamelessly revealing the content and character of the media and politics. Had I lost my sense of humor?

"You provide not just news and entertainment, but wisdom about the human condition. You save lives by warning about flood, hurricanes and other natural disasters. And charities also save lives by using your stations to raise hundreds of millions of dollars every year."
    "Last year broadcasters relayed video messages from soldiers in Desert Storm to the United States. The cheerful words, "Hi Mom, I'm in the desert. I miss you!" brought together not just families but whole countries."

Meanwhile I stood remembering Arcata's sanctuary resolution. Rather than uniting a nation, I saw a war within our own. He made Desert Storm sound like a summer camp, "Hello Mudda, Hello Fadda, here I am at Camp Grenada."

"Broadcasting has transformed our universe. Radio and television waves are a sixth human sense - the extra dimension of the twentieth century. This invisible energy inspires humans to be human - to learn, to laugh, love, hate, go to war, or join together in peace. Instantly.
    "Radio and television waves are the Paul Reveres of the universe. They are liberators undeterred by icy tundra or trackless desert. You tear down Berlin Walls, uproot bamboo curtains and destroy dictators."

Some of that was true. Radio and television, combined with print media, have transformed the world. Brainwashing works! The White House put out 15 to 20 press releases a day, while Bill Moyers, who worked the White House as a news correspondent, emphasized, "Most of the news on television is, unfortunately, whatever the government says is news." With as many as 13,000

PR people working for the federal government, to the tune of 2.5 billion a year in taxpayers money, what else could we expect?

Austrian Scholar Karl Kraus summed it up, "How is the world ruled and led to war? Diplomats lie to the journalists and then believe those lies when they see them in print."

"Reporters are puppets," said Lyndon Johnson, "They simply respond to the pull of the most powerful strings."

While the government, the military, the nuclear industry, and the corporate monsters led the world in arms sales of $22.2 billion, over 70% of the world's international market, their media machine spoon fed us violence so that by the age of sixteen the average American had viewed over 200,000 televised acts of violence.

Reagan said to the convention, "You destroy dictators," but he neglected to mention they install them as well. Rather than Paul Reveres announcing, `the redcoats are coming,' the media are the redcoats discrediting the modern Reveres as a boy crying wolf.

Reagan continued his sycophantic dialogue with a brief synopsis of his radio career and ended that segment with,

"And not willing to leave well enough alone , I ran for President and ended up having to leave my beloved California for eight years in public housing in Washington."

I stood dumbfounded. Maybe my mouth was hanging open. Had he just alluded to the White House as a hardship of 'public housing'? I remembered my many homeless friends, the supposed suicide of Mitch Snyder, and his Walks for the Homeless to the steps of what Reagan loved to call "our little bungalow". Yet the Reagans had often been criticized for the conservative estimate of $44 million they spent on refurbishing that *bungalow*.

Forty-four million dollars, while people sat sleeping on the sidewalk in snow covered, cardboard box houses two blocks from the United Nations, sleeping on sewer grates to keep from freezing just across the street from Ronnie and Nancy suffering in their *public housing.*. The NAB crowd roared with laughter as they chugged their Budweisers.

Under Reagan, the rich got richer and the poor poorer. In 1980 there were 4,414 individual tax returns filed listing more than a million dollars in adjusted gross income, while in 1987, the heyday of Reaganomics, there were 34,944 such returns. By 1989, the richest two-fifths of families had the highest share of national income while the poorest two-fifths had the lowest share in the forty years the Census Bureau had been compiling statistics.

After eight years as president, he claimed on national television that "a large percentage" of the homeless were "retarded" people who had voluntarily left institutes that would have cared for them.

Yet here he was the "Great Communicator," the Johnny Carson of national politics, the 'amiable dunce,' as described by Clark Clifford. Syndicated columnist George Will, who spent many hours with the man, wondered how anyone so uninformed could reach the top of the American political system.

Reagan startled congressmen by telling them that bombers and submarines did not carry nuclear missiles. He did not know one missile system from another, nor could he describe the simplest government procedures.

At the same time, he claimed, from his volumes of Readers Digest quotes, that "Government does not solve problems, it subsidizes them." Depending on the threat of mutual nuclear annihilation to keep the peace, Reagan had said, was "a sad commentary on the human condition." While claiming that a "nuclear war can never be won and must never be fought," he invented the Strategic Defense Initiative, "Star Wars," in the hopes of protecting American citizens from what he believed to be Armageddon. But Reagan did not know enough about nuclear weapons systems to formulate a policy to accomplish his objectives. He was susceptible to manipulation by advisors who shared his militant anticommunism but not his distaste for nuclear deterrence or arms control.

As an individual, I had no animosity towards Reagan. Actually, I recognized him as the most manipulated president in U.S. history. His live words brought me back into the Hilton convention hall.

> *"In those early days, some well-meaning people also feared the rise of television. In a terrifying book called <u>1984</u>, George Orwell predicted Big Brother would use a `telescreen' to control his own subjects. George Orwell, bless his heart, was wrong about the telescreen."*

I heard the words coming from the mouth of each head on the giant screens as he looked down on the people. 'Yeah, sure! Pay no attention to the man behind the curtain.' At that point I almost screamed, 'That's him, that's Big Brothers puppet, right there; and he's using double speak, telling you that Orwell was wrong. That is General Electric's boy Friday, still touring the nation, pitching nukes for GE, and not even knowing what he's doing.' My emotion was drowned in a sea of applause.

I looked at the stage steps just fifteen feet in front of me, the purple-velvet cord accenting the opening between the two gold stanchions inviting me to join Orwell in calling a spade a shovel, a nuclear detonation a deadly bomb.

Oh, was this really the right thing to do? My sweaty palms made it impossible to hide my fear from myself. I maintained the poker-face of a detached reporter, but I felt weak. Where was my power?

A young face came into my mind, a weak smile in the center of her bald head, her hair fallen out from chemotherapy. I saw her mother's tears, huge heavy drops rolling off into the streets of downwind St. George, Utah. I heard her voice, "I could never believe that our own government would lie to their own people, but they did."

I heard the voice of the Soviet poet Olzhas Suliemenov as I watched him in front of the White House, "No defense strategy justifies the actions of a government against its own people."

I saw bare chested women from the South Pacific with withered craters on their chests where full, round breasts used to be, and I saw the pockmarked satellite photographs of the test site, each lunar crater another mastectomy on my Mother.

Then I was looking into the eyes of Anthony Guarusco, the president of the Alliance of Atomic Veterans. His head tilted toward one shoulder, as if it had been ripped off and set back on crooked. In his eyes I saw young, baby faced US soldiers, St. Christophers still hanging from their necks, sweethearts in their eyes, running across the desert towards a demonic nuclear genie, freshly escaped from an atomic lamp, billowing, mushrooming up into the sky. As they ran, a sickly flash and a puff of smoke turned them to skeletons, to ashes. They fell to dust on the ground and the quivering dust piles glowed.

The wind blew. The dust was carried off and took new shape. Bighorn sheep appeared running from the hurricane cloud. Deer and rabbits jumped from the dust, desert tortoises were baked in their shells, horny toads toasted, and swooping, fluttering birds emitted tormented chirps as their feathers fell from their wings.

As I gazed into Anthony's eyes, the bighorn ran zig-zagging, attempting to escape the monster of heat and fire. Tufts of fur smoldered and burned, lesions and tumors popped out of their hides. Hunter's Trophy? They fell. A deformed calf half crawled out the hind end of it's torched mother and spewed glowing red ashes from it's nostrils. The wind took hold again. Dylan's prophetic words whispered from my lips, "How many deaths will it take till they know? The answer my friend, is blowin' in the wind." My soul puked as I choked on my heart.

I looked on the floor, as an etherous, foul fog floated and snaked through my legs and feet. "Get up and do something," it commanded. "Walk up there on that stage and tell these people, tell the world. It doesn't have to be like this. We can't live with these bombs. I looked to Reagan for a cue, some opening, the right time for my announcement.

My time was running out. The speech would end soon, the event would be over, and I would be just one more silent, complacent blob, overcome by my own 'psychic numbing,' shuffling through the lobby out into the zombied existence of Las Vegas.

My eyes came once again to the tables, the white cloths, the silver bowls, the great god Budweiser poking from the white snows of ice. The waxen faces laughing at jokes that weren't funny.

And then there I was, standing at the entrance to the temples and this wild eyed bearded man, Jesus, comes running through the money tables, grabbing the money, throwing it towards the streets, flipping the tables over, dragging his arms across and flinging everything in his path aside, coins flying. He screamed, "This is my Father's house!" It was so loud I thought I had screamed it myself, but no one noticed me.

> *"In the spring of 1989, shortly after the students rebelled in Beijing, Mr. Ted Koppel did the impossible. He sent a live report from one of the most tightly guarded places in the world, Tiananmen Square.*
>
> *"Like a spy in a movie, Mr. Koppel rode a bicycle under the noses of the Chinese authorities. A microphone was in his shirt and a miniature camera was mounted on his bicycle. A satellite bounced his report back to New York and into the homes of millions of Americans."*

That must be my cue, I thought. *'Like a spy in a movie.'* I'm here to send a live television report to the world from the most tightly guarded place in the world, Big Brother's headquarters, the NAB.

The camera panned to the crystal eagle, and Corbin's song brought me back, Hey na na na nay, Hey na na na nay, the eagle feathers fanning my nostrils with sage. I breathed deeply.

"Creator," I prayed, "if you want me to do something, give me the strength, the courage. You know I'm weak. It's up to you, I'm here to do whatever you want. I surrender!" I remembered that courage is not lack of fear but action in spite of it! As Reagan continued speaking, I saw my right foot step forward. I was as committed as a cliff diver when he feels his toes leave the rock.

> *"America, the Cold War victor, stands triumphant on the world stage."*

I walked the five steps to the stairs, purposeful but in no hurry. I mounted the stage totally thoughtless, moving in another world, a deathless dimension. I strode towards the podium. As I came aside the Formica pedestal, fifteen feet from the podium, I found my body turning to face it squarely. I was drawn to the eagle like a magnet.

> *"But can our nation handle peace as well as war? Or will we become a self-absorbed nation of couch potatoes?"*

I placed my hands firmly on the solid, frosted crystal base. I raised it over my head in offering.

> *"I may be old fashioned on this subject. But I believe the communications business has a key role in strengthening the spiritual values that knit our society together."*

In the clearest, most meditative moment of my life, that eagle came down on the pedestal with the power of over 900 nuclear bombs detonated at the Nevada Test Site. It appeared to disintegrate into a fine mist, the base still whole in my hands. I dropped the base to the floor and proceeded to the podium. Mr. Reagan was moving away from the podium, so there was room for me to stand in front of the microphone. The teachings of my elders, my Mother and Father, took priority.

"Excuse me, Mr. President," my voice announced.

My next sensation was that of being swept backwards off the stage. I was later to learn that I was smashed, tackled into the podium, knocked to the floor, pounced on by a variety of Secret Service officers, jerked to my feet, and carried away. I came back to my senses, center stage, in front of the curtain, my mission still holding my thoughts. "Help" I screamed, "there's a nuclear bomb test tomorrow!"

A hand slapped to my throat and another cupped over my mouth, muffling my words, choking, I let go of the effort to speak. I was carried behind the curtain, my feet flapping half on and half off the floor. Like a herd of buffalo stampeded off the cliff, the four agents forgot the stairs behind the curtain and we fell and tumbled to the floor below.

Someone jumped on me and twisted my head like I was some wild dog needin' killin.' Others jumped on my back, my stomach was pressed to the floor, and held tight. The man on my neck was determined to see I never moved again and continued twisting my head to the right, my nose smashed into his armpit. I felt a hand grab mine from behind and get a handcuff on my wrist.

My cervical vertebrae came to the end of their rotation and I felt each one standing bone to bone on the edge of breaking. I yelled into the black of an armpit, my anger clearly evident,

"You're breaking my neck!" The pressure eased up enough for me to realize I had been thrown down on top of my right arm. Instinct told me that the sooner I was cuffed, the sooner I was safe. I pushed hard against the weight on top of me to wriggle my arm loose and get it in back of me. They snatched it up. I heard the click, click, click of the cuff as they crammed it together. A hand under my arm raised me from the floor, and I was standing, walking into a side room, accompanied by a group of angry strangers.

* * * * *

"Our children see the craziness, the absurdity of the arms race. Like the kid in the fairy tale who loudly proclaims, 'The emperor is naked!' todays child sees right through the hypocrisy .... — Alice Evans <u>Watermelons Not War</u>

* * * * *

Entering a room on the west side of the stage, I was plopped into a plastic chair. Hands from behind jerked at my tie and threw it to the floor, unbuttoned my shirt and pulled it to the sides, my shoes and socks were removed and thrown out of reach. My wallet was jerked from my pants and splattered on the table to my left, business cards were pulled from my shirt pocket. Every hand I saw was shaking with the worst case of Parkinson's disease I've ever seen—the quivering vibrato—tweaking on natures own crank, adrenaline.

I turned my neck back and forth to see if I had become the exorcist with full neck rotation, but to my surprise, I was still just normal. Actually, my neck felt looser, somehow better. A stupid idea for a chiropractic joke came to mind, but I let it go.

"Just what the hell do you think you're doing out there?" A blond, clean-shaven man of my own age demanded in frustrated wonder.

"I was trying to announce a nuclear bomb test tomorrow. It's poisoning our world," I responded near to tears. It wasn't fear or my own pain or remorse, but the tears of the downwind child—the sad understanding that this act was necessary.

Get a grip on yourself, I commanded silently, this is no place for tears. But the child in me cried silently, knowing what leukemia teaches a child about death and being shortchanged in life.

I looked to the heavens and air about me and prayed, amazed at what I had just done, "Creator, I hope that's what you wanted me to do because there's no turning back now!"

Three officers stood facing me as two stage hands entered the room from the left. The officers looked up, assessed as I did that they were stage crew, and gazed back at me in wonder, figuring out the next procedure. As they looked back at me, they allowed the two stage hands to walk across the room and then directly behind them. As I gazed in their direction, the stage hand in front looked me in the eye and gave me an emphatic, silent 'Yessss,' with a thumbs up sign. It was the expression you see when a gymnast nails a gold medal performance.

Probably less than one minute after the action, one piece of the Creation told me, "You did good!" Somebody got the message of the Broken Eagle. I silently tucked that support into my heart and sat up straighter.

The man whom I discerned to be the lead officer, stormed out of the room. "Keep an eye on him," he demanded, disappearing somewhere behind me. I bowed my head, realizing that for better or for worse, I had torn through the wall of complacency.

"Well, you certainly are an unusual activist," he told me as he re-entered the room, with a hint of respect in his tone.

"I'm afraid that's what it takes to get the message out there," I informed him.

"Yeah, well, I'm not so sure of that." As he stepped aside, another attempting-to-look-stern yet equally flustered face appeared. His face was pink from exertion. He was an overweight policeman, 280 sloppy pounds at 6'1", round baby face cheeks, friendly, probably a dork in high school, but overall just another good man doing his job. I liked him.

The blond grabbed my wallet. He pulled out the contents with thumb and forefinger. It was probably a fascinating array of cards for him. Due to my recent efforts to license our event, I had cards from Greg McCurdy, Metro police special events officer, Art Besser, head of county business licensing, Michael Ford, In Music Magazine, and even my brother, John, from LAPD in Los Angeles. "Geez, ya got enough credit cards here," he spread all six on the table, B of A, a covey of Visas, AMX Gold, and a Chevron.

Round Face, whom I later learned was Secret Service Agent Mike Fithen, introduced himself and explained he was going to read me my Miranda rights.

I asked if my handcuffs could be loosened, as they had broken the skin, and my wrist bones, although they normally had a space between them, seemed to be flexed to contact. At the same time I needed a stretch and proceeded to stand up, trying to give my shoulders a little relief. I noticed at that point that something strange was on my face. It was indeed, my nose, but it felt quite different. If they had broken it, my only hope was that they did it the opposite way than my brother did in our youth.

Round face came back rather disgusted and looked me square in the mug. "Now tell me, don't ya think that was kind of a prick thing to do, I mean, ya just storm out there and rain on the old man's parade?" He said, revealing his personal feelings on the action.

"Well, no, I don't, but now that I know how you feel, I don't want to talk to you anymore without my lawyer!"

Sensing somehow he'd blown it, he was willing to loosen my cuffs. He seemed like Barney on Andy of Mayberry when he asked me, "Now you're gonna be a gentleman and not try anything funny, aren't you?"

I assured him with a curt, "No problem."

They really were good to me. I don't know if they were just friendly, well-mannered fellows, if they thought I was somebody not to mess with, or if it was some strategy to get me to confess that the rest of the gang was waiting in the alley.

I overheard the walkie talkies between the security people. "There's a woman outside asking about that guy. What do you want me to do with her?" The little box asked. "Keep an eye on her for now," the guard in the west side responded.

The west door pushed open, and in the brief crack I saw Sue Navy standing there trying to look in. I couldn't believe it. Well, there was no doubt she had her own mind, but I wasn't sure where she'd left it. Pretty soon they would pick her up and there we would be, a conspiracy. The thought of her going along for the jail ride did not make me happy. Doggonit!

Fifteen minutes later, I heard her voice off to the left saying, "Hi, Rick." I felt like some senior day care refugee, busted again after my escapades through town, my medication overdue. She kissed me on the cheek, somehow proud and happy to see her charge rounded up and safe again. "Rickey really is a nice boy, ya know," I expected her to say.

"Are you all right?" She asked, noticing the tear on my left pant leg in the middle of my thigh.

"Yeah, I'm okay. Bumps and bruises, they about broke my neck and maybe my nose, but I'm all right," I assured her.

She walked back out of range at the guard's request, and what enters the room but my bag of tricks. "NOOOOO!" Not my black bag, I thought. They set it on the table in front of me, that faithful bag! With both the bag and I busted, I knew one of us would spill its guts. I had left it in Sue's car, and now they had it. Sue continued to converse with the fellow Ron and the other guards as if they were all buddies. Maybe they were planning to have a few beers at the end of the day, judging from the casual smiles and gestures.

"You gave them my bag?" I exclaimed in disbelief. She musta turned state's witness already. I realized what I had become, nothing more than a Day Runner and a Rollodex. I had succumbed to "it's not what you know, it's who you know." I later found out that Sue had spent the past hour talking to the Secret Service, assuring them that I was not some homicidal maniac. No doubt, she and many others did much in the following days to save my twisted neck.

The hotel security came over to address me with what they thought was some important business. "Okay Mr. Springer, I have a statement I am going to read to you."

"The Las Vegas Hilton Hotel does hereby renounce and revoke all hotel privileges to Mr. Rick Springer. You are no longer allowed to use hotel facilities of any sort and will be arrested if you fail to abide by these rules. Entering these

grounds constitutes trespass and will incite legal prosecution to the fullest extent of the law.

"Do you understand what I have just read to you, Mr. Springer?"

The smart alec kid of my youth desperately wanted to answer this statement with a theatrical plea, "Oh no, not my Hilton privileges; where will I ever stay in Vegas? Why, it's always been like my second home! Don't you think you're being a bit rash about this?"

Fortunately, I held my tongue, "Yes, I understand."

Another officer came from behind me and said, "OK, Mr. Springer, we're going to be transporting you to the Federal Building in downtown Las Vegas." A moment later, a hotel guard announced, "They're here," as if the getaway car at a bank robbery had just arrived.

Little did I know, some were perceiving my action as an assassination attempt, and historically, assassins have a short life span. The police were trying to make sure that I didn't get shot, at least not while in their custody. My shirt was thrown over my head. I felt like the rapist instead of the victim.

"Get this thing offa my head. I'm no criminal!" The shirt came off, and I was firmly grabbed by the arms and whooshed out the door.

There it sat, an unmarked car, waiting under the green walkway canopy I had entered two hours ago myself. Through the Hilton parking lot and onto the street, I noticed the marquee sign out front, "NAB NOW," it said. I thought maybe I could come back for a little night action and change the first two letters to CT: CTB NOW, Comprehensive Test Ban Now!

I saw the flashing lights of a Metro police escort in front of us. Our unmarked car made its karate Keeii, Whaaaaa, as the accelerator pedal hit the floor. There goes a half gallon, I thought. The risk to other traffic really didn't seem worth it, but it was obvious I was along for the ride. Ambulance drivers on a code don't go that fast in traffic that thick. The light turned red, the siren was flicked on and we ran right on through. In the next block we passed our Metro escort because he wasn't going fast enough. "Pass him," was the impatient order. We turned left, and left again into a covered parking area, still rolling through the tight parking at 30 mph, squealing into our slot. We slid out and stood at the elevator entrance. A card was inserted into a slot and voila; the door opened.

The grip on my arm could have been a tourniquet. Robocop's mechanics seemed to be frozen: his grip didn't loosen in the elevator. Out and "To the right." Driven by my arm, the words seemed superfluous. I went where it went. Door after door, we finally found our own little cubicle to call home, at least for the moment. "Face the wall," he told me as he undid my handcuffs. "Have a seat. You need anything, water, the bathroom?" He cuffed my left hand to the wooden chair. "Now, you're still gonna be a gentleman?" The question struck me as odd. How else do you answer that question? `Well, no. I'm gonna jump on you, beat you with this oak chair cuffed to my arm, steal your keys, and blow this pop stand at the first possible convenience!' I answered "Sure."

My fatigue settled in. My back was tired. This chair, the same as in schools, was designed to keep people from falling asleep. I couldn't remember any food that day. Vitamin Coffee, that was it.

Round Face came back into the room with a cup of water. "Well, we contacted your brother in LA, and he says you're a good guy, although he doesn't agree with your methods. He told me to say he could get you a lawyer if you need one. He says you're the most nonviolent man he knows. So that's good. We're trying to determine if you're stable and that kind of thing. We have to go through the booking process and then we'll take you over to the county jail and you can get some rest. You'll get an arraignment tomorrow," he explained.

"Can I get something to eat?" My stomach asked.

"No, they'll get you something at County. We have to do some fingerprinting. Have you ever been fingerprinted before, Rick?".

"Yes, when I worked with Youth Services Bureau with abused teenagers I had to get fingerprinted. I worked with child welfare and the juvenile justice system, and they want to make sure the people working with these kids have no records."

"That sounds like good work. Why'd you get outta that?" He rolled another finger into the ink.

"I didn't like all the time spent on the bureaucracy, all the paperwork, rather than working with the kids themselves. It was too frustrating."

"I hear that. You have no idea of the paperwork you've created for us. You've caused a lot of trouble."

"That's nothing. You have no idea of the mess the nuclear industry is creating of our world, not just for you and me, but for our grandchildren. I wouldn't be here, but for nuclear insanity."

We finished several sets of fingerprints before four officers surrounded me for the walk downstairs and the hustle into the next waiting car at the curb. I suspect they were wearing bulletproof vests. We drove the four blocks to the county jail. As we approached, a face I recognized lifted my spirits. It was Norb, an elder of the peace movement. He stood next to the gate as we rolled by and put his hand out to me. His eyes glowed with compassion, his tan, weathered skin pulled towards his ears in a shared knowing smile. "Well, they know where I am," I whispered.

* * * * *

"Nevada is ranked one of the most punitive states in the nation, 300% to 400% greater than Minnesota or Utah. Nevada is among the ten most punitive on all scales."
— *Selke* <u>*Prisons in Crisis*</u>

* * * * *

"Who's that guy at the back gate?" Ron asked on his radio. We sat in the car for a moment.

"Yeah, we see him on the camera screen. He's with part of that guy's group. He checked in already. He wants to see him." A voice came from the radio. We left the car, Ron on one side and Mike on the other. They dropped their badges into a slot like a drive-through teller and we entered the first set of doors. Mike walked me to the corner and positioned me towards the wall. I turned enough to see them remove their guns and drop them in larger bank slots. Mike grabbed my arm again and we entered another set of doors into the world of the county jail.

Yech!!!

Trustees mopped the shiny, gray, well-worn floors, while monotonous voices yelled "Trustee" from cells. The trustees ignored them and kept on with the swish, swish of the mop, dragging their bucket and folding yellow "wet floor" sign as they went. Ron checked at a window while Mike held my arm. One of the county officers approached. "So this is the guy that bonked Reagan, huh?" His voice seemed to say it wasn't a bad idea.

"I didn't bonk anyone," I corrected.

Mike was perturbed by the question, and ignored it. Ron sauntered back like he was collecting overtime, hands in his pockets, pulling his pants up. "It'll be a couple of minutes," he informed us. I felt eyes checking me out like they somehow already knew who I was. I still felt I had done the right thing, but boy, was I whipped. I remembered a line from that old sonnet of wisdom, <u>Desiderata</u>, "Many a fear are born of fatigue and loneliness." I kept sucking the now stagnant air from the basement and bowels of Las Vegas Detention Center.

The Secret Service officers left me with the county jailers for a property check, a pretend physical, photos, more fingerprints, and off to a jail cell.

The door closed behind me, Klunk, klunk. I was alone. It was home for however long, so I decided to take the tour. It had all the necessary features of a fine home for a rat in a cage, although it could have been upgraded with a running wheel and cedar shavings to sleep in. Behind a steel wall with thirty coats of paint on it sat a stainless steel commode and sink all built into one. Made you wonder if the toilet water recycled into the sink. No matter, since my toilet was clogged with a half-roll of TP. I pushed the bubbler button, and sure enough, water spewed out; yum, lovely downtown Vegas water. The cutest feature was the built-in round hole in the side of the sink for the TP, empty at the moment since mine was lodged in the throat of the toilet. A maple butcher block counter was my bed for the night. Now, as an advocate of the simple life-style, you'd think I would appreciate these Spartan quarters. But it was a clever rascal that figured out exactly how narrow to make a bench so your buns could park on it but you couldn't sleep on it.

I decided to lay on the bench in an act of defiance, and tucked my hand and part of my arm into my pants so as to keep it from falling on the floor. I looped my other arm under my head as a pillow and tried to get a nap. Some meathead (a tofu eater wouldn't do this) kept banging on my door every five minutes as he strolled by.

I thought maybe I dozed. I opened my eyes. Yes, a face was in the door. I pushed my stiff body into a sitting position, and from a stupor asked, "Yeah, what's up?"

"We have to get another set of fingerprints, so get up."

I stood up and moved towards the door. It opened and I went into the hallway, my body and face heavy. I sucked more air, but it was as thick as old paint, glopping into my nostrils and mouth. The guard walked behind me, kicking out directions before each move. "Into the elevator." "Walk to the back and stay facing the wall." "Turn around and walk out of the elevator."

More halls and doors, Orwell's horrors of 1984, came to haunt me as a guard passed me, leering, "Don't like Reagan, huh?" I had just enough left for an empty gaze of insolence. Fingerprints again and back to my cell.

Bang, bang, bang, "You've got a visitor," someone was saying through my door. I sat up again and my door opened. It was a woman guard, tailored clothes tight enough for a dancercise class.

I be a gooood Toby. I knew the routine, walk in front, follow directions. I wondered, how much would it take to whip me, to break my spirit?

At the entrance to the elevator, she didn't like where I was standing, so she jerked me to the right six inches. Must be a hard life for a woman in a mostly male jail.

How many years and generations had the native people of this land been oppressed, demeaned, their language and religion outlawed? Still, some of them had a spirit, a connectedness to the Mother Earth. That was it. The Mother Earth. Forget everything, your name, your face, your birth, your likes and dislikes, but always remember your Mother Earth and you will never lose your spirit, because they were one and the same. I gave myself a pep talk.

On another floor, I was escorted to a small closet of a cell and there was Norb, on the other side of the glass, a leprechaun of the desert. His once black hair turned gray and silver; his skin was bronzed from vigiling at so many weapons manufacturers' gates in the sun and wind. His moustache was thick and silvery, his eyes sparkled with some hidden mischief. Although his face was familiar, I really didn't know him well. His voice was heard often enough at actions. He was an elder, and deserved the respect he garnered. I knew he had been on several peace walks, here in America and the Soviet Union. As a veteran of foreign wars, he had done much to patch the communist/capitalist rift. I was pleased to see him.

He put his hand to the window in a show of friendship, and I put my palm to the glass. "How are you doing? Did they hurt you?"

"Oh, a couple of cracked ribs, a smashed nose, bruises, but all in all, I'm okay. Mostly I'm whipped, just tired. They're keeping me in a holding cell with no bunk or blanket. I don't have much strength for shivering. I missed dinner somehow, but I'll make it. How do I look?"

He shook his head up and down, indicating I was all right. Rarely had I felt such compassion from a long or a short time friend. It felt as though he had been on my side of the window several times before.

"So how is everybody at the Monkey House?" I asked.

"Oh, they're concerned about you, but they're okay. It's a little bit frantic. The press, the media calling constantly. It's a Monkey House! So what happened?"

"Well, I went into the conference and decided I should announce tomorrow's bomb test. I kept praying for guidance, and as I finally walked to the podium, I was inspired to break the eagle. I tried to make an announcement, but the Secret Service jumped on me. What do you know about it?" I asked.

"It's in the media everywhere. Front page of the Review Journal, headline story on TV. I'm pretty sure it's gone national. They're saying you attacked Reagan!"

"I never touched Reagan. He was moving back as I came to the podium. I hardly even looked at him. I just wanted to announce the bomb test," I exclaimed, dismayed at the misrepresentation.

"Well, I'm glad to hear that. I'll tell everybody you never touched him, 'cause we really didn't know what had happened." We fell silent for a moment.

The door behind me opened, "Your time's up." It seemed I had just arrived. I pressed my hand tight to the glass and gave my best stiff upper lip as I pushed off the stool. "Tell everyone I love them."

Left, left, left, right left, I marched and followed orders back to my cell. "Could I have a blanket, please?" I asked as the door was closing. "We'll see," the guard answered, betraying no emotion. Either I was going to hang myself with it, pee all over it, or in their minds I was already guilty and this was a part of the punishment. Something positive, gotta keep my spirits up. I did good. I made a statement, regardless of what the press said. I won! I did. I struggled to convince my soul, while I felt my body had lost. I started making up a childlike poem:

> If one man won
> Then two can too
> And three could be
> Four war no more
> And five could strive
> To give up sticks
> And seven to heaven
> Would be eight at the gate
> If nine cross the line
> Then ten stop the end

Who needs sheep? I fell into a stupor on my bench. It was a hellish night, rolling from maple to concrete, shivering, hearing the madhouse voices in the hall. My neck stiffened, my recent chiropractic work coming to haunt me. My kingdom for a few pounds of fat to lay on. My hip and butt bones told me just how fast I would have bedsores if I were bedridden in the old folks' home.

That's where I'd spend our $200 million in savings if we cancelled the next bomb test; padding for all the bedridden old folks. Hey, maybe we'd even get them some therapy, a few more nurses to help them to the toilet, rather than a suppository once a week. Oh hell, send them home to their families where they could be with their grandchildren and die like they were supposed to, not like some decrepit meat lot leftovers for wealthy morticians.

I dreamed of an old, old man as he ran out the side door of an old folk's home. Into the night in his bedclothes, the splattering rain soaking his shoulders and buttocks. He looked both ways, then ran across the street and into the woods. He had some secret that made him chuckle and smile, making that rickety sound only the very old can make, the sound of sucking gums and rusted hinges on the farmhouse gate. Through the woods and into the hills, the wiry, bony legs hobbled. He finally lay down, crawling under a manzanita. He lay there shivering, but chuckled, coughed, and died, a queer smile frozen on his lips. One man won. He died uncaged.

I felt his shivering and woke, realizing it was me. I tried to straighten my neck. I paced my cell and thought of the walkers out there that would be on their way to the test site. For two years I had said that the walk through the desert would be the frosting on the cake, the payoff, a blessing, and now here I was in jail. Another deep breath. Oh well; I decided to walk with them for a while even though I knew it was night. I could walk in their dreams.

The desert was in bloom like I'd never seen before. The rains that threatened the event had watered the garden. The desert garden was splattered with colors, but mostly with green. No one believed the desert could be that green. It was the green of Irish sheep pastures. As in a Van Gogh painting, the colors separated themselves the closer you got and became splashes of the rainbow. Every color was there. The yuccas and Joshua trees bloomed torches of ivory whites, bugs busy inside with an important job. Yellows of the desert trumpet, lime greens of the barrel and oldman cactus, pinks and purples of the cholla and beavertail, each blossom was a sensuous centerfold of the wildflower gazette, spreading, inviting, opening to attract and delight the world, in unabashed sexuality, inviting bees to mix pollen and humans to make love in the spring sun.

While the visions of the desert blossoms passed through my mind, I remembered the faces that would be out there walking: Jason and Jim, Carla, Susan, Hillary, Peter, Laura; people of every age and stereotype. Although the press would lump them into one group, they're unlumpable, a very unique band of rebels, rebelling against the waste and pollution of nuclear arms. I realized again how much I loved them all. I felt comforted.

Bang, bang, bang, the door rattled. "You've got a visitor, get up."

There was a young man waiting patiently for me, fresh out of law school, glasses, a cross between Poindexter and Beaver Cleaver. I slid the chair under my rump and settled in.

"Hi, my name is Daniel Snyder. I'm an attorney. I've been talking to some of the people at the Monkey House, and we feel you could use some legal representation. I'd like to offer my services." He pulled a delicate breath.

"So what are the charges, have you seen them yet?" I asked.

"No, I haven't seen them, but I talked to the Federal prosecutor's office and the charges are Assaulting a Former President and Resisting Arrest." His manner was so quiet and peaceful, I had to wonder if he knew how to get angry or impassioned.

"So, I'm not guilty, can you help me get off?"

"Well, I don't know about that, but we can certainly work for the least penalty possible. My father is a long time attorney in Las Vegas and has a lot of pull." The 'pull' he threw in with a little dot of his pursed lips.

"Well, I really appreciate your concern and willingness to help. I need to consider if I really need an attorney or if I should be representing myself. Also, you should know I have no money, no collateral, and lots of debt."

"I'm sure we can work something out. I would be willing to get started, knowing that."

I liked him, but not necessarily as my attorney. "Okay, let me think on it for a while and I'll let you know how we might work together as soon as I figure it out."

"Here's my card, give me a call." His round, somehow naive, boyish smile betrayed his idealism, normally something I liked, but my guts said if I wanted an attorney, I wanted a shark. I could get hung by myself.

Like a yo-yo, I went to my cell and back to the visiting room, again and again. Two men, dressed in grey suits, briefcases open on their counter, stood as I entered the room, as if they were going to shake my hand through the glass. I nodded and sat down. They followed my lead. They looked like G-men to me, but turned out to be another attorney's helpers, paralegals.

"Hi, I'm Terry Care and this is Sam Boyd. We're with the law offices of Hunterton, Naylor. We're here representing William Carrico, attorney." They lost me already. My thought process was rather feeble by this point. "William Carrico is in court this morning, but sent us over to get the preliminary information."

"So, what do you need to know?"

"Well, we need to start getting a witness list together so you could tell us some people, locally, who can give a good character reference and how we can find them. Also, you should tell us some details of the event and how you would wish to plead."

"Uh, well, Sue Navy," I started.

"Yeah, we've spoken with her."

I was beginning to be impressed with these guys; they already did their homework. "Bill Rosse, native American elder. Sue will know where he is. Holly Hutcheson, she's either on the walk or in the office. My mind's drawing a blank. Matteo Ferriera. That's all I can do for now."

Well, that's a good start. You're scheduled to be in court at 3:00. We'll do some research and be back with William at 11:00. Now for the story in brief, your version," he continued.

"I went into the NAB convention with a bona fide press pass."

"How and from whom did you get this pass?" He interrupted, wasting no time.

"Rose Davis from *Indian Voice* knew I wanted to do some sort of action, so just two days before the convention it turned up. But I don't want to drag her into this any more than we have to." I cautioned.

"I think she's already in."

I took a deep breath, feeling guilty about having left Rose's business card in my shirt pocket. The Secret Service zoomed right in on that one. I gave Terry and Sam the brief version, finishing with, "when I went by the crystal eagle statue, I turned, grasped it firmly, raised it over my head and smashed it on the pedestal."

"How far was that from Reagan?" He continued scribbling notes.

"About fifteen feet, I think," I stopped to imagine that space. "Oh, has a bomb test gone off today?"

"Not that I'm aware of," Terry told me.

"Yeah, they probably won't do a test with this kind of publicity happening. So anyway, I moved to the podium, and the rest is history. The Secret Service jerked me offstage, cuffed me, and here I am."

"All right, I think we've got enough for now." He started loading his brief-case.

Once again a couple of business cards slid under the slot in the glass. William Carrico, attorney at law, sounded like some TV show to me.

"Uh say, you guys know I don't have any money, yes?"

"Yes, we know. William will talk with you about details. Is there anything we can do for you?" He closed.

"Yeah, get me outta here!"

"We'll see you at 11:00 AM." They pulled their bags off the counter and were gone.

My goodness, what to think. Well, I certainly like that, two hot shot para-legals show up to do the prelim before I ever even meet the real attorney. They sure seemed on the ball. The guard appeared, and I was the yo-yo again, back to the cell.

11:00 AM:

My stupor seemed to be hanging there, looking to graduate into a full scale headache. I just let go. Someone else was gonna have to run this show. Auto pilot in the sky, it's up to you, my old friend. You broke the eagle!

Back in the prison conference room, I sat down and Terry Care introduced Mr. Carrico. So, was this my shark, I thought? The way he held his jaw and mouth said 'yes.' This guy's face said district attorneys were the breakfast of champions. With his eyes wide and discerning he was reading me much faster than I was reading him. Of course, maybe he had lunch and a nights sleep. Here he was with two helpers sitting next to him, taking notes and voila. We had a team. I began to realize what an asset these guys could be. We could get the nuke testing issue in the public's complacent face.

"Pleased to meet you, Mr Springer. We've got the law book copies of your charges here. Let me read it to you. I also brought you a copy of the grand jury indictment." He slid it though the slot. Yipes! They were charging me with assaulting a former president, a federal felony.

I tried to listen as William explained the charges, the penalties, our options, and what we should be doing to prepare for this afternoon's court. He sent his team off to round up character witnesses and get them to court by three. They were off to track down The Walk.

"A friend of mine called me from Washington, DC and told me about your case. There's somebody in your Hundredth Monkey office whose mother knows some good attorneys. I'll take the case Pro Bono, with your approval."

I knew enough of legal jargon from my mentor, good old Mr. Steward, to know he was offering his services for free. "What's in it for you?" I asked point blank.

"Publicity... the opportunity to ensure that you get good legal representation." He seemed a bit curt and business like, a wise demeanor for a first meeting. We may never become drinking buddies but hey, I don't drink.

"Well, I would like you to be my attorney today in court."

"Very well, I'll see you there at three," he said, departing with the buzzer.

I sat staring at my copy of some 'Oh fishy al Doc U ment'... not impressed. Well, they were going to try to nail me on this one. I never even touched the guy. I said, "Excuse me," just like my Pappy taught me. I laid my head in my arms and dozed until they came for me.

Finally we were off to the Federal Building. I knew I had become someone special when handcuffs were no longer sufficient. They decided to prepare me for the Siegfried and Roy Houdini act. My feet got shackled to each other, my wrists shackled to my waist. Next, I was expecting something on my neck, and then into the river with cement shoes. Maybe I'm getting Houdini confused with Hoffman. Good gosh, I hoped the nuclear war didn't happen now.

The Federal building hadn't moved, and there it was four blocks up the street. Ron and Mike were still my official escorts for court. We mazed our way to what I was later to learn was the third floor. They housed me in another cell, very similar to the county facilities, but instead of the traditional maple bench, they'd gone modern with the decor: 'frozen snot' as we call it in the wooden boat world, molded fiberglass. Looked like something they salvaged from a New York Bronx RTD. My lunch arrived. "I asked for vegetarian," I reminded him as he handed me a brown paper bag.

"Yeah, well, that's what you got. Just take the bologna outta there and you got vegetarian."

Nice to see how helpful these people could be. With lunch over, we had business. Something different, yeah, fingerprints, believe it or not.

I tucked my faded black corduroy shirt into my torn grey-corduroy trousers. I was sure I looked a little rough. I was. With my chaperones, Ron and Mike, on either side, we entered the courtroom.

They sat me down in the choir pews, front row. The marshals removed all the hardware they had chained me up in to walk fifty feet down the hall. They had their rules, no doubt. I tried to awaken by stretching my eyes and face in a Yoga technique called the Lion. If anyone had seen me, they probably would have reshackled me. The facial posture resembled a roaring lion, mouth and eyes wide as if roaring, tongue sticking out like some federal building gargoyle. In spite of my weariness, I managed to feel somewhat nervous. My action still remained controversial, even in my own mind. I was sorry such actions were necessary.

My attorney entered the room and sat at a table up front. He gave me a reassuring nod. People started shuffling into the courtroom, sitting on what was once an oak forest. I shook my head. I looked up to see Sue Navy, Holly Hutcheson, Norb, Bill Rosse, Sr.... I needed more air, 'Don't pass out now!' I told myself.

I saw Sue and Holly's faces, the expression bordering on pity. I could hardly look at them. I was ashamed, not of my action, but for being here, being caught, a chained dog, my pants ripped, my eyes sunk in my head. I felt like a prisoner of war. I saw a motherly concern in their eyes: love, wanting to help, to fix things, to stop nuclear testing as any Mother who understood would. To stop nuclear testing because they knew it was killing me. It had me like a disease; nuclear weapons had broken my nose and cracked my rib cage. I was now another casualty of nuclearism, joining the atomic veterans, the clan of the one breasted women, and the leukemia babies.

"All rise for honorable judge Lawrence R. Leavitt," the bailiff announced. A black robe walked in from a door behind the bench, gray hair and thin gray moustache bespeaking a sense of dignity. I rose with the room. *"You may all be seated."*

THE CLERK: United States of America Versus Rick Paul Springer, Magistrate 92-0092-M-LRL.

THE COURT: Mr. Springer, you're presently charged with threats against a former President of the United States. Do you have a general idea as to what you're accused of?

THE DEFENDANT: Yes, I do.

THE COURT: Mr. Ham, what is the government's position regarding bail?

MR. HAM: Your Honor, the government asks for detention in this case. He is an appearance risk and a flight risk. He has no ties to the community. In fact, he doesn't really have any significant ties to any community. He's led a nomadic life-style while he's engaging in his protesting of social issues.

His father felt that he was not a flight risk, however his father was unwilling to take third party custody of him.

Although he has no prior criminal record, contact with his brother, who is also in law enforcement, revealed to us that for approximately the past year and a half he has been obsessed with protesting social issues. And obviously, he is an opportunist who seeks an audience to further his cause.

He's forty-one years old, he obviously makes conscientious obsessive decisions to violate the law. As to a bond, he apparently earns no money at this time because he's engaged in these nonprofit organizations for which he is not paid. Yet he carries three major credit cards. He also has a cellular phone. He has apparently access to unknown sums of money.

Finally,– a final note, the Secret Service in this case has received numerous phone calls threatening the life of this individual. Based upon these reasons, I believe that detention is appropriate in this case.

THE COURT: *All right. Thank you, Mr. Ham. Mr. Carrico?*

MR. CARRICO: Your Honor, I think what you have before you is an individual who is more than deserving of being released O/R. There are a number of people in the courtroom today that would be willing to talk about his extensive and long ties to a community of people, his responsibility in acting upon issues which are of concern to him, his peaceful nature and how he is able to always rise to any responsibility and carry forward. This man is as good as his word.

Obsessed perhaps, but for protesting social injustice and protesting on behalf of peace, I would that more of us were so obsessed. It's a coincidence, and worth noting, that on Easter weekend, the time when the government is most afraid of this individual, we would commemorate the death of another peaceful individual who was so obsessed with protesting peacefully that we all commemorate it today. And someone living in his image should be able to walk about and in fact work to raise people's consciousness about certain issues without being called obsessive or a danger to the community.

There are numerous calls perhaps from people who would threaten this individual, but there are numerous people who would call to support this individual. I spoke with his brother just before coming over here. He said he is the most nonviolent person that his brother's ever encountered, a veteran of many years with the Los Angeles Police Department.

His access to significant monies, You Honor, is just a misstatement. He works for an organization which by the seat of its pants helps people to organize peaceful protests. So I think what we have before us is an individual who he can be counted on to be here for every appearance.

THE COURT: Thank you, Mr. Carrico. Well, the report prepared by the Pretrial Services Agency certainly does not reflect, or draw a picture of a man who has led a violent life.

And Mr. Ham, I don't view the defendant quite in the nomadic sense that you wish to portray. The clear impression I have is that the movement has been with a purpose, to be tied to the organizational activities he's been involved in for some time.

I frankly do not, based on this record, find any evidence that the defendant poses such a serious risk of flight that no condition would reasonably assure his appearance.

Consequently, it is going to be the order that the defendant will be released on his personal recognizance.

MR CARRICO: Your Honor, I wonder if the court would entertain a motion on his behalf to attend the culmination of the last year and a half of his labors, which is the end of the walk now on its way toward the Test Site. That's in Nye County. I think it would be appropriate for the court to see its way clear if he could at least attend that. Specifically, that service is a Nevada Desert Experience Easter Liturgy.

THE COURT: And that will occur on Sunday? Mr. Ham?

MR. HAM: Your Honor, I think the court has been more than reasonable in the conditions that it's fashioned. This is a very serious offense which the Government is not going to take lightly. I would oppose the recommendation.

THE COURT: Well, Mr. Ham, I don't see a serious problem with it frankly. Mr. Springer, you will be permitted to venture into Nye County this weekend, Saturday and Sunday.

Somehow it all seemed as it should be, as if justice was prevailing. William was a clever shark indeed.

I was being escorted out of the room, back to my cell, when I thought, 'he even got me the freedom to attend the walk and rally. Oh, that's great. I'm being released today. Hooray!!'

I'll never quite understand how I missed dinner again. Must be another policy. If you're getting out in the next eight hours they don't have to feed you. Well, it wasn't like I missed anything. Salisbury Dogfood, wheatless biscuit, two year old peas, and lard cookies with real fake chocolate chips. I could hear them describing it from the cell down the hall during TV commercials.

After my lifetime in purgatory, so it seemed then, the door opened. I was led to the original entrance lobby, down the hall and eventually into the public lobby where Sue, Holly and William were waiting. I pushed through a waist high swinging door and into open arms. Hugs, hugs, and a handshake. I was recovering already. "Let's get outta here," I suggested anxiously, "This place gives me the creeps."

Chapter Eight
MEDIA MANIPULATION
AT ITS FINEST

We drove around the block to William Carrico's 7th floor office. As we entered a locked Bank of America lobby, we walked by a fifteen foot tall bronze statue of an Indian in the lobby entrance. If the Indian was local, he'd be Paiute, Mohave, or Shoshone, people that lived in the desert that is now the radiated Nevada Test Site. I marveled again at how we love to romanticize that which we've damn near destroyed!

An elevator whooshed us to the ninth floor and we filed into the law offices of Hunterton, Naylor. I melted into a plush padded chair in the Honduran Mahogony conference room.

"Well, do you want to give Channel 3 a call?" William reminded me.

"So tell me, why do I want to give an exclusive to some TV station. Don't I want to get this story out to as many people as possible? What's the advantage? What are they gonna do for me?"

"Well, they'll get your message out in your own words. They're the CNN affiliate, so they'll link it to them and it will go out on CNN. Mostly it's an opportunity to say what you want to say. When the rest of the press gets a hold of you they will ask what they want and edit what they want."

"Are you sure you're up to this tonight?" Sue asked, "It's almost 9:00 o'clock. Maybe you should just go to bed and deal with it tomorrow".

"That's not a bad idea," I conceded.

"Well, why don't you watch the TV news coverage of the incident and think about it. We've got a half hour or so before we have to call." William opened the matching mahogany wall cabinet to reveal a television, fumbled through a few videos and inserted one onto the proper slot.

"Hello, this is Nightside with Melissa Jue."

I watched the screen, mesmerized, as former President Reagan talked away. Suddenly there was a crashing sound and chips of flying glass hit Reagan in the side of the head. He turned, startled by the sound and the glass, staring in horror as I entered the screen. Standing at the podium, I began, "Excuse me, Mr President".

"Oh my God." I had no idea that the glass had hit him in the head like that, however small the shards. "Oh, No."

Immediately, a Secret Service linebacker tackled me into the podium, knocking me to the ground.

I watched myself in wonder as I struggled to roll onto my feet and other Secret Service agents bounced me around before picking me up and escorting me towards the center of the back curtain. It was at this point, I yelled, "Help, there's a nuclear bomb test tomorrow." I was whisked backstage, behind the curtain. The film showed Mr Reagan regaining his composure, and I have to give him credit, even making a joke, "Was he a Democrat, by chance?"

The film then showed Reagan speaking again to the cameras outside the event hall. "He hit me with a fist, but it just bounced off."

I couldn't believe it. "I never hit him. I never even touched him."

The commentator said, "Mr. Reagan finished his speech and wanted to have a few words with Mr Springer." The film then showed Reagan pulling up his sleeves as if for a fisticuff affair out back. "I think I'll go have a few words with that guy." What a showman, I thought.

The commentator continued, "Mr. Springer is being held without bail until tomorrow's hearing in Federal court."

We proceeded to see a variety of news clips, and I was dumbfounded. The glass hitting Reagan put a whole new twist on the action. My gosh, if he had been hurt, I would have been busting rocks in Leavenworth, all right. I was thankful he wasn't hurt.

William came back into the room, "I suspect the Secret Service was rather pissed off at you. I'm afraid you made them look pretty bad. That's their job, to make sure people don't do what you did – walk right up to the president. They were sleeping."

"It seemed they were there pretty fast to me," I said. "Heck, I was about to give my whole antinuclear speech".

"You shouldn't have even got on the stage," William shook his head. "So you better call Channel Three and let them know your decision."

I got Melissa Jue on the phone and let her know I was gonna pass.

"What, you're not coming!" She shrieked in disbelief. "We had an exclusive," she related, as if I'd signed a contract. "We built our whole show around you; there's nothing I can do now to fill those holes. I'm screwed," she dumped.

"OK, OK, I'll be there in twenty minutes," I conceded, in my exhaustion. "But I want to mention the nuclear bomb test and talk about the testing issue as well."

"OK, no problem. Thank you. Get here as soon as you can," she finished. God, this woman was brutal and it worked.

I lay the phone in its cradle, wishing it was me in the cradle. More breaths; I wondered at what point I would just drop to the floor.

"Well, let's go. We're off to TV," I announced into the mahogony room.

"Well, you wanted coverage for your cause. You've paid for it. I'll drive you," William offered, not surprised by my change of mind.

William knew right where he was going, and pulled into a slot with a man waiting for us. Hhhhmmmmmmmm, I was beginning to feel like a commodity already.

We almost ran in the back doors and were whisked into the hustle of a news office. With her makeup just right, an attractive polynesian woman greeted us and extended her hand, "Hi, I'm Melissa Jue, I'm sorry to pressure you, but we really did build the show around you." She didn't sound sorry but it was the right thing to say.

"Well, let's get ready. I have a series of questions I'm gonna ask you and if you just give your honest answer, we'll have it," she coached me.

This wasn't exactly the way I wanted to make my television debut but it wasn't my show. Like William said, I paid for it; maybe I'd be paying for a long time.

I can't be certain of what I said that night. I was so exhausted, I was on autopilot. Efforts to get a copy of the show failed repeatedly. I brought them a blank video, as requested, but they never did give me a copy, and after a while they just blew me off.

Melissa and I wrapped it up and left the studio. "You did good," Sue Navy encouraged me.

"Yeah, it was good, Rick," Holly agreed.

I was introduced to some of the reporters on the way out. They were sincerely sympathetic to the cause and the action. "Let's go home" I pleaded.

"That's a good idea," William agreed. We made our way to the freeway and back to Monkey Land.

The Monkey House was still alive at a quarter to twelve. "Oh please, don't hug me very hard. I think I've got a couple of broken ribs." I felt pretty fragile. My breathing was painful and would be for days.

I had to check my messages; there was a pile, with several requests for interviews. It was midnight by now; my eyes ached in their sockets.

Lisa Law, our event photographer, explained an interview schedule. With her experience from Woodstock, she seemed to have a clear picture of how to handle the onslaught of press. "I've been setting up times for them to call you. If you're up for it you can do a live New York radio show this morning at 2:00 AM which is 6:00 in New York", she judged from my expression that I wasn't up for it. "I didn't think so." She continued, "We're working on a press conference for tomorrow noon in front of the federal courthouse."

"That sounds good, but I'm gonna call it a day for now," I finished. I looked for a piece of floor space in the first bedroom, and passed out on my way to the floor.

Morning came early, as someone stepped over my curled body. The aches of my front stage tackle football game were starting to reveal each point of impact. I must have smashed my ribs on the podium during the first tackle, bruised my left thigh bone on the fall down the stairs, and broken my nose and tweaked my neck in the Secret Service scramble to gain control. I was not so mobile this morning. As I crawled to my feet, I noticed the bodies around me. The smell of coffee filled the house in the faint blue, dawning light. I found a cup, filled it, and went to sit at my desk. "Is there anything white to put in this coffee?" I begged.

"No" Sue answered.

Five hours of sleep was a start on the forty-eight hours I needed but I almost felt worse. I took a slug of black coffee, "Yech," and followed Sue's advice to go back to the bedroom floor. The radio stations were going to call me, so all I had to do was answer the phone. Somewhere off in slumber land I heard a ring, and it was beginning to bug me when I awoke for the first call. I picked up the phone, a foot from my head, and answered, "The Hundredth Monkey, Rick here," Someone was talking from my mouth. It sounded like they knew what to say, so I went back to sleep.

I had finished a dozen interviews before 10:00 AM, all of them lying on my back. The interviewers all seemed to work from the same question sheet. "Mr Springer, how did you manage to sneak by the Secret Service? Have you ever been in a mental hospital? What do you have against Reagan?" It took the morning to catch on, to learn how to either ignore the question or bend the answer around to be relevant to the nuclear testing issue.

How did I sneak by the Secret Service? "Well, how does nuclear testing sneak by the American public. Over 900 nuclear bombs have been detonated in our own backyard and most Americans are unaware of that fact."

Have you ever been in a mental hospital? "Well, I was born in the United States. What kind of insane society allows its schools, its homeless, its roads and social programs to go to waste while investing in radioactive bombs that poison all of us. This sick society is one huge mental hospital."

What do you have against Reagan? "Mr Reagan's appearance was simply coincidental. I didn't know he was going to be there and wasn't going to let his presence stop my announcement of a nuclear bomb test."

Some of the broadcasters wanted to publicly denounce my act and asked pointed questions. "Did you ever consider what might happen to the eagle as you smashed it on the podium, Mr Springer?"

"Well, first off, I didn't smash it on the podium. I broke it on a pedestal about fifteen feet away from the podium. It was a spontaneous act and not really thought out. I'm sorry for the flying glass that hit Mr Reagan." I responded honestly.

"Well really, don't you think the whole thing was kinda hairbrained, actually pretty dumb?" He poked at me.

"No, not really. The truth is that nuclear testing is hairbrained, and *really* dumb, and most Americans don't even know it's happening. The press doesn't give it any coverage. I think the act was appropriate in light of the situation. The

Soviets aren't testing, the French aren't testing. It's time for the United States to join the world and let go of the fears and market morality that propagate nuclear weapons," I bantered.

I could hear him click off the live feed, "Well, ladies and gentlemen. That was Rick Springer, the man who attacked President Reagan. He thinks we should just drop all our defenses and be buddies with the world."

I picked up a newspaper off the floor and looked at the cover photo of Reagan and I. I noticed my hair flying (a slightly wild look in my eye), and then noticed that the hand wrapped around my waist was not mine. The photo was taken at the exact moment when the Secret Service agent was tackling me into the podium. My eyes were just beginning to bulge as my ribs and solar plexus made contact with the wooden edge of the podium. The air was ejected from my body as effectively as if an EMT had performed the Heimlich maneuver.

I decided that *LIVE* rather than recorded talk shows were the only way to go. You could say what you wanted until they cut you off, and most didn't. Many shows were sympathetic and were willing to hear medical facts about the testing programs as well as what was happening on the political front. We had four phones lines in the house, and all of them were constantly busy.

As a Zombie, I walked into the living room. There was Jeff, the bass player from Clan Dyken, a rock and reggae band who practiced what they preached. Not only did they write and play the most empowering, healing music of the movement, but they worked their asses off doing the grunt work as well. They set up the solar stage, they raised funds, and like many others, spent every penny of their own money to work on the Hundredth Monkey and every other test site action.

Jeff gave me a hug and pulled me over to check out the press conference statement they were working on. I looked it over and made a couple of comments, but overall it said what needed to be said. Almost everyone in this office could rap off the facts and figures of the nuclear issue. They were taped on every wall among the posters and Welcome Home murals.

Jeff handed me a note from Mark Dyken and Matteo. "We're with you, Brother. Keep the faith." I heard that Matteo and 27 others were arrested at the DOE action after I left on Monday.

Lisa yelled from the kitchen phone, "Hey everybody, CNN is sending a camera crew out to the walk." Hoorays came from all the rooms. It felt like something was happening. Maybe we could really get this thing into the spotlight.

Sara Seeds ran into the room and briefed me on the order of events. "Now, Rick, we're gonna have you go last and try to incorporate the whole movement, get the spotlight off of you and onto the issue, OK." She half asked, half told me in Sara style.

"Sure, sounds good to me," I responded, pleased to get back to the issue.

"Time to go!" I heard Sue Navy rounding people up as she leaned in the door. I loaded into the Dodge Dart and glanced over the professional press packet the office had put together. As we approached the Federal Building, I remembered the many times I had seen Father Louis Vitale and Peter Ediger of Nevada Desert Experience walking the courthouse sidewalk, carrying signs protesting nuclear weapons.

Good gosh, you think they've got enough police here!" I told Sue as I motioned towards the squad ahead. We walked towards the corner to cross and intercepted a few officers.

"You guys all here in my honor?" I joked with one of them.

"Well not exactly. We've had a few death threats and we just wanna be sure."

"Well, we're happy to have you here," I said, but I realized that one call was probably enough to prompt overtime for a dozen officers.

While we were crossing the street, I glanced up to see two officers positioned on the roof of the federal courthouse, rifles in full view. I took another deep breath, just on the long shot that it might be my last. We were early, so we meandered to the front steps. Sara was there to steer me away from the early press people. "We don't want a bunch of little interviews before we get going, so hold out until they're all here and then we'll do the whole thing. Got it?" Sara looked over the rim of her glasses to see if I was coherent enough to understand.

"Got it," I responded. The press finally was complete, with *Reuters, Associated Press,* the main three television stations, *The Review Journal* and *The Sun,* about a dozen in all. We gathered like tug-of-war teams, peaceniks and pressniks. Sara jumped right in, her old acting career paying off. The words 'Stop Nuclear Testing,' were in her first sentence.

The expressions of the camera people in front of us varied. Mostly I could see that they were edgy, not there for the nuclear issue, but for the story of the Broken Eagle Incident. The camera rolled, and a few notes were scribbled as Sara wrapped up the details of the walk and the Easter weekend action. Bill Rosse, Sr., with his weathered hat, was a cross between a cowboy and Indiana Jones. He stepped into the sun to speak his words on the Western Shoshone position regarding nuclear testing. I saw a couple of the cameras shut off and wait impatiently.

I waited my turn patiently while Judy's kids played at my feet, two sisters dressed for a Shirley Temple rehearsal. Most of the cameras remained idle while Solange Fernex poured her heart out. The press all realized by now that they were going to have to pay a price to hear my statement. Maybe some of this would sink in and affect them unawares, but changing human attitudes was too slow for me.

I looked down to see the younger sister falling asleep on her older sibling.

I bent down and picked up her sleeping body. She was out, her head flopping as I raised her in my arms. Even while I settled her in, I realized I must look like a politician kissing babies. Oh well; she was there and I wanted to hold her. This beautiful child was the reason I broke the statue and caused all this ruckus in the first place. What world would she grow up to? Do we love our children?

Sara stepped up to introduce me. I read my statement, apologizing for the glass chips that hit the former president, while maintaining my position that overall, in light of the media ignorance of the issue, I believed it to be an appropriate action.

A dozen predictable questions scurried from the reporter's mouths. It was a familiar TV scene: microphone poles jutting forward, some furry mics in outstretched arms, all clamoring to ask their questions first. A chatter ensued while they settled down to hear my response.

"I think the Secret Service did a fine job. If they aren't going to put the president in a bulletproof bubble, then people can get to him. I didn't sneak or run, I walked casually. I have heard that people in the front rows assumed that I was a sound technician – I walked like I had a job there and I did!

"I had no idea President Reagan was going to be there and I was surprised to see he was. The action was spontaneous, but I believe, in light of the press coverage, we can see that it worked." I saw a couple of grimaces on that comment.

With the press finally satisfied, or at least out of questions, we moved into private meetings with different press representatives. I bounced from one to another while Sara introduced me to them one at a time.

During a brief pause, I turned to the lawn and absentmindedly took a couple of steps on the grass. A tall, long-armed young man in his early twenties moved my way, his face covered with a menacing scowl. I was too tired to prepare to block, but I unconsciously pulled my shoulders up and turned my body slightly to the side. Something dark and grey about his eyes said he knew the ins and outs of the crank business. He walked right up, swaying his shoulders as if ready with each sway to throw an arm and fist into it. He stuck his jutting face into mine while extending his hand. His facial and hand gestures were not in sync. I took his hand as he demonstrated his belief that manhood was a powerful squeeze. His jaundiced, pale-yellow eyes stared into mine with an intensity I'd rarely seen.

"The name's Manny. You ever have a job like that to do again, you let me know and I'll do it. You hear me?" I began to sense his anger when he threw my hand down. Although I was confused about his intent, I felt a sense of having upstaged him, a feeling that he thought, `now why didn't I think of that.' I looked back into `the deep' of his eyes and told him, "I'll let ya know, Manny."

"Good," he pronounced with a sense of wild, hateful command. I wondered about his childhood.

I remembered a youth I had worked with in the wilderness of the Trinity Alps in northern California. His parents had lit the house on fire when he was just a toddler and left him in it. His face, his arms, most of his upper body were covered with burn scars. He had so much anger. I had once asked him, "What kind of world would you rather have, a world where your sister can play outside on the streets free from the fear of rape, where you can leave your bicycle laying around and know it's gonna be there when you come back, a world where people smile at each other and trust and support the neighborhood? Or do you want a world where everyone is strung out on drugs, willing to steal anything they can get their hands on for the next fix, and they all want some perverted sense of love so bad that they rape your sister and leave her beaten and stabbed on the streets?"

The twisted, scarred tissue of his face twisted even more as the eyes peered from the reconstructed sockets. "That's the world I want," he said, referring to the latter, "Cuz then I can find the bastards, and stick 'em, give 'em the shank." He pretended to perform the act of stabbing someone in the guts half a dozen times with a hate and vengeance born of the fire that scarred him. He was only seventeen.

It seems that our society is doing that kind of thing with nuclear weapons, lighting the house on fire and leaving the children to burn in it.

Back in front of the Federal Building in downtown Las Vegas, I glanced to the roof and down the street to see the officers smoking, joking with each other. I realized they were there to cover their own asses, not mine. Anyone could walk up to me or drive up to the curb and blow me away, because the press said I attacked Reagan. If there was an attempt on my life, then maybe the police would shoot them before they got away.

We loaded the cars and drove back to Ellis St. in North Las Vegas. I climbed out of the car to the neighborhood jeering. "Hey, das da man, whut slapped Reagan upside da head. Scuuzze me, Mistah Prezzy dent. Yeah!" They all laughed.

I made my way into the house and sat at my desk. "Rick, you have a 3:30 and a 4:30 radio show," Sara reminded me. "Same phone, we'll wake you about ten minutes before."

I looked out the window at the rental truck loaded with the stage, all rented on my American Express card. I decided it was time to get that gas drinking monster back to LA.

"Sue, can you call Jerry Rubin and see if he could set up a press conference for tomorrow afternoon? I think I'm off to LA."

"I don't think you should go by yourself. You're too tired. You need someone to keep you awake." Sue expressed her concern.

"Okay, why don't you come along?" I asked.

She got on the phone with Jerry Rubin to set up a full scale press conference in the Santa Monica Monkey office on Lincoln. I called Pretrial Services, the branch of the judiciary responsible for monitoring individuals such as myself, and convinced them that since my name was on the truck and stage rental agreement, I would have to drive to LA to return it.

We adapted our leftover press packets for LA. I was informed that CBS This Morning wanted to do a live interview on Friday morning. They would send a limousine over to get me at 4:00 AM so I could go on the air live in New York on the 8:00 AM news. The thought of live national TV was exciting. Media-wise, this is what we'd always wanted... to get the issue out to America. 'This Morning America' maybe could 'wake up America.'

We got out to the truck at around 9:00 AM; no clothes, no bags, just a few snacks, a set of keys and my black bag. I took a walk around the rig to check the lines. They were a bit slack, but they would work. I noticed one of the latches on the stakesides next to the cab not hooked and tried to get it in place. I jerked and jimmied to no avail and decided to keep an eye on it when I realized they had the stakesides on backwards.

I turned the key, fired it up and heard it roar through a half gallon of its hundred gallon tanks. The automatic choke just kept screaming as I slapped the accelerator to let off. It never did, so I jerked into drive and we jackrabbited on down the road. The load creaked, but held. The roar of the engine got to me immediately. It was gonna be a long haul.

Rolling down the grapevine was especially exciting, worried about the stage. I'd seen big rigs dumped on this grade too many times; recently was the foggy 102 car pile-up. We made it to the flats outside the foothills of Cucamonga. Cucamonga: all you had to do was say it and you were primitive again, living on the open lands of the heaven southern California once was. Then orange trees ate the fields of white sage and pearly everlasting and then asphalt and malls finished the job.

I was getting sleepy behind the wheel, and Sue was getting sleepy behind the windshield. Sue decided it was time for a haircut, anything to wake me up. She pulled a pair of scissors from her bag. Sue was destined to become some Senator's wife. Always at the ready, operating the front from the back, she had that innate talent for getting what she wanted done and making it look like my idea.

I told her she was nuts, but she wasn't remotely phased. "I'm traveling with you, aren't I?"

I let go, not of the steering wheel, but my attachment to my hair. She snipped away until I thought I probably had a pretty thorough job, at least on one side of my head. Punk was not exactly the mainstream look I was hoping to offer the press. I can't imagine ever having another haircut while driving full tilt boogie into four-in-the-afternoon LA traffic. I leaned forward as she commanded and she gleefully danced her scissors around the other side of my head.

She ignored me but for a grin.

"'Comin' into Los Angeles, bringing in a couple of keys.' Hey, whatever happened to Arlo Guthrie? Is there any chance he will make the Easter weekend after the walk?" I asked.

"We still haven't heard anything as far as I know! There, not bad for a bouncing truck haircut, if I do say so myself." I glanced in the mirror and was surprised. Short, but not the mess I had expected.

I realized that we didn't have time to drop off the stage and the truck if we were to get to the press conference on time. We kept bouncing on Interstate 10 through downtown LA and on to the coast.

I was in that slap-happy sleep mode, struggling to stay awake. No matter how much I shook my head, I could barely make my eyes focus. Sue started pinching my thigh, but decided more serious action was appropriate. The prospect of having last rites performed in a freeway wreck in LA smog, with a rental truck for a coffin, was too much. I felt her hand sliding up my thigh, lingering and brushing her fingers just long enough to plant a seed of thought in my slumbering Neanderthal consciousness, which was, of course, the thought of planting my own seed. It worked! I immediately awoke, some parts more than others. My eyes managed to open up wider and the focus became much more distinct. I now had a worthy challenge, namely, paying attention to the highway regardless of what other exciting sensations I was experiencing. Sue was good enough to check in occasionally, "You are paying attention, aren't you?"

"Yesss, Ma'am," came my emphatic response.

Pass the Harbor Freeway exit, the straightaway down the Santa Monica freeway towards the coast, under the Interstate 5 overpass and here it comes, the Lincoln exit. Gosh, it was work staying awake like this. We parked the gas monster, locked it up and ran down to the office. Up the stairs and there on the deck was a hearty handshake and hug from big John Quigley of Earth Day. "Well, you sure shook things up, didn't you? Now I want you to know I don't agree with the BC office. They bailed on you, dude. But hey, no matter. I stuck up for you. How're you doing?" He blurted out in one fell swoop.

"I'm hangin' in there, but that's about all. I gotta figure out a way to get that stinking rental truck and stage back. I've got to get on the phone."

I had just picked up the phone when John Leddy of the SUN Campaign (Support the United Nations) walked into the room. I put the phone down. "How ya doin', John?" I asked, seeing his hurt expression.

"Well, I'm pretty unhappy," he said on the verge of tears. "You let us down," he stated like an angry father. "You're supposed to be an advocate of nonviolence."

"I am, John. I didn't do anything violent." I told him straight.

"Oh come on!" His brow wrinkled in disbelief, "You risk Reagan's life with flying glass, destroy someone else's property, push an old man around, get knocked all over the stage, and you call that nonviolent?"

"First off," I said, raising my voice, "John, I never touched the man, never made any contact whatsoever. The flying glass I continue to apologize for. It was an accident. I didn't think about that possibility. I'm sorry I didn't. Next time I'll throw a towel over it."

Sue Navy had heard our voices and entered the room as a calming presence. She interupted. "Excuse me, some of the press are here."

"John, let's talk more later. I appreciate your feelings, but I don't agree." He turned and walked out the door into his own office where he could listen to the press conference. I was sorry to start the onslaught of persecuting press on that note. Air was my savior. I took a few deep breaths as I wondered how much of that conversation the on coming piranhas had heard. They love a story of dissent in the ranks.

They set their cameras facing the desk, which must have been an interesting perspective with the full wall mirror in the background. The cameras showed clearly in the glass behind me. I avoided individual questions to keep from repeating myself and I started the conference with a more impromptu version of what I had read the day before. "I must begin with an apology to President Reagan for the flying glass shards that hit him. As an advocate of nonviolence, it was not my intent to harm him or anyone. The breaking of the crystal eagle was a spontaneous act and not thought through. My intention was only to get attention to the issue of nuclear weapons testing at the Nevada Test Site." I went on to quote my usual list of test site horrors. They heard me out, and we turned it to question and answer.

With that job dispensed I turned to see Jerry Rubin's smiling heart all over his face and sleeves. We hugged and he told me he would do anything for me, help in any way. Jerry was a long time LA activist. He had personal experience with controversial actions: he smashed a piece of cake in Edward Teller's face at a UCLA pro nuke speech.

I looked up to see John Leddy standing, confronting me in the door. The controversy I had created was blatantly apparent. I approached John to hear him out although I suspected some other baggage was motivating him.

"It was violent, Rick," he insisted. "As a leader of an organization you have a responsibility to set an example. I'm ashamed of that example. I put the SUN Campaign endorsement with The Hundredth Monkey, but that is not an action I would endorse." Ah, he's afraid of the old guilt by association, I thought.

"That's often the problem, John, is that organizational leaders become powerless trying to please too large a faction of supporters. I, as an individual, will never give up my right to personal actions no matter how UNITED we get. The group cannot slip to the lowest common denominator. We have to be free to express the highest." My volume now matched his.

"Well, that's certainly not the highest," he concluded.

"I'll tell you, John, the whole action is still not fully reconciled within my own soul." I shared, trying to be honest, struggling to end on some patched, bandaged sense of brotherhood.

But he wouldn't budge. "I'm not surprised." There was no confessional priest in him that would understand today. I had breached his opinion of nonviolence and succumbed to the temptation to do harm. There could be no sense of ironic symbolism, no glimpse of poetic justice for John. I noticed Sue was there again as he walked out.

"Boy, he just won't let go, will he," She said.

"Oh, he's just trying to sort it all out himself. But yah, I wish he would lighten up a bit. Now we've got to jump on the freeway and get this truck over to the stage rental," I said, getting on with business.

"I called them, and they're waiting an extra hour for us to get there." Sue knew her job, anything that needed doing. Heck, I'd hire her if I had any money.

After realizing that I had locked the keys in the truck, we dropped back to punt. Thank goodness for Auto Club. John Quigley saved the day and handled the return of the truck.

I booked an 11:10 flight back to Vegas. We headed for Chow Mein dinner. The time somehow had gotten away and we now had to hustle to catch our plane. Sue patted my hand as we settled into our seats. A half empty flight gave us some room to move. I spread out, turned the lights out, and passed out.

Sue had called ahead for a ride home: Jeff Jones was waiting there at the gate as we bobbed out of the tunnel like we'd already used up our Vegas free drink tickets. "Who am I, where am I, where the hell did I dine?" I muttered lyrics in a stupor.

Jeff, always helpful, retorted, "You're Rick Springer. You're in Las Vegas, and I don't know where you ate." I nodded.

I bumped through the doorway into a silent house, bodies strewn on the floor. Jeff whispered, "I'm gonna wake you up at 3:30 for the limousine. I'll be going with you."

"Good," I muttered and crawled into the back of the old Blue Heron, my beat-up 64 Chevy pickup. I heard the neighbors across the street wrapping up the last crack deal at 1:10 AM.

Two hours later it was still black out, and I heard a voice, an urgent whispering. Someone in my body responded, "Okay, I'm up." I rolled over and fell on the cluttered plywood floor. 'Okay,' I told myself, 'national television. America, here comes nuclear testing.' I pulled on yesterday's clothes and found my loaned sport jacket. I crawled out and in my socks stepped into the dusty dirt drive. I sat my butt on the bumper. I pulled the holes in my socks together as I stuffed them into my shoes, jerking off the remainder of the broken shoelace. They were more like slippers than shoes now. Prosecutor John Hams comment, "He seems to have access to unknown sums of money," was accurate in one sense. We didn't seem to know any money.

Jeff came out and cheered me up with his bubbling presence, "You ready, dude?"

"No doubt, let me at 'em," I faked.

"We're outta coffee, so we'll get some on the way," he told me.

"How's the walk doin?" I asked.

"They're doing great. There's about 500 of them and today is the last day. When are you going out?" He asked.

"Today, this morning, after we get back from this interview. That's it, I'm off to the walk." I told him, "I can't believe I've missed the whole walk but the last day. Well, at least I'm gonna walk the last day to the test site. Where's that limo? It's 4:05; he's supposed to be here."

A couple more minutes and up rolls a black stretch limo. We hopped in; my first time in a limo. It seemed rather ludicrous. We could've been towing a water-skier with that boat. Jeff sat on the other bench, far enough away to have a spit wad fight. Only one last job here in Vegas and I was a free man in the desert!

"Mr. Springer, thanks for coming at this hour," a technician told me. "Right this way."

"Thanks for helping us get the issue out there," I responded.

We entered the studio, being careful not to trip over the myriad of cables and cords running around the floor. We made our way to a lone chair in front of a curtain where I was instructed to sit. I buttoned my jacket as a woman came over to insert the mike under it and clipped it to my tie. "All set, now. Should be about five minutes. You're going to be early in the show," she informed me.

I sat there waiting, pushing my nervousness back into the recesses of my foggy mind. Would they try to make me look like a fool, or were they really interested in the message behind the broken eagle?

A woman came over to explain what was going to happen. " you see they're going to be showing the little picture in the corner of the screen to start and then they bring it in full size while you're talking. This is going live to New York." I nodded my head in understanding. It seemed as if we were still just setting up when I heard the command, "Everyone ready!"

I could hear Harry Smith in my earphone:

"Antinuclear activist Rick Springer says he never had any intention of hurting former President Reagan earlier this week. Springer says he just wanted to make a point. Still, the incident startled Mr. Reagan and jolted the Secret Service. Springer is with a group called The 100th Monkey, which

opposes all nuclear testing. And he joins us this morning from KLAS-TV in Las Vegas. Good Morning. What were you trying to accomplish earlier this week?"

"Well, I have known about the National Association of Broadcasters convention for approximately six months, and I thought that this was incredible timing as relates to our project to stop nuclear testing. I thought this was a great opportunity to address the NAB and to let them know that nuclear testing does continue just 60 miles north of Las Vegas."

"What was smashed when you went up onto the stage next to former president Reagan?"

"That was a crystal statue of an eagle, a symbol of freedom to the Western Shoshone, whose land nuclear testing continues on today."

"And did you smash it intentionally? What exactly happened when you got on the stage up there?"

"Well, you know, I stood at the side hearing Eddie Fritz's speech for approximately 10 minutes, and then Mr. Reagan was on. I was trying to get my nerve up. It was, you know, pretty scary to know I was going up there to make this announcement without permission, and as I approached the podium, I had no intention of doing anything to the statue, but I found myself turning to the statue and raising it over my head and breaking it on the pedestal."

"Did you give any consideration to what might happen to you when you went on that stage?"

"Well, actually, I did. While I was standing at the side, I had many visions, and I did consider the possibility that the Secret Service may shoot me in the process of trying to make my announcement."

"The question everybody has is how did you get so close?"

"Well, you know, it was a convention where you had to have passes to get in. I casually walked on stage, and I have heard from many people that they thought that because I was moving in a confident, casual manner, that I must be a sound technician. And of course, when I approached the podium, I wanted to announce to the attendees that there is a nuclear bomb test scheduled for this week, and that France had discontinued their nuclear testing program, and it was time for us to do likewise."

"Did you have any IDs? Did you have any of the requisite, sort of media passes?"

"Yes, I had been lucky and a friend of a friend had just gotten a press packet to me two days before. I hadn't even had time to read the packet until I was en route to the conference, and it was just at that point that I read that Mr. Reagan was receiving an award. I didn't even really believe at that point that he was going to be there in person."

"Mm-hmm."

"But when I did enter the room, I found he was there."

"Are you surprised at all that they let you go?"

"No, not really. I believe that my life is an indicator of my commitment to nonviolence. In fact, this entire project, The Hundredth Monkey, is based on the nonviolent teachings of Gandhi and Martin Luther King, Jr."

"Do you have any regrets about what you did?"

"Well, I certainly must offer an apology to Mr. Reagan. I am very sorry that the Secret Service jostled him in an effort to get me off the stage. I have no regrets as to the fact that I approached the podium, and I think the coverage I have received due to this act is an excellent example of what it takes to wake up and startle the media and, indeed the American public, whose apathy is responsible for the continuation of nuclear testing to this day."

"Mm, Rick Springer, thank you for joining us. Do appreciate it. Twenty two after. Wasn't that interesting?"

Paula Zahn, the co-host, commented, *"I loved that segment."*

Mark McEwen, the meteorologist, added, *"He could talk. Most of the time you get people like Squeaky Fromme—you remember?"*

"Well, as it turns out this guy is a well known —I don't know about well known, but there is lots of tape of him leading nuclear—antinuclear demonstrations and stuff. I mean, that's really what this guy is all about. That's because he was released so quickly and everybody said, "What? Excuse me. And he has a real track record of pacifism, so..."

Mark continued, *"I thought that was great. So you think you're going to jail? 'No, I think they're going to drop the charges,' which I thought—I don't know if I would have said that. I'd say, Oh please—oh, please, oh please."*

"But he did apologize for hitting the former president with the shards of glass."

"Absolutely."

"It's just amazing—just amazing..."

There it was, done, however short. I brought up the nuclear testing issue again. I wished I had brought a 1-800-PEACE-92 card in my sleeve so I could have flashed it on the air. I was just about to announce it and the interview ended. "You did ggrreat," Jeff complimented me. Somehow I was never quite satisfied with these interviews, though. They just seemed to be short sound bites and over before I knew it. I just barely touched on the issue, although once in a while I got in some statistics on the medical effects. I needed a whole show like Donahue or something like that.

Everyone thanked us, including the station manager. I felt a real sincerity from them as individuals, but they were not yet willing to make a stand.

The limo was there ready to whisk us off, and we sank into our couches as we floated home to monkey-land. "I'm ready to get to the walk."

"Good, let's check inside before we go," Jeff agreed.

I hardly knew what to grab so I decided to rough it for the weekend. I laid

The message, the media, and manipulation at its finest

After he strolled past a professional security team Monday and livened up former President Ronald Reagan's speech by shattering a glass statuette, Rick Springer of the 100th Monkey Project anti-nuclear group resembled nothing so much as the 101st simian.

Although sometimes exclamation is the point, Springer's attempted message was convoluted.

Of course, having a cadre of embarrassed Secret Service agents hanging from one's neck tends to garble a political statement. It's something to remember in an election year.

Springer was yanked from the stage like a hack vaudevillian, booked for presidentus interruptus and later released on his own recognizance. If anything, Springer's action showed two things:

First, good security help is hard to find.

Second, the wild-looking Springer knows more about attracting the media than a gaggle of blue-suited Congressmen.

In the time it takes to say "No Nukes is Good Nukes," the photo of Springer barging into the National Association of Broadcasters ceremony at the Las Vegas Hilton was flashed across the nation. The media are painfully slow at picking up

John L. Smith

on some issues, but we know news when we see it.

The arguable logic of atomic weapons testing is a small story; breaking glass trophies belonging to ex-presidents is a big one.

By Tuesday afternoon, his defense attorney had compared Springer to Jesus Christ.

Good lord.

By Wednesday afternoon, Springer and a contingent of other anti-nuclear activists addressed the waiting media and warned at length about the evils of nuclear weapons testing. A couple dozen cops stood within shouting distance just in case he decided to break someone else's statuette.

At this rate, by Sunday Springer will replace Bill Clinton as the latest Democratic hopeful. He's already come closer to beating a Republican than the others.

As I stood Wednesday near the steps of the Foley Federal Building,

when we see it.

The arguable logic of atomic weapons testing is a small story; breaking glass trophies belonging to ex-presidents is a big one.

it was difficult to stifle a laugh. Not at the anti-nuclear activists, although their outfits brought smiles to the faces of some of the cops. And not at the cops, whose overreaction in the wake of Monday's under-reaction is worthy of a few Johnny Carson gags.

I almost laughed at the television and print reporters, myself included. Only days earlier, most of us would have been extremely reluctant to give yet another long-haired, bearded fellow in well-worn clothes two minutes in the name of the anti-nuclear movement. The reporting trade's inherent cynicism demands that if you've heard one no-nuker's idealistic spiel, you've heard them all.

By many accounts, Springer was just another anonymous demonstrator until Monday. Now he's movie-of-the-week material. He quoted Gandhi at noon Wednesday on a local television station.

Gandhi?

Holy cow.

Although the courthouse news conference appeared impromptu, it wasn't. Springer's statement was prepared and appeared carefully worded. Before he answered questions, reporters were treated to the atomic admonitions of a member of the Western Shoshone nation, a

terribly sincere woman with a French accent, and a singing youngster. Although the messages were littered with the slogans that mark the movement, Springer was kept from the media until all the rhetoric was released.

All this fuss for an incident involving a wild-eyed guy who by his own admission got the notion to upstage Reagan at the last minute?

Obviously, it worked.

But imagine what would have happened had Springer the-new-nuclear-savior turned out to be a weirdo with a felony record or something similarly disagreeable. Then the 1992 edition of the anti-nuclear cause would look more like a mon-key than a movement.

Anti-nuclear activism is filled with many well-meaning groups. Perhaps it cannot have too many speakers. Perhaps.

As the no-nukers' Easter gathering at the gates of the Nevada Test Site draws near, I am left with two simple thoughts:

Hopefully someone is guarding those warheads better than they are watching over former presidents.

And wild-eyed Rick Springer isn't so crazy, after all.

John L. Smith's column appears Wednesday, Thursday, Friday and Sunday.

Reprinted courtesy of Las Vegas Review-Journal/Sun

my still bruised bones down into the squalor of Jeff's mini-pickup front seat. We gassed up and with the dawn of day, headed out of town, chased by the urban sprawl up the Vegas valley. We rolled through Indian Springs and on to Cactus Springs where the walk was camped. The sanctity of the desert valley in the morning dawn brought me back to healing power of Mother Earth. Even at 7:00 in the morning, the drums were playing in camp. I was glad to be home.

* * * * *

"He didn't have a gun and he didn't have a knife
And you don't say 'excuse me' when you threaten someone's life."
   – Robert Hoyt, folk musician

* * * * *

In 1983, Ben Bagdikian, professor emeritus at UC Berkeley and the author of The Media Monopoly, pointed out that "twenty corporations control more than half the 61 million newspapers sold every day; twenty corporations control more than half the revenues of the country's 11,000 magazines; three corporations control most of the revenues and audience in television; ten corporations in radio; eleven corporations in all kinds of books, and four corporations in motion pictures." These same corporations, and conglomerations thereof, make much of their profit on US military contracts and international arms sales. Raytheon alone, major test site contractor, grossed $9.3 billion in 1991 with 53.7 percent of that total from the US government. The distinction between government bureaucracies and corporate management is often vague and indistinguishable. And that interlock is compounded by the interlock between the media and corporations, creating in essence one entity or conglomerate of government, corporation, and media. Former President Eisenhower called it the "military industrial complex."

Robert McNamara, Defense Secretary under Kennedy and Johnson, recently retired from the board of directors of Washington Post Co., the second most influential paper in America. Former cabinet rank officials also populate the boards of other major print media including the *New York Times, LA Times* and *Readers Digest*.

In 1990, "The corporate boards of three major television networks were studded with government power brokers. Harold Brown, Carter's Defense Secretary, was director at CBS, along with former Secretary of State Henry Kissinger. General David Jones, chairman of the Joint Chiefs of Staff during the Reagan years, was on the board of GE/NBC, as is former Attorney General William French Smith. And prior to becoming CIA director in 1981, William Casey held sway as chief counsel and board member of CapCities, which gobbled up ABC early in Reagan's second term, " say Martin Lee and Norman Solomon in their hallmark "guide to detecting bias in news media," Unreliable Sources.

The monopolistic incest between government, corporations and media was exposed clearly in a 1979 study by Peter Dreir and Steven Weisberg, showing interlocked directorates in major newspaper chains. Gannett, the largest paper chain in America shared directors with Merrill Lynch (stockbrokers), Standard Oil of Ohio, 20th Century-Fox, Kerr-McGee (oil, gas, nuclear power, aerospace), McDonnell Douglas Aircraft, McGraw-Hill, Eastern Airlines, Phillips Petroleum, Kellogg Company, and New York Telephone Company.

Exxon, the worlds largest corporation in 1983, had two directors on the board of Citibank, alongside directors of Mobil and Standard Oil of California, General Electric, Westinghouse, General Motors, Ford Motor company, Du Pont, AT&T, IBM, and RCA.

Corporations employ thousands of lobbyists and political action committees (PACs) that work daily within congress to manipulate opinion and budget spending. They are employed to secure government contracts and insure policy that will guarantee future contracts. The way of capitalism has spawned in America what Cornell West, the head of Arfro-American studies at Harvard terms "Market Morality," where people judge their self worth by their material possessions.

Eddie Fritts, the head of the National Association of Broadcasters, was also a key Reagan advisor during that presidency. The mainstream media response to the Broken Eagle Incident on April 13 of '92 was aimed at manipulation of the public response opinion. It was the classic example of Orwellian media manipulation, as directed by what Orwell referred to as the "Ministry of Truth."

No matter how much the public (and even the people involved in the peace movement) are aware of the medias ability to twist stories, the truth is that lying to the press works. Studies conducted during presidential campaigns found that it took eleven times as much press to correct an error. Campaign lies are an effective strategy tool in politics. "You can say anything you want in a debate and 80 million people hear it," George Bush's press secretary stated shortly after the vice presidential debate in October of 1984. "If reporters then document that a candidate spoke untruthfully, so what? Maybe 200 read it."

Three motion picture cameras were rolling, showing clearly that there was no contact between the former President and I, and in fact revealing to the discerning eye the accidental grazing of Reagan's head by a Secret Service fist. Still the headlines accompanying the photo read, "Arcata Man Attacks Reagan," "Reagan Jostled in Activist's Attack." *Review Journal* photographer Jim Laurie's photo appeared in US News with the caption, "Stunned, Reagan and his attacker.""

Reagan was credited with being the most manipulated president in history with one of the most successful PR teams to manage the White House. The White House issued 15 press releases every day. The Air Force alone released

600,000 (yes, six hundred thousand) news releases in 1980, the last year such stats were made available.

The media had been a tool of the government corporation of nuclear industries since the Manhattan Project. Every aspect of the arms race and the Cold War had been cleverly manipulated. "Lying to the press goes back to the beginning of the republic," says David Wise, a former editor of the New York Herald Tribune. Norman Solomon reminds us that "institutional lying took on new dimensions at the outset of the Cold War, as clandestine operations began to multiply like rabbits. The proliferation of covert actions required a plenitude of cover stories, and cover stories, lest we forget, are lies."

While former Secretary of the Interior Stewart Udall exposes the early lies regarding the Germans' proximity to the discovery of the nuclear bomb, he tells us in his book The Myths of August, the truth that we torched 18 of our own soldiers in Hiroshima and kept it from the public. Journalists were expelled from Hiroshima after reports appeared in the *London Times* of the ensuing radiation sickness.

The supposed missile gap was a hoax, as confessed twenty five years later by the *New York Times*. While the *Times* alleged that the US lagged far behind the Soviet arsenal, the United States actually had 2,000 long range missiles while the Soviets less than 100.

Bill Moyers, who worked the White House, as well as print and broadcast media, made a similar point regarding power, "Most of the news in television is, unfortunately, whatever the government says is news."

And it continues. In the summer of 1985 the Soviet Union announced the start of a unilateral moratorium on nuclear testing. Gorbachev invited the US to join the moratorium, but the American mass media immediately dismissed the initiative as an empty ploy.

CBS evening news depicted the Soviet offer as mere "posturing." Lesley Stahl used the word "propaganda" four different times in the networks first report on the Soviet moratorium. The *New York Times,* the *Washington Post* and the *LA Times* misreported the following morning that the Soviet policy shift was only a proposal.

The truth remains today that the Soviets observed three unilateral moratoriums totalling almost 3 years while the US Department of Energy maintained it's average of 12 to 18 bomb tests per year. The American public heard almost nothing of it.

Confusion "keeps us powerless and controllable," states psychotherapist Anne Wilson Schacf. "No one is more controllable than a confused person; no society is more controllable than a confused society. Politicians know this better than anyone, and that is why they use innuendos, veiled references, and out and out lies instead of speaking clearly and truthfully."

The action of sounding the nuclear fire alarm by breaking the glass of a crystal eagle, not only embarrassed the Secret Service, but angered the media, the nuclear industry and the government. They knew just how to manipulate an upstart pauper such as myself.

In the *Atlanta Constitution* the uncredited dialog states, "It will take a heap of rational arguments to win over Americans who were appalled at the sight of Mr. Springer getting rough with a man twice his age."

The people in the front row, Larry King among them, said "He was so casual, we thought he was a sound technician," yet the Associated Press article by Robert Macy appearing in the *LA Times* was headlined Man Rushes Reagan. *The Las Vegas Review Journal* claimed Springer "stormed the podium." However distinct the difference between 'rushing' and 'casual' were, the media chose to create an image guaranteed to discredit the action.

There was no physical contact between the former president and I, yet the press still wrote, 'Springer pushes Ronald Reagan aside.' *The San Francisco Chronicle* ran headlines, `Man Grabs Glass Bird From Reagan, Breaks It,' while the bird was actually lifted from a pedestal fifteen feet away. *The Review Journal* later labeled me Reagan's heckler. Almost all the international media articles were copies or rewordings of the original articles from the Associated Press.

In the press my name was changed to Richard, an unresearched assumption. All ID confiscated by the Secret Service was printed clearly Rick, as well as birth certificate records. My residence in Arcata in far Northern California was turned into Arcadia in the LA basin, sparking a debate in Humboldt County media over the really important issue of where I did or didn't reside. *The Times Standard*, fearing guilt through association, printed, "Arcata takes a bum rap in assault on ex-president", while in their second paragraph, the editorial states, 'This is a textbook case of how bad reporting spreads and how reluctant the media is to correct their mistakes" Next sentence, the *Times Standard* begins, "As all North Coast residents know by now, Richard Paul Springer, 44, an antinuclear activist." Rick Springer was born in 1951 but mathematics evaded the Times Standard that day.

They continued, "Particularly perturbing to this paper, as an admirer of The Associated Press, was that AP did not report the correct address until five hours after we repeatedly informed the SF Bureau on Tuesday. We rely on AP to be as accurate as possible and quick to clarify or correct factual mistakes." In the next paragraph, "Reporting on the Springer incident reminds us of the time in 1963, after Lee Harvey Oswald was killed in Dallas, when CBS and other networks repeatedly called Oswald's assailant 'Jack Rubenstein.'" Our local reporters jumped on the opportunity to further the connection to assassins.

Still, the *Times Standard* refused to run *my* editorials clarifying the unfortunate fact that the Secret Service accidentally hit Reagan in the head as they dove on me from behind. This fact is so clear on slowed film, where the tackling officers fist brushes by Reagans forehead, that Judge Lawrence Leavitt stated just 24 hours following the incident, "An interview with the defendant certainly does not reflect or draw a picture of a man who has led a violent life or is a flight risk or a danger to the community." Nonetheless, media in Los Angeles ran a special program on presidential assassins, and concluded the airing with clips of the Broken Eagle Incident,.

Two weeks after the event I appeared in LA for an interview on Friday night, 9PM News, on NBC . On arrival at the Burbank station in Southern California, I briefly met Reverend Madison Shockley, a black peace minister with roots in the Martin Luther King, Jr. Civil Rights movement. He was presently a practicing minister in Southern California. We were both handed papers from the station, encouraging us as opponents to "interrupt whenever necessary" and "jealously guard your positions." It became apparent that the Cross Talk segment was hoping to portray a disjointed and fragmented peace movement response to the action.

In the midst of a crammed and bustling NBC/GE news studio, Shockley and I were separated and seated at desks out of view of each other, but with a camera trained on each us. A makeup woman came by to fuss over my face, but I declined, as I suspected her instructions were to make me look bad.

The news began and shortly entered into the Cross Talk introduction, "This evening on Cross Talk, we have with us the man who attacked former president Ronald Reagan and Reverend Madison Shockley of Los Angeles."

I was outraged, "Well, first I have to correct that I didn't attack anybody and the fact that I was released on my own recognizance 24 hours after the event is evidence that the courts agreed. As an advocate of nonviolence, I have to apologize for the shards that accidentally hit Reagan."

The news team, eager to manipulate the session, cut short any comments that would correct the impression they sought to create. Fluster became apparent in the caster's demeanor when she asked Reverend Shockley in a leading tone, "Well, Mr. Shockley, do you think Mr. Springer accomplished his goal by this type of action?"

"Well, we're here on TV, aren't we?" Mr. Shockley quipped.

The past two weeks had prepared me for live interviews. I kept on issue. The studio director grimaced in concern as he sat next to the camera in front of me. As he watched the response, he decided to cut short the intended show. He gave a wrap-it-up hand signal, and the newswoman cut me off mid-sentence, announcing quite frankly, "Well, we didn't come here to discuss that this evening. Thank-you."

Judge Phillip Pro told me at the sentencing hearing, "I don't doubt for a minute, Mr. Springer, that you hold very strong views and that you are sincere in the views that you hold. I don't question for a minute that when you took that stage you had no intention to harm a former president." Yet when I returned to Arcata, *The Times Standard* again headlined its piece, "Activist returns to Arcata, defends attack on Reagan."

My greatest regret is that the action was manipulated into a statement against an individual rather than an indictment of a nation. The message of The Hundredth Monkey is that each common individual is an added force that brings us closer to tipping the balance towards a clearer knowledge; towards the understanding that violence is not an effective tool for conflict resolution.

Jeff Cohen and Norman Solomon wrote an article that got some coverage, at least in the *Minneapolis Star Tribune*, "Media bomb again on nuclear testing." The informative article closed with, "National media seem as oblivious to events at the Nevada Test Site as the gamblers who fill the Las Vegas casinos an hours drive away. You'd think that nuclear explosions ranging up to 150 kilotons would be hard to ignore...... Think again." The caption under the Jim Laurie photo stated, "As usual, the action photo replaced the deeper issue."

Professor Bruce Lincoln concludes in his book <u>Authority, Construction and Corrosion</u>, "So hysterical is the rhetoric, and so obvious the financial interests being defended, one is tempted to think the *Wall Street Journal* felt threatened by Rick Springer, and viewed the spectre of him on network TV much as Odysseus viewed Thersites in the center of the Homeric assembly: So wrong a person in so right a place."

Sadly, the established media swiped at Judge Lawrence Leavitt for daring to release me the following day on my own recognizance. Journalist John Smith of the *Las Vegas Review Journal* responded to what he called "the McLaughlin Mob, an erudite bunch of bar brawlers. The McLaughlin Group spent a few heated moments slicing to pieces the Secret Service and its $500 million annual budget, then took after Leavitt for having the audacity to release the bearded pacifist. Why, they even suggested the magistrate get his head examined."

"Someone may call for psychological work ups all around before this federal fiasco is finished. So far Leavitt appears the only official to have acted rationally," Smith commented.

In a radio interview on the Los Angeles Michael Jackson show, one caller insisted, "They should drop you down the next nuclear bomb test hole and detonate it with you in it." Some of the peace movement itself bought the sensational media, hook, line and sinker. Long time associates asked, "Why did you hit Reagan?" "You let us down." "Your action marginalized the movement." It caused great debate within the nonviolent movement as to what constitutes violence, but the issue was clouded by the initial headlines, "Reagan Attacker Released."

I went on tour and participated in over 120 radio shows and twenty TV interviews in just six weeks. I explained what I had experienced and found that most concerns were eased with my story.

The Oregon Peace Worker ran an article displaying a variety of responses,

Fellowship of Reconciliation (FOR) member Susan Davis said she did not regard the action as violent, but recommended that Springer replace the statue. Calvin Hecocta of the American Indian Movement said: "I think it was an appropriate action. I would like to see it done the same way again. Watching the action was a piece of inspiration for me."

Betty Rademaker (FOR) questioned how we can "Pierce the embodiment of evil" that is the established order, suggesting that "we have to be true to our own inspiration."

Jay Penniman: "I see it as a violent action and I can't condone it, but people have to be woken up. We have to change our mode of operation from the use of violence."

Fairborz Pakseresht, a Middle Eastern peace activist, reminded the group, "The element of understanding is missing from our lives, and we judge peoples actions without knowing what motivated them."

Peter Bergell, *Peaceworker* editor said, "If any of us knew how to end the arms race, we would have done it by now. It is not necessary for us to sit in judgement of others actions. However, if we want to communicate, we must take responsibility not only for being clear about what we say, but also for what others hear. Smashing the eagle allowed the broadcasters to ignore the message about testing and apply the label of violent to Springer."

Paul Krassner's *The Realist* ran my own response titled <u>Why I Did It</u>. "They say a picture is worth a thousand words, but the media missed the real picture. It is not the picture of former President Reagan with an unknown antinuclear activist at the podium. The real picture is the image of the sacred symbol of freedom, that crystal eagle, as it shattered into a thousand pieces. Shattered by over 900 nuclear bomb tests on Newe Segobia, the sacred lands of the Western Shoshone people. Shattered by the incarceration of Clifford Dann, by the Rodney King verdict, by the deaths of over 13.5 million children under five starving worldwide this year. Shattered by every bomb dropped on Iraq, but ultimately shattered by the apathy of a nation that thinks freedom is free."

Part Two

The Degradation Ceremony

Chapter Nine
FUGITIVES FOR JUSTICE

The Easter/Passover events and arrests of The Hundredth Monkey completed two years of organizing. What media the Broken Eagle Incident brought to that ten days of events came to an abrupt halt with the Rodney King verdict, wherein the police were found innocent of brutality in the appalling beatings of that man. Black communities across the nation rioted in the worst race riots in US history.

The Hundredth Monkey office, in the heart of the black neighborhoods of North Las Vegas, just six blocks from North Las Vegas Detention Center, weathered the storm untouched. Our neighbors had accepted us from the beginning with curiosity. I think they had an understanding that while our focus was different, the black people and the antinuclear movement were up against the same opponent. Nuclearism and racism go hand in hand, with nuclear testing conducted on indigenous lands around the world; the Shoshone in Nevada, the Kazakhs in the Soviet Union, the Uighur in Lop Nor, China, and on Maohi lands in the South Pacific. Racism is, in fact, an intrinsic aspect of nuclearism. The US government has kindly granted permission to the British to bomb the Shoshone over 22 times at the NTS.

With the Event, the Walk and the Action completed, the members of the office were anxious to continue the push to halt nuclear testing. After all, the goal was unfulfilled. We agreed to launch a Nevada initiative to allow the citizens to vote on whether nuclear testing could be allowed within the state. We had gathered over 8000 signatures of the 30,000 we needed, when we gave up. The citizens were supportive, but we didn't have the staff or funding necessary for a full scale initiative campaign. At a minimum, the campaign was successful in keeping the issue alive through press coverage.

The Broken Eagle Incident became the dictating force in my life. I was facing state and federal charges. International law professor Francis Anthony Boyle advised me to accept a plea bargain with the feds because they would not allow me the Necessity Defense in court. "You don't stand a chance," he said. I accepted his advice, and with the aid of William Carrico, worked out a deal with the federal prosecutors. I admitted that I was guilty of `Interfering with the Secret Service,' a misdemeanor which we more accurately described as `Embarrassing the Secret Service.' They dropped the felony charges, Assaulting a Former President and Resisting Arrest, both of which I was innocent of. I've learned since the government strategy: scare the hell out of you with charges carrying 20 years, and you'll be happy to plead out to charges carrying two to five. This strategy results in plea bargains in 9 out of 10 federal convictions.

The State of Nevada wanted their own piece of the eagle action, and charged me with Malicious Destruction of Property. This was the arena Professor Boyle advised I make my case in. From a strategy perspective, that word 'malicious' offered much more opportunity to bring out the nuclear issue. State courts would often hear the necessity defense, which allowed expert testimony as well as cameras in the courtroom. The possibility of Carl Sagan and Helen Caldicott testifying in my case was a goal worth working for. The state charges of malicious destruction demanded that the government prove that my motive for breaking that glass bird was malicious. That, in turn, allowed me to prove that it was not malicious but appropriate, in light of the atrocity. I had to be allowed to prove that an atrocity existed.

Although the state and federal governments often bicker on political issues, they are generally united on the prosecution of common criminals and work together with the intent of nailing you one way or another. They ultimately postponed the scheduled state trial because they wanted to see how the feds could deal with me first. They knew as well as I did that the state court was my arena.

For almost a year and a half following the Broken Eagle, I was on pretrial supervision, reporting twice a week to pee in the bottle, while Hector Huerta and Ron Pease gazed on. I didn't realize that it was only the beginning of the government's 'degradation ceremony.'

After closing the Vegas Monkey office, I retreated to the shores of Lake Mead, just over the mountains to the southeast, where I worked on recording the details of the Hundredth Monkey organizing story and the Broken Eagle Incident. I baked like a cookie in an oven---I love the desert heat.

In September of that same year, 1992, a group of Belgians arrived from the Walk Across America for Mother Earth. In conjunction with the 500 years of indigenous resistance to the invasion of Columbus, they had departed from New York in the January snows and walked across the nation, stopping along the journey to pay respects to native tribes and peoples. After nine months of following 'the trail of tears,' they were to arrive at the Nevada Test Site for the Healing Global Wounds ceremonies. Before them, a small group, about ten of those 100 peace marchers, arrived to plan some backcountry actions, hoping to get the press aware of coming events.

Backcountry, August 1992

The quote, "Those who make nonviolent revolution impossible make violent revolution inevitable," is proven throughout history, and in gradations at test site actions as well. Within the peace movement the commitment to nonviolence is strong. But as the need to alert the public becomes ever more urgent the actions escalate with the risk to the opposition minimal, the personal risk great. It may be justifiably argued that creating situations where one may be injured themselves is a form of violence but Gandhi believed that enduring personal suffering was not only redemptive, but helped aggressors to transcend as well.

The media report on test site actions based on three key criteria. First is to ignore as much as possible any stories about nuclear weapons that may arouse the public. Second, they must report on events if it is apparent that word of mouth will deliver the story regardless. The illusion must be maintained that the media is unbiased and tells us what we need to know. Third, actions that will sell enough newspapers to justify the negative exposure must be covered. Capitalism is capitalism, after all. These factors are based on the valid premise that a public saturated with negative news remains overwhelmed and incapable of response. I spent four years myself trying to sort out information and decide where to invest my energy.

Actions at the gates of Mercury became old hat to the media as fast as Martin Sheen was arrested after his publicly announced plan to civil resistance at the test site entrance. Although a variety of celebrities continued to be arrested with the masses, the media dropped the coverage to three paragraphs, sixth page of the local section. Activists became bolder, and 'Backcountry Action' was born. Dan Elsberg is reputed to have been in one of the first teams to enter the test site in an effort to discover the location of a test and block it's detonation by human presence. Other actions followed. A team of British women went in and to some degree, the press responded.

But it is very risky business. The trick is to get to Ground Zero (G.Z.) after the area has been evacuated but before the bomb is detonated. The risk of radiation exposure is high. Death is possible, as some craters subside over a hundred feet.

I worked with the Belgian team on two actions. There were four Belgians from Walk Across America for Mother Earth that were willing to enter the test site to halt a test. We went into the desert for a shake down hike and briefing on desert survival, medical concerns, and basic strategies. Having vacationed as a youth in the Mojave and Southern Nevada deserts, I was well acclimated to the desert heat and lack of humidity. I understood how the human is capable of acclimating to a variety of climates, but only over time. While these intrepid Earth patriots had the will, as an EMT, I wanted to make sure that they fully grasped the ways of the desert: how distances are deceiving, how cactuses and snakes do not appreciate personal contact, how moisture is sucked from your body and how reluctant the desert is to give it back.

We have our people out doing reconnaissance work on the test site quite often. We also have people listening to the test site scanners, so we know when they are going to do a bomb test, because the NTS staff go through a series of dry runs to test all of their equipment before each test.

The Belgies, as Sue Navy affectionately called them, organized a media and support team. I was the medical support and driver. Other activists had taught me the ways in and out of the mountains surrounding the test site. It is the most rugged four wheel driving I've done. I thought Baja was tough, but that was in the daytime. And then the backcountry of the Navaho reservation on Big Mountain was wild in the Blue Heron, my 64 Chevy, but the test site took the cake, the yellow cake in this case. (Yellow cake is what they call raw uranium as they take it from the ground.)

One night, after a week of planning, we drove, as far as possible with no lights out into the hills. We drove off of hills that I would have been intimidated by on a motorbike. We crawled up sandy washes and over rock escarpments weaving through a valley barely wide enough for our vehicle. Finally we hit a narrow gorge just over a pass. Hanging from a cable strung across the road, a sign read, NO TRESPASSING! We believed our Western Shoshone permits superceded any US government signs. The four Belgians and two guides departed into the starry night. They hiked all that night and hid in the day. They had several close brushes as test site patrol trucks drove by. I drove the truck out that night, since it's hard to hide a truck on a desert mountain top, especially from air patrols.

The team was successful in getting to N tunnel for Hunters Trophy, the test postponed by the broken eagle. N tunnel is also the location of past NTS testing accidents that resulted in worker deaths. The Belgies got right up to the tunnel entrance and chained themselves to the entrance gates.

They got some local publicity, and some in Belgium. They were being arraigned in court while I was out to pick up the guides at our designated time and location. The critical factor on backcountry actions is water. It's hard to carry enough water to stay out there for more than a couple of days. We try to cache water around in different locations for emergency backcountry exits, but we don't have the US Treasury to print money for us.

The government claims that they test the water all around the test site at 22 locations to determine radioactive contamination. Yet I have never detected a single well cap disturbed. On the 1970 Baneberry test the DOE says, "The exact cause of the venting still remains a mystery. The original explanation postulated the existence of an undetected water table." They also admit that over 100 underground tests have been conducted directly in the groundwater, yet somehow they claim that the radiation is just sitting still and not moving.

The second Belgian backcountry team went in on bicycles. They had little time to move. We dropped them off at 1:00 AM on a cold and black desert night. They had seven hours to peddle sixty miles across the cholla covered desert. Through sandy, rocky roads they had to get to the test location before it was detonated. Somehow they did it.

The next morning, their support team called the DOE at 6 AM and explained that foreign citizens were at Ground Zero and the test would have to be postponed. The DOE claimed they saw no one, and the test moved forward as scheduled. The support team called the Belgian consulate, begging for help while they remained in contact with the DOE.

The support team had radio communication with the bicyclers, so they knew that the protestors were at G.Z. The action team described the location, and as the DOE helicopters flew overhead, they set off flares and colored smoke bombs. Not just auto flares, these were the industrial size from army surplus. The flares were so big, the team was afraid that the helicopters might think they were being fired at.

Still, the DOE claimed they never saw anyone. The four activists and the guide, who had stayed with them to insure they found the site in time, listened to their radios, staring at the tower in front of them, while the countdown continued. As you might guess, they thought they were cooked. They didn't know what to do. They knew they couldn't get away fast enough. The guide told them to stay on their feet to absorb the shock. Ten, nine, eight, they were in a panic....three, two, one, ZERO!

The DOE blew off a nuclear bomb test, knowing full well that five people were standing at Ground Zero. The ground swelled under their feet like a giant snake.

These tests are full scale earthquakes. They get measured by the US geodetic survey in Golden, Colorado. Many are 6.0 and above. Earthquakes in the Pacific Rim have doubled since the advent of nuclear testing, according to research conducted by Professor Whiteford of the University of New Brunswick. The DOE claims once again that there is no relationship.

I drove back into the test site to pick up the guide. After the test, the four Belgians rode their bikes to the Area 3 Support Facilities. They unfurled a banner which read "Stop Nuclear Testing Now," while wearing their radiation suits. They were arrested one hour after the bomb was detonated.

The guide wrote this statement shortly after I picked him up, "Just after we started towards ground zero, I heard the information that the test was probably going to happen in about thirty minutes. Can you say `adrenaline rush? Even though we had just traveled the entire night, with no moon, on some very rough jeep trails, I was wide awake. Next, we heard on the scanner, 'T-minus twenty minutes to zero time.' This is when I realized that I was scared; scared for my Belgian friends who had come halfway across the world to risk their lives in defense of Mother Earth, scared we might not make it, but most of all nuclear bombs just scare the shit out of me. I realized, shit, they're gonna do it. Twenty seconds ...fifteen...ten..9...8...7...6 ...5...4...3...2...1. zero time - beeeeeee.

"For just a moment there was total silence. I froze, waiting, listening, my heart pounding, and then the ground started trembling and it lifted me up, I don't really know how much. It wasn't enough to knock me down. The trembling lasted for several seconds. And after that was over, an intense thundering noise came from deep within the ground. Our Mother Earth had just been raped one more time by the United-States-Department-of-Energy-George-Bush-Military- Industrial-Complex."

The Belgians continued with a variety of actions, often joined by American activists. To bring home the continuing atrocity against the native people and their lands, the activists were determined to close the test site. They locked themselves to the cattle guard at the entrance, forcing the cars either to stop or drive over a body. It takes a lot of guts and commitment: there is always the possibility that a test site worker will come unglued and refuse to stop. They planned it early in the morning to stop the morning shift.

Bus load after bus load of test site workers come from Vegas and on that morning four people were lying in the road, locked to the cattlegaurd. They lay face down on the cold steel, put their arms around the steel I-beams, inserted their hands into a 5" steel pipe and locked their wrists together. The only way to get them off is to cut the pipe, which is under the cattle guard or convince them to unlock themselves.

Nye County Sheriff Jim Merlino was there to diffuse and make protest actions as ineffective as possible. He had witnessed action after action after action at the site and he knows from experience that these protestors are committed to nonviolence, yet every year he allowed the brutalization of protestors. If you refuse to cooperate, like going limp or refusing to walk, the Wackenhut thugs would stick their billy clubs into pain spots, under your arms or behind your ears. They would twist your wrist just shy of breaking.

Chris Stercks, a small Belgian woman with a giant spirit, was the last person still locked to the cattle guard that morning. I stood there watching, while buff weightlifters with beer bellies used nunchakus, a martial arts weapons, two wooden handles with a foot long chain. They wrapped the chain around her ankles and then her upper arms, using the handles to tweak the chain; making her scream and cry. The American tax dollar, hard at work torturing citizens while at that point, not even one vehicle was being stopped by the action. They could have easily set a road block and let her come off in her own time. Nobody would have been hurt or stopped. It is another example of the philosophy that justifies violence.

Wackenhut is a private security corporation, in direct violation of constitutional law. They are a private standing army with over 30,000 armed employees on its payroll. Basically they're mercenaries that hire out around the world with offices throughout the U.S. and in 39 foreign countries. The DOE hires them to brutalize protestors and provide security at the DOE headquarters. "It is known throughout the industry," said retired FBI special agent William Hinshaw, "that if you want a dirty job done, call Wackenhut."

156

The Belgian back-country team, (back) Chris Stercks, Caroline Dossche, (front) Wim and Luke, traveled around the globe to hike across the Shoshone desert to lock themselves to the entry of N tunnel in an effort to halt the nuclear bomb test, Hunter's Trophy, and bring media attention to this continued atrocity.

The Belgian bicycle team. The team pedalled over sixty miles across the desert from midnight to seven AM to witness a nuclear bomb test firsthand. The US DOE and the Belgian consulate were unwilling to halt the bomb test although they were informed of the activist's presence at ground zero (GZ).

Photo by Caroline Dossche

The Wackenhut security was dumbfounded when it occurred to them what had happened. In a joint US/Belgian citizen action, the test site was briefly shut down by four people willing to lay their bodies on the line.

Photo by Caroline Dossche

This activist was stomped on after being handcuffed and pushed to the ground by a Wackenhut employee . Other NTS workers looked on without concern.

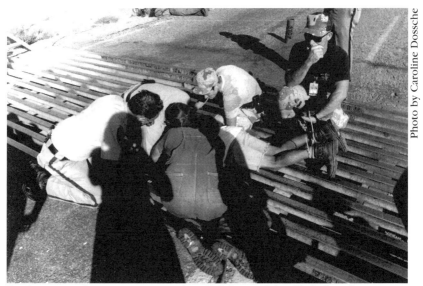

Photo by Caroline Dossche

For her commitment to stop testing, Belgian activist Chris Stercks was tortured by US DOE Wackenhut security. The Wackenhut employee, calling himself Mike, used nunchaku to tweak on Chris' ankles and upper arms. No traffic was being blocked at this point.

Photo by Caroline Dossche

The same activists at midnight as they departed into the black, starry Nevada Test Site. I was very impressed by the no-nonsense commitment of the Belgian back country teams. It was an honor to work with them.

Photo by Caroline Dossche

N tunnel in the middle of the Nevada Test Site. This is a horizontal tunnel used for weapons related tests. To test its ability to withstand an atomic blast, equipment is placed in a closed section of the tunnel. The Belgian team approached the tunnel entrance in broad daylight and locked themselves to equipment. N tunnel is a part of the Department of Energy public tour.

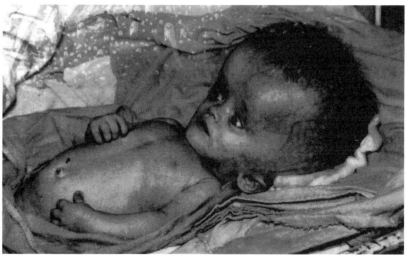

"The number of children and grandchildren with cancer in their bones, with leukemia in their blood, or with poison in their lungs might seem statistically small to some, in comparison with natural hazards, but this is no natural hazard—and it is not a statistical issue. The loss of even one human life, or the malformation of even one baby—who may be born long after we are gone—should be of concern to us all. Our children and grandchildren are not merely statistics toward which we can be indifferent."

John Kennedy, July, 1963

As individuals, they refuse to tell their names or wear identification. They could easily bring stretchers and carry away the limp protestors, but instead they torture them to make them move. I have seen them torture young women and old people, with a smile on their face.

On October 12th, 1992, 500 years after Columbus launched the perverted destiny, known as manifest, hundreds of modern citizens gathered to reflect on our history and remember that Columbus did not discover America. Rather than warring on the lost 'boat people', the indigenous cultures helped them survive.

Healing Global Wounds, a week long ceremony was designed to heal the wounds of lies. For the BLM it was an opportunity to destroy any modern attempt to revive indigenous cultures. Randy, a BLM officer, arrived at Peace Camp, across from Mercury, with his government pickup. He attached a rope and pulled down the 10' carved Peace Pole that had been erected as a part of the ceremonies. I've watched the BLM tear up beautiful sculptures of mothers and children and rip up stone circles placed by hundreds of protestors. While primitive cultures created what is often now preserved in National Parks, modern cultures are not allowed to create ceremony or art on public lands. Culture must be bought and owned.

In the late fall I felt it was time to return to Humboldt County. After selling The Heron, I took off by bicycle to pedal the 1000 miles home. It was a wet journey for Hobo and I, but it was good to ride day after day. The debts of the Hundredth Monkey left me broke and $20,000 in debt, so I slept on the beach and dumpster-dived on the journey home. I towed the cart piled full of my gear, with Hobo on top. South of Frisco a woman approached me as I repaired a flat tire in the rain. Seeing Hobo's head sticking out of the tarp covered pile, she handed me a $20 bill and asked that I get Hobo some treats. "Hobo, the president of Pitbulls for Nonviolence, thanks you, and I thank you," I told her with a sweeping bow. Another older man approached to tell me while he was petting Hobo, "I like your style. Especially that Visualize World Peace sticker on the bike cart."

It was a soggy winter in Humboldt County; the odds are good for that. I needed to repay some debts while awaiting the court sentencing date in February. I lived incognito in the barn of the old Mad River farm. While building kitchen cabinets in the shop upstairs by day, I renewed my EMT license by night. I slept where the cows had once been milked and fed, in the manger.

Sue Navy and I continued our long distance romance, from Crested Butte, Colorado to Arcata, California. Fortunately, she shortened that distance in February and brightened my winter with a visit. She couldn't quite believe it when I met her at the Arcata Greyhound station with an extra bicycle strapped across my cart. While she indulged me, I suspect peeing in the soggy cow pasture on a rainy, foggy Humboldt night was not the romance she'd fantasized.

Early in January I received the Pre-Sentence Investigation Report (PSI). It stunk. Theresa Brown of the Vegas office invited me into her office on a day six months prior to view a wall of her favorite portraits. Three of my heroes were there; Martin Luther King, Jr., Mahatma Gandhi and John Kennedy. Little did I realize that these were her examples of successful government assassinations. She began immediately by telling me that she wouldn't 'blow smoke up my ass' and later added that she wouldn't 'jerk me off.' Her recommendations to the court proved quite to the contrary, though.

Clinton was running for office at the time of our interview so when she asked about my drug use, I jokingly told her "I smoked pot twice but I didn't inhale." She included this in the report. With clever wording using insinuation, interpretation, and slander, she used her report as the cheering section for the prosecution.

On January 18, 1993 I flew to Vegas to receive my slap on the wrist for my slap on the eagle. In detailed meetings, Carrico had explained that my point total guaranteed that I was ineligible for jail time.

Surprise! Running into the courtroom from a stormy plane flight, I witnessed Carrico's concession speech on my behalf. He was kind enough to wave my banner, complain about the PSI tone, and plead for mercy, but my guts tell me, he knew what was coming down. Judge Pro, the man now in charge of the case gave me a brief verbal reprimand, sentenced me to four months in jail and left the bench.

As I stood there soaking in the reality of 120 days in jail, William couldn't help himself. Maybe even he thought I was just a bit too cocky. "You look like someone just kicked you in the balls?" His question was just a couple of seconds too early. He should have been computing the sentence like I was. He didn't have to because he already knew it, which I later learned is often the case in plea bargains. Your attorney and the prosecution bargain with your life. An attorney is like a real estate agent or an arms dealer, they just want the deal to close, and they work both sides of the fence to make that sale. Win or lose, their job is done and they get paid regardless.

Judge Pro was kind enough to allow me to complete my in-progress EMT renewal, and in that four months fate changed for me. Clinton let it be known through the Robert Bell Commission that he expected to restart nuclear testing at the end of the moratorium. This was a possibility that made me shake my head screaming, "NNNNOOOOOOOOOOOOO!" The Soviets, the French, the Brits were all observing the moratorium and had clearly expressed that they would resume testing if the US did.

If I went to jail, the US would resume testing during the middle of my sentence. I was tormented. I felt like I would be deserting my post to go sit in a prisoner of war camp while the bombing resumed. I was also aware that a refusal to surrender created another charge, with a whole year in prison. I take a deep breath even now.

I wrote the court for a stay of execution of sentence until my appeal was exhausted. They answered, "No dice." Surrender on June 2, 1993 to the Shasta County Jail.

Two days before I was due to surrender, I walked through the Arcata Co-ops anniversary tent event. I silently said good-bye to a community, or as close as we get to one these days. With Hobo in the cart and Laura Stec and John Bogner, peace marcher friends, riding along for cover, we pedaled Highway 299 out into the central valley. Fate is as gentle as the mongoose is with mice. Without planning we pedaled through downtown Redding just after lunch on June 2. I waved at the Shasta County jailhouse doors, rolling on by. Fate just wanted to know if I was sure about this fugitive thing and gave me one more chance to change my mind. I kept pedaling.

I issued a press release that same day to the major papers of the nation, *LA Times, New York Times, Boston Globe, SF Chronicle*, etc., "Why I Refuse to Surrender." I talked about the Western Shoshone elder Clifford Dann who had lit himself on fire in protest of the BLM roundup of Western Shoshone livestock, about how he was brutally extinguished by government employees and then charged with endangering a federal officer. This absurdity should have been enough but then the feds convicted him and sent him to prison in Lompoc.

I talked of the nuclear testing issue, the possible restart and my commitment to do whatever I could to halt it. I talked of the dysfunction of the courts and judiciary that supported the nuclear industry. I said I could not surrender to such an oppressor nation.

Becoming a fugitive is a challenging experience. As was often the case in my spiritual journeys, I didn't feel strong enough. But like the eco-rock band Clan Dyken sings, I knew I had to 'stand by my watch,' for what it was worth.

John Bogner pedaled back to the San Francisco Bay. Laura Stec got off in Oroville to become a macrobiotic cook and nutritionist. I pedaled out through Nevada and up into Idaho. While I lamented my fate as a fugitive, there was something incredibly free about it. It was a paradox. I pedaled into the mountains outside Oroville, struck by the beauty of the rivers strewn with house size boulders. I remembered Ishi, the last of the Yahi, a native man whose tribe was slaughtered around him. He remained the last of his kind in those mountains for many years before loneliness drove him into the white man's camp. I felt like Rickey, the last of the Yeehaw.

In Idaho, I worked with my old friend Bill Chisholm on organizing a rally in Twin Falls. We marched through town with a couple dozen protestors carrying signs calling on Clinton, "No Nuclear Testing!" I was on the front page of the local paper, but it's a big country.

Our labor paid off! At the first of July, Clinton responded to the public outcry and extended the moratorium. And with that came the end of my reasons for not surrendering. I began to make plans for a public surrender. If I was going to jail, I wanted all the press I could generate for nukes. We still had to complete the Comprehensive Test Ban.

I called former attorney general Ramsey Clark and he liked my idea of a public surrender to Janet Reno. He also advised me that communicating with the district attorneys office was a waste of time for a fugitive.

The problem was, I was broke and it was a long pedal to Washington, DC. I couldn't dumpster dive bicycle spokes, and towing a hundred and fifty pounds of laptop, bubble jet printer, a Nicaraguan first aid kit, and my camping gear was popping three or four spokes a day. I needed stronger wheels, which cost a couple hundred bucks. Still, I took off towards DC, rolling day after day, down through Nevada and out into Utah, through Salt Lake and down through Provo, and up the valley to Soldier Summit.

It was a queer thing how right at the bottom of that grade coyote was waiting to test me. These two guys came rolling down fresh from the east coast, on an Atlantic to Pacific bicycle tour. They explained in detail to me how Soldier Summit is one of the toughest grades in Utah. While I had pedaled over the Rockies in my early twenties, I had yet to tow a 150 pound cart over a thirty mile grade. Still, I was not to be daunted. Those who pale at the thought of an entire day of first gear grunt should never attempt such a climb. The truth is, you have to be a bona fide fool, oblivious to the reality of a long day of burning muscles and the inevitable blood sugar deficits that will leave you whining in despair. Then you must be prepared to continually lie to yourself that you're almost there; the summit is around the next turn. Such a fool am I. Regardless of the horror the two east coast tourists painted of the grade ahead, I took off with a kick-butt attitude.

I bid these (obviously mamby-pamby) East Coasters farewell and began the grade, immediately giving Hobo the signal to bail off the cart and begin the trot over the Rockies. I was a couple hundred yards up the grade, when what comes chugging alongside up the valley but a Hobo's dream...a freight train. With the train track running alongside the river bed and me on the grade the engineer and I were at eye level. He could see me pedaling and Hobo trotting. He gave me a loud 'toot-toooooot' of encouragement, and I raised my fist, thumb high in the air to let him know we were unstoppable.

I have groveled in a Minnesota snowstorm, slithered into an Alaskan purse seiner's hold full of salmon, and pounded nails in a 115 degree Mojave desert. On that day, as a fugitive, I rode the rails like a gypsy king. The Creator likes certain types of fools. That day I got an endorsement.

By the time that train came to a halt, the engineer must have been a quarter mile up. That an open box car sat directly across the tracks from me was either an example of Casey Jones expertise or random fate. 'Could a mile long freight train have come to a halt to pick up a lone cyclist and Hobo dog?' I asked myself. `Hell, yes!'

The challenge was to turn around, roll the hundred yards to the dirt road, rattle down the rutty road fifty yards, get my bike and trailer across the eight tracks between me and the open boxcar. Then I had to get my cart full of junk, the bike, and Hobo into the boxcar. All this before the train began to move again. Go for it!

I had the trailer three quarters unloaded and Hobo smelling the remnants of the prior tenants when I heard that farting-train sound, 'Ppssssshhhhhh' that everyone knows instinctively is the release of the brakes, "uhh-ohh."

They say that a small woman can lift a car off her husband when the adrenaline flows. My bike and cart became feather weights as I imagined Hobo and the train rolling off without me. I tossed them in with a surge of energy and hopped the five feet up into the car as it began to roll. We were hobos.

I waved at the cars that had passed me just that morning . Ahhh, romance at it's finest. The clackety, clak of the steel wheels on the track were music in my ears as we climbed slowly into the heaven just north of the "Big Rock Candy Mountains, where you never have to change your socks, where they hung the jerk that invented work, and there's a lake of stew and ginger ale, too."

The fugitive life has it's high points. I rode that freight train clear into Grand Junction, and as I sat in the 100 degree shade of a liquor store, a man came out with a buck thirty nine quart of icy beer. He silently assessed me and the cart, dumped the quart in my lap, scratched Hobo's ear and left us to toast the day.

We camped by a Colorado creek that night. I was on my way to Sue Navy's cabin in Crested Butte. I was in need of an intimate friend. Loneliness can almost be exacerbated by a full life. A world of wonder with no one to share it with can become a burden even greater than an empty life.

I was broke and needed to make a few bucks before my final assault on DC and public surrender to Janet Reno. During our time together at the Hundredth Monkey, Sue and I had been uncertain as to how and if we could turn our feelings into something more permanent. Now I was concerned about her being watched. How much effort the government was going to make to find me was anyone's guess. I was not a criminal in any true sense, but I had pissed off some powerful people, and I was another threat to the secrecy of the nuclear club. As Judge Pro had said, "An example must be made that such action will not be tolerated."

Sue Navy, while she didn't agree with my fugitive move, was again supportive of my insistence on following my commitments and inner guidance. She was a dear friend, willing to take personal risks. After my arrival in Crested Butte, we ran into the mountains for a week. We camped at the base of a glacier, where the ribbons of runoff glistened in the afternoon sun, creating a golden mane of hairlike threads. Mother Earth is a sensuous creature. For those with open eyes, drugs are superfluous.

I got a job at a ski condo pounding nails, but fate was cruel again. I got a brutal stomach flu, and while I fought my way through the week, I just couldn't crawl out of bed on Saturday morning. I was that weak. Hired as the crew leader, they canned me as a slackard. Still, I got $500 bucks in my pocket and had time to decide that, rather than travel to DC, I would prove the old adage correct and return to the scene of the "crime," nukes in Las Vegas.

Sue convinced me that Hobo, if arrested with me, would be at risk in the hands of government officials. A sweet, loveable old dog, she was also a pit-bull owned by a public dissident. The thought of putting Hobo into an animal shelter and then accidentally or otherwise disposing of her was not far fetched. So I not only left Sue behind, but Hobo, too.

It took me four hours, but I got one ride from Grand Junction, Colorado to Las Vegas, Nevada with a trucker. I slept in an abandoned car on the outskirts of Vegas. The next morning I made my way to the Nevada Desert Experience Hiroshima/Nagasaki events at St. Mary's church.

It was August 6, Hiroshima day. I attended all the weekend events in the sanctuary of a Catholic Church---meals, prayer circles, discussions, songs---but the real lesson came from a walk with Dan Berrigan. He knew my status and was kind enough to advise me on my efforts to bring media coverage to the nuclear issue.

"No one should have to go through that alone," he commented on my upcoming arrest. "It should be done with the support of a community."

I drove with the NDE people to the NTS ceremonies but went into the mountains to pray on my own. I wasn't ready to be arrested that morning and Jim Merlino, the Nye County Sheriff, might recognize me. I hiked to 'Black Woman Altar,' my own name for the altar built on a mountain overlooking Mercury. It has children's toys, crystals, money in a jar (for those who might need it), prayers on paper, plastic animals and more. It was the right place for my prayers. I wasn't ready to be recognized by the Nye county sheriff and arrested that morning.

August 9th, 1993 -- Nagasaki day:

Monday morning I met for the first time with Susan Quig-Terrey, the attorney that had consented to take my case. We had pancakes together. I explained my plan to do a media tour after breakfast and remind society about Nagasaki day in the hopes that error would never be repeated.

Susan Quig-Terry was an attractive professional woman in her early thirties. Her hair was black, shoulder length and she wore makeup with red lipstick. She had researched the failure to surrender charge and confirmed my understanding that it carried a potential one year sentence.

After breakfast we parted company as I began my planned media tour on foot. Channel 6, across from the cemetery, was the closest to the pancake house. I entered their back door and announced that I was Rick Springer, a fugitive, and that I was there to make a statement to the press. They immediately got the cameras. Al Tobin, whom I remembered from his days as a court reporter, was now the Channel Six news manager. I made my statement, focused on Nagasaki Day; the horror, the deaths, the mistake, and tied that in to the continued mistake of nuclear weapons research, development and testing. I also stated my solidarity with Clifford Dann, the Shoshone elder, and his unjust and absurd incarceration.

Al asked me a couple of revealing questions. "Aren't you concerned that you'll be arrested?"

"Of course, I'll be arrested sometime soon. I'll be in the media. They'll know I'm in town. I'm not avoiding the law. I'm using the media as a public surrender."

"So you're going to all the media stations today?" Al asked.

"Why, do want an exclusive?"

"We always want an exclusive." Little did I know just what he would do to guarantee one.

I headed out into the August desert heat to make my way to the *Review Journal* newspaper to arrange an interview. As I walked into the entranceway of the *R.J.*, a car came racing from the back of the lot. I knew I was going to be arrested, but I didn't expect it quite that fast.

Lo and behold, it was agent Mike Fithen again, the same Secret Service man that had booked me on the day of the Broken Eagle Incident.

He and a younger partner jumped out of the car and I stood still as they relieved me of my black bag and frisked me.

"You don't have guns or weapons, do you, Rick?"

"Of course not! You know I'm opposed to guns, Mike."

They loaded me into the car and whisked me off to the federal courthouse.

"We were afraid you ran off to the Dann land up there in north Nevada to join that AIM movement," Mike commented.

"Why were you afraid of that, Mike?"

"Well, they're a bunch of cop killers, ya know."

"No, Mike, the cops are a bunch of Indian killers is more realistic. I think you should read In The Spirit of Crazy Horse by Peter Mathiesenn, which I think is a more accurate portrayal of the relationship between cops and Indians in the American Indian Movement."

"Is that right?" He sounded earnest. "Hey Rick, how's your book going? I hope you aren't going to be too hard on us in the Secret Service?"

"I'm gonna tell the truth as best as I can, Mike."

We squealed into the courthouse parking, just like on TV. Another officer hopped out of a parked car and came to open my door and drag me out. Squeezing my arm tightly, he got in my face, "We're gonna send you away for a long time this time, Springer."

I could have responded, "You've got the wrong man," after all I'm just a nonviolent anti-nuke activist, but his melodramatic style was a bit to much for me. "You've been watching too much Miami Vice, my man."

He glared at me like he'd love to punch me in the gut. Instead he fed me off into the bowels of the dragon once again.

I spent four days in a fifteen by twenty holding cell, crammed in with thirty other guys. I watched convulsions and confessions, DTs and drug trips, crying, fighting, vomiting and diarrhea, all in front of my face.

I decided to begin a fast, in solidarity with Clifford Dann. Besides, I needed to get grounded and spiritual to endure. Fasting was not all that simple in prison. The guards insisted I take a tray. Some inmates fought over food.

In about ten days I was transferred to North Las Vegas Detention Center, NLVDC. It was a city-run prison that had just been opened a year earlier. My first cellmate was a lifelong alcoholic who claimed he had worked his life for Hughes Aircraft in public relations. His job had been to wine and dine foreign customers. He was an arms merchant. I guess it should come as no surprise that he was in for threatening to murder his wife. He was clever, witty and demented. The nurse arrived twice daily to see he got his lithium and almost every night at about 3 AM he was up and looking out our cell window slot imagining he was on an ocean liner cruise.

He was mentally ill, but even more, he was spiritually ill. Other inmates asked just how I could stand him, but I felt compassion for him. When you hear someones life story, it often makes sense that they would go crazy as they did. I knew that Tom had drank away too many brain cells while selling bomber contracts. He told me several stories of illegal activities in the line of Hughes Aircraft duty.

Some of the inmates encouraged me to eat. It was hard for them to understand the spirituality of fasting. To them it was just a slow suicide and they hated to see anyone give up. I lost a lot of weight. Fortunately or unfortunately, I go quickly when not eating. Some last for a couple of months, but I think I'd be gone in about three weeks. It was obvious how weak I was getting. My cellee one night observed with a wicked smile that I was so weak, I couldn't stop him from "fucking you in the ass if I want to." I mustered enough strength to lean up on one elbow. I told him that if he spoke that way again he'd have a new cellmate immediately. He liked and respected me enough that he never joked that way again.

Anyway, on the 18th day I went to sleep with numb legs. My body was so clean and empty I felt that the totality of my physical body was my heart, my aorta, and my left femoral artery. With each beat, I felt my life pump up and over the aorta, whooshing down unimpeded into my leg. It was a moment of reckoning.

Gilbert, the nurse, had explained to me how I would be strapped into a hospital bed, hooked up to an IV and fed intravenously if my fast continued. My personal hit is that I could have died before they realized I was gone. The prison medical staff had little if no understanding of the physiology of autolysis, the process of dissolving your own body, and the idiosyncracies of each unique metabolism.

I asked the Creator that night if it was time to come home. I couldn't help but mull over the admonitions of an elder Greek man who became my prison mentor, George the Greek.

"I respect that you have to do what you have to do, Rick, but we need you here, too!"

I decided that while I was willing to die for this beautiful Mother Earth, I was even willing to take the harder path. I was willing to live. I asked Gilbert for a bowl of vegetable soup and some rice cakes the following day. He was pleased to grant my request but I have to confess I reconsidered when they delivered greasy chicken bouillon cubes with saltines in a styrofoam cup.

And with that, I joined the daily prison scene of North Las Vegas Detention Center, a cross between *One Flew Over the Cuckoo's Nest* and *Apocalypse Now.*

Man who shattered Reagan's crystal eagle is pro-Earth

John L. Smith

When Rick Springer decided in June to become a fugitive from justice, he didn't exactly slink out of town.

He pedaled.

The nuclear testing opponent made his great escape by bicycle with his 60-pound pitbull, Hobo, watching for FBI tails from the attached trailer.

A pedaling fugitive?

It wasn't the quickest getaway on record, but Springer succeeded in his goal to avoid reporting to jail until President Clinton stopped wavering and signed a moratorium on nuclear testing. A month later, Springer began serving a four-month sentence at the North Las Vegas Detention Center for embarrassing the Secret Service by smashing a 30-pound crystal eagle near former President Reagan during a broadcasters convention at the Las Vegas Hilton.

Just so no one gets the wrong idea, the pitbull is as different as her owner.

"She's the president of Pitbulls for Nonviolence," Springer says, laughing in an interview room at the North Las Vegas jail. He appears about as comfortable as a man can be when serving federal jail time. "Pitbulls just happen to be little, strong, energetic animals. She's great and playful and not the least bit aggressive."

A pacifist pitbull?

After spending a few minutes with Springer, the bearded fellow who interrupted Reagan's monologue and wound up making international news, it becomes clear he would own nothing else.

He is not merely a member of the unwashed masses who assemble outside the Nevada Test Site each year for a chant of protest and a token arrest. He is not an aging hippie on some long, strange trip.

In fact, Springer was not always active in the anti-nuclear movement. Nothing so political could describe his spiritual evolution; nothing so simple could capture his indefatigable optimism.

Springer, 41, was raised in Altadena, Calif., near Pasadena. He attended John Muir High School, and his family includes a brother who is a detective with the Los Angeles Police Department.

When Springer left home, he took a backpack and a bicycle and combed the country for the better part of a decade. He was a merchant marine, a salmon fisherman in Alaska, a boat builder and finish carpenter in Massachusetts and Maine, a camp counselor and social worker in California.

He once owned a 28-foot sloop in Massachusetts and a 45-foot cutter in Maine. He has had a fair number of material possessions.

Although Springer left nature when necessary, it did not leave him. The giant redwoods and the ceaseless sea tugged at his spirit.

At 30, he found himself studying American Indian culture, customs and religion. It was then he began to understand his feelings.

"I had a lot of real time in nature," Springer says. "Native American people, they have had practiced for generations, I had discovered."

Namely, that the Earth was too beautiful to let die.

"Look at Red Rock," he says.

"You've got to be spiritually numb not to be awe-struck by that beauty."

Springer is not anti-nuke so much as pro-Earth. He considers weapons and weapons testing a threat to the planet. He believes the deterrent is not as great as the danger.

He is paying for his belief.

"Almost everybody feels this way," he says. "People just don't feel empowered to act on this. It is the accumulation of all our small efforts that will make the difference."

He is not a politician, but his speech brims with ready rhetoric. He is not a jailhouse lawyer, but he already has begun taking up his fellow inmates' causes.

Springer is not some crazy old hippie star-struck by his 15 minutes of celebrity. He does not hear voices, except perhaps for the opera sung by an ocean breeze through redwood trees.

"We pay now, or our grandchildren pay later," Springer says before the guard comes. "Now that we've got it rolling, we've really got to push."

A pedaling fugitive with a pacifist pitbull.

A rail-thin fellow who cries at the beautiful Earth and has devoted his life to preserving it, jail cells and G-men be damned.

Rick Springer is out to save the world. On bicycle, yet.

Those who doubt he'll do it should look how far he's come.

John L. Smith's column appears Wednesday, Thursday, Friday and Sunday.

Reprinted courtesy of Las Vegas Review Journal/Sun

Chapter 10
NECESSITY OR NOT NECESSITY!

* * * * *

"Court mandated prisoner rights are sometimes manipu-
lated and ignored even in the other phases of the criminal
justice process, it is not surprising that rulings on the rights of
inmates often have little impact in the closed prison environ-
ment. The most debilitating aspects of prison life result from
the lawlessness and unfettered discretion in closed institutions."
ACLU *Civil Rights Violations in the United States*

* * * * *

The passage of time becomes the science of mathematics to inmates in prison; counting, division, and increments of all varieties; minutes, days, months, calendars, and even lifetimes. But even beyond science, it became philosophy, the philosophy of paradox. Sleep became a state of consciousness often indistinguishable from awake, as daydreams blended into naps and night-mares awoke other nightmares. Is this today's nightmare or yesterday's? How long have I been asleep? Did I cheat the system out of some real time?

"Springer, Attorney visit!" Officer England broke into my maze of naps. His presence seemed appropriate in that ugly, fear laden dream world I'd been sweating in. The knot in my stomach was still there. . . still.

There he stood, a dark-haired, butch-waxed young prison guard with thick, black-rimmed glasses and a cookie duster moustache. I was hustled from the dead air of the lockdown unit and into the slap-together, prefab-plastic Intake Unit. England's portly frame carried his roly-poly belly well, but then he was still only 25.

"Hey, Springer, I voted for Reagan, ya' know."

"Really, well, I'm glad to hear you voted, England, but next time maybe you oughtta' research *who* you're voting for."

"You sure this isn't your girlfriend, Springer?" England asked, referring to my attorney. Another door buzzed and allowed us entry into a gauntlet of halls. There were seven of them, each with a door to buzz to get to the front door.

Buzzer after buzzer, I kept my mouth shut. The fact that Susan Quig-

Terrey was an attractive woman was only a distraction, from my point of view. I still needed a landshark in court, and she looked more like a rabbit. Carrico was off to bigger trials

Through my prior trials and appeals I had followed every lead, every contact suggested. I had scoured ACLU lists, followed Lawyer's Guild suggestions, written, phoned, faxed, and after sorting them all, came up repeatedly with Susan Quig-Terrey, Esquiress. My several letters and phone calls to get her to accept my case had finally paid off.

"Under no circumstances are you to defend yourself," I remembered Anne Fagan Ginger, the head of the Miekel John Civil Liberties Law Library telling me. "I don't care how smart you are, how wise, clever, committed or spiritually grounded you are. The federal government will eat you up in procedure."

Officer England and I entered a small room with a wall of glass on the hall side. Susan Quig-Terrey rose. I hugged her like I'd hug anyone in the peace movement. I needed assistance of counsel. I also needed a friend. England stood rudely staring on the other side of the glass, departing only after we took particular note of him.

"How are you doing?" She asked.

"I've been better," I managed a weak smile. "We've got a lot of work to do, as I see it. How are you?"

She apologized for missing our Friday appointment and explained that her personal life was a bit hectic with the kids. She listened patiently while I explained my perception that the City of North Las Vegas was so deep in debt in building this prison that they had opened before they were ready. In order to cover expenses, they were gouging inmates on phone services, medical supplies, clothing, and health care, as well as recreational supplies and activities. I asked her to file a grievance against NLVDC. I believe their violations were criminal, but as an inmate it was impossible to gain access to the files and BOP policy manuals that could prove it.

I explained to her the connection between the prison system and nuclear weapons. With the resources our societies invest in armaments we could easily provide health care, jobs, housing and education to every family around the world. Forty percent of all state inmates are unable to read. Only 25% of prisoners nationwide have completed high school. Our schools are packed with 25 to 35 kids per classroom, despite the fact that one teacher is not able to effectively educate much over 15. That leaves 10 to 20 students that not only fall through the crack but widen it by distracting the entire classroom.

Eisenhower called each bomb "a theft from those who hunger." That was not a rhetorical supposition, it was a true reality. The tales of my fellow inmates proved it.. Many stories I heard made complete sense in that their path to prison was so predictable; No father from birth...Mom on welfare doing drugs with numerous boyfriends...Brother shot to death at eleven...Began doing drugs at 9...Minimal attendance at school...Into prison at 18...Sentenced to fifteen years. What were the options? Could I have painted a different picture with my life in those circumstances?

I asked Sue Quig-Terrey to file a grievance with the American Civil Liberties Union, the Bureau of Prisons and the Public Defenders office because I honestly believe that NLVDC is worthy of a *Sixty Minutes* story.

I told her, "Inmates are deprived of critical medications. Ray Jefferson's teeth got smashed out by another inmate while chatting on the phone, and he's suffered for two months now with two front stubs, and all they give him is Motrin. They still haven't taken him to a dentist. But hey, he's black, so that's okay, huh?" I glanced at her with a twisted face to see that she got the sarcasm. "Imagine laying in your bunk day after day, with raw nerves exposed on two broken teeth. Might make you a bit cranky, huh? But then, get outta line and the guards'll beat your head with a black stick or fill your face with mace.

"Now here...good old George Christakis, a Greek elder, here's a copy of his request for meds. He's even offered to buy his own. It's his blood pressure medicine. They're messing with people's lives. Ya' know how we communicate if we need something from our cells? We wave a towel out our food slot and hope someone will see it.

"Then, there's the phone system. When you finally get out of your cell to stand in line for an hour, it's collect calls only with an intro from Inmate Phone Systems." I impersonated the generic phone voice, "`You have a collect call from an Inmate at North Las Vegas Detention Center.' Half the people you need to talk to won't even accept.

"But the worst is that they charge not only the collect price but jack it up for an extra profit for the phone contractor and the city jail both. So the poor inmate, broke already, probably why he's into crime, is desperate to call wife and kids, and in one month runs up an $800.00 phone bill on all local calls. Then his phone is disconnected cuz his wife is broke also and now she's got no phone and he won't have one for job hunting when he does get out.

"Then there's the commissary. They tell me that most prisons issue you socks, underwear and t-shirts, but here you have to buy those things or you don't get them. They issue one pant, one shirt and one pair of shower slippers. That's it!

"You get one blanket and they think that the colder it is, the less germs, so you shiver under your blanket, fetal position, all night and most of the day. Of course, you can buy sweatshirts from their commissary, seconds at a premium, if you have money on your books.

"Speaking of commissary, you can buy all the candy bars or Fritos you want but you can't get vitamins unless you've proven you're anemic or pre-coffin. Prevention is not a viable concept in this facility.

"Same thing with shampoos, soaps and cosmetics. The Crawford brand they sell you here is free in other prisons. The standard issue soap is so caustic with lye that people have constant rashes and dry itchy skin, but hey, you can buy Dove with a quarter cleansing cream, if you got a buck in your account and you get to help pay off the prison loan at the same time." I thought maybe I was boring her, but she insisted that she was with me. She assured me she would file the grievance.

"Yes, and also you should know that much of my mail is not getting through. All my papers from the first county jail have never been returned, although I've filed three grievances. This prison's own rule book states they will respond to a kite within 72 hours. Yeah, they call the grievance form a kite, because you might as well go fly it."

She gave me a copy of the prosecution's response to our motion to present the Necessity Defense, an old defense which basically allowed for the violation of a law in order to prevent a greater harm. The classic example is that a crew can mutiny a ship if they know the ship is unseaworthy. It was clear to me that testing nuclear bombs on Spaceship Earth was akin to blowing the canons off into the bilge or polluting the water casks while at sea.

The necessity defense consisted of four key requirements before it would be allowed in court. A person must be faced with a choice of two evils and choose the lesser. I believe failing to surrender to sit four months in jail was a lesser evil than allowing our earth to be shattered, our water and air supplies to be tainted and our grandchildren's inheritance radioactively pissed into the wind by restarting nuclear testing.

The second requirement of the necessity defense is that one must act to prevent imminent harm. Third, one must reasonably anticipate a direct causal relationship between their conduct and the harm to be avoided. I hoped my fugitive status would generate more media coverage of the issue and arouse public opposition to a restart of nuclear testing.

And the fourth requirement -- a sticky one and hard to prove -- one must have no alternatives to violating the law. If soldiers in war had a duty to escape, then I certainly had a duty to refuse to surrender to the United States government's nuclear war.

I explained to my attorney how critical it was that the US not restart testing at the time of my decision to refuse to surrender. The US, Great Britain, France and the Soviet Union had all made it quite clear that if the US resumed testing, then they would do likewise. One must understand that it is not the nuclear war we might have, it is the nuclear war we are having. After 45 years of blowing off nuclear bombs around the world, it was all quiet on the testing front. It was a cease-fire we could not afford to violate.

In about two hours I gave Susan Quig-Terrey the impacting facts that had brought me to the commitment that interrupted the UN, set that crystal eagle free, and made me a fugitive and a prisoner of war. I took a deep breath, because I sensed she understood, for the first time, the real horror of nuclear weapons.

We delved into the International Laws that make nuclear weapons illegal and the very cogent arguments by international law professor and activist with the Lawyers Guild on Nuclear Policy, Francis Boyle. The testing and development of nuclear weapons represented yet another series of broken treaties by the US government. Boyle used the US Army Field Manual to show that our own laws as well as the Nuremburg Principles prohibit the use of weapons that cannot distinguish between combatants and noncombatants.

I explained to Ms. Quig-Terrey that even the Declaration of Independence demanded in the first two paragraphs that "It is not only our right but our duty to change, alter or abolish any government that becomes injurious to our basic rights of life, liberty and the pursuit of happiness." I don't think anything in history has been so clearly injurious to those rights as nuclear bombs, from start to finish.

The expert witnesses I felt could best present my defense were Professor Francis Boyle, to cover the illegality of nuclear weapons, any one of Drs. Rosalie Bertell, Carl Sagan, John Goffman or Ernest Sternglas, to cover the radiological effects and imminency of the harm to be avoided, and journalist and author Norman Solomon, Ben Bagdikian or Noam Chomsky to present the mainstream media cover-up and complicity in the nuclear industry.

The most compelling argument to me was the spiritual argument, one that had been instilled in me since Vacation Bible School. The truth of 'Thou shall not kill' is nearly instinctual. No matter what the government of man decided, it was my belief that the will of God superceded that. Our pledge of allegiance states, 'One nation under God.' I believe On God, as Earth is my God. Though it seemed like a bastardization, even money the root of all evil, claimed "In God We Trust." Gods of all faiths claim, "Thou shall not kill," and a man touted as the son of God, Jesus, took it even further, saying "turn the other cheek."

My studies with Corbin Harney instructed me to recognize and respect the sacred in all the Earth's Creation. Not in all of man's creation but in what Mother Earth created. And respect for uranium, like a grizzly bear, meant giving it a wide berth and leaving it alone. Dr. Rosalie Bertell and Dr. Sternglas have discovered clearly why.

Bertell is a sweet, white-haired nun who is a wizard mathematician and researcher with a Ph.D. Early in her career she worked at the National Cancer Research Center in Buffalo and then specifically on the Tri-State Leukemia Survey. She published her research showing that low-level radiation caused leukemia and premature aging. She found that the federal government allows the general public to receive up to five hundred millirems per year. This is equivalent to a hundred chest X-rays per year. Nuclear workers were allowed to receive up to five rems, which is equivalent to 1000 chest X-rays a year. She learned that the average time interval between men's participation in nuclear tests and their diagnosis of leukemia was 15 years. Multiple myelomas took twenty years to diagnose and solid tumors take twenty to fifty years. She joined radiologists around the world in claiming, "There is no known tolerance level for radiation." She was also the one that opened my eyes to the fact that nuclear power plants are just another facet of the nuclear weapons industry. Every nuclear reactor produces plutonium 239 as a by-product. This is not only the most toxic substance known, it's also the most convenient material from which to make fission bombs. Edward Teller, a physicist and bomb proponent was asked, "Don't you think that third world countries are eager to get nuclear power so they can then build nuclear bombs?" He answered, "Yes, that's true. Unfortunately, it's already happening."

Dr. Ernest Sternglass discovered the relationship between nuclear fallout and decreased SAT scores. Due to nearly undetectable thyroid damage from the effects of radiation on fetuses, our children are actually getting stupider. He proved that, while 1957 was the year of greatest atmospheric release of radiation from nuclear bomb tests, eighteen years later, 1975 was the year of lowest SAT scores in history. To dissuade sceptics, he showed that the decrease did not appear upwind in California but in direct relation to downwind fallout patterns.

He proved that man, especially during the early stages of embryonic growth was thousands of times more sensitive to radiation than anyone had suspected. Even one pelvic X-ray in the first trimester of pregnancy doubles the child's chances of getting leukemia.

It's all documented from government statistics, but like with Bertell, the nuclear industry and the media did all they could to discredit Sternglass. I was convinced that if a jury heard these facts from credible experts then they could see why I felt it was necessary to take such seemingly drastic steps.

I shared many of the details of my personal life with Ms. Quig-Terrey, who insisted I call her Sue. I felt it was important for her to know that I had not lived my life in a vacuum; that I had plenty of other interests, that I had lived and loved and it was that diversity of experience that had brought me to community service, because I felt a sense of indebtedness for this incredible earth and life. Through all the experience I've had, the diversity of life on earth drove me to a state of wonder.

Officer Ritzman opened the door of the attorney/client room and stuck his red, freckled head in. "I'm sorry but we gotta wrap this up. It's almost chow time. Maybe another ten minutes, huh?"

Ritzman was a constant reminder that stereotyping the prison guards was as unfair as stereotyping the inmates. He knew you get more with honey than vinegar. Ritzman was not a party to the degradation ceremony.

I tried to get a commitment from Sue to meet three times a week, two hours at a shot to prepare for trial, but she wouldn't go for it. She said it was hard to get baby-sitting that often, better to do more time in fewer meetings.

Sue Quig-Terrey had studied law. I had studied nuclear weapons and testing. With enough preparation, I thought we stood a chance in spite of Francis Boyle's warning, "Stay out of federal court."

We hugged briefly before Ritzman led her away. She walked out the front door to the heat and Casinos of Las Vegas, and I was escorted back to gamble on mystery meat. A dog food tray slid through a slot in my cell door.

* * * * *

"The concept that `one should not be punished when an act of breaking the law prevents more evil than it caused' is an essential and basic one to our system of law. A history of reported cases provides ample criteria to either justify or discredit any claim of necessity. However, courts have usually suppressed proof of this criteria when faced with citizen intervention cases....Nevertheless, when such a defense has been put to a jury, the defendant has usually been acquitted. This fact raises the question of whether courts are really effecting justice by denying the necessity defense or whether courts are acting upon political motivations."
— *Aldredge/Stark, <u>Santa Clara Law Review</u>*   1986

* * * * *

October 1993

The sixth amendment states that "the accused shall enjoy the right to a speedy and public trial, by an impartial jury; the right to have compulsory process for obtaining witnesses in his favor and to have assistance of counsel for his defense." The amendment does not state which witnesses or which defense. The judge does that.

Sue Quig-Terrey and I appeared in court to argue that I should be allowed to present the necessity defense. We began with a reprimand from the judge for Ms. Quig-Terrey's tardiness. "This is Federal Court," reminded Judge Pro.

After an apology, Sue argued, "It would be our position that Mr. Springer's action was an act of direct civil resistance."

Our hurdle to jump was a case titled "US vs Schoon" in which protesters had chained themselves into the lobby of an IRS office as an act of protest against US policy in El Salvador. The judge in that case had ruled that their action was *indirect* civil resistance. The IRS does not set policy and has no ability to affect the situation in El Salvador. This point, valid or not, has been the tool by which many protestors are denied the necessity defense. Expert testimony, films, and a variety of other evidence are denied when the court accepts the Schoon case as applicable to the case at hand.

Ms. Quig-Terrey continued, "It is our position that Mr. Springer violated the order to surrender because putting him into incarceration would remove his ability to contest and fight the resumption of nuclear testing."

"All right. Mr. Springer, let me hear what you might add, and then I'll hear from Mr. Ham."

"I see that the law states clearly that a crew can mutiny if they see that their ship is not seaworthy. And what I see is that the government is the captain of this planet ship Earth, or the United States, and the allowance of nuclear weapons to resume is a similar analogy. You know, the crew, and myself, being part of the crew, it is allowable that I mutiny in this situation because we are about to start bombing our own ship here.

"And because there is some gray area, I say that it is appropriate that we allow a jury to make this decision. That's very key to the whole process, in my mind, because you yourself are a party to the captain and the authorities that are being mutinied. So in essence we're being tried by the captain to some degree."

"All right, Mr. Springer, well, you will be permitted to testify as to why you failed to appear. Mr. Ham."

"Well, Your Honor—I'm not going to belabor this point because it is so obvious. There is nothing to distinguish Mr. Springer and his perceptions of what he did with the Schoon case. It is directly on point.

"As to the uncontrollable circumstances as an affirmative defense of the failure to surrender charge. This was a volitional act by Mr. Springer. In effect, he was mad about the possible restart of nuclear testing, and so he said, well in protest, I'm not going to obey any of the government's laws and this is the first one that I can clearly break, this requirement that I surrender. It's similar to a teenager who's given a 10:00 o'clock curfew and says, well, in protest I'm not going to clean my room."

The Court agreed, but Sue gave it another shot anyway. "He felt that to go to jail would be like walking away from someone who was murdering a child to go comply with a surrender order. And I think that the jury has a right to hear the danger that he perceived, what he perceived was his moral and legal duty to do to prevent that danger. That's a decision for the jury to make."

Susan Quig-Terrey was asked to explain what expert testimony would offer... what Carl Sagan or Dr. John Goffman or Noam Chomsky might present. Still, Judge Pro was not persuaded. Judges expect to be persuaded about expert evidence by someone who has no expertise in that field, the attorney. I was exposed to another of the judicial methods of control.

"All right. Mr. Ham."

"Your Honor, the testimony that they're seeking to present through experts relates to the defense of necessity where you have harm or threat of imminent harm and you have to balance that harm to determine what is best for you or for society. The defense of necessity is not going to be allowed in this case."

That was exactly my point. I needed experts to prove that the harm and the threat of harm existed.

Ham and Pro were singing the same song. "All right. Counsel, I'm going to deny the motion for expert witness. As I've indicated, certainly he's free to testify as he chooses."

Mr. Ham had other concerns, "My concern is, regardless of what takes place out at that test site, Mr. Springer is merely going to use this courtroom as a forum to present his views. Mr. Springer has from the inception of his contact with the federal government sought a forum. And whether it is legal or illegal, his actions have been in furtherance of his political views. He's going to be making statements about a conspiracy by the government, by me, by some policy here to silence him. Mr. Springer is going to create I think a circus attitude or a circus environment. I would object particularly to him being given the chance to make a closing statement."

I struggled to get the court to look again at the Necessity Defense. "Could you explain to me why this action in your mind does not fall into the direct? I believe that I am being tried as a political prisoner and that the prosecution is doing everything in its power to silence me and keep me from expressing why I took the actions I took. It's my belief that if a jury hears and knows what I know about the issue, that they will say, yes, that was an appropriate action. There is no question in my mind that I'll be acquitted."

Judge Pro was becoming impatient, "Okay. Well, you're right, I am ruling on issues as to evidence that will be permitted in this case. And I don't expect you to agree with every ruling I make. I understand what the indictment is, I understand what orders were entered in the case and what the previous sentence was, and I'm not going to haggle with you about that."

I suspected the orders in the case were simple... conviction! "Can you explain why it's direct or indirect?"

"I thought I just did. It's analogous exactly to Schoon."

"A mutiny of a ship, is that a direct argument against the laws of mutiny? No. They're just saying, let's not go to sea. I'm not trying to change the law as far as the surrender is concerned. I'm saying in this particular situation that the law must be broken to avert a greater harm from taking place."

My hearing was up. "Look, I understand you disagree with me but you've got my ruling and that's it. Anything else that the parties have? All right. We'll see you all on the 25th then for trial with the prospective jury."

Chapter Eleven
BLOOD IN, BLOOD OUT

* * * * *

"As one of the most important conditions of confinement, given violence in prisons, the availability of medical care is a pressing issue inside the walls. The Newman v. Alabama (1972) case was the first in which the court decided that the medical care in an entire state was constitutionally unacceptable.

"The Supreme Court addressed this further in Estelle v. Gamble (1976) and created the basic medical standard of evaluation. It must be shown that there is 'deliberate indifference.' Of course this guideline has made it very difficult to direct further attention to medical care provided by prison authorities. It is difficult to show that a prison staff was deliberately indifferent." — Selke, <u>Prisons in Crisis</u> 1993

Status Epilepticus

The cold concrete slab, 25' wide by 60' long was the central living space for us 80 to 100 inmates filling the NLVDC lockdown facility. When not locked in a cell, we were allowed out to sit at tables with formica chess boards, to play Scrabble, Monopoly or to sit on plastic stools watching Geraldo dissect the latest Aryan Brotherhood hate crimes before his live audience.

I gathered with half a dozen men for a push-up and dip workout. There were no weights, although Director Brown promised a weight machine monthly.

Another inmate stood up from his stool and glared into cell number 12, just behind the TV. "Hey, what's wrong with him?" He asked to anyone listening.

I finished my thirtieth push-up and joined the others to stare in the cell. Officer Miller had noticed us gather and was there at the cell door to see for himself what was up.

As the door popped opened, a young Hispanic man came into full view. I realized, "He's having an epileptic seizure. Get some pillows under his head." I noticed the man was smashing up and down on the concrete floor. I started to enter the cell to help but Miller turned, "Get out of here, Springer!" He ordered in a half panic.

Officer Miller was five foot eight, about a hundred and fifty pounds, and had a slight belly with a sway back posture. His face was that beet red of the chronic alcoholic. He was mean, even when he was joking, and was generally considered one of the power tripping jerks of the guard staff. He was in his forties. It was a real nightmare when his girlfriend, a barbie look-a-like blond guard with teased hair, worked the same shift. Miller's Apprentice, we called her. He liked to show off how tough he was for her.

The thrashing continued as Miller grabbed the young man's shoulders to restrain him. Officer England pushed through the eight men crowding the doorway to view the scene and asked Miller, "Do you need some help? Should I call the nurse?"

"Yes, call the nurse," I gently urged him..

"No, he'll be fine. I saw a seizure once. He'll come out of it."

I was leaning in the door of the cell as England turned and put a hand on my chest to push me out. "Get some pillows under his head, England." I suggested.

"There aren't any pillows, Springer!" He yelled.

"Well, pull the mattress off the bunk or pop the next cell and get some pillows." I told him calmly.

"Springer, get outta here," Miller ordered, yelling in a tone that said `lockdown' was next. I backed from the door in silence but remained to witness the pathetic entertainment of the day. The seizure continued until Miller conceded, "Get the nurse."

England pulled his radio from his hip and communicated the message to control. In another minute the young man was quieting down and starting to slowly regain consciousness.

The chubby nurse waddled in with a stethoscope hanging from her neck, but nothing in her hands. She entered the cell to find the patient coherent but weak. During her first questions he fell back into another seizure and the spasms began again.

"Status Epilepticus," I whispered. "This can be a true life threatening emergency," I quoted from my EMT textbook. But hey, we're only dogs. If ya lose one every now and then, so what. They're criminals anyway. The world's better off without em." I commented.

Eventually the second seizure came to an end, and the patient was helped out of the cell. A recent bullet wound, the slot beginning above the eye and tracing back in a groove just past the temple, was clearly evident.

"Disperse" Miller hissed as he walked by. Then he said to the nurse, "Nobody told us he had medical problems.

"Well, we didn't know either," Claudia, the nurse, complained in defense. "He didn't tell anybody. It's not on his medical chart."

We returned to the workout corner. "Your turn, Springer," Lewis reminded me.

"I just did it," I argued.

"Well, nobody here was takin' a break while you were on your ambulance call," he insisted, "hit the floor."

"One, Sir, Two, Sir, Three, Sir," I joked in military style.

"All right, let's do dips now," Lewis suggested.

As Rick Lewis started his set, Miller came into the corner. "Hey, you guys are done. That's it."

"We do this every other day." Lewis argued.

"Well, not today, you're not," he trumped, glancing with a barely perceptible nod directly at me.

As Miller walked away Lewis said, "All right, let's do em off the toilet seat in our cells. Don't anybody cheat. I want five sets of 30."

"You got it," we all agreed.

"With respect to staff assaults the court asserted that 'the record is replete with incidents, in many cases substantially undisputed by government officials, where the use of force by prison correction officers was far in excess to the need for force, with serious injuries resulting.'

"In the 1989 case of Tillery v Owen another federal judge noted that these numbers were in reality far higher, as many inmates failed to report assaults for fear of retaliation."

— ACLU, <u>Human Rights Violations in the United States</u> 1993

The doors started popping open down the rows of cells as the door monitor flicked the panel of switches in the lockdown unit. The inmates pushed out like dogs through rows of flapping doors.

I joined George in the central promenade and fell in for a few laps to stretch it out and settle my meal. We took the wide lap, ducking under the television on each round, excusing ourselves as we passed congested chess games. We settled into killing time, attempting to strangle it by the throat, but it refused to die, it's incessant, interminable heart...tick... tick...t...i...c...k...i...n...g.... The caged bird of time, known as tempest fugit, had been arrested with broken wings, and in prison could barely crawl.

"Hey, Springer, get them to pop my door," Jeffel Mike yelled through his food slot.

"Sure, no problem," I looked up at the control booth and flashed them first one finger and then two, indicating door twelve. The 260 pound woman sitting at the control panel stuffed another Fig Newton in her mouth and shook her head, as we continued our laps.

"Hey Miller, pop number twelve," I asked.

"He's on lockdown, Springer."

We came by Jeffel's door again. "You're on lockdown, he says."

"Why? I didn't do anything!" Jeffel puzzled. "Ask him why."

I broke out of the track to stand by Miller's desk careful not to allow my toes over the duct taped line surrounding the desk area. "He wants to know why he's in lockdown. He doesn't know," I informed Miller.

"Springer," Miller stated in frustrated disgust, "everyone wants to kick his ass."

"I don't want to kick his ass. Hey, George, do you want to kick Jeffel's ass?" I yelled as George passed.

Behind door number twelve, the small black man began an insistent banging. Though perhaps only 5'5", 125 pounds, Jeffel Mike had the physique of a Baby Tyson. He was a wizard at bible verses. His hair was short cropped. He kept a clean appearance and was usually seen reading his small dog-eared testament. He had a positive attitude.

"No," said George, shaking his head. "I don't want to beat Jeffel."

"Springer, it's none of your business. Now move on." Miller ordered like a Marine Corp drill sergeant.

"Seems if someone wants to kick Jeffel's ass, then you should lock up the guy who wants to kick ass, not the recipient of the ass kicking." I tried to convince him with logic.

"I can't lock down the whole unit, Springer," his temper shortened. "Do you want to join him?"

I was already walking away, sensing Miller's limit. I shortened the lap to avoid door twelve as the pounding and yelling continued. Officer Shaffer, with sandy red hair and a cookie duster moustache, walked in a brisk, 'I-mean-business' strut to door twelve and signalled to the monitor.

As the door opened, he pushed Jeffel roughly against the wall, grabbing his ear at the same time. Jeffel slapped Shaffer's arm off and yelled in his face. "I only want to talk."

The officer attempted to grab the smaller man again, but was pushed away with another yell. "What are you doing? I only want to talk."

Seventy inmates stopped walking, dropped their cards and ignored the TV as the scene escalated. Shaffer walked out of the cell, slamming the door in his wake, but the force of the slam caused the door to bounce open. Jeffel followed him out the door. Shaffer struggled to gain control of the situation by jumping on Jeffel, but the young man threw him off easily with a quick jab to the face. Like a dazed boxer, Shaffer walked towards him again as Jeffel screamed at him in utter frustration, "Is that what you want?"

The second punch dropped Shaffer to the floor. Jeffel stepped over him and punched him twice more. Blood splattered with each punch, as Shaffer's nose and lips suffered like a juicy steak under a tenderizer hammer.

Jeffel backed off, and in dismay turned to the wall and leaned his arms and head against it. He knew his physical victory was actually a costly moral failure.

Miller snuck up from behind and grabbed him in a full nelson as several other guards stormed into the room, hustling into cell 12 behind Miller as he forced Jeffel in.

George and I ran over to the cell door, fearing for Jeffels safety, yelling, "No violence, we're watching you."

"Don't hurt him. It was Shaffer's fault," we continued.

"LOCKDOWN!" Another guard yelled. "Get to your cells immediately".

I sat in my cell typing a statement on the Jeffel Mike incident. I wrote the statement like Joe Friday of Dragnet said: "The facts, ma'am, just the facts."

After our cells were opened, I passed the papers around the unit and got 8 signatures of those who saw the incident and 30 others who were in agreement about the guard problem.

"Officer Martine, I need you to sign these kites, please," I asked.

"I can't sign these, Springer. We don't accept group kites. If you insist on turning these in, then everyone whose name is on here will go to lockdown." Martine played his prison card.

I decided that the best strategy was to get the story out to the media by way of an attorney. I passed the group kite to Susan Quig-Terrey, who said she would follow through and send a copy to Jeffel's parents back East. Several people wrote up individual kites and turned them in to Director Brown. No response ever appeared. Jeffel Mike disappeared from our jail.

* * * * *

"In fact, jailed detainees [awaiting trial] are more apt to suffer abuse than are sentenced inmates in prison facilities."
— *ACLU, 1993*

* * * * *

Fifty of the eighty men held in the NLVDC lockdown unit began to line up along the west wall when Officer Donelly yelled, "Rec Yard." The remaining thirty or so inmates slumbered, still in their bunks at 10:30 AM, trying to cheat the BOP out of time. After twenty minutes of standing with no sign of rec yard happening, most of us began to return to chess, TV and other occupations.

"Do you guys want to go to rec or not," Donelly yelled after five more minutes.

"Yeah, well, let's go then," an inmate yelled.

"Well, line up so I can get a count."

The daily routine of hurry up and wait continued, until finally the doors slid open. In clumps of ten at a time, we were allowed outside.

Donelly proceeded to lead the first group across the short yard to the locked gate and eventually allowed us to file into the chain-link fenced asphalt yard, bordered on top by the woven rolls of razor wire draping just a foot overhead. Scotty took off as soon as he got inside the yard and began his laps; each loop one-twelfth of a mile, we figured. He had a gazelle-like lope: springy and covering distance.

I joined in after the first lap. "Good gosh, what's the hurry, Scotty? Got to get to the insurance office on time?" I was pleading for a more reasonable pace.

"Now don't try to keep this pace, Mr. Springer. I would hate to be responsible for your return to the infirmary, or was it the geriatric ward," he taunted. "Remember your ankle, your heart, your diet; perhaps you're constipated this morning. I wouldn't want any of that to fail on my account."

"Oh vile infidel, has your life grown so dull, that wish to end your career?" I challenged him as I caught my breath on the third lap and picked up the pace.

"Did they issue the Geratol on morning pill call, Mr. Springer." Scotty poked between breaths.

"Ah, a young whelp such as yerself still droolin' on the mother's teat is no match for a mature homo sapien in his prime." The pace was now approaching the brutality of a one mile race. Conversation slowed down as the guards and inmates perceived the competition.

"Oh, Sccaughttteeee, I think he's gaught you," Rick Lewis sounded like an ancient Moor on tour in Scotland.

The pace continued, both of us punishing the other by refusing to back off. After a dozen laps, I began to sense my stamina fading. Instead of easing up on the pace, I realized my only hope was for a kick, and burn him out now. My slip-on K-Mart tennys slapped the pavement harder. Maybe it was an act of mercy, but Scotty faded after another half lap, letting me sprint down another 30 yards of the basketball perimeter.

I caught my breath for a quarter lap and then began dancing on my toes in a victory lap. I rammed Scotty with my shoulder, "Let's go."

"All right, Mr. Springer. I'll give you a run on another day," he threatened.

We continued, lap after lap, as the basketball flew around the court, full teams working out their own frustrations -- trying to get tired enough to lie around for another three days, or until the next rec yard.

Scotty and I kept the jogging meditation going, swerving around slower walkers and those sitting, sunning against the A-dorm wall. We turned left at the north end of the court. All of a sudden, we were confronted with inmates Olson and Bingham flailing into a fight. Scotty and I split, one on each side of the tussling pair, in an effort to avoid the battle. They were swinging wildly like two pre-schoolers who had yet to find their coordination. I had to leap in the air to clear Olson as his body dropped from a blow to the side of the head. I stumbled, but caught myself to remain standing. I turned to see Bingham jump on Olson and begin to pound his head into the asphalt. As Olson tried to lift his head and protect himself, Bingham would punch him, slapping his skull down again.

Officer Donelly ran with his shiny black belt bouncing. He grabbed Bingham by the hair, tilted his head back and sprayed mace directly into his eyes, nose and mouth. Amazingly, Bingham let loose two more blows before it dawned on him that his body was beginning to convulse. He stood, drawing his hands to his face and wandered off towards the stucco A-dorm wall; he banged roughly as a blind man without his cane. Donelly followed down to Olson, still struggling to get to his feet, and proceeded to flock him with mace as if he were whiting a Christmas tree. The tree ran away to the other end of the yard, where most of the other inmates had moved rapidly to avoid the heavy hanging droplets of mace waiting to light on any passerby.

Meanwhile, the entire scene unfolded on the TV screens in central command before the bored women staffing the screens. The alert was sounded and the yard door on the intake unit popped open to release the responding guards rushing to assist. Officer England, having seen too many Bruce Flea karate movies, attempted to vault the railing in a direct line to the rec yard, but the toes of his black polished shoes caught on the blue painted rail, rolling him like the humpty dumpty he was. He managed to tuck his head and land on his shoulder. He kept rolling across the pavement through a full somersault, regaining his feet in an awkward half crawling effort to act as if nothing happened.

A yard full of inmates, persecuted by England's power ego, broke out, laughing their heads off, happy at any opportunity to humiliate one of the hated officers.

"Did you see that fat mother fucker come tumbling off that railing?" Said Crockett, just released from lockdown. "That Mo Fo think he Chuck Norris." Several inmates covered their mouths as they sputtered and pointed at England. England dusted off the torn elbow of his shirt as he inspected the oozing raspberries within the tear.

He and Miller grabbed Olson roughly, jerking him through the gate and off to segregation. Donelly held Bingham against the wall, cuffing him behind his back, until Jablonski and Zach arrived to take him off.

"All right, everybody up against the fence for a count," yelled Donelly, listening to his radio. We lined up under the razor wire on the west fence, while Ritzman followed Donelly down the line, counting as he went. After he and

Ritzman conferred, they began a recount. Any fight or distraction in the yard was treated as a potential cover for an escape.

"Are there any requirements to the guard job, besides a willingness to wear a uniform and beat heads?" I wondered.

"Counting is not one of them, we know that much," George commented.

"I can see the job ad now, George." I mused as a radio disc jockey, "The North Las Vegas Detention Center is seeking a few good men as proud prison guards. Can you take orders without asking questions? Will you do what you're told for a fat paycheck? Do you have natural tendencies towards child abuse? Well, here's the opportunity of a lifetime. Enjoy your chance to beat on handcuffed inmates, the power to manipulate the lives of America's toughest criminals, and all this while munching Big Macs and Fritos. It's a job for a patriot."

"All right, back to the unit," Donelly ordered.

"What was that fight about?" I asked Rick Lewis.

"Who knows. Olson gonna get his ass kicked by everybody in here before he's done."

"It's been about half already," George agreed.

The unit door lurched open, the hydraulics already becoming sticky in the tracks. Ten inmates entered as the door closed behind. We stood for three or four minutes, waving to the camera, waiting for the door monitor to open the second door. The dead air accosted our nostrils on entry. "Lock 'em up," Miller yelled as we noticed the arc welding machine zapping away on a door in the corner.

"We can't stay in those cells while you weld on the doors," Lewis complained. "Those fumes are poisonous."

"We haven't been sentenced to death by gas chamber," I supported.

"Get in your cell," Miller ordered unsympathetically.

"You wouldn't put your child in there, Miller." Lewis argued.

"Sure I would." He insisted as he slammed the door behind him.

"Yes, he would," I reminded Lewis as I reluctantly entered my cell. Blam, Miller slammed the door after me and rattled it roughly to ensure it locked.

The rattle of my cell door had become connected to my medulla oblongata, scraping my nervous system from the base of my skull to the end of my tail.

I looked over at the door as the welder continued welding the remaining food slot flaps. The fumes flooded through the slot, amidst flying sparks. I struggled to minimize the inhalation by putting my blanket over my mouth as a filter. With the welding completed, the welder finished the job by spraying blue paint over the flap and hinges. I watched as the stream of paint flowed into my five-by-ten cell. We remained locked down for the remainder of the day, because the workers were nervous about being around us criminals.

Chapter Twelve
THE MESSAGE OF THE CRICKET

"Nuclear power and nuclear weapons are two sides of the same coin. Nuclear power is life threatening in three independent ways, each in itself formidable.

"First is the threat of a nuclear accident in nuclear power plants. Those great realists, the American insurance companies refused from the beginning to insure nuclear power plants. Hence, we have the Price Anderson Act which lays the bulk of liability on the "government" i.e.. the taxpayers.

"The second is that every nuclear reactor now in operation produces the artificial element plutonium-239...the most toxic substance known. It is also the most convenient material from which to make fission bombs. Every nation that now possesses a nuclear reactor can begin to make nuclear weapons.

"The third life threatening aspect of nuclear power and weapons involves the disposal. No one knows what to do with them."

— Dr. Ernest Sternglass, Secret Fallout 1981

* * * * *

"All right, visitation," came the officer's yell as inmates gathered to be ushered to the intake building for the highlight of the day, or week, or month.

"Springer, you got an attorney visit," England informed me.

Each inmate's name was yelled, followed by a "Yo," or "Here," or "Mmmhhhmmm." People were slicking down their hair and preening their moustaches, picking lint off their grays or running to gather legal papers and a two inch stubby pencil.

"Hey man, now don' be dissin' me now," one black man cautioned another.

"What trash you talkin, foo! I don' be dissin' nobody."

"Well, you jus' stomp on my Nike, Motha Fucka."

"Sho wahn't me." Mike insisted. "I think it musta been Springer," he motioned with a thumb to the lean white man on the left -- me.

"Ah, Springer, you dissin' me, stompin on my Nigh-kee, he interrogated, turning to square off.

"Well, Kilo, let me see here now? Does that dirty track on your Nike match up with this here plastic shower slipper?" I asked him, raising my slippers to view the sole. "No, that ain't no match," I deduced. "You messin wit da wrong nigger, my man," I raised my empty palms.

"Now dig Springer here," Kilo responded looking at Mike, "He da blond haired, blue eyed devil in-car-nate and he say, 'You messin' with da wrong nigga.' You crazy as Olson, Springer."

"Well, jes lissen up, my man. Cuz I'm gonna give it to ya, the straight and the skinny," I talked in the jive of my youth in Altadena, California, known to locals as Afrodena. "You can buy the propaganda of the man, Mr. Farrakhon, and don' git me wrong, I agree with much of what he say. But when it comes to the racism issue, I follow the teachings of my main man, the good Doctor, Martin Luther King, Jr."

I was a curiosity to many of the blacks in jail. They knew why I was there; they had heard my nonviolence rap. But how would I operate when put to a test? I had the floor as a couple of other faces turned to listen. "Yeah, and Dr. King say, 'We must learn to live together as brothers and sisters, or we will perish together as fools.'"

"Shut up, Springer, you are a fool," yelled Newson. "You guys want visitation or not?"

The line fidgeted but quieted down.

"I'll git back witcha, Springer," Kilo whispered over my shoulder.

With the names checked twice, the steel door clunked open, and 18 men jammed into the vestibule before the door clunked closed. We stood packed like sardines while the door monitor cleared the count and accepted the signal before opening the second door to the delicious smoggy Las Vegas air outside.

"Who farted?" Mike yelled, "Whoooeee, somebody in here is rank. Newson, is dat you dem fumes risin' from?"

"Shut up, foreskin!" Newson retorted.

The second door finally lurched open, pouring bodies out like Cheerios from a box. Officer Taylor stood outside waiting. "Two lines on the white line," he commanded. Bodies milled around, creating two sloppy lines; the constant subtle resistance, the minuscule but ever present reminder to the guards that although you treat us like dogs, you have not whipped our spirit.

We marched into the intake building, cameras watching, waiting for the officer's signal or voice on the radio.

The U-shaped visitation room was filled with little stalls looking to the center of the U. A phone receiver was attached to a receiver on the other side of the thick pane of glass. There was no paper passing, no fingers to touch, and even the sound was cut off with the flick of a switch.

"Springer, you can wait in the library until your attorney arrives," Taylor informed me.

"Hey Scotty, how you doin," I asked, entering the law library.

"Good," he lied. "I've been shelving the new law books for Director Brown. We still need a lot more, but it's better than nothing. They have to provide us with a law library, but it seems like an afterthought," he confessed.

"Yeah, here we are going up against a federal prosecutor with a whole team of support staff, paralegals, the marshal's office, pretrial supervision, and the judge who was once himself a prosecutor . Add that to a computer system plugged into WestLaw so all they have to do is punch in a key word and up comes every case in history," I complained. "I feel like David up against Goliath. How the heck do I find cases on the necessity defense?"

"Sounds like you better get a slingshot, Mr. Springer." Scotty showed me the Federal Reporters and case referencing systems.

"Where's the card catalog? I go to those long, skinny little drawers, look under "necessity" and it tells me where to go. By the time I figure out this system, I'll be rattling the bars at Leavenworth."

"Well, yes," agreed Scotty. "I'm sure you've heard, `He who defends himself has a fool for a client.'"

"Yeah, well, with that confirmed, I had to defend myself, but you must rememba, Grasshoppa," I mocked in guru jest, "He who know he a foo, is not biggest foo."

"You bofe sounds like foos to me," another voice joined.

"Rick, do you know Cal Springer?" Scotty introduced a bull of a man with deep chocolate skin glistening in the glare of the slotted window he was leaning on.

"No, but he musta stole my name," I threw out as a joke.

"Yeah, Motha Fucka, like your Grandaddy raped one of his slaves, my great grandma," Cal ripped, not appreciating the joke.

"My grandpa didn't rape anyone," I back paddled, realizing my blunder. Open mouth, insert foot.

"MmmmmHhhhhmmmm," Cal dropped in disbelief.

"Springer, your attorney is here," Taylor peered in the library door.

I walked into the attorney room noticing the visitation windows across the hall, still occupied by inmates, a phone stuck to their ear, while friends, families, and lovers tried to make contact.

I turned to see Sue Quig-Terrey. She dressed in jeans and a faded denim shirt with embroidered flowers. After two months in jail, I was excited by Good Housekeeping bra ads. Sue Quig-Terrey, dressed like a Humboldt Honey, looked very good.

"How're you doing?" She asked, genuinely concerned.

"Oh, it's up and down. I've been better, but hey, I ain't dead yet!"

"Well, you certainly don't look dead."

"Well, I do have my zombie days. The 75 watt bulb two feet from my face, 24 hours a day, the constant cold. It wears you down," I whined. I put my hands to my head making a lunatic face of bulging eyes and tongue. "But hey, I'm fine, really. I'm out of lockdown."

"Well, that's good. I'm sorry I missed our last appointment. You know we're going to trial on the 26th?" She asked.

"Yikes, we have a lot to do. What happened to our Friday appointment?" I asked, my disappointment clearly evident.

"Well, I'm really sorry, but I was in the hospital over the weekend." She confessed.

"Really? What's wrong?"

"Well, I was having chest pains for a couple of days, and my son finally convinced me to call the hospital on Thursday. They took me in, and I ended up spending the whole weekend. I just got out two days ago."

"Whoa, that's a problem. We're supposed to go to trial in ten days and you just had a heart problem. What did they say it was?"

"They don't know for sure but they gave me some medication and told me to take it easy," she smiled weakly.

"Well, as an EMT I have a decent grasp on the ills of the heart. I have serious concerns about you going to trial under these circumstances. You know how stressful court can be."

"Well, I'm sure I'll be fine." She tried to sound convincing.

"I'd like to talk to your doctors to confirm that. I'm having mixed emotions about you going to trial in this situation. What did you eat for lunch?" I pried, assuming the EMT role.

"Oh, I had a Sprite," she confessed sheepishly.

"You need to get some real food. You probably had coffee for breakfast," I chastised. "Time to pay the piper, Sue!"

"Okay, okay," she chewed on her pen, red lipstick staining the tooth marks.

"All right, let me have your doctor's name. I'll try to give him a call, but for now we'll move forward. What can I do to make it easier on you. Can I write more motions? Do any other research? Anything?"

"Well," she dawdled, "you can tell me I'm beautiful and send me some flowers."

"All right, that's easy, you are beautiful!"

"Did you get the copy of John Ham's motion that I sent you?" She asked getting to business.

"Yeah, I got it. It's ridiculous! I mean check this out. Here he says, he starts off, `COMES NOW,' where do they find this formal crapola? These law people are lost in some primitive Shakespearean festival of stockades. It's still witch burning and commie hunts." I became Hamlet, "`Comes now, by and through, John Ham, United States Attorney, and moves this court In Limonaid.'"

"In Limine, Rick."

"Yeah, sure, `to instruct defendant's counsel not to mention, refer to, interrogate concerning, or attempt to convey to the jury in any manner, either directly or indirectly, and instruct defendant's witnesses of the same, evidence of or relating to the use, testing, possession, or proliferation of nuclear weapons, national or political matters relating to such weapons, national defense, or international armaments treaties," I concluded, humbly bowing my Shakespearean head.

I continued, not hiding my disgust: "Perhaps I should beg my ladies' pardon for expressing such open disdain for the pomp and circumstance of the legal aristocracy, but as the famous poet Gina Rosetti pointed out, "A rape is a rape," and the reason I failed to surrender was to halt the restart of a planetary rape. And although I abhor profanity as the attempt of the weak mind to express itself forcefully, I find no more succinct application of the term "Mother Fucker" than the nuclear testing industry! No industry on Earth debases the sacred quite so thoroughly."

I noticed Officer Taylor glancing into the room through the wall of glass. Taylor went to return the inmates from visitation. I saw that the other inmates were now looking into our room, pointing at us. I ignored them. Inmates gawked at women during visitation, and Susan Quig-Terrey was a woman.

"Am I entitled to a defense or not?" I asked.

"I don't think they're going to deny that, but you've seen from the pretrial hearing that you will not be allowed expert testimony to support it," she said. "Here's a copy of the Rules of Evidence. You should study them."

"Yeah, well let's send a copy of the constitution for the prosecution and the court to study. Am I a madman or has the world gone crazy".

"No, you're right. It's crazy."

"Okay, let's go over our witnesses. Claudia Petersen, the mother whose little girl died because they lived downwind of the test site in St. George, Utah. She was a very powerful influence on me. It is not only her daughter, but also her community that has suffered so dramatically. I mean, St. George, Utah, staunch Mormon stronghold, America, love it or leave it. Don't ask questions of the patriarchy. This town did commercials for the Atomic Energy Commission in the 1950s to help alleviate the concerns people were having about the poisoning effects of testing.

"Now the same people from those AEC films are doing films for the antinuke effort saying, 'We can't believe they lied to us. We were a strong healthy people, and now were all dying of cancer.'

"I want Claudia to tell her story because it will affect the jury. This same woman has gone to the Soviet Union and met the mothers over at the Soviet test site and cried with them over the needless stupidity that took the lives of their children. Do we hate our enemies more than we love our children? I think you should question her on the stand."

"Sure that sounds good.   Could you make a list of questions for each witness. We'll try to let them see them before trial. What about Bill Chisholm?" She asked.

"Bill is walking history.   He is doing more as an individual to halt the desecration of Idaho and the planet than the entire federal bureaucracy of the Environmental Protection Agency.

"I want him because he has done direct action and been successful, not only in achieving substantial media, but in actually halting the shipments of radioactive waste into Idaho. He's been to jail for his beliefs, and he continues. His story is proof that I had reason to believe that I could have an effect on Clinton's decision to restart nuclear testing. And we did: he extended the moratorium instead.

"I'll question Bill Chisholm. What about Bill Rosse, Sr.? Did you get a hold of him?"

"No, but I talked to his wife, and she says he will be back from DC by then. He has some doctor's tests in Reno, but he should be able to make it."

"Now that man is a wonder of nature. He was shot by friendly fire in WWII, became diabetic in mid life, had triple bypass heart surgery, and goes and goes like he invented Energizer batteries. Not a big man size wise but what a heart.

"Corbin is the Spiritual leader of the Shoshone. Bill and Corbin are my spiritual mentors. They are the tribal elders that I respect and honor. What of Chris Brown of Citizen Alert?"

"Yeah, he'll be there," she confirmed. "I talked to him yesterday."

"How you doin? I think we covered enough for today."

"Oh, I'm okay, but I do have to relieve the baby-sitter."

"When can I see you again? We still have to cover my testimony and what you are going to ask me."

"Yeah, well, I'll try to make it later in the week." She didn't sound convincing.

We stood to say good-bye with a hug. It seemed both of us had broken and bleeding hearts in need of mending. Her broken heart landed her in the hospital and mine in jail. In the peace movement, we hug a lot. It's an ugly issue. We sometimes lead a transient lifestyle. We take what good energy and support we can when and where we can. I didn't consider the propriety of hugging my attorney. She obviously didn't either. I think we were both desperate for some warmth and healing.

"God, she's cute, Springer," officer Taylor commented on the escort back to A Dorm, "How'd you get her?"

"She's done a lot of ACLU work, Taylor. She came highly recommended and I kept asking her to take my case."

"She must be expensive," he dropped with a lewd innuendo hanging in the air.

"She took the case Pro Bono." I noticed a light furrow in the officers brow, "That's means free, Taylor."

I entered the unit, wishing for a butter knife to cut through the thick and foul locker room air.

"Hey, hey, Rickey," Lewis strolled alongside after I had dumped my legal work in the cell and decided to walk a lap or two before lockdown.

"That woman is your attorney, Springer?" He asked.

"Yeah, that's her."

"She is hot on you, young man," he advised.

"And why do think that?" I was amused, but not really concerned.

"Hey, we were sitting there watching you two from visitation. We got eyes. She's lookin at you, boy!" He insisted. "We could see her heart throbbin."

"I think you guys are checkin out what's on top of her heart. I just wish she would come more often to prepare this case. We're ten days from trial and I don't feel at all ready."

"Well, all I'm tellin' you is that she is ready."

✳ ✳ ✳ ✳ ✳

"I have the audacity to believe that peoples everywhere can have three meals a day for their bodies, education and culture for their minds, and dignity, equality, and freedom for their spirits. I believe that what self-centered men have torn down, other centered men can build up."
— Martin Luther King, Jr.

"Springer, attorney visit," Newson yelled through the popped cell door. "C'mon, I'm not waitin' all day."

Newson escorted me past the attorney rooms into the library. I walked in to see Sue Navy, fresh from Colorado, sitting with Sue Quig-Terrey. Sue Navy and I embraced and kissed briefly in the open of the NLVDC law library. It was an awkward, somehow painful kiss, an honest kiss that told the truth about the feelings we both shared; the pain of nuclearism, of separation, of incarceration, of suffering. It was a kiss of the letters I had written her describing the daily brutality of my life.

"How'd you get in here?" I asked.

"She's my paralegal aid for this case." QT laid the line, providing the foundation for her presence.

"Yup, I'm here doing research on Springer versus the Feds," she agreed, "I'd like to do some research on you!"

"Not much room to move in here."

"Well, at least another hug behind the bookshelf." She offered.

We stepped behind the one row of shelving, hugging again, betraying that desperate pain familiar to every prisoner longing for freedom, for touch. There would be no intimate consolation dinner following this meeting, no taste of skin to skin, no nurturing press of cheek to breast, no fondling of a female mate, and no love for months or years. We returned around the shelf; QT averted her eyes in a 'see no evil' gesture. "Well, three days to trial."

"How are you feeling? I couldn't get through to your doctor. Imagine! His receptionist wouldn't accept a collect call from an Inmate at the North Las Vegas Detention Center. I tried to scam it as an attorney call but I still couldn't get through."

"Well, I'm fine," she drawled clear from South Carolina. "We have to get the rest of our prep together today."

"So, do we have our witnesses confirmed?" I asked.

"They'll make it. What we need to work on is your opening and closing remarks, and then your testimony," she pushed, more businesslike than usual.

"Bill Chisholm will be here tonight," Sue Navy confirmed, squeezing my hand under the table.

We moved through the details of trial preparation, trying our best to pull together a defense capable of reaching a jury in spite of the handicaps and handcuffs.

"Springer, time's up," Newson ordered. "I have to get him back for chow," he explained gruffly to the women.

I hugged them both briefly, trying to maintain the stiff upper lip, while Newson tensed his jaws impatiently.

"You look good," Sue lied, while noticing my gray pants and smock, the garb of the inmate.

"Oh, Sergeant Parker, are you going back to the lockdown unit?" Newson asked of the squat, swaggering black woman entering the hallway at the same time.

"Yeah, I'll take Springer back." She released Newson to other duties.

"Attorney visit, Springer?" Sergeant Parker inquired as we made our way door by door to the outside.

"Yeah, trial on Monday."

"Well, you sure got some cupcake for an attorney," she commented, her broad hips swaggering and jingling her key ring with each dip. Her SWAT team commando sweater concealed the woman inside. I could only imagine the stress and pressures of being a black female prison sergeant. Her pimping walk said "don't mess with me, I can jive with the best and lock up the rest." Still, there was something more, something pretty and soft inside her bulldog exterior. Concealed in layers of self protection, I sensed a heart.

"Springer, just what do you think you're doing?" She inquired frankly.

"What do you mean, Sergeant Parker?" I queried for parameters.

"You know, you out there trying to save the world, and you know you ain't gon' do sheeeitt. It's over, Springer. Are you blind?" She didn't wait for an answer. "The world is going down, and you can't do a thing about it. The signs are everywhere," she insisted, as we stopped outside the unit door in the gray afternoon light.

"Well, you can take that attitude, Sergeant Parker. Most do, and that is the most certain way to guarantee it does go down. But what I see is the greatest challenge in world history. You can either take the challenge or lie down whipped and whimper. Me, I'm goin to that mountain that Martin King, Jr. talked about, and I may not get there with you but..."

She interupted me with open disdain for this stubborn white man quoting her own people, "I want you to know that we as a people will get there." She seemed offended now. "Hey, I'm not sittin on my fingers, Springer. I spend my free time with poor children teaching them how to read."

"Well, then, Sgt. Parker, you do have hope!" I gloated.

She frowned, "No, I don't have hope, but I want these children to be able to read for themselves."

On that, she pushed the button on the radio clipped to her sweater and the door slid open and the flood of stale air accosted us.

"So help me out here, Parker. You want these kids to know what it is they don't have?"

"Oh, you're a gem, Springer. No, I want to give them the opportunity to decide for themselves if they can hope or not."

"Ah, so you hope they can hope. Well, example is the best teacher."

✳ ✳ ✳ ✳ ✳

"I'm no fool, no siree, I'm gonna live to be a 103
So I play safe for you and me, Cuz I'm no fool!
  — Jiminy Crickett, Walt Disney

I sat there in my cell, trying to tune out the blaring TV only ten feet from my head. The cheap television speaker had been tweaked to maximum so often it now rattled and rasped with the rales and ronchi of a forty year cigarette smoker.

Tomorrow...my trial. I didn't feel well prepared. I was disappointed at how little time Susan Quig-Terrey and I had actually spent. I knew that in order to win, we would have to go at it like I was a wealthy client, money or time being no object. Such was not the case.

I imagined how it must feel to sit on death row and know that tomorrow morning was the last day of life. How senseless it must seem. Or maybe it was a relief?

I mulled over all the things I might say to a jury, trying to commit them to memory. At the same time I felt silent, a strange cloud between my mind and the recognition of what my eyes saw. I didn't really want to have to talk. I felt like I had never really recovered from my entry fast of 18 days. My mind was greasy bouillon cubes and jello. Still, I decided to eat an evening snack. Reaching under the bunk, I pulled out the reused styrofoam cup they handed out for KoolAid, and looked at the spaghetti noodles I'd saved for the ten o'clock munchies.

I hate spaghetti. Tomato sauce just don't work in the vat of bile constantly gurgling around in my stomach. But I was determined to gain back some weight and get some carbos for tomorrows gauntlet.

As I stared absently, I noticed a motion from under the cell door. A desert cricket walked in, taking a tour of NLVDC, free to come and go under any door.

I missed Hobo as much as many of the inmate fathers missed their kids. She was twelve years old now, a fawn color female pitbull of sixty pounds with a white chest and paws. As sweet as dogs come.

"Hey buddy, how ya doin? Come for a visit before my trial? I could use some support." I spoke to the cricket. I remembered the vision quest of the native people and how important each little creature was, each detail of its appearance and behavior. Often the seeker would return to the elders to learn just what his experience meant. Just how far removed could one be from that world, I thought?

"But you, my friend, are a good omen. What do you have to tell me? Maybe you're are an elder yourself. How ancient are the cricket people? How long have your ancestors lived in this spot in this desert valley?"

The cricket made its way across the concrete cell floor. Patience was no requirement in prison, only endurance. I watched. I had all night. The cricket crawled over my new K-mart high top tennies, issued as a medical aid to my sprained ankle.

I pulled a noodle out of the cup, pinched a half inch section with my thumb and forefinger and dropped it to the floor in front of the cricket. I kept eating and watched as the cricket used his feelers to find the noodle. He ate more than half of that piece of noodle. Musta been hungry.

Grasping at straws, I took what comfort I could that all would be well tomorrow. I picked up Gideon's small white testament and opened it up looking for a spiritual noodle. My soul was hungry for some sustenance. I opened the book and read.

✳ ✳ ✳ ✳ ✳

"But when they deliver you up, take no thought how or what ye shall speak: for it shall be given you in that same hour what ye shall speak. For it is not ye that speak, but the Spirit of your Father which speaketh in you"
Matthew 10 : 19-20

Chapter Thirteen
WHITE MAN'S MOCCASINS

A cold voice rousted me in the early morn of dark thirty. "Are you on the razor list, Springer?"

"Yeah," I had learned in the Merchant Marine to respond to any question from a dead sleep.

"How many razors you want?"

"One face, one razor," I heard my ecological self reply. But my stomach had already remembered the upcoming day's event and had another thought: one throat, one razor.

A cheap, orange, disposable razor was set on the narrow door ledge of the food slot. Some men ordered three of the cheap dull razors to get through one shave. I pushed the button on the stainless steel sink and water spewed out of the combination spigot/bubbler. Rubbing the prison issue lye soap across my cheeks, I scraped the ragged steel edge down the center, stopping just above the chin bone. I puffed my cheek out like a hamster and scraped upward against the lay of the stubble. At forty-two years old, I had managed to escape the so-called, manly art of shaving, so successfully in fact, that red droplets now covered the bare patches in proof. "What a mess!" I proceeded to butcher my whole neck in the same fashion, looking as if I had fulfilled my stomach's suggestion. I toweled off, making a pink mess in the rough white cotton.

The door popped open, the razor was collected by the guard, I was then escorted to the intake lobby for the before-trial, hard-boiled egg breakfast.

The Marshals arrived and began the frisking and shackling process. I was in my own thoughts but managed to mention, "My court clothes were dropped off here last night. At least, that's what Miller told me."

"Well, Springer, your clothes are supposed to be brought to the court house. We don't run a tailor delivery program here." The cranky officer informed me.

"Well, I didn't make the arrangements or even ask for them to be dropped here. My attorney dropped them last night and I got a note, that's all."

"Well, we aren't taking them, Springer. That's all."

The van jerked in and out of traffic as we made our way across town past the casinos and topless bars of Lake Mead Boulevard. We pulled up by the federal building back ramp to a half dozen waiting cameras.

I unloaded, stopped and began the now standard, mini-press conference looking directly at the cameras. I was determined that if the press wanted to show me on TV shuffling in shackles and cuffs, they would also have to show me waving a peace sign. I pulled my waist-shackled hand up next to my face, holding my fingers in the peace/victory sign. The Marshals stuffed my file of legal papers under my arm, determined not to be bookboy to criminals.

"CTB in 93. Please write Bill Clinton and encourage him to convene the United Nations Comprehensive Test Ban Conference and sign the CTB treaty ending nuclear..." The Marshal grabbed my arm, pulling me away from the cameras and off towards the entrance ramp.

"...Ending nuclear weapons testing for all time," I kept talking as I shuffled up the ramp. "So now is an important time to write President Clinton." The Marshal had a firm grip on my arm to insure I kept moving. He realized that, given the opportunity, I was liable to turn this into an antinuclear lecture.

The journey through the courthouse was now familiar. I was uncuffed, guided into the holding cell on the third floor and took a seat to look over the papers for my trial..

The rattle of keys forewarned of the coming Marshal.

"Springer, there are some suits here on this rack. Choose one of these and get dressed for your trial," the officer instructed.

"I have my own clothes that my friends went to a lot of trouble to gather for me. I'll just wear my prison clothes, thank you," I told him resolutely.

In a few minutes I was ushered down the stairs to the cell behind the paneled court wall. I sat and prayed, remembering the message of the cricket, "Though ye be brought before judges and kings in my name, fear not what ye shall say."

The young dapper Marshal, tassels dangling from his Italian loafers and his hair slicked back for the cover of *Gentlemens Quarterly*, fumbled with the huge crib size keys. What was he? Twenty-five, twenty-eight, young, bright blue eyes, one of America's finest, the US Marshals. He was the showpiece.

He returned from the paneled court door and announced, "Showtime" with the vigor of a Barnum and Bailey circus M.C. I stood with the weight of a firing squad candidate. My recently issued K-Mart high tops stepped out of the cell delivering my naked arm into the young mans firm grip. He led me into the court, but just as I caught site of the room full of people, the Marshal jerked me back in. I stood a moment while the judge gave the Marshal further instructions and came back.

"Well, I hope you're happy, Springer. We have to send a van over to pick up your clothes at North Las Vegas," young Gucci nodded with a tight jaw.

"Couldn't care less," I answered honestly, quite content in my spandex pocketless greys. The court room was cleared of prospective jurors and I was brought into the room again.

Judge Pro began, "Mr. Springer. It's my understanding that the clothes were brought over to the jail by Ms. Quig-Terrey and the Marshals are tracking those down so we can allow you to have your suit.

"But I just wanted to spend a couple of minutes addressing a couple of matters. I've reviewed the voir dire questions that the parties have provided, and will ask virtually all of them in one form or another.

"That raises in my mind, as one of the question areas that is posed or suggested by the defense focuses on whether the jury had seen any media coverage of the incident involving former President Reagan and the breaking of an award at the National Association of Broadcasters Convention. I will ask that but I want to stress the fact that they are not being called upon to render a verdict in this case concerning that event." Judge Pro continued leisurely, stalling until the clothing arrived.

"It is your duty to find the facts from all the evidence in the case. To those facts you must apply the law as I give it to you. You must follow the law as I give it to you whether you agree with it or not. And you must not be influenced by any personal likes or dislikes, opinions, prejudices or sympathy. You will recall that you took an oath promising to do so at the beginning."
—Jury Instructions CR-S-93-215-PMP (RJJ) United States of America vs Rick Paul Springer

* * * * *

"Most Americans are aware they have a right to a trial by jury, but very few know that the jury has more power than anyone else in the courtroom. In addition to the facts, the jury is free to judge the merits of the law itself, its use in the case at hand, the motives of the person, and anything else necessary for it to reach what it feels is a just verdict.

If juries were only supposed to judge the facts, their job could be done by computer. It is because we, the people have feelings, opinions, wisdom, experience, and a sense of right and wrong that we depend on jurors, not machines to judge court cases."
—Fully Informed Jury Association FIJA

* * * * *

An hour later, dressed in Sue Quig-Terreys choice of designer jeans, dark blue tie and Bill Chisholm's powder blue sport coat, I walked into the court room. As I spotted Bill and Sue Navy, I felt somewhat reassured and walked by, lifting one foot, displaying my ill matching tennis shoes. I proclaimed, "White man's moccasins."

They somehow felt right. It seemed dishonest to be dressed so nicely when I had spent the last three months in hell and was returning there at the end of the day. I felt like a doll dressed up for a show; Mr. Bill about to get burned.

I sat down next to Sue Quig-Terrey. "You look very nice."

"And you look quite sharp yourself. Thank you very much for the flowers." I had Bill and Sue Navy send her some flowers as she had requested.

The jury selection process began with 22 citizens being chosen for us to sift through to compose the petit jury of 12 with 2 alternates.

Judge Pro dove right into the concern of possible prejudice.

THE COURT: I'd like to know whether any of the prospective jurors have any personal knowledge regarding this case, and firsthand knowledge of the facts of this case? Ms. Caguimbal, all right.

MS. CAGUIMBAL: I wouldn't say it was knowledge, but I know how he first started, you know, from seeing him on TV...

THE COURT: Okay, I'm going to come to that, in fact. Do any of you recall having read any news accounts regarding this case or perhaps having viewed any accounts on television or heard any accounts on radio concerning Mr. Springer and this particular case?"

The entire jury raised their hands.

THE COURT: Okay, let me go back to an earlier event. I want to stress that Mr. Springer is not on trial for this particular event that gave rise to the earlier sentence for which Mr. Springer's charged with failing to appear. And that revolves around an award being given by the National Association of Broadcasters to former President Reagan in the form of an eagle, crystal eagle, which was broken during the course of that award. That's not the case for which Mr. Springer is on trial.

The judge continued through the prospective jurors, one at a time.

THE COURT: And do you feel that what you saw or read would interfere with your ability to serve as a fair juror in this case?

Those jurors that felt they could not be fair were eventually brought to side bar to be questioned in private to prevent prejudicing the other jurors.

Several people were excused for prejudice during the initial voir dire questions regarding prejudice formed from the original news media. Mr. Taylor was kept in spite of his admission that in his mind he'd already convicted me, was an employee of Government Sales Corporation, made deliveries to the Nevada Test Site and had just the week before been convicted of prowling.

THE COURT: Mr. Garrity, why don't you go ahead and explain to us what your problem is?"

MR. GARRITY: I worked at maximum security for twelve years. My body's a mess, I'm out on disability, numerous phone calls to kill my family, obscene phone calls to my wife, my daughter over the years even though I kept changing my numbers. I have definite opinions.

MS. QUIG-TERREY: Move to strike.

THE COURT: Yes, it's clearly appropriate in Mr. Garrity's case.

I learned that the jurors most biased against me were exactly the ones the prosecution most wanted to retain. Justice was not the goal of the prosecution but rather maintenance of the federal conviction rate. Mr. Ham worked to that goal by creating simple sentences to elicit a positive response.

MR. HAM: Mr. Adkins, are you willing to follow the instructions of the court, to separate evidence in this case from the evidence dealing with that earlier incident?

MR. ADKINS: Yes.

The peremptory challenges began with both prosecution and defense allowed to exclude three potential jurors each. With defense contractor employees, military personnel and police there was no way to get rid of all of those I believed may be prejudiced. Judge Pro read the jury instructions and upon completion, Mr. Ham asked the judge at sidebar to advise me about Rule 602 regarding evidence.

MR. HAM: Well an attorney would know what the boundaries are in an opening statement.

THE COURT: Mr. Springer as his own attorney is still held to the standards as an attorney. I assume you've had a chance to talk about this.

MS. QUIG-TERREY: We've discussed the hearsay rule but I'll tell you, we studied that for weeks in law school.

✳ ✳ ✳ ✳ ✳

"The legal system is concerned with law and law is pledged to Power. As a consequence, law will most often stand against such human rights as threaten Power....Power, by definition can never permit itself to be subordinated to the individual. As a consequence, justice will be delivered to the people only when it is in the best interests of Power to deliver it."
— *Gerry Spence* *With Justice For None* *1989*

✳ ✳ ✳ ✳ ✳

PLAINTIFF'S OPENING REMARKS

MR. HAM: Thank you, Your Honor. And may it please the court, Mr. Springer, counsel, ladies and gentlemen. My name is John Ham and I'm the Assistant United States Attorney. I have been assigned to prosecute the matter of United States versus Rick Paul Springer.

As you know the defendant has been charged with failing to surrender and this may not be a serious crime as you would have expected when you came to federal court, but it is an important case nonetheless. It is important because you are going to be asked to decide several things.

You're going to be asked to decide whether the defendant is above the law or subject to the law. You are going to be asked which has supremacy, the laws of the United States which have been passed by our duly-elected officials, or a moral cause which the defendant holds. You're going to be asked to decide the guilt or innocence of Mr. Springer. This case is unique for a number of reasons. It's unique because of the nature of the defendant, Mr. Springer.

He is a person who is an opportunist, he seeks an opportunity to further his cause which is no doubt very important to him and he wants to promote it.

Another unique aspect about this case is what this case is not about, and what the defendant most likely would want this case to be about, and that is nuclear testing, the amount of money spent by governments or corporations for nuclear testing and other forms of defense. Ladies and gentlemen, this is not a referendum on nuclear testing or on how the Test Site is used; this is not a referendum on Government spending or possibly Government waste. We have established a process: we elect officials, and we elect them for various reasons. And that is where this type of issue should be handled. Whether you or I disagree or agree with the defendant or his politics is not the issue in this trial.

Now the law, in this case, requires that you shall surrender to serve your sentence also provides for a defense. It is called an affirmative defense. This defense is referred to as the defense of uncontrollable circumstances.

I'd like to list the four elements of that defense. First, there must be some type of uncontrollable circumstance; second, it must prevent you from surrendering; third, you must not contribute to the existence of that circumstance and fourth, when that circumstance ceases to exist you must then surrender. Ladies and gentlemen, I submit that you will find that the defendant has tried to put a square peg in a round hole; the defense will simply not work in this case.

In sum, the defendant was told to surrender and he chose not to. And at the conclusion of this case I'm going to ask that you find the defendant guilty. Thank you".

Mr. Ham straightened his papers on the podium and returned to his seat

by Jim Davy, the US Marshal that booked me upon the Nagasaki day arrest.
THE COURT: Thank you, Mr. Ham. Mr. Springer.

I took a deep breath and approached the podium behind which I was ordered to stay.

THE DEFENDANT: I'd like to thank you for being here. I do believe this is an incredibly important responsibility of citizenship.

We have a unique situation here and it is going to require that you open your minds, and expand the parameters of the past.

I broke down in a flood of tears. Streams began running down my cheeks as the words choked in my throat.

I'm going to ask you all to bear with me, because this is very difficult.

The words came sputtering out through the tears. Sue Quig-Terrey began to stand at the table expecting to relieve me. But I kept talking through the cracking voice and looking at the jurors through bleary, tear flooded eyes. I forced myself to focus.

I did not want to have to address this issue. I wish it had already been solved. I consider nuclear weapons testing unquestionably the greatest atrocity in human history. I believe that when you know what I know about nuclear testing that you'll agree with me that I not only did not break a law but was actually obedient to several laws which invalidated the prior law for which I am being charged.

There's a Chinese proverb that says `a wise man feels what he should, not all he can.' Perhaps that is my greatest crime, I feel too much. When I learn the facts and statistics and the pollution, the immorality of nuclear weapons testing, I'm just – astounded.

The tears slowed to a trickle and I started to gain a flow despite the nasal sound of my speech.

You know, it hurts me in my soul that humanity is capable of doing this. Mr. Ham made a couple of comments right at the start about perhaps I'm above the law. Not at all. In fact, I feel as though I am commanded constantly to abide by the law, and so I pray a lot. I put a lot of spiritual effort into making these decisions.

I think I should address the initial action that started this court process rolling because there has been a lot of disinformation that came out in the media. I went to the NAB convention in the hopes of announcing a nuclear bomb test that was scheduled for the next day. We had five hundred activists who were leaving Las Vegas in a civil rights style protest march to the Nevada Test Site. I did not know Ronald Reagan was even going to be at the convention, he was no target of mine in any form.

I continued describing the Broken Eagle Incident, apologizing again for the flying shards, but stating,

Nonetheless, there's no question at this point that I believe that action was appropriate as a fire alarm to the issue of nuclear weapons testing.

I explained the Secret Service accidentally hitting Reagan from behind and the fact that it was on film.

I can guarantee you this is not the life I want to live. I would rather be in my community working with abused teens, growing a garden and living a life like everyone else. But I have come to this awareness and I see there is no future for humanity so long as we embrace violence as a means of conflict resolution, so long as we allow our governments to lead us down this path.

It is not only your right, but your duty to change, alter or abolish any government that is injurious to our basic rights of life, liberty and the pursuit of happiness. And nuclear weapons is injurious to all those.

I informed them of their jury power and rights by reading from a pamphlet supplied by the Fully Informed Jury Association, FIJA.

This is what Thomas Jefferson said in 1789; he said, "I consider trial by jury as the only anchor yet devised by man by which a government can be held to the principles of it's Constitution.

When the constitution says it is your duty to change or alter a government that is injurious to our rights, I said, okay, I'll do my duty. And it is not only my constitutional duty, it is my spiritual duty, because everything I believe in says killing is wrong. And these bombs are portable Auschwitz ovens and we're paying our tax dollars for them. I looked up justice in the dictionary and Websters New Collegiate says that justice is the principle of right action, conformity to the principle righteousness,' Then I looked up righteousness, `acting in accordance with divine or moral law.' Each of us as individuals must decide what is divine or moral.

When this court is concluded I believe you will agree with me that my action to abide by the US constitution and my spiritual beliefs was appropriate. Thank you.

The jury was excused for lunch hour.

✳ ✳ ✳ ✳ ✳

"What is happening in America that we should provide our citizens with 2.67 lawyers per thousand people while Japan needs only .1? Two-thirds of the lawyers on earth live in the United States, while we account for only 6 percent of the worlds population." — Gerry Spence <u>*With Justice For None*</u> *1989*

✳ ✳ ✳ ✳ ✳

The Marshals descended on me like vultures on a carcass to escort me back to a cell. "I need to confer with my attorney," I informed Marshal Gucci as he latched onto a piece of my flesh.

"You can talk with her upstairs."

Upstairs, I was escorted into a windowed booth with a grey screen over the glass. A sack lunch was delivered, (the treat of going to court), a turkey sandwich, (On wheat, no less), Big Grab BBQ chips, a maple donut bar, an apple, and a large Sprite in a styrofoam cup. I nibbled slowly, knowing I should eat, but with little appetite.

The door opened to admit Susie Q, which is how she signed her correspondence to me. I exhaled deeply, blowing between pursed lips, a silent whistle. I couldn't help noticing how good she looked. In a professional sense, she was dressed to kill, as they say.

"Hey," I joked, "Don't you dare come here dressed like that again. You're ruining my concentration."

"I thought for a moment there, you were going to have a breakdown." She told me.

"I am. And that's probably what the jury needs to see." I felt my eye sockets burning. I squeezed and opened them wide trying to exercise and relieve my sagging lids and bags. Strange how the entire eyeball burned, even on the back side clear into the brain.

"What are you drinking there?" I noticed her huge styrofoam cup full of some cola?

"Soda."

"You have got to eat some real food. How's your heart feeling?"

"Oh, I'm okay." She seemed to be avoiding. Our roles as attorney and client, pro per defendant and assistance of counsel, EMT and patient, nuturer and nurtured, friend and friend, flirt and flirt, were vague and etherous, flowing back and forth with confused alignments. I was as vulnerable as a crumbling divorcee on the psychiatrists couch while my facade, the false front of spiritual and physical endurance, told jokes and gave orders with specific instructions. `I'm tough!' My aura said while my guts kept calling `Mama!' I couldn't tell who was telling the truth!

I got demanding, "Hey, with a heart condition and a high stress job you have to quit coffee, all that sugar shit, and start eating healthy. You owe that much to your kids."

"Okay" she agreed glancing at the floor like a reprimanded child. I wasn't totally sure the heart condition was even real. Maybe it was one of a hundred excuses the professional attorney used to explain why they couldn't show up. If you're gonna lie, make it convincing, something that no one would dare to question. Attorneys are actors by profession. Who said, "A jury is twelve people gathered together to see who has the best attorney?" Thank goodness I felt confident that Sue Quig-Terrey believed in my script.

* * * * *

"A Time Magazine Poll showed that 76% of the voters in the
U.S. support a nuclear freeze"
  – Ken Keyes The Hundredth Monkey 1981

* * * * *

The prosecution presented five witnesses, each testifying in one form or another to the facts, just the facts, ma'am. That Mr. Springer had promised to surrender to serve a four month sentence, that Mr. Springer had failed to show up at the Shasta County Jail in Redding, California, and that Mr. Springer had subsequently been arrested after two months as a fugitive.

Eventually I cross examined Mr. Jim Davy, the US Marshal booking officer who had been kind enough to offer his business card and 'off the record' support.

I had, during the months following the Broken Eagle Incident, noticed a unique phenomenon. Supporters of the action from around the world had sent encouraging letters, empowering poems, crystals from sacred places as far away as Chile and Alaska, eagle jewelry, eagle feathers, and eagle talons. They bought my breakfast, lunch and dinner, handed me bags of groceries, while taxi drivers waved the fair. The real wonder was how constantly individuals *within the system* offered their personal support in private. The directors of TV stations made a point to introduce themselves after TV appearances and while holding eye contact and firm handshakes would say, "Thank you for your good work to halt nuclear weapons testing." US Marshals, prison wardens, even the prosecuting attorney, John Ham, offered their personal support, catching me in private, always qualified with the subtle interjection, "Off the record, I'm one of your greatest supporters". They each had a paycheck to consider. It made me realize that the difference between a good American and a good Nazi was the difference between a gas oven and a microwave, Auschwitz and Fat Man.

I thought that the fact Mr. Davey, the booking marshal, had told me he supported my work was a good example of the phenomenon. I tried to bring this before the jury. I found out exactly what 'off the record' meant.

"And so, Mr. Davey, my understanding that you told me off the record that you were in support of my work is–is erroneous?"

Mr. Davey glared coldly, steeling himself to the lie.

"I did not tell you I supported your work, sir."

But he couldn't hide the hiss when he pronounced 'sir'.
"Thank you, Mr. Davey."

* * * * *

Bill Chisholm, an Idaho activist, was employed by the Federal Emergency Management Agency (FEMA). He was my first defense witness. Bill had proof of the power of the individual to get a political ball rolling. His actions to prevent the illegal shipment of nuclear waste into Idaho had received statewide press. He had stopped a nuclear waste truck by simply standing in front of it. That was the Imcon Incident. Later he doused a nuclear train with red paint to mark it. In a few months after Bill's actions the shipments were halted. In my trial I hoped he could established the need for individual action, corroborate my beliefs that my actions were necessary in light of a restart of testing, and confirm that I had travelled by bicycle. When Ms. Quig-Terrey questioned Bill about his understanding of the Nuremberg Principles, Judge Pro interupted,

THE COURT: "Counsel, on instructions on law, that'll have to come from the court."

MS. QUIG-TERREY: "Your Honor, I was seeking to establish the common perception of what was required among the social activist community of which Mr. Chisholm and Mr. Springer were members. It was Mr. Springer's reliance upon his interpretation of his duty under those laws which led him to take the actions that he did."

THE COURT: "Well, I'll deal with that at the appropriate time, but I'm not going to allow this witness to testify as to international law. Okay, call your next witness."

In fact, Judge Pro never explained any aspect of international law while in earlier motions he had denied the admission of international law experts. Christopher Alan Brown was sworn in for testimony.

MS. QUIG-TERREY: "Good morning, Mr. Brown. Could you state your employment, please?"

A   I work for Citizen Alert, which is a statewide environmental watchdog organization based here in Nevada for the past 18 years and I'm the Southern Nevada Director since September of '88."

Q   What do your responsibilities include?"

A   I supervise programs that involve the Nevada Test Site, one of our main program areas, nuclear wastewater, and toxic issues. I do fundraising, supervise two other staff, research on particular issues, testify at hearings, coalition work, and organize grassroots participation in various lobbying and public advocacy activities around the issues.

Q   Are you familiar with the federal governments policies concerning nuclear testing?

A   That's been my primary work for a number of years. Before Citizen Alert, I helped organize the American Peace Test. I've been working on nuclear testing issues since 1985.

Q   In May and June of '93 were you involved in nuclear testing debate?

A   That was a very intense time in early May. The President floated a proposal that would allow testing to continue under a purported Comprehensive Test Ban Treaty. Despite the generally accepted definition of that treaty as meaning no nuclear tests, he actually floated a policy option that would allow testing to continue at one kiloton or less. I'm part of a national coalition of 30 groups. We met in mid-May of this year in Washington, DC with National Security Council staffers to hear their explanation and explain our concerns about not just US policy but also about international policy and the fact that other countries would be far more likely to continue to develop nuclear weapons if the US tried to pursue this one kiloton testing regime.

Q   In June of '93, was the nuclear testing debate resolved?

A   At the end of June, to the surprise of a lot of people, we won the fight completely with Clinton backing off his earlier proposal and proposing a fifteen month moratorium.

Q   Has Citizens Alert continued to work on the nuclear testing issue from June to the present?

A   Absolutely! One of our biggest projects this summer was clean-up of the test site. We want to keep jobs from being the momentum that pushes the United States back into nuclear testing. And so we're trying to advocate jobs for clean-up.

Q   Have you witnessed individual action impact on national policy concerning nuclear weapons?

Mr. Brown responded by telling of congressmen and journalists that had been impacted by individual and group backcountry actions, where citizens were willing to risk their own lives by trying to stop a nuclear test. The result had caught the attention of congress and several important bills were passed restricting test site funding. He stated:

A   It's fairly clear that congressional members thought that individual activities, especially these more high risk activities were bringing the issue to light in Washington, DC.

Q   Based on your experience with Citizens Alert has media's coverage of nuclear testing and the protest against it been an important factor in changing federal policy?

MR. HAM: Your Honor, I don't see the relevance of that.

MS. QUIG-TERREY: Your Honor, Mr. Ham cross examined Mr. Springer extensively about his unreasonable belief that he could have any impact upon federal policy. Mr. Springers response was—

THE COURT: Well, go ahead, I'll let him answer.

A   I'd say coverage by the media is fairly critical to shaping the opinions of policymakers, especially by the major east coast media outlets.

Q   To your knowledge have Mr. Springers activities been reported in those east coast publications you've referred to?

A   I think they were reported in practically every publication, every TV show that ran. They got attention nationwide, and probably world wide. It certainly got everyone's attention.

QT concluded her questioning as Ham approached for redirect exam.

BY MR. HAM:

Q   Mr. Brown, is it safe to conclude then that a defendant gets attention when he violates the law?

A   That's one aspect of the whole Gandhian philosophy of nonviolence, is that when you cannot get attention through regular channels of governance that you have to go beyond those in order to draw peoples attention to the injustice going on.

Q   Mr. Brown, these questions are going to be simple, they call for a yes or no answer. All right? Now Mr. Brown, your wording was with regard to the moratorium being extended, 'we won the fight'. What channels were you working through in order to win that fight?

A   At Citizen Alert, we worked mainly with national coalitions that lobbied both congress and the public. That coalition had a full page ad in the *New York Times*.

Q   So you lobbied? You contacted legislators? You performed public activities, and you wrote editorial boards. All of these are lawful acts, isn't that right?

A   Yeah

MR. HAM: Nothing further.

MS QUIG-TERREY: I have one very brief question. Would you claim that your organization was solely responsible for 'winning the fight', as you described it?

A   Absolutely not.

The next witness called for the defense was Anthony Guarusco, the director of The Alliance of Atomic Veterans. His long gray hair was pulled back in a neat braid with his bushy moustache twisted up at the ends. I approached to address the witness myself.

Q   Good morning, Anthony, Could you give us a brief description of your background in the nuclear weapons issue?

A   Well, I'm a World War II veteran, served in the Pacific during that war; I'm also a Korea War veteran. And in between I was ordered to participate in nuclear experimentations at the Bikini Atoll in 1946, which consisted of two nuclear explosions: both were twice the size of

Hiroshima.

MR. HAM: Your Honor, I would object to this as being cumulative. Mr. Springer had full opportunity to take the stand, to testify as to what impacted him.

THE COURT: What is it you want to elicit from Mr. Guarusco?

MR SPRINGER: I'm trying to explain to the jury that I saw an incredible movie. The impact of the movie is not going to do much to them by me saying, it was a great movie. Whereas if you see the movie, you are devastated yourself and find yourself in tears. Mr. Guarusco's impact on me they cannot understand–they have to experience it firsthand from the man.

THE COURT: So what do you want Mr. Guarusco to tell the jury?

MR. SPRINGER: I want him to cover his personal experiences with being exposed to the nuclear bomb tests and the detriment to human lives.

THE COURT: Okay, the issue is not whether bombs cause incredible damage to human life. I don't find that that's relevant to the case. So I'm not going to allow that type of testimony.

MR. SPRINGER: I beg to differ regarding the fact that the bombs cause harm to personal life; that is exactly relevant to this case, and that is the issue. If it wasn't causing harm to life, we wouldn't be here.

THE COURT: Well, that's all right, Mr. Springer. You can disagree with me, but that's my ruling. So I'm not going to allow Mr. Guarusco to testify as to that area.

MR. SPRINGER: Mr. Guarusco, were you personally exposed to nuclear bomb tests?

A   Yes, I was exposed to –

MR. HAM: Your Honor, I would object.

THE WITNESS: – nuclear bombs.

THE COURT: Mr. Springer, if there is nothing else you want to elicit from him, then...

MR. SPRINGER: Due to corporate interests that benefit from nuclear testing, the media has largely kept the information from the public. In all probability the jury has not been exposed to the details of what nuclear testing actually does.

THE COURT: Mr. Springer, all the jury needs to concern themselves with is the charge against you. This is not a referendum on nuclear testing. I've given you wide latitude to testify as to areas that motivated you, but I'm not going to allow this, it's that simple.

MR. SPRINGER: The jury cannot understand or validate my defense without knowing what it is that motivated me to that defense.

THE COURT: I understand you disagree with me, but that's my ruling.

MR. SPRINGER: It seems as though I'm being denied a defense.

THE COURT: Let's not debate any further in front of the jury. Why don't you step back and consult with your counsel, Ms Quig-Terrey, for a moment.

(Colloquy between defendant and advisory counsel)

BY MR. SPRINGER:

Q   Since your exposure, Mr. Guarusco, have you been involved in efforts to stop nuclear testing at the Nevada Test Site?

A   Yes, I have. I have personally been involved in attempting to stop nuclear testing since the late 70s when the atomic Veterans were coming forward in terms of the latency period of having had certain types of cancers that were connected with nuclear testing, such as polycyphemovera, cancer of the blood.

MR. HAM: Your Honor, this is not responsive.

THE COURT: I'll let the witness finish. Go ahead.

THE WITNESS: Thank you sir. At that time veterans were coming down with different types of cancers that the Government accepts as being radio-genetically connected, and the Veterans Administration now accepts and let the vets come in to spend their last time before they expire. And those were the cancer of the blood that usually precedes leukemia, or multiple myeloma, which is a cancer of the bone marrow that we've seen in the survivors of Hiroshima and also at Chernobyl. "So my interest in stopping testing was to see if we could stop this insanity of using people as guinea pigs, such as myself and other—a large number of 250,000 men and women who were in the military were used in these experiments. Our concern for the downwind people of St. George, Utah, the people of Las Vegas who had been irradiated. Everything I'm mentioning has been documented by the US government.

Q   Are you familiar with the Radiation Victims Compensation Act?

A   I certainly am, and we certainly don't take any part in it.

Q   Could you explain why that is?

MR. HAM: Your Honor, I don't see the relevance.

THE COURT: Yeah, sustained. It's not relevant.

Q   Do you enjoy this work?

A   I don't enjoy this work. I feel that all of us have an obligation to stand up. And sometime maybe somebody should stand up and refuse to serve an unjust sentence even.

The next witness, Claudia Peterson, a sandy, short haired blond woman from St. George, Utah, took the stand. She had an attractive motherly aura about her with her floral print, beige, mid calf dress. She explained that she worked at Albertsons in St. George as a checker, and was involved with the Mormon church and the American Cancer Society.

Again, I questioned the witness.

Q   What led to your willingness to participate in this process?

A   Because I think it's really important that people know what's happened in our area and what's happened to my family and my neighbors family members as a result of what the Dept. of Energy and the US government did to us because of nuclear testing.

MR. HAM: I don't see how this is relevant.

Judge Pro and I went through another round of debate on what testimony would be allowed. While Pro supported Mr. Hams position again.

Q   Before my decision to surrender I viewed a film called "Bound by the Wind" by David Brown, which heavily impacted my decision. You appeared in that film. Could you briefly describe your part and why you appeared?"

A   I appeared in that film because of what has happened to my family and what we have been through. In my family, my father died from a brain tumor, my thirty-seven year old sister died from melanoma and I lost a six-year old child to leukemia, as a result, I truly believe, from being exposed from the nuclear testing.

It's really important that they didn't resume testing and I understand why it was so important to you. Because as Dr. Rosalie Bertell and Dr. Ernest Sternglass and other doctors have proven, that those of us who were exposed...

MR. HAM Your Honor, I object."

THE COURT: Sustained as to what other doctors have proven.

MR. HAM: And further, Your Honor, it seems Mr. Springer is taking a circuitous route to get to what the Court has already precluded him from doing.

THE COURT: He is, he is. I'm trying to be flexible. But go ahead, Mr. Springer, have you got something else you wish to cover?

Q   Is St. George downwind of the Nevada Test Site?

A   Yes, it is.

Q   Have any members of your community been compensated by the Radiation Victims Compensation Act?

MR. HAM: I would object—

A   Several.

Q   Could you explain what activities you've been involved in to stop nuclear testing?

The intimate story of Claudia Peterson's six year old child never came out before the jury. But her child's untimely death from luekemia could be heard in Ms. Peterson's voice as she stated with a childless mother's conviction,

A   I call the White House, call my congressmen, my Senators, I call Anthony Lake's office.

BY MR. HAM:

Q   And all these activities of yours were lawful?

A   Yes

Bill Rosse Sr. was called to the stand. An older dark red Indian man walking with a slight twist of the hips approached the bench.   Bill Rosse was a testimony to the power of a commited cause. As the Environmental Protection Officer of the Western Shoshone National Council (WSNC), he had traveled the world in his old age, on a bare bones budget. He rolled broken car after broken car to rally after rally protesting the abuse and desecration of indigenous lands, particularly at the Nevada Test Site. He served on the board of directors of Citizens Alert, American Peace Test, The Shoshone Council, Walk Across America for Mother Earth, The Hundredth Monkey Project, and Nevada Desert Experience. In the peace movement, he was a walking legend. He stood no taller than Gandhi, was as soft spoken, but his cowboy hat, long grey streaked hair and thin trimmed moustache were the trademarks of the head of the Reese River Rosses, his family band that had entertained at several actions. It was expected that after his coffin was lowered in the hole and the first shovel load clodded on the wood, Bill would kick around inside the box and demand that he was only resting.

Mr. Ham objected in advance to any discussion of indigenous treaties, aboriginal claims or land rights regarding the test site.

Bill testified that he had been at many actions issuing Western Shoshone permits to enter onto Shoshone land. He explained the Shoshone permit system and the 1863 Ruby Valley Treaty.

"I have toured with Mr. Springer in California, all up and down the coast and into Oregon, speaking about the issues here at the Test Site and inviting people to be a part of the demonstrations."

With Bill Rosses' testimony completed, my defense was complete.

The jury instructions began after lunch with Judge Pro demanding, "In following my instructions you must follow all of them and not single out some and ignore others."

Mr. Ham was called on for closing arguments.

MR. HAM: The case before you that you've listened to for the past day and a half illustrates a problem in society. Nowadays everyone wants to be a law unto themselves. I would like to read some of Mr. Springers comments. "I have decided to deny the Courts order for my surrender. It is time for a change with the US Government that is not capable of happening from within the established structure. I do not recognize the authority of the US Government. The US government is not only incapable of serving justice, but through the dictates of capitalism and materialism are leading the world in the destruction of our planet. The people of America are composed largely of a nation of spoiled brats seduced into a stupor of complacency through comfort convenience, materialism and entertainment. It is via the support of the American taxpayer that the oppression continues worldwide. Democracy does not exist in America and therefore democratic methods will not work."

Ham paused after reading from the statement I had sent to the press and the court the day I became a fugitive, titled, "Why I Refuse to Surrender."

MR. HAM: "You mix frustration with the political process with someone's belief as to their moral duty, and you blend that in with what that person perceives to be the will of the people, and presto, you have a higher moral law. George Washington, who I think probably understood the Constitution better than Mr. Springer, said, "Laws made by common consent must not be trampled on by individuals."

Mr. Ham worked through the components of the uncontrollable circumstance defense attempting to convey to the jury that I had not fulfilled the required elements.

MR. HAM: "The fourth element, did he surrender as soon as circumstances ceased to exist.? And the key word is "as soon as". Sixty days—over sixty days after he was to surrender he was arrested. He did not surrender at any point. His own words were he knew he, "would be arrested sooner or later" when he started going to the media. He did not surrender.

"In order to accept the defense that Mr Springer has alluded to you would have to disregard the proof which has been established, disregard that he has not established a legal, lawful defense for his actions, you would have to disregard the instructions and you in effect would be asked to legislate to set federal policy. You and I recognize something that Mr. Springer does not recognize, and that is a strict observance of the laws of this land are one of the highest duties of good citizens. "Mr. Springer is far too quick to dispose of the system that we have in this country. It's got flaws, but it's the best in the world."

Again Ham closed by asking the jury for a guilty verdict. I stepped to podium.

MR. SPRINGER: Greetings again. In some respects I'm disappointed or sorry with the knowledge that the outcome of this situation hinges on debating skills. I think Mr. Ham is doing an excellent job. I feel safer knowing that he is going to be prosecuting murders and that type of crime but I can't help but wonder what did that failure to surrender actually cause. How was society harmed?

I didn't show up on a particular date because of a greater cause and call. If I did not want to deal with this situation, if I was not a responsible citizen, I guarantee you, I wouldn't be here today because this system made efforts to track me down and as we know from recent media, from the woman that spent 26 years in Oregon, you don't have to surrender until it's time.

Tears flowed down my cheeks again. I tried to explain to the jury that they had been denied the opportunity to hear any expert testimony. Ham objected and Judge Pro insisted I move on.

Sociologists estimate that 85 percent of American families are dysfunctional. What does that give us? That gives us 85 percent dysfunctional systems on all fronts. And we all know it. It's in the papers constantly. We're not fooling anybody. Are we in denial about this? Let's get real here. We are in a serious situation. We are stumbling, going down. You know, people have got to start screaming, you know, hey, we gotta wake up, this system is not functioning for us.

Vice President Al Gore said on Sept 7, 1993, 'The United States government has grown stale, wasteful, inefficient, bureaucratic, and is failing the American people."

Mr. Clinton himself stated, "It is outrageous for the government to have rules and regulations which take peoples money from them and spend it on things that cannot be justified."

Stewart Udall, former Interior Secretary regarding Navaho uranium miners just stated recently, "These people were sacrificed in the name of national defense." Sacrificed.

There is no question that the US constitution is one of the finest pieces ever written. Unfortunately, from day one people didn't pay any attention to it. Ask the Native American people. Treaties are the supreme law of the land and we've made over three hundred and ninety-four and every single one of them is broken. You just call up the International Indian Treaty Council. Talk to the tribes about how they feel about it. Oh, you got this reservation. Oh, then they found uranium on it and they came back and took this chunk of it. Now they're offering you a big chunk of money because they want you to accept the waste on your property.

John Adams, the second President of the US had this to say about the juror. 'It is not only his right, but his duty to find the verdict according to his own best understanding, judgement and conscience though in direct opposition to the direction of the court.'

I went into the several international treaties that made nuclear weapons illegal. The Hague conventions of 1899 and 1907 established clearly that a nation cannot use weapons that cannot distinguish between combatants and noncombatants. The Genocide conventions of 1925 passed rules prohibiting unnecessary suffering. Then after Hitler, the Nuremburg Principles came into effect further ratifying the Hague and Genocide conventions and adding responsibility to each individual for his actions in war. A superior order is not justification for war crimes.

I explained the 1963 Partial Test Ban Treaty, John Kennedys greatest achievement, the international agreement that forced nuclear weapons testing underground and I read the first paragraphs, "Proclaiming as their principle aim the speediest possible achievement of an agreement on general and complete disarmament under strict international control in accordance with the United Nations, seeking to achieve the discontinuance of all tests explosions of nuclear weapons for all time, determined to continue negotiations to this end, and desiring to put an end to the contamination of man's environment by radioactive substances."

Mr. Ham interupted, "He's introducing law, he's defining words, he is testifying, he's presenting new evidence."

But I was done with that section and moved on.

I'm an Emergency Medical Technician and I take my oath and duty very seriously. They say an ounce of prevention is worth a pound of cure but with the nuclear industry we're talking kilotons and megatons.

I guarantee you that if I made a decision to 'not' deal with this system, I wouldn't be here dealing with it but there is nowhere to run on this planet. You want to go to the South Pacific, we got the Bikini Atoll contaminated out there. You want to go to France, hey, they got nuclear reactors leaking all over out there.

Nuclear weapons begin by pulling uranium out of the ground and that's when it begins killing people. The seventeen nuclear support facilities from Hanford to Rocky Flats, Savannah River to Fernald, everyone of them is a Super Fund clean-up site. November 9th, Time Magazine said 'the US military is the nation's number one polluter' and they didn't even consider the Department of Energy in that equation.

I closed with a quote from Corbin Harney. '

We only got one earth floatin' around out here, we got one air, one water, and we're all downwinders.' Thank you.

Sue Quig-Terrey stepped forward to address the law side of the argument. She also went through the elements of the uncontrollable circumstances argument proving in simple but effective rhetoric that we had fulfilled all the components.

MS. QUIG-TERREY: "The first element is uncontrollable circumstance. Now Mr. Ham has tried to do some little dance around the meaning of uncontrollable but you've got real life experiences and common sense, you know what uncontrollable means. It doesn't mean you could have absolutely no control over a situation. And I think you all know that. You've got the common sense to realize when someone's trying to play a word games.

"Second important word is 'prevented'. Did the circumstances prevent Mr. Springer from surrendering.? If your children are in a burning house, of course you're capable of getting in the car and say, "bye' and going in to surrender. But almost no one is going to do that.

"As the judge directed you, we're only considering Mr. Springer here today. Did the circumstances, the threat of nuclear testing, given Mr. Springers knowledge of the threat, his fear of nuclear testing, did that prevent him from surrendering. Not would it have prevented Mr. Ham from surrendering, not would it have prevented me from surrendering but did it prevent Mr. Springer, was that something comparable to his children being in a house fire so that he could not just go forward and ignore the situation. That's what prevent means."

"The final element, did he surrender or would he have surrendered as soon as the circumstances ceased. Again, that's something you've got to decide. That's not a question of law."

She closed by thanking the jurors for their attention. Mr. Ham, as the law allows, was on his feet to offer his second rebuttal closing. His rather stolid closing was full of quotes demanding obedience to written laws. I was close to sitting up and barking.

That concludes my comments to you ladies and gentlemen. This final request, that you abide by the law that the court has given you in this case. If you do that, you're going to find that Mr. Springer is guilty as charged.

"Thank you, Mr. Ham" Judge Pro proceeded to give the remaining jury instruction and with that the jury was excused to deliberate.

* * * * *

"Your awareness is needed in saving the world from nuclear war. YOU MAY BE THE HUNDREDTH MONKEY! You may furnish the added consciousness energy to create the shared awareness of the urgent necessity to rapidly achieve a nuclear free world." — Ken Keyes <u>The Hundredth Monkey</u>

* * * * *

Present since my initial intake into NLVDC, the constant knot in my stomach was like an unraveling electrified golf ball with a poisonous core. It only amplified to the point of nausea as I sat in the holding cell praying for the jury. I sought refuge in my copy of <u>The Hundredth Monkey</u>. After explaining my charges to the man in the next cell, I pulled the book from my legal file and began reading it out loud to pass the time.

After reading three quarters of the book, I realized that my neighbor had gone to sleep. I closed the little red and yellow book and began a series of push-ups and dips, trying to work off the boiling chicken fat, bubbling through my central nervous system, causing shivers and near convulsions in my body.

I hoped for, I prayed for, internally, I cried for an acquittal but the jury didn't seem all that responsive. They all just seemed to stare with no emotion (although the Hispanic woman in the front row did smile once).

The clanking key sound made it's way into the cell bank. I was cuffed for the walk down the stairwell and uncuffed to enter the courtroom. The judge had a note from the jury.

Judge Pro began, "The note reads; 'Your Honor, what does 'as soon as' specify with respect to time following the July 3rd resumption of a moratorium.'"

"My initial reaction is, that's for you to figure out, members of the jury."

I jumped in adamantly, "I certainly agree with your opinion." Sue Quig-Terrey supported my comment.

"Mr Ham, do you have any alternative suggestion?"

Mr. Ham struggled to find a comment that could be supported by law and confirm the term 'as soon as', but the end result was a note passed back to the jury stating, "I can give you no further definition as to the phrase, 'as soon as'.

I was led again back to the cell and sat fidgeting, jaws clenched until called to discuss dismissing the jury for the evening. The foreperson, Mr. Edwards, had written another note, "We cannot reach a unanimous decision and expect to remain deadlocked regardless of further deliberations."

My breath caught at the reading. Could it be we would get a mistrial? I was weak at the thought of another trial. The emotions were too much to live through again. The jury was dismissed for the evening at 5:00 PM. I was returned to NLVDC and a cold dinner. After dinner lockdown, I tried to walk the circle to burn off some more of my energy. Ron Stevens, the old brothel pirate, came alongside with the days *Review Journal*.

"Check out your press today, Rick."

The headlines read, "Man Says Cause Above The Law."

"Well, that's cute, they quote John Ham and make it look as though I said it. Ah, the Spin Doctors hard at work. That stinks," I complained. "I said I was following several laws that superceded the court order."

"Oh Yeah, they're wizards at twisting things. They have me portrayed as the head of a biker gang and kingpin drug dealer because I own a couple of bars and cathouses. But what happened today?"

"The jury is deadlocked. I might get an acquittal".

George and Scotty, walking behind, burst out in a great roar of support. Scotty could hardly believe it, but the ear to ear grins were good to see.

"I don't want to have to go through another trial."

"Oh, they'll drop the charges if you get a mistrial. They don't want you getting all that publicity," George thought out loud.

Early the next morning, I was dragged to the holding lobby to wait for the Marshals again. I'll never forget the callousness of the female duty officer as we shuffled by to the van, "Ah, men in chains, my favorite sound." One male and one female Marshal picked up the court inmates that morning. The female dressed smartly for court, poked fun at me as I shuffled down the court hallway. She complained I was the slowest inmate she'd seen in shackles. I kept my mouth shut, not really in the talking mood. The lack of nutrition made each day a push. Ingenious how the system had learned to nutritionally starve one to death in front of the public's eye.

After waiting until 9:30 another note from the jury prompted my appearance. "We are irretrievably deadlocked and are unable to reach a unanimous verdict. With respect, we ask you to declare this a hung jury."

The jury was brought in to hear a booster called the Allen charge designed to encourage them to push beyond the block. "You should not hesitate to reexamine your own views and change them if wrong. However, you should not change an honest belief for the mere purpose of returning a verdict."

They departed to deliberate again. Later they asked for a transcript of my testimony. They were allowed a cassette player and a tape copy of what I'd said before them.

The jury deliberated as I paced to keep warm in the dark and cold cell. At 2:52 PM the jury was brought back into the courtroom and the most recent note, stating the same hung jury opinion, was read. The jury was polled to insure that each juror agreed with the deadlock.

Judge Pro addressed the jury and formally declared a mistrial, briefly explaining that they had not failed, and then he thanked them. They were dismissed. Sue Quig-Terrey moved for an acquittal which, with Ham's objection, was promptly denied.

Mr. Ham argued to insure that I remain detained in prison. "Mr. Springer is deemed a flight risk and his present time is not being credited towards the original sentence."

My trial on State charges, Malicious Destruction of Property, was due in just two weeks and was used as another reason to keep me detained. I was led out by the Marshals and after undressing, while they watched, suited up in the prison greys to return to North Las Vegas for yet another asshole inspection and strip search.

As I walked in late to the unit, a dozen inmates ran over to hear the days news.

"I got a mistrial. I hope they drop the charges."

Hoots and hollers bounced from the ceiling as the word spread. George walked up with glassy and supportive eyes, offering his hand, "Congratulations, Rick". I was not pleased with the prospect of another trial, but I still smiled. The cricket was right.

Chapter Fourteen
A CAGE TO A LEASH

"Gentlemen of the jury, look at this—this—this boy. I almost said man but I can't say man. Oh, sure, he has reached the age of twenty-one, when we civilized men, consider the male species has reached manhood, but would you call this—this— this a man? No, not. I would call it a boy and fool.....Look at the shape of this skull, this face as flat as the palm of my hand—look deeply into those eyes. Do you see a modicum of intelligence?....

Gentlemen of the jury, be merciful. For Gods sake be merciful. He is innocent of all charges brought against him. But let us say he was not ... Why I would just as soon put a hog in the electric chair as this."
Ernest J Gaines A Lesson Before Dying 1993

"Between 1885 and 1930 there were 3,246 recorded lynch-ings of blacks in the southern states." Gerry Spence With Jus-tice For None 1989

* * * * *

"Springer," Officer Reed called to me as I walked the circle with George.

"Yeah, what's up? I asked approaching the central desk.

"I got something for you from your attorney." He said quietly, "I'm not really supposed to do this but I told her I'd give it to you since it's only a week till Christmas. I asked her if she was sure this wasn't gonna' bum you out and make you hang yourself in your cell or somethin', but she said you were tough enough," as he finished he handed me a new book.

I took it from Reeds hands and looked at the title, A Lesson Before Dying by Ernest J. Gaines.

I nodded "Thanks Reed," before walking away to my cell to stash it and then returned to my laps with George.

"What's up?" George asked.

"Oh, a little Christmas gift from my attorney. I don't know why she didn't come in to see me, though. I've been calling her since the mistrial."

"I tell you, she's a woman scorned. You haven't been responding to her advances."

"What advances, George? I would hardly call a couple of hugs and supportive letters advances."

"Rick, look, listen to me." George stopped walking, "That woman is attracted to you. I've watched her in the visitation room and she is looking at you with ga-ga eyes. I think the letters are an example also. How many attorneys sign their letters, "Love and kisses, Susie Q" or lipstick kiss the letter?" George dropped his trump but I didn't want to operate on that premise, true or not. "You still have those letters, don't you?"

"Unless the guards stole them already, yes. George, she's impressed with my politics, my commitment, my knowledge of the subject. She knows I'm struggling in here and she's trying to make it easier."

George's head bobbed in a patronizing nod, "Yeah, sure, don't believe me. I'm just an old Greek who knows nothing of love."

"Oh George, com'on," I pleaded. "Hey, I'm not going to deny she's attractive, the guards, and inmates oogle over her. But my attraction is based on the fact that she is genuinely interested and supportive of the issue. We worked great together in court. I'm convinced that I couldn't have gotten the mistrial without her as a team member.

"Yeah, Rick, but all I'm saying is that if you were to pay a little more attention to Miz Quig-Terrey she would probably be more attentive to you."

"George, I told her she was beautiful and I had Bill and Sue send her flowers. What do you want me to do? Invite her to my cell for a romantic blaring light bulb dinner. Sure, that's right. You have waiter experience. You could serve up our roasted shoe leather in ham gelatin with the delicacy of instant mashed potatoes au rotten, highly salted whether you like it or not, canned green peas from the WWII vintage stock of K-rations, and finish the meal with jello flambeau. Yes and we'll swill Koolaid syrup till we get pleasantly drunk, then wash it down with hot brown water. No doubt she'll be impressed with my choice of dining."

"Okay, I'll drop it, Monsieur Springer."

"Besides, George, they are probably going to drop the charges so my relationship with Miz QT is close to an end.

They aren't going to drag me into court again with Hazel O'Leary's December 9th nuclear guinea pig confession to America. 'I was shocked, appalled and deeply saddened'. Hey the head of the Department of Energy compared her own agencies 'Cold War' practices to Buchenwold, Nazi Germany, George. Human guinea pigs for the DOE radiation testing program. This is proof that I had reason to believe the nuclear testing program is the imminent threat. If they drag me into court again I'll resubmit my motion for expert testimony based on new information."

"Yeah, that makes sense to me, but I have learned from my experience that these government people do not operate on sense. They operate on agendas, egos and personal politics. I hope you're right and they release you, because if anyone doesn't belong in here, it's you."

"Thanks George. Ham is still insisting that I stay in jail. He keeps this lie going about my lacking community and family ties. I know more people in this town than he does. I lived six blocks from this jail for six months. My family has been coming to this county to our house trailer at Lake Mead for 30 years. I've organized in Vegas for test site events for four years, working with Metro police, county commissioners, and the local Indian community".

"Okay, Rick, you've convinced me."

"Listen to this one," I quoted from my legal papers. "'The defendant is of the mistaken belief that an argument or request repeatedly raised, gains credibility and merit.' He seems to think it works for him and the government knows it works."

"The standard DOE line for the justification to continue nuclear testing is 'Safety and Reliability.' Every time Senator Reid is in the paper or public arguing for the continuation of testing that's what he says, `We have to continue for Safety and Reliability.' That's all he says. He never gives examples or explains why. They have chosen catch words that they know the public wants and relates to, safety, reliability, we all want it so whenever they mention nuclear testing they use those words, again and again. The media prints those words over and over. I'm sure Raytheon, General Electric and EG&G just love their safe and reliable profit margin.

"The nuclear industry is perhaps the most profitable in the world. The drug cartels are moving into weapons grade plutonium as the worlds most profitable smuggling resource. Forget cocaine and China White, the big buck is in yellow cake. Hell, in 1991 Raytheon alone made over $5 billion off the American taxpayer.

"Hey, check this out, George." I pointed to Officer Newson pulling Olson from his cell again. With his hands cuffed behind his back, Newson escorted Olson by the arm, down the stairs and towards the exit doors. I looked over to see Crockett and Chris standing under the stairs looking maliciously at Olson. Newson escorted Olson by the left arm right past the inmates. It seemed so staged. They held Olson out like bait. Crockett glared as Olson got within range, but Olson knew what was coming and spit in Crockett's face. It was hard to say what came first, the spit or the punch, but Olson got nailed in the head and dropped to the floor. With cuffed hands he was up and scampering like a rabbit full speed into the center of the room and under the ping-pong table for protection. Crockett and Chris, the Italian, were on him as Newson made his way to the desk phone to call for backup.

Chris grabbed at Olson to drag him out from under the table but Olson wrapped his body around the nearest leg and was not to be removed. A couple of brutal punches to his head and shoulders and then the team started kicking him in the body. Hate and anger flooded out through each kick.

George and I watched as the staged event unfolded.

Baby Huey, a huge, clumsy officer, along with Jablonsky and Miller entered the room and ran to break it up. Crockett and Chris were pushed over to the west wall while Olson was helped out and led to the opening door.

Miller leaned on Crockett pushing his face to the wall. Crockett put his hands in the air as an act of submission, but Miller insisted on keeping him pegged while the doors slid closed.

"Just another day at North Las Vegas Detention Center. Seems like any fool would've seen that one coming," George commented. "It really is a wonder how the mood and energy shifts with the different guards. Life is miserable when the guards with chips on their shoulders are on duty."

"And here's Miller with us now." I pointed.

When the ruckus died down Miller walked around rattling doors. I watched as Miller went by cell 36. Miller stopped, peered in the window slot and motioned to the door monitor to pop the door.

"That's my cell. I better go check this out."

I walked in as Miller was cramming the manual typewriter into it's case upside down like he was trying to break it.

"What's the problem Miller?"

"You're not allowed to have this typewriter in your room. It's supposed to be for everyone to use."

"It is for everyone. Little Ray used it today, I just got it back two hours ago. Cal used it yesterday." The veins in Miller's nose and cheeks stood out in the stark cell lighting. How long ago was his last beer or shot of Jack Daniels?

"Besides, George has the electric one in his room. Director Brown knows I have it. I'm writing motions for my case."

"I'm just doing what I was told Springer. You can take it up with Brown."

"Let me put it in the box the way it's supposed to go," I offered.

"It's fine." He slammed the door locking me in. I put my towel through the food slot to get out but the door remained locked. I looked out the cell window to see a flock of winter birds diving in unison on a roller coaster of air current. The bare branches over the prison wall waved in the cold winter wind.

I looked at the stainless steel table and picked up the new book puzzled, "<u>A Lesson Before Dying</u>"? Merry Christmas, Humph!"

* * * * *

*"A creature, human or otherwise, that has had it's free-
dom compromised has been degraded. In a subconscious
reaction that combines guilt, fear, and contempt, the keepers
of the caged—even the observers of the caged—are degraded
themselves. The cage is a double degrader. Any bar, whether
concrete or intangible, that stands between a living thing and
its liberty is a communicable perversity, dangerous to the sanity
of everyone concerned."*
— Robins from Selke, <u>Prisons in Crisis</u> 1993

* * * * *

"Springer, get up. You got court today." It was Donelly at my door.

I slid on my tennies and there I was, dressed. I slept in smock and pants and still shivered much of the night. The cold air blew out of the vent right onto the top bunk. I nearly fell on the sink as my left ankle gave out, but I caught myself still wondering that the nerves in my legs had not fully returned after the 18 day fast over four months ago.

Court, yech, but it was the only hope that things would change. I hadn't heard a word from QT. Was she was gone for the Christmas holiday? I grabbed my packet of legal papers, a ragged and overflowing manila envelope. I slid my stubby pencils into my smock pocket: gray, green and red colored ones for highlighting.

The door popped open and I eased, unescorted, down the steps, slowly warming up my ankle. Young Crawford, a nineteen year old black man, his hair fluffed in a neat afro, rather than, his usual corn rows, was also off to court.

"Have a seat," Donelly ordered, after taking us up front to intake. He motioned to the bench in front of the holding cell window. Inside, bodies lay strewn around like dirty rags on a linoleum floor, trying to sleep and stay warm in the refrigerated environment. The many faces of misery, stared vacantly or slumbered in fits.

"Hey, can you get me a smoke?" A voice inquired through the door. "I'm jonesin', dude".

"Can't he'p you man," Crawford shook his head.

We sat on the cold steel bench for an hour and a half until the US Marshalls arrived. To my surprise it was Marshal Davey and G. Lucia again. Marshal Davey, lawman, investigator, transporter, prosecutor's assistant, perjured wit-ness, and judge puppet: all those hats on one head.

"All right, let's go," Davey motioned us to stand up. "Good morning, Rick" he said curtly. "I'll take your papers," he told me, sliding them out from under my arm, and setting them on the counter.

"Well, I need those to prepare my case today," I thought I'd better remind him in case he might misplace them, so to speak.

"Well, we'll see." Davey stooped to hook up the ankle shackles and snap them in place. He took his keys from his belt and used a small tool to lock each one. He then stood, grabbed another chain and wrapped it around my waist, sliding one end into the appropriate link to make it snug. Grabbing a set of handcuffs from his back pocket he slid them through the waist chain and I assisted by putting my hands, one at a time into the cuff as it was locked. This was a stale routine by now.

Marshall Davey proceeded to frisk me as an afterthought, "Let me see in your mouth." Then sliding his hands under my arms and around my chest, he found the 2" pencils. He removed them from my pocket ignoring my protest.

"I need those pencils to prepare my case today. I have some more notes I need to highlight before I get in the courtroom."

"Well, you can't have the pencils" he told me bluntly.

"I've had them every other time. The law says I'm entitled to the tools necessary to my defense and I believe pencils or writing utensils would be considered necessary."

"Look, Springer, I just follow the rules. You can take it up with my superiors."

"Well, I believe in complaining before the rape rather than after and besides, I've learned that officers will lie whenever necessary anyway."

His face glared, as we stood eye to eye, in cold recognition of the implication. He began with a slow challenging tone, "Are you suggesting that I perjured myself on the witness stand?"

It's a strange space to be in, so totally vulnerable. It punctuated what could happen with an exclamation, but I returned the gaze regardless, "No, I'm not suggesting." My stomach muscles flexed instinctively.

Davey grabbed my arm and turned me roughly towards the exit. We were loaded into the van for the ride to the courthouse and in moments pulled up to the back of the Foley Federal Building. A milk crate labeled Anderson's Dairy, a donation from Anderson's no doubt, was set on the ground as a step because the shackles weren't long enough to step to the ground in one move. The van door slid open and we were reminded to watch the step. Crawford and I shuffled out to the pavement, up the ramp, and through the hallways.

Lucia stood in the elevator, hand on the buttons, waiting as I shuffled in. As I entered, the sliding door lurched forward, ramming me in the side and shoulder.

"Oh, I'm sorry, Springer" he said in thick syrupy mockery. "Now face the wall," he ordered.

We unloaded on the third floor, passing again the Marshals hall of fame SWAT team photos. Holding huge rifles, they looked like well equipped guerillas with black masks. It was hard to imagine that they liked that image of themselves as the faceless man about to pull the guillotine or swing the ax or as in this case, pull the trigger. In the photo, there was no way to separate the Marshal from a black suited mercenary.

"I need my papers and pencils," I reminded Lucia as he pushed me into the holding cell.

"Yeah, yeah," he put me off. His tone said, 'yeah, and people in hell want ice water.'

Crawford went into the cell at the end and when he reappeared he had on a sharp business suit. He no longer resembled the hostile young man of the lockdown unit, willing to fight over a TV station.

"Hey, you look great, Crawford," I tried to encourage him as they led him out.

"Thanks, Springer."

The hall door stayed open and the fish eye mirror that was installed to allow the Marshals to view the inmates from the hall also gave me a view of the Marshals. I watched in disbelief as Lucia pawed through my papers.

Crawford was returned in an hour. "The jury got to liberate. Keep your fingers crossed for me, Springer."

I did my push-ups off the fiberglass benches, then I did dips, stomach crunches, hung off the wire cage like a monkey. Eventually, I tired and layed down to doze fitfully; my ever present, prison headache nagging.

Crawford came and went as the jury deliberated. The waiting was hard, minute after minute, hour after hour, the time moved slowly in the chilled cells. I pulled my arms into my smock and tried to breathe into the short-sleeve, V-neck, canvas shirt.

Finally, at 4:15 I walked into the court, empty but for the Judge, John Ham and Ron Pease of Pretrial Services. Pease was the man who had watched me pee in a bottle every week for six months after the Broken Eagle incident.....Ron Pease?

"Mr. Springer, this is a detention hearing to decide if you should be released," Judge Pro explained.

I listened in wonder as Judge Pro and Ham debated the detainment order. Surprise, Mr. Ham, an argument repeatedly raised does seem to gain credibility.

"Mr. Springer remains a flight risk and has demonstrated a will loyal only to his own political agenda," Ham argued.

Still Judge Pro decided, "Well, regardless, I'm going to release him anyway. The release effective today."

I was in a stupor being led back to the holding cell to wait for Crawfords verdict and the trip back to NLVDC. After almost five months I was being released. Tonight? I didn't really believe it. I was missing something. I was suspicious. My release was just another trick to tweak my emotions, to break my spirit, another elevator door.

The doors clunked open, one after another as Crawford re-entered the poorly lit cells. He kept his head high as he passed but the hostility had returned and the suit couldn't hide it or hold it in. It bubbled out the collar and cuffs of the stiff white shirt.

"Any word, Crawford," I asked.

"Guilty as a Mother Fucker, they say," his voice was thick with resentment.

The Marshalls stood as Crawford undressed and replaced the suit on the row of loaners hung just outside the cell.

Crawford was silent on the drive back to North Vegas. I let him be. There was nothing I could say that would help or console him any more than silence. I certainly had no wisdom for him, no silver lining to this justiceless nightmare that said a nineteen year old who accompanies his big brother on a crack cocaine sale should be imprisoned for fifteen years.

The chattering of the Marshalls, as they cursed at the five o'clock traffic, gnawed on the silence like rats on a box of cornflakes.

"Fuck you, asshole," Lucia yelled to a honking driver he had just cut off.

"Now wait a minute." Davey corrected, "I thought we had decided to be more professional."

"Yeah, when these assholes get more professional, we'll be there. Okay!" He threw back in Davey's face, not hiding his contempt.

I wondered if Davey had any idea how the other Marshals had ridiculed him on the last ride from court.

"Can you believe that twirp, Davey? Giving Springer his business card in court like he's some celebrity."

It was hard to believe the Marshalls would bicker as they did in front of the inmates. No different than parents in front of their kids, I guess. The profanity, the arguing, the ignorance betrayed the thin line between the lawman and the lawless, the parent and the child.

An imminent release didn't preclude the evening strip search, what I hoped was my last complete orifice inspection. After an hour of sitting on the bench again, Crawford and I were returned to the unit. Dinner was over, the hall buzzing with cards, chess, and TV.

Scotty and George approached to hear Newson say, "Springer, get your stuff, you're outta here."

"Outta here?" George exclaimed in disbelief.

"Yeah, to my surprise, today was a detention hearing and Pro is releasing me to the Halfway House."

"No shit! Well, good for you!" George was truly happy.

"Springer, get going and get your shit or you're staying here." Newson insisted, "I'm not waiting all night."

"Newson, are you gonna be an asshole until the last minute?" I asked loud enough for others to hear, pushing the weight of my release order to the edge.

"Yeah, that's right. Now get your shit," he ordered. "Or you can spend another night here."

I jumped the stairs, two at a time, my ankle miraculously healed. I loaded my papers, plastic cup, Gideons bible, and the world map Sue had sent me, my 'escape map', into a hefty garbage bag and went back down to say good-bye.

"Hey, I'm losing my workout partner," Rick Lewis told me affectionately.

One by one the inmates came over to say good-bye. Newson had left in impatience, intent on launching his final trump, 'You don't make me wait, I make you wait.'

Although I had never experienced war in a foreign land, I knew now what it was like to say good-bye to army buddies after battle. We saw a lot of blood in this unit and each face was a story of suffering, some deserved, but most not. I felt like I was starting to choke. Each pat on the back and word of encouragement almost hurt.

"You take care, Springer," Harry O told me in earnest. "You a good man and God got a job for you"

"Thanks Harry," I was fighting back the tears now.

The exit doors opened to admit Newson, "Springer, let's go."

A dozen men stood at their stools and cheered and clapped as I grabbed my plastic bag and walked through the doors for the last time. It was too much. I was crumbling again, succumbing to the exhaustion of five months of imprisonment, nutritional deficiency, and trials. I tried to suck the tears in. Newson was not the man to cry with.

I sat in the front intake lobby while they got the 600th set of fingerprints and a departing photo. Officer Owen, her violet eye shadow as perfect as ever, cheered, "So you're going home, Springer. That's good."

Somehow her soothing voice just brought the tears welling up. Owen hadn't lost her sense of compassion, but she didn't quite understand my response. I doubt very many inmates cry when they're being released.

The remainder of my inmate account was returned to me in a check despite the fact that the prison took it from my wallet in cash.

"Is there any way I can cash this? I don't have any way to get across town to the halfway house."

"No banks open at this hour, Springer," another officer told me as he guided me to the one door all inmates long to see opened. It closed behind me.

I stood there in the biting cold of a December 23rd desert night at 10:30 PM in the August T-shirt I'd been arrested in, the brand new loafers QT had bought for my trial, no socks and stiff new jeans. I hefted the plastic garbage bag onto my shoulder and headed across the vacant lot towards Lake Mead Blvd. Right to the very end, they degrade you. They dump you out like a bad dog on a cold night, but the stars were awesome. . .

I saw that solidarity is a burden, but also what Marvin Gaye pointed out, "He ain't heavy, he's my brother." I, Rick Springer, walked out of prison today but I, George Christakis stayed behind; I, Scotty Murdoch stayed imprisoned; I, Rick Lewis still in the cage; I, Mordechai Vanunu still in solitaire; I, Leonard Peltier, still behind the wall. Tears rolled down my cheeks, the cold dry air biting at the tiny rivulets.

I knew the truth: while others are imprisoned, none are free. I began reciting a song of freedom as I removed my shoes and walked barefoot on the icy pavement. The cold was less painful than the blisters formed in the first two blocks.

> "Old pirates, yes they rob I
> Take I from the merchant ship
> Minutes after they took I
> From the bottomless pit.
> But my hand was made strong
> By the hand of the Almighty
> We forward in this generation
> Triumphantly"
>   – Bob Marley

I gazed up at the stars like old friends. They were unconcerned with the 100,000 watts of Vegas. "Orion, I missed you, and Sirius, Pleiades, Cassiopeia." It finally dawned on me that I was out and I started singing to the sky, "Won't you help me sing these songs of freedom, That's all I ever have, Redemption songs, oh, redemption songs."

The cold bit at my nearly numb toes. They seemed to belong to someone else. I slid the loafers on and knocked on the door of an old two-story motel with bars. It sat directly across the street from the nine story Clark County Jail.

I walked into the warmth of the hotel lobby and was greeted by a tall, fat man with glasses and white hair. The man's plaid shirt and brown slacks were distinctly different from the prison guard uniforms.

"You're Rick Springer? Good, have a seat. I'm Bill." Several forms and a polaroid photo later he announced, "Now we get the urine sample and then you can go to your room. Here's a copy of the rules and a bottle. Let's go." I followed him around the corner, into the long hall of doors. He opened an office door and directed me to a bathroom. Bill stood at the door glaring at my ice-shrunken worm-of-a-penis barely peering from the opening of my stiff jeans.

I tried to relax and let the urine flow into the bottle but my mind was on Bill, staring. During all the pretrial testing I'd gone through I never got used to someone standing there staring at my dick while I tried to pee. Dick seemed to sense this was not a safe environment and refused to pee no matter how I tried to persuade him.

"This is ridiculous" I said giving up and buttoning my pants. "I don't have a drug or alcohol problem."

"Well, if you don't give us a sample, we have to list it as a refusal, in which case you violate our rules and will be sent back to the jail. That's the rules."

"Let me drink some water and try in a while."

"That's okay, but you have to sit in the lobby chair until you go. We want to keep an eye on you." Bill showed me the coffee pot in the lobby and I began to down cup after cup after cup. Two hours and three tries later Bill watched me fill the small plastic jar with the vindicating yellow liquid.

At 1:30 AM I was led to a room at the end of the hall on the second floor complete with a view of the jail across the street. Exhausted, I flopped onto a full-size bed. Can I get an extra blanket?" I asked before Bill departed.

"No, just turn the heat up. The controls are on the unit by your bed," he said, closing the door behind him.

I glanced around in wonder at the change of scenery. Two queen size beds, a dresser, a round table with chairs, carpeted floor. I wandered into the bathroom and absentmindedly filled the tub with hot water.

I unpacked my Hefty garbage bag suitcase, laying my papers and cup, tooth brush and comb in the drawer. I got undressed to lie down, ears submersed, in the womb of a hot plastic tub. I was asleep in seconds.

* * * * *

"Approximately 3.2 million offenders were on probation and parole in 1992, compared to 1.3 million prison and jail inmates."
    — The Edna McConnell Clark Foundation, <u>Americans Behind Bars</u> *1993*

* * * * *

The Clark Center halfway house was located in the crack neighborhood of downtown Vegas and sat directly across from LVDC, Las Vegas Detention Center, where I'd spent my first ten days of imprisonment. The spot where white-haired Norb had stood waving his fingers in a peace sign on the day of the Broken Eagle Incident was right across the street from my window. He remained a ghostly sentry at jail entrance, a reminder that I wasn't alone. Father Louis Vitale had spent time in this very half-way house, maybe this room.

The Clark Center was a converted motel. The windows had bars on them. The front lobby was operated by an electric door release controlled at the lobby desk. An outdoor parking area had fencing with a razor wire cap. A set of beat up plastic weights sat in a corner of the yard, which was also an area used for smoking. Cigarettes were only allowed outside.

My counselor, Phyliss, weighed about 180 pounds, and stood 5'5". She drank coffee and smoked cigarettes constantly. She was the drug addiction counselor; helping the residents organize their lives.

Group drug counseling was required, but many people just showed up at the end to sign their names on the roster. The woman who led the group had been a prescription drug addict but since she got her drugs from Eli Lilly she never had to do any jail time. She hated the government and shared her IRS nightmare story. Most residents were not impressed with the one hour weekly group session.

The director of the center appeared to be a speed freak. He was bone skinny, addicted to caffeine and nicotine, and on occasion, actually wore his shoes on the wrong feet. I kid you not!

Residents were required to find work and give 20% of their pay to the Clark Center. Food was provided by some industrial catering outfit in the same Rubbermaid dog food trays as at NLVDC. The perk of this halfway house was that you could go outside to your job or to seek new employment. As time went on, individuals were allowed to stay overnight at home on weekends. Families were allowed to visit in the lobby. You could hug and kiss your wife and kids.

I arrived at the Clark Center two days before Christmas. Christmas could have been what my adopted grandmother Josephine McGillicutty used to call, 'the loneliest day of the year', but a visit and gifts from Cindy Burkehart, one of the hundred monkeys still in Vegas, broke the lonely veil. A whole pile of little gifts, chopsticks, an eagle claw, and a book of poems written by her father in Montana changed the mood to a remembrance of how lucky I really was.

The halfway house was half way to freedom. I had come from a cage to a leash. Like any caged animal, I felt the leash as a vast improvement, but just like the cage is a double degrader, degrading the caged and the cager, so the leash does likewise. Like an untrained dog, I wanted to see how far that leash could stretch or better yet, if I could break it.

* * * * *

"Any society that depends on only two sentencing options—confinement or nothing at all—is unsafe and unjust. We need a full array of effective sentencing tools that actually suit our various sentencing purposes."
— Micheal Smith, President, Vera Institute of Justice

* * * * *

The Monday after Christmas I was framing on the outskirts of Vegas, up

Highway 95, out by the Santa Fe Casino. First I wandered Vegas collecting pawn shop carpenter tools and in the afternoon landed a job as a framer in a town that is eating the desert for 6,000 new residents a month, . The foreman complained that at forty-three I was too old to be a framer so I ran the pants off his twenty year olds. He raised his eyebrows. I taped up my blisters and became an aspirin junkie.

The crew members were as curious as any about the Broken Eagle, but after the story, were verbally supportive. "I just have one question," they asked, "How'd you get that close and miss."

During my four weeks with that crew, I came to feel that two of the other framers were government agents. Elder friends of mine have said that sooner or later, agents mess up. They fumble their lies and I found that to be the case. One carpenter, Tom, claimed to be a free lance writer and by chance knew several of the movers and shakers in the antinuclear movement. When pressed later, he confessed he hardly knew them. He seemed to be backpaddling.

* * * * *

"Institutional lying took on new dimensions at the outset of the Cold War, as clandestine operations began to multiply like rabbits. The proliferation of covert actions required a plenitude of cover stories, and cover stories, lest we forget, are lies."
— *Martin Lee/Norman Solomon, Unreliable Sources 1990*

* * * * *

I finally decided that the Clark Center staff had jerked me around long enough so I just left with the other church goers and hitchhiked out Charleston into the desert. On the way, I stopped at the mini-market at the edge of town and picked up a gallon jug of water. I threw it on the counter, while the manager looked at me intently.

"Hey, you're Rick Springer, aren't you? I want to shake your hand. That Hundredth Monkey group was good people and I appreciate your action with Reagan. The water's on me."

After sticking my thumb out, a beat up Volkswagen dune buggy picked me up. The driver looked like I would in forty years, if I survived. Long, white hair and flowing beard. He still had sparkling eyes, a good sign. He dropped me just past the Red Rock museum entrance.

I wandered off to the church with no walls, but with more majestic cathedrals than man can build. I listened to a pastor who spoke no words. I heard the choir singing: Rustling Leaves, Babbling Brook, and Whispering Wind, my favorite hymns. I saw my mentors: the antelope squirrels who live and dance in the spiny chollas and I understood that sermon. I felt the power of God and gave thanks.

The Lokota people say you only have one possession in this life....your body. I could have easily disappeared that day or any other, from the Clark Center or the state of Nevada. I took my one possession back into Vegas to make an offering in the hopes that the church would thrive. . . The Earth Church!

Chapter Fifteen
A LESSON BEFORE DYING

* * * * *

"Under the Speedy Trial Act, a defendant must be brought to retrial within 70 days following the declaration of a mistrial. 18 USC 3161e. In the present case, Mr. Springers, trial was declared a mistrial on October 28, 1993. His second trial began 83 days later, on January 20, 1994. Thus Mr. Springer was tried outside the 70-day limit."
    — Appellants Opening Brief

* * * * *

"Springer, you have a visitor in the lobby," someone announced over the Clark Center intercom. I jumped up and headed downstairs.

"All right, Bill!" It was a total surprise to see my Idaho buddy, Bill Chisholm "What the heck are you doin' in town?"

"Well, I'm here for your trial," he told me kind of puzzled at the question. "To testify tomorrow."

"What trial? I just got home from pounding nails all day. I haven't heard anything about a trial. I'm defending myself. They have to at least tell me so I can show up."

"You haven't heard anything about it? Susan Quig-Terrey phoned me a week ago."

"Well, she didn't bother to tell me. What the heck is going on? I haven't heard a word about it. But hey, she was supposed to be here tonight, at least I got a note saying she would be here at seven for a meeting. I thought we were going to discuss a Motion to Dismiss for violation of the Speedy Trial law. It must be two weeks past that seventy day limit now."

"Well, that's what I came here for, your trial. But it's great to see you on the other side of the glass."

"Thanks. Let's go outside and get some air. It's getting stuffy in here." My prison knot, the unraveling golf ball in my stomach released a little more poison thinking about another trial. My nightmare had arrived. "Whoa, I don't believe it. She told everyone I know including Marsha, my aunt and uncle, and Cindy that they were going to drop the charges. I haven't been able to talk to her since my first trial."

"That doesn't sound good. I'm supposed to be off for a FEMA call in LA but I told them I would be a couple of days late so I could make your trial."

"I'm really getting disappointed with Susan Quig-Terrey. I don't understand why she hasn't been able to come by before. I have seen so many inmates screwed by their attorneys, it's pathetic. The public defender program is just a rubber stamp to nail anyone who can't afford an attorney. It would be easier if they just screwed you honestly. Instead they go through this game like they are gonna give you a fair defense and then they screw you. April Fools, the joke's on you."

"Yeah, I know, I'm still in the Idaho courts on appeal. It's not very impressive at the state level either but no doubt, the feds are even worse."

"All to create the illusion of justice. 'Well, it may not be perfect,' says John Doe Ham, Flag Wavin' Patriot, leaching off the taxpayers, 'but it's the best in the world.' Yeah, if you ignore the fact that we are manipulating our own citizens and the rest of the world to maintain our decadence and consumption."

"You don't have to convince me. You know I'm on your side." Bill put a hand on my shoulder as a statement of support. "Hey, I live in a tipi and a school bus."

"Yeah, I just can't believe we're going to trial in the morning. I'm exhausted from work. My shoulder is falling out of the stinkin' socket. I've become an aspirin junkie just to sleep from ten to four," I complained, "I'm not prepared for trial. We haven't discussed what witnesses we can get this time. I haven't even seen the woman in over two months and now we're gonna jump into court."

"Well, you sure look better for this round. Looks like you've been out sun bathing."

"Pounding nails in the sun."

A voice called over the loudspeaker, "Springer, you have a visitor in the lobby."

Bill and I walked into the lobby to see Sue Quig-Terrey. "Hai thar," she drawled with her usual South Carolina belle accent.

"Hey, what's going on?" I was unhappy but willing to hear an explanation.

"Well, we better prepare for the trial, I guess." She offered as though she had talked to me the day before.

"I didn't hear a thing about a trial until about an hour ago when Bill showed up."

"My secretary left a message for you. Didn't you get it."

"I got a post-it note that says you were coming for a visit on the 17th and I figured we were gonna talk about a motion to dismiss since you've told everyone but me that they're gonna drop the charges. Especially with the Hazel

O'leary DOE release, 204 Secret Tests, Human Guinea Pigs, comparisons to Nazi Germany."

"Oh no, I'm sorry. I thought you knew. You didn't get anything from the court?"

"No, nothing, not even a party invitation."

"Well, we better go prepare as best we can. It's pretty much the same trial with the same witnesses so we have that much together. How about if we go over to my house so I can watch the kids while we talk. I couldn't get a baby-sitter."

At 8:30 PM, we walked in the front door of a suburban home to two boys greeting Mom with a demand for pizza. She approved; they were on the phone, modern boys of five and nine, ordering their own pizza delivery.

Sue disappeared into another room while I laid out my defense papers that I hadn't thought about in a month. We spent an hour going over the old defense notes. I realized there was no time to do any other defense than a repeat of the first trial which Ham would be prepared to disempower at every turn.

"I'm going to resubmit my motion for expert testimony due to Hazel O'leary's press release. I want to be sure to introduce the motion before the jury so they can be reminded about the government feeding radiation to pregnant mothers and how that information justifies my opinion that the public has been kept in the dark. Now that we know strontium and cesium have been leaking into the bilge and the captain has kept the truth from the crew, I suspect they may support a mutiny. The youngest boy entered the room with pizza sauce all over his face and dove into Sue's lap.

"Then, even if they reject my motion, the jury at least heard the argument. Is there a time I can do that in front of the jury?"

Sue looked up from her fidgeting child to answer, "Yeah, right after jury voir dire, you can submit new motions."

The night wore on to 11PM. We were not really functioning anyway so we said goodnight with plans to meet in court in the morning.

"Well, what do you think, Bill?"

"I'm afraid they're putting you on the railroad, my man."

> Ooey Gooey was a worm...
> A mighty worm was he...
> He climbed upon the railroad track...
> The train he did not see...

* * * * *

"A defendant has a constitutional and statutory right to an impartial and fair judge at all stages of the proceedings."
— Marshal v Jerrico, 446 US 238 1980 , Wounded Knee Legal Defense/Offense Committee v. Federal Bureau of Investigation 507 F2d. 1281

"It is a general rule that appearance of partiality on part of judge is as dangerous as the fact of it; thus many cases exist where the mere appearance of partiality suffices for nonwaivable disqualification." — 28 USCA 455 (a,b)

* * * * *

I left the Clark Center to walk the four blocks to the courthouse in silence. I entered the rear doors with my legal files under my arm and set them down on the small conveyor belt to have the papers X-rayed for contraband.

I walked through the arch setting off the buzzer with my belt buckle, pocket change and small knife.

"We'll keep the knife here for your return, Mr. Springer." The door monitor told me as he slid it into a drawer. "It looks like you have some newspapers in this file so we'll have to keep this also."

"Well, those are evidence and a part of my defense. If you check the dates you will see that they are clippings from old papers. I need them for my case."

"Well, no papers are allowed so you'll have to clear that with the court. We can send them up if the court so orders"

I stepped into the elevator with nothing, not even my legal file, feeling as though I had just got the first whack in a long gauntlet.

Debarking on the third floor, I made my way to the courtroom of Judge Lloyd George. On one wall were a series of photographs at the entrance to the court. I recognized almost all the faces, Pro, Leavitt, Johnson. At the top of the hierarchy of faces was the head of the Nevada district courts, Judge Lloyd George.

I later learned that Lloyd George was an Idaho Morman and an Air Force flyboy in the 1950s. I suspect that he bought the nuclear propaganda, hook, line and Enola Gay. With the other judges having failed to secure a conviction, the boss man decided to handle it himself. Appointed by Reagan in 1984, the least he could do was put this pauper in his place.

Sue Quig-Terrey arrived about 30 seconds before the 8:30 convening. Her arms were loaded with papers of all sorts, almost tumbling out of her grasp.

"You look nice."

"Why thank you," she beamed.

"They took my papers at the front door."

We walked in and had a seat at the table on the right side of the court. Proceedings began promptly at 8:30 AM.

Judge George entered the room in his black, priestly robe. "Will counsel approach the bench please." His seventyish white hair neatly trimmed, his pink martinied skin freshly scrubbed, conservative black rim glasses, he portrayed the generic federal judge. Just one of over 204 federal judges appointed by Reagan during his successful stacking of the US courts.

Along with Prosecutor Ham and Ms. Quig-Terrey, I approached the sidebar, out of sound of the others in the court.

"Mr. Springer, I understand you had a motion you wanted to make?"

"Yes, the motion is that due to the seventy-day time lapse on the retrial of such a case as this, I would submit that this case be dropped, in lieu of the fact that the time has passed."

"Counsel, what do you say?" He addressed Ham.

"This is the first I've heard of the motion. I'd like to look at the statute."

"Well, I'm going to deny the motion for the time being. Okay?" He impatiently continued.

He turned away from the microphone with a private comment meant to set me, but not the record, straight.

"Mr. Springer," he began with an air of contempt, "I want you to know that I have reviewed the transcript of your first trial and quite frankly, I can't understand how any of that testimony was admitted." He glared into my eyes as he continued, "I want you to know that this is going to be a *very different* trial." He returned to his majesty's bench.

As we turned to walk back to our table, Sue Quig-Terrey, cupped her hand over her mouth to direct the sound towards me. "We're screwed!" She informed me.

"You may go ahead and call the case," Lloyd informed the court clerk.

"The United States of America versus Rick Paul Springer, Criminal case Number CR-S-93-215 LDG(RJJ)" Anita, the court clerk announced.

"Thank you. You can go ahead and start to seat the jury, Anita," he instructed her.

The clerk proceeded to call thirty-two names and each prospective juror entered the jury box until the overflow filled other benches.

THE COURT: Ladies and gentlemen, I'm delighted to welcome you to the beginning of this jury trial. I think I know of no other area of citizen responsibility any more important, than perhaps service in the military in time of conflict.

I covered the microphone at our table while I whispered to Sue Quig-Terrey, "Well, we've got his citizen priorities pegged, convicting criminals and going to war."

THE COURT: I have been trying cases for a very long time, I have probably tried well in excess of 300 jury trials.

You'll find that I ask a lot of questions. Why do we ask all these questions? Well, to determine whether or not there's any basis for a conclusion that you cannot serve as fair or impartial jurors, and secondly, to obtain information to enable the attorneys, or in this case the defendant, to exercise what are called peremptory challenges. Peremptory challenges are challenges that permit attorneys or defendants to excuse a person who's otherwise qualified, without stating any particular reason.

THE COURT: Okay, are you employed, Mr. Cawlfield?

PROSPECTIVE JUROR CAWLFIELD: Yes, I'm a senior systems and application specialist with REECo, at the Nevada Test Site.

THE COURT: What kind of work do you do, Mr. Griffith?

PROSPECIVE JUROR GRIFFITH: I'm with the parking enforcement unit, the City of Las Vegas.

PROSPECTIVE JUROR JUSTICE: I'm a quality engineer manager for the M&O Contractor on the Yucca Mountain Site Characterization Project. My wife is a professional trainer for the same company.

PROSPECTIVE JUROR HADLOCK: My husband was a senior scientist for Hughes Aircraft Corporation.

PROSPECTIVE JUROR ELLIS: I'm the head electrician for the City Light Sign Company.

PROSPECTIVE JUROR BEROLDI: I work for EG&G special projects.

THE COURT: Well, we've got enough electricians here we could start a company of our own. Mr. Beroldi?

Reynolds Electric (REECo) and EG&G, both electric companies, are the NTS' largest local contractors. Questioning went on to reveal that the jury pool had several electricians, a Hughes aircraft scientist, two police officers, the constable's father, a border patrolman, a National Guard MP, city employees, a meter maid, several others that were friends to law enforcement and Ms. Booker.

THE COURT: Ms. Booker, you know all the police officers, don't you? And I take it, most of the US attorneys. Would that affect your judgement?

MS BOOKER: No.

THE COURT: Ladies and gentlemen, while this case is a totally different case and involves a different question, Mr. Springer was charged in an earlier case that involved former president Reagan and the breaking of an award that was being given. Are there any of you who are familiar with that case? Okay.

As in the first trial, every juror's hand went up.

THE COURT: Are any of you unable to listen to this case and keep an open mind to make a final determination as to this case that involves a totally different question? Allright. Do you want to come up to side bar please?

PROSPECTIVE JUROR JUSTICE: I'm aware of some of Mr. Springers activity, I've worked in the nuclear industry all my life, I have very strong views about that and besides being familiar with what happened with Reagan, your views and mine don't even come close.

The prospective juror addressed me personally.

THE COURT: Well, that really isn't the issue, the issue is whether or not you can make an assessment of the factual case itself, and then apply the law that I'll give to you. Do you think you could be able to disregard your own personal feelings about these matters?

JUSTICE: To be perfectly honest, I don't think so.

Mr. Ham pursued him as a juror ruthlessly.

JUSTICE: I think that's the same question I've been asked three times and I don't see why I should give a different answer than I have before.

THE COURT: Do you have any problems excusing Mr. Justice. All right, we'll excuse you, Mr. Justice. Ms Browder? Are you employed?

PROSPECTIVE JUROR BROWDER: Yes, I'm an office assistant for Reynolds Electrical and Engineeriing.

THE COURT: Any reason that you can't serve with total impartiality both towards the Government and the defendant?

BROWDER: "I don't believe so."

THE COURT: Okay, Have I missed...yes? Mr. Cawlfield.

PROSPECTIVE JUROR CAWLFIELD: Yes, your Honor, I was trying to wave in the affirmative at that...Well, as a test site worker, we tend not to be entirely, you know sympathetic to our —

THE COURT: Well, sympathy doesn't play any part in this kind of a case.

CAWLFIELD: Sure. I would do my best to be impartial but I just want to point out that I come from the opposite side of the camp here.

THE COURT: Well, we appreciate your being candid and well, I don't know if we need to put ourselves in one camp or the other. The important question is could you assume him innocent until he's proven guilty by the government and follow the instructions of the court.

CAWLFIELD: Yes, I believe I could.

MR. SPRINGER: I'd like to ask a question. From what you understand of the nuclear issue could you hear the facts that may be presented contrary to those beliefs and consider those facts unbiased?

THE COURT: Well now, let me just take a moment. That isn't at issue here. What's at issue is whether or not you violated the particular statute, and that's where the focus of this trial is going to be.

CAWLFIELD: I believe I can hear the matter at hand.

THE COURT: Okay. Anything further?

MR. SPRINGER: I guess I'm confused about —

THE COURT: Well, if you're confused, the issue is not whether nuclear testing is good or bad, the question is whether or not there was a legitimate reason for your failure to appear.

MR. SPRINGER: And they may be one and the same in this case.

THE COURT: Well, you'll be permitted some latitude, but that's the issue that I'm going to require be addressed. Do you understand?

MR. SPRINGER: I understand that I will be granted some latitude in that.

THE COURT: Okay. Have any of you formed an opinion as to the guilt or innocence of the defendant in this case? Mr. Alvarez, did you serve in the military before?

PROSPECTIVE JUROR ALVAREZ: No, I didn't. Yes, I did six years.

THE COURT: What branch did you serve in?

ALVAREZ: I was an M-1 tanker in the army.

THE COURT: Okay, Mr. Beroldi?

PROSPECTIVE JUROR BEROLDI: I served in the US Air Force on a classified project that was later the Stealth Fighter.

THE COURT: I see, okay. Well, I was a fighter pilot in the Air Force. So you're in the right branch. Would that affect your judgement?

BEROLDI: Not that — other than the fact I've worked at the Nevada Test site before, things like that.

THE COURT: Mr. Gonzales, do you want to come to side bar please?

PROSPECTIVE JUROR GONZALES: Okay, I have a doctor's appointment for chemotherapy, I have cancer —

THE COURT: Oh.

GONZALES: And I don't know if I'll be sick or whatever during the next couple of days or not.

THE COURT: When is the appointment, Mr.

GONZALES: It's at 1:30 today.

THE COURT: Anybody have a problem with excusing Mr. Gonzales?

As Mr. Gonzales passed he put his hand on my forearm and gave a gentle squeeze worth a thousand words.

THE COURT: Anyone else? Mr. Schiller?

PROSPECTIVE JUROR SCHILLER: I was a nuclear weapons technician for four years in the air force. No, I don't think it would affect my judgement.

THE COURT: Mr. Abdalkarim? You have a problem with this case?

PROSPECTIVE JUROR ABDALKARIM: Well, I don't consider the young man to be my peer. You know my sensibilities are strictly Islamic, and I would think of him in that light. I worry about the moral issue of my judging him to start with. You know I would much rather — really make a mistake on someone who is innocent, I'd much rather have the guilty go free.

In my book, the Koran, it says that," *Mr. Abdalkarim spoke in his native tongue,* "It means I wash my hands, I take refuge, you know because the weight of judgement upon another human being is very, very – I would hate to –"

THE COURT: You're telling us you simply do not want to make a moral judgement. All right, you'll be dismissed.

MR. HAM: Your Honor, may we approach the sidebar? Your Honor, How many peremptory challenges are we allowed?

THE COURT: Six.

MR. HAM: I understand by statute there should only be three.

THE COURT: Oh I'm sorry. I just assumed that we were trying a felony. We're not trying a felony? I never try misdemeanor cases.

MR. HAM: Well, according to statute it's three and the defendant is entitled to four.

THE COURT: Do you have a twelve person – I've never tried a misdemeanor.

MR. HAM: Yes, twelve person. It's correct, your Honor.

THE COURT: Well, I guess that makes sense if the underlying charge is a misdemeanor. Well, we've gone through a nice exercise and met a lot of interesting people. Well, we have now stipulated to the jury.

Judge George went on to instruct the jury in the mechanics of their duty, the locations of cafeterias, the rest rooms, how to line up to enter the court room, etc.

THE COURT: Faithful performance by you of your duties is vital to the administration of justice. The law that's applicable to the case will be contained in the instructions that I'll give you during the course of the trial as I'm doing now and it will be your duty to follow all of the instructions."

From time to time, it may be the duty of the attorneys to make objections, and when they do, it will be my duty to rule on those objections and to determine whether or not you can consider certain testimony or evidence.

And you mustn't be offended by either side that chooses to object, they will act to ask the Court to make such determinations, and you don't want to keep count of how many objections was made by one side or the other. You must not concern yourself with the objections or with the court's reasons for those rulings. You must not consider testimony or exhibits to which objections are sustained, or which have been ordered stricken.

* * * * *

*"Well known for their pioneer work with radium, both
Marie Curie and her daughter, Irene, died of leukemia".*
— Helen Caldicott, <u>Nuclear Madness</u> 1978

* * * * *

THE COURT: Counsel, can the parties stipulate to the presence of the jury. This is day two in a jury trial. Ladies and gentlemen, we will start the process with opening statements, Mr. Ham.

Mr. Ham's opening remarks were a repeat of our first trial while he attempted to accent, ' what this case is not about.'

MR. HAM: I suspect the defendant will use this opportunity to express to you his political and spiritual beliefs. And his political and spiritual beliefs may be well and good, and in many respects may be laudable, but that is not why we are here today.

This case is simply about one thing, the defendant's obligation to obey the laws of this land as those laws are determined by the democratic process and not by Mr. Springer's determination.

Ladies and gentlemen, at the conclusion of this case, I will ask you to return a verdict of guilty for the crime of failure to surrender.

Judge Lloyd George would not allow Quig-Terrey and I to split the opening and closing remarks.

OPENING STATEMENT BY MS. QUIG-TERREY:

May it please the court, my name is Susan Quig-Terrey. I am serving as an assistant or advisory counsel for Mr. Springer, who's representing himself in this proceeding. Mr. Springer has a deep and abiding respect for the Constitution and believes in putting into action—imposing them on our daily lives.

Mr. Springer is charged with failure to surrender for service of sentence on June 2nd, 1993. At that time, the evidence will establish that there was a crisis facing the country regarding the issue of nuclear testing. There had been a brief moratorium of nine months which was about to expire. There was every indication that the Clinton administration intended to renew testing. They were under tremendous pressure from the defense industry and the military. Mr. Springer and other nuclear activists were in a state of panic and alarm. His testimony and other evidence will establish that he had no choice but to act in this situation.

In order to establish this, we are going to have to open up Mr.

Springer as a man, his philosophical beliefs, his spiritual beliefs, everything that comes together in him that mandated his course of action. You will have to step outside yourselves to analyze what motivated Mr. Springer.

Mr. Springer will testify concerning his extensive knowledge of nuclear testing, of the deception by the Department of Energy, of his awareness that the media and the DOE were hiding facts concerning the dangers and the likelihood of the resumption of testing. He will testify that he had every reasonable basis to perceive the resumption of nuclear testing as a threat to the very existence of his country and his own life as well as everyone around him. That's an uncontrollable circumstance that can actually prevent a person from surrendering, no less than a car accident or an earthquake. Mr. Springer will testify that the magnitude of harm at risk by the resumption of nuclear testing far exceeded an earthquake.

The evidence in this case will show that Mr. Springer, on the anniversary of Hiroshima and Nagasaki bombings, went public, went to television stations and to newspapers here in Las Vegas, knowing full well that the federal authorities knew he was in town and would incarcerate him. He was making a surrender in a manner of a public statement to get his message across.

We would therefore urge the jury, to determine that Mr. Springer, given who he is, his beliefs and what has motivated his existence for the past several years, had no choice but to continue fighting the resumption of nuclear testing. Thank you.

THE COURT: Thank you Ms. Quig-Terrey. Call your first witness, Mr. Ham.

MR. HAM: My first witness will be case agent Marshall Davey.

The prosecution presented the same testimony but Judge Lloyd had read the first transcript and knew what to expect.

Q   Did you obtain information on August 9th of '93 from a confidential informant?

A   Yes. Part of my investigation was to develop informants. If I couldn't talk Rick in, I wanted to find out where he was. A confidential informant stated he was in town and he could—-

Q   Did you forward the information to any other agency?

A   Yes, the Secret Service was assisting the Marshals in finding Mr. Springer.

Q   And do you know if on that date he was in fact arrested by the Secret Service.

A   Yes. He was arrested within about fifteen minutes of my first becoming aware that he was in town.

MR. HAM: No further questions, Your Honor.

THE COURT: Okay, cross examination, Mr. Springer.

BY MR. SPRINGER: Good morning to all, Mr. Davies, you've been with the Marshals for 23 years. Would you consider yourself an expert in your field?

A   An expert? I'm an experienced deputy.

Q   Thank you. Are you being paid to be here?

A   I'm on duty. Yes, I'm being paid.

Q   You are the officer that originally booked me, is that correct?

MR. HAM: Your Honor, I object to the relevancy of the booking for the initial arrest.

THE COURT: What is the relevance, Mr. Springer?

Judge George wasn't going to let me even get close.

THE COURT: Mr. Springer, please move on.

MR. HAM: Your Honor, the governments next witness will be Curt Alcorn. I think he'll be here in a moment. I apologize for the wait.

THE COURT: That's fine, Mr. Ham. If you would like to stand up and stretch, you are welcome to do so.

Two more US Marshals were sworn in and testified to documents regarding the surrender and the fact that I had not surrendered on June 2nd. The prosecution again flew in from the Shasta jail, county sheriff Charles McCorison, to testify that I had not surrendered there. Next was Bill McAfee, special agent to the Secret Service.

MR. HAM: Mr. McAfee, upon receiving information from the US Marshals on August 9th, did the Secret Service respond and what did you do?

A   Yes, myself and SA Mike Fithen responded to the area of the Las Vegas Review Journal. We thought he might possibly attempt to gain an interview.

Q   All right, where did you go and what did you see?

A   We generally cruised through the area of the Review Journal and as we started to exit, we noticed the subject who was in fact, Mr. Springer, walking towards the entrance.

Q   And —

A   We stopped our vehicle, identified ourselves and placed him under arrest.

MR. HAM: No further questions, your Honor.

THE COURT: Okay, cross examination.

BY MR. SPRINGER: Good morning, Mr. McAfee. Do you remember if I made any attempt to escape from the situation?

A   No, you didn't. Not at all.

Q   Did I cooperate with you officers at that time.

A   Yes, sir.

Q   Thank you.

MR. HAM: I'd like to redirect, Your Honor. Mr. McAfee, how big are you and how much do you weigh?

A   I'm six one and weigh two ten.

Q   What about agent Fithen?

A   Agent Fithen, I believe, is six three and weighs two hundred and eighty pounds.

MR. HAM: Nothing further, Your Honor.

Judge George called the attorneys and I to sidebar. He looked as though he had some expectation.

"Do you have anything for me before you start your case?" He demanded impatiently.

I didn't want to make my renewed motion for expert testimony at sidebar where the jury couldn't even hear but it seemed I had no option.

"Did you have a motion that you wanted to make?" Sue Quig-Terrey asked, prompting me.

"Yes, I feel due to the phenomenal release of new information from the Department of Energy that it is time to resubmit our motion for expert testimony in this case to show that my beliefs were founded and that my actions were justified, that the uncontrollable circumstance did exist, and that the US government was considering a restart of a program that risked polluting our people again."

"Counsel?" George looked at Ham to assist in his rubber stamp `DENIED'.

Rule 702 Whether the situation is a proper one for the use of expert testimony is to be determined on the basis of assisting the trier. There is no more certain test for determining when experts may be used than the common sense inquiry whether the untrained layman would be qualified to determine intelligently and to the best possible degree the particular issue without enlightenment from those having specialized understanding of the subject involved in dispute."
— Federal Rules of Evidence

THE COURT: Ladies and gentlemen, the Government has now rested their case. The defendant may now call witnesses and he may testify himself and if he does he's to be judged as any other witness. And I'll give you the standard by which you can make assessments with respect to witnesses.

MS. QUIG-TERREY: The defense would call Terry Tempest Williams. Could you tell us your occupation please?

TERRY TEMPEST-WILLIAMS, DEFENDANT'S WITNESS, IS SWORN

A   I'm a naturalist at the Utah Museum of Natural History and an author of seven books, two for children, a book of poetry and other creative nonfiction works about natural history and my family.

Q   Are you involved in issues concerning nuclear testing?

A   I have been. It's something that has concerned my family. I'm six generations Morman. My family is very conservative Republican and we have not been involved in these issues, yet nine women in my family have all had cancer.

MR. HAM: Your Honor

THE WITNESS: Seven are dead.

MR. HAM: Your Honor

THE COURT: Just a moment.

MR. HAM: I don't see how this is relevant to Mr. Springer's mental process.

THE COURT: How is it relevant?

MS. QUIG-TERREY: I was simply trying to get some background into her perception of the status of nuclear testing in June of '93 to provide evidence that there was a crisis.

THE COURT: Well then, you ask questions and get responses.

MS. QUIG-TERREY: How long have you been involved in nuclear testing issues?

A   Since the death of my Mother and my grandmothers and my aunts when we realized–

MR. HAM: Your Honor, that not responsive.

A   My Mother died in 1987.

THE COURT: I feel that you have an anxiousness to go beyond the question. Just listen to me. You may proceed counsel.

BY MS QUIG-TERREY:

Q   Could you tell us the status of the testing of nuclear weapons in the US in June of '93?

A   We were very concerned and anxious that the Clinton Administration may lift the moratorium because of the commission reports and shutdowns of military bases, the controversy around the gays. We were worried that this might be a wild card that Clinton might give away. So in June, it looked like nuclear testing would resume to the detriment of our health.

Q   How long have you known Mr. Springer?

A   I met Rick Springer in New York City at the Comprehensive Test Ban Treaty meeting in January of 1991.

Q   In the summer of '93, did you discuss with him the US policies concerning the resumption of testing?

A   We had corresponded through letters and we both shared our concerns
      of what our government might reopen and our concern about our
      health, of ourselves, our families, and the health of the land.

MR. HAM: Your Honor, at this time. If I may object? It seems irrelevant.

MS. QUIG-TERREY: Did he discuss surrendering with you?

A   In our correspondence, you know, he was –

MR. HAM: Your Honor –

THE WITNESS: I'm just trying to answer the question.

THE COURT: The question is a very simple one. Did he discuss with you
      surrendering?"

THE WITNESS: Yes

BY MS. QUIG-TERREY:

      Can you tell me when these discussions took place?

A   It was during June.

Q   All right, can you tell me the substance of what Mr. Springer told you
      concerning his intentions?

MR. HAM: Your Honor–

*While the court had admonished the jurors not to keep track of who had
the most objections, I did. Court transcripts reveal 51 prosecution objections
within less than three hours of defense testimony.*

MS. QUIG-TERREY: Could you state the reasons for surrendering in Mr.
      Springer's letters?

A   Yes, the letters stated that my family's story had a great impact on his
      actions, and that he was concerned about the moral issue of surrender-
      ing because of this window of time of great uncertainty. So as a result of
      my family's story, the Clan of the One Breasted Women of the women in
      my family all dying because of nuclear testing –

MR. HAM: I object, Your Honor.

THE COURT: Sustained, it will be stricken.

MS. QUIG-TERREY: Thank you, I have no further questions.

MR. SPRINGER: The defense calls Bill Chisholm.

      Through numerous interruptions, Bill attempted to provide a holistic foun-
dation for his activism and a basis for support of my actions.

BY MR. SPRINGER: Could you state your profession please?

A   Well, it's a diverse background. I was a firefighter for BLM. I've also
      been a certified yoga instructor for seventeen years. I was an emergency
      medical technician, a wilderness survival guide, during which time I
      worked with disadvantaged youths in the mountains, using Native
      American survival and spiritual skills to help these kids learn self esteem
      and self control. For the last ten years, I've worked for the Federal
      Emergency Management Agency on disasters throughout the United

States and it's territories. My main function is damage assessment and hazard mitigation, trying to prevent these disasters from happening.

Q   During our relationship, could you explain the details of what we imparted to youth.

A   Well, we tried to teach them about two wildernesses. One was the wilderness outside, the natural environment, to respect and take care of the environment. We tried to teach them you had to balance your needs with the needs of the future generations. And because most of the kids we worked with were abused, we tried to teach about the inner wilderness, to give them the skills and self-discipline to go on and face that aspect of life.

Q   Mr. Ham, in his opening remarks, said that an earthquake was justification for a failure to surrender. If I was allowed expert testimony, it can be proven, in fact, scientifically, that indeed nuclear testing has been related to earthquakes since 1945.

THE COURT: Let me remind the jury, incidentally, questions are not evidence. And so any of these – the dialogue that you're listening to is not evidence for you to consider.

MR. SPRINGER: That's why we would like the response from the witness.

THE COURT: Take a moment to tell us what your effort has been but abbreviate it.

THE WITNESS: Okay, well, I started asking a whole lot of questions. I wrote congressmen trying to get answers, but what I came up with was more questions. I organized conservation groups in Idaho. I joined anti-nuclear groups. I ran for political office five times, trying to force the dialogue on this topic but always the information was held back. Then finally I found myself, somewhat similar to Rick, being involved in civil resistance and coming before the court.

The thing you have to understand, the radioactive nucleides are very dangerous and however they get in.

MR. HAM: Your Honor, again. This is not responsive to the question.

THE COURT: Objection is sustained. What else is it you have that you want to ask this witness?

MR. SPRINGER: What importance do you place on the power and responsibility of the individual in preventing these disasters?

A   I think there's a whole series of things morally and spiritually that says that we have to be responsible. That has even been manifested in international law such as the Nuremburg Principles that said that if you believe that something is wrong and a danger, no matter what sort of authoritarian figures above you–

MR. HAM: Your Honor, Again, I object.

THE WITNESS: – you have to stand up..

THE COURT: Sustained, Sustained, the objection is sustained. It will be stricken. Do you have anything further of this witness?

BY MR. SPRINGER: From your experience, do you believe that I was justified in perceiving an emergency by the potential restart of nuclear testing?

MR. HAM: I object.

THE COURT: Sustained.

MR. SPRINGER: Have you been personally imprisoned for your efforts to halt nuclear weapons testing?

MR. HAM: Your Honor, I object to –

THE COURT: Sustained. I don't know what that has to do with this case.

MR. SPRINGER: What it has --

THE COURT: The objection is sustained.

MR. SPRINGER: It's a fascinating concept of a defense, I must say. Mr. Chisholm, do you believe that you can be as effective in jail as out of jail in achieving these goals?

THE WITNESS: No, you have to have the ability to move around and provide leadership. I myself have experience in Idaho where I had to stand in front of a nuclear waste truck—

MR. HAM: Your Honor, I object.

THE WITNESS: —that effort galvanized the –

MR. HAM: I object to that.

THE COURT: The objection is sustained.

MR. SPRINGER: Mr. Chisholm, thank you.

MS. QUIG-TERREY: We would call Corbin Harney.

Corbin Harney was sworn and gave his name. He bowed to begin his own prayer of honesty. He began in his own tongue, an ancient Western Shoshone prayer. But the court was determined to interrupt even that.

A   Let me say a thing.

THE COURT: There is no question, Mr. Harney. Mr. Harney, there are no questions. If you will stand.

THE WITNESS: I'm talking with you in my heart. I say nah [phonetic].

Corbin was finally allowed to finish his prayer.

THE COURT: Oh, go ahead.

BY MS. QUIG-TERREY: Mr. Harney, you've previously stated that you are the spiritual leader of the Western Shoshone Nation. Could you tell me what your responsibilities are?

A   Well, this might be a little longer to talk, but the spiritual leader means that I have to be protecting all the life on this Mother Earth, the life, the water, the air, all the living things. Those are my concern, those are the things I try to teach my young people. Today, we are all included in this as a people. We're all concerned with our water.

MR. HAM: Your Honor, this doesn't seem to be responsive to the question.

MS. QUIG-TERREY: Could you tell me what your day to day tasks are?

A   In the morning, early in the morning, at sunrise, we have our ceremonies, thanking the Earth, the water that we drink, the air that we breathe, the Mother Earth that we walk upon. The Mother Earth is the provider for all the living things. Those are the things that I have to thank.

Q   And do you instruct followers in the principles that you just set forth?

A   People are beginning to understand why the spiritual leaders are important on this Earth. We have to take care of what we got left. From the nuclear testing, I'm against that all the time. Those are the things that's ruining our Mother Earth. Today, throughout the —

MR. HAM: Your Honor —

THE WITNESS: —the world —

MR. HAM: Your Honor, again

THE COURT: Just a moment.

THE WITNESS: We don't have much water left.

BY MS. QUIG-TERREY: Do you know the defendant, Rick Springer?

A   Yes, you know he's been working with me for quite a while.

Q   Have you instructed him on the tenets of the Western Shoshone faith?

A   Yes, I have.

Q   And do you know whether he is an adherent to those tenets?

MR. HAM: Your Honor.

THE WITNESS: Yes, he does.

BY MS. QUIG-TERREY: Could you describe briefly what the Western Shoshone faith requires it's followers to do to care for the environment?

A   Like I said, we got to protect what we got, all animal life, the bird lifes, our water, our air, our Mother Earth. I taught him his part, to teach his people to take care, to stand together as human people throughout the world.

MS. QUIG-TERREY: I have no further questions, your honor.

I took the stand before my second jury and told the story again. The tears were no longer there as in the first trial. The aggressive stance of Judge Lloyd George created a more combative environment.

MR. HAM: Your Honor, at this point, I object to the relevance?

THE COURT: Well, in any event, and I think his responses have not been responsive to the questions that have been asked—

MS. QUIG-TERREY: Your Honor, I would ask for a little leeway. I mean the essence of this case is—

THE COURT: You have been given a great deal of leeway, counsel. Move on.

MS. QUIG-TERREY: Did there come a time when you were arrested by federal authorities?

A   Yes, I was arrested by the Secret Service for attempting to announce a

nuclear bomb test to the world, in which I appeared on stage with
Ronald Reagan and broke a crystal eagle to get attention to the fact that
they were planning a nuclear bomb test the next day. It was to my
utmost surprise that Ronald Reagan was even there.

MR. HAM: Your Honor, I object. That's irrelevant.

THE COURT: It is irrelevant.

THE WITNESS: No, this is highly relevant.

THE COURT: Now just a moment.

THE WITNESS: Incredibly relevant. That is why I am here today.

THE COURT: Well, now you're the witness and I'm the judge and I have
ruled that it is irrelevant.

MS. QUIG-TERREY: Have you received any instruction in the principles of
civil resistance?

A   I studied Gandhi and Martin Luther King Jr. I realized that nonviolence is
the only hope for existence on earth.

MS. QUIG-TERREY: Did the instruction you receive impact your decision to
surrender?

A   Unquestionably, I believe there is a spiritual, moral mandate, from what
I learned from the Western Shoshone, to care for this planet. Synony-
mous with our constitution, it is my duty, my spiritual duty. I labored
over this decision. Like everybody, I want to validate our system. I want
to believe in America. I knew that by denying a court order to surrender
I was invalidating this system yet I searched my own soul. I looked at
international, moral, spiritual law and I said no, I have to do all in my
power to stop a restart of nuclear weapons testing.

THE COURT: You've answered the question.

THE WITNESS: Yes, I did.

MS. QUIG-TERREY: What was the nature of your developing plan?

A   Well, my plan was to continue petitioning the government until I got
arrested or we got a continuation of the moratorium. Then I could deal
with the court system because we wouldn't have the threat of nuclear
bombs.

Q   Was it always your intention to surrender once you felt the situation had
been resolved?

A   I have innumerable people, Ramsey Clark one of them, who would be
willing to testify that I was planning —

MR. HAM: Your Honor, objection to—

THE COURT: Sustained. It will be stricken. Let's move on.

MS. QUIG-TERREY: What did you do after the events commemorating
Hiroshima and Nagasaki?

A   I was blessed with two hours with Dan Berrigan, a renowned priest
from New York City. Dan Berrigan has been imprisoned on many

occasions for efforts—

MR. HAM: Your Honor, I object.

THE WITNESS: to stop nuclearism.

THE COURT: Sustained.

Q   When you began the media coverage, were you aware that you were likely to be arrested?

A   There is no question about it. I was going to be on television and in the newspapers. I was going from station to station. It's on film with Channel 3, me being asked, "Aren't you concerned they're going to arrest you," and I said, "Of course, they're going to arrest me."

Q   Was it your intent to permit them to arrest you?

A   It certainly was. My hope was that I would communicate with as much media as possible.

Q   Why didn't you just go to the US Marshals office?

A   If I'm going to be arrested, I need to utilize it. I'm sorry to say that the media has been blockaded to the issue of nuclear weapons for a long time, and we have just now seen lately—"

MR. HAM: Your Honor, I object. This is not—

THE WITNESS: the horrors—

THE COURT: Just a moment. Sustained.

MS. QUIG-TERREY: Prior to your decisions not to surrender, did you have knowledge of the plutonium injections and the —

MR. HAM: Your Honor.

MS. QUIG-TERREY: The matters that are just now—

MR. HAM: Your Honor, I object—

THE COURT: Just a moment"

MS QUIG-TERREY: — being disclosed?

MR. HAM: It's totally irrelevant.

THE COURT: Sustained

MS. QUIG-TERREY: I have no further questions.

THE COURT: Mr. Ham do you have any questions of the witness?

MR. HAM: Yes, I have quite a few questions, Your Honor. You did not surrender at the Hiroshima ceremony. Is that correct?

A   That is correct.

Q   It is also correct that you did not surrender at any point. You were arrested, isn't that correct?

A   Well, you asked a question about those two hundred and eighty pound police officers, but you didn't ask how fast they run.

Q   You're — Mr. Springer, that's not responsive.

A   I realized it was the Secret Service.

Q   Mr. Springer—

THE COURT: Mr. Springer—

THE WITNESS: and I said fine and I surrendered.

THE COURT: Mr. Springer, Mr. Springer.

MR. SPRINGER: Yes, sir.

THE COURT: Respond to the questions.

MR. SPRINGER: I believe I did respond.

THE COURT: Mr. Springer, you seem to have an overwhelming desire to run everything.

MR. SPRINGER: That's your opinion, sir.

THE COURT: Just a moment. I have an obligation to manage this court, Mr. Springer.

MR. SPRINGER: I think you have.

THE COURT: And I intend to manage it as I feel I must.

MR. SPRINGER: Yes, for a particular conviction.

THE COURT: And I'm telling you, Mr. Springer, listen to the questions and now we're going to finish with your testimony.

MR. SPRINGER: I am answering the questions to the best of my ability.

Mr. Ham spent the next half hour of precious court time retracing my summer fugitive journey with the precision of a travel agent. He used a classroom size map of the United States to draw a red line on the bicycle route I had traveled.

Q   And each of those towns had law enforcement officers, is that correct?

A   I was advised by Ramsey Clark that communicating with the federal government was inappropriate at this point. I was responding to Ramsey Clark's suggestion.

Q   That's not responsive.

A   But it's the truth.

THE COURT: Well, it's not responsive.

MR. SPRINGER: He's trying to make a point and I'm responding.

THE COURT: Mr. Springer, I have no intention of turning the operation of this court over to you.

MR. SPRINGER: I don't believe you are. It's in your hands.

THE COURT: You respond to these questions as directed.

MR. SPRINGER: I'm doing the best I can.

THE COURT: Well, you pay attention.

MR. SPRINGER: I am paying attention.

"What, do I look like I'm sleeping through my own lynching party?" I thought.

THE COURT: You may proceed counsel.

MR. HAM: Each of these towns had law enforcement. Is that correct?

A   I assume so.

Q   But you did not surrender, did you?

A   Before the moratorium, no.

Mr. Ham introduced another exhibit: a large calendar to show the dates of events.

Q   You were going to surrender under conditions which in your mind would bring about significant press coverage, is that correct?

A   Correct

Q   So that was a condition you placed on your surrender?

A   The condition I placed on my surrender was that I would do what I could to continue the effort to stop nuclear weapons, yes.

MR. HAM: I have no further questions, Your Honor.

THE COURT: Redirect? Ms Quig-Terrey.

MS. QUIG-TERREY: Yes, thank you. Mr. Springer, why didn't you contact the federal court or federal authorities after June 2nd, 1993?

A   Because my communications with former Attorney General Ramsey Clark indicated that the court was not receptive in any way to communication once you had become a fugitive.

Q   After the extension of the moratorium, did you believe the threat of resumed nuclear testing had been eliminated?

A   Certainly not totally, but partially.

Q   After the extension of the moratorium, did you believe it was important to arrange a public surrender?

A   Unquestionably so.

Q   Why did you take a job working in Colorado for one week?

A   Because I was broke.

Q   Is media coverage important to the effort to halt nuclear testing?

A   I think we've witnessed by recent coverage, it's everything to public awareness.

MS. QUIG-TERREY: I have no further questions, Your Honor.

"The irony we fail to appreciate is that the more justice the people enjoy, the fewer crimes they commit. Crime is the natural offspring of an unjust society."
— Gerry Spence, <u>With Justice for None</u> 1989

Henry David Thoreau claimed that, "In an unjust society a just man's place is in jail." Judge George agreed with him

THE COURT: "You know, I'm a fan of Thoreau and I read Thoreau when I was young, and I understand the position taken in some of these matters, but one must be prepared to suffer the consequences of civil disobedience."

My personal belief is that we are ready to move beyond Thoreau's acceptance of an unjust society. It's time to decide that if an individual's actions can be proven to be in the greater interests of the whole then they should not be punished.

MR. SPRINGER: Certainly the reason that we asked for a jury trial is so that the jury could make that decision. I've requested my right to a fully informed—

THE COURT: Congress may have already made that decision.

MR. SPRINGER: Could you wait until my sentences are completed?

The anger in Judge George was clearly evident. His pink skin turned a couple of shades closer to red and his voice was just shy of a yell.

THE COURT: Well, I intend to ask you questions as you proceed. My position is a little different than yours, Mr. Springer.

MR. SPRINGER: You don't have to respect me, but I'm supposed to respect you. Furthermore, Mr. Pro in the last—

THE COURT: Judge Pro!

MR. SPRINGER: Judge Pro allowed the jury to decide. On that premise, I think it behooves the court to err to the side of justice in this case and allow the jury to make—

THE COURT: I have an obligation to decide on the side of justice and you know justice includes the whole process.

MR. SPRINGER: Exactly, my point.

THE COURT: Well, I don't think that is your point.

MR. SPRINGER: Well, we certainly disagree, don't we?

THE COURT: You think with a narrow focus. I think we do disagree.

MR. SPRINGER: I requested a trial by jury, not by judge, and I would like the jury to decide on it.

THE COURT: What does the government have to say?

MR. HAM: I feel this defense is totally inapplicable as applied to the facts here. It is the Courts right and duty, when there is insufficient evidence to present this type of defense, that it not be presented to a jury because it would simply misguide or confuse a jury.

THE COURT: Well, I'm not convinced that the moratorium creates some uncontrollable circumstance in the first place.

MR. SPRINGER: Why am I not surprised?

The real trial before judge continued at the sidebar as Ham and George agreed with each other on why to disallow the uncontrollable circumstance defense thereby disallowing any defense.

MR. SPRINGER: I think you are setting a particular time frame here. You say ten days to surrender is extreme, forty three is absurd. But you live in a different world.

THE COURT: I hope so.

MR. SPRINGER: You're not traveling by bicycle. You do not operate with the minimal budget that I do. It takes an entirely different time frame.

THE COURT: You could have gotten on a telephone and called within minutes.

MR. SPRINGER: I did testify about Ramsey Clark's suggestion that it's a waste of time to talk to the court.

THE COURT: Ramsey Clark doesn't run this court or, thank goodness, the country.

Judge George's irate contempt was not hidden.

MR. SPRINGER: He was the attorney general and a man I respect.

THE COURT: Well, I don't have any problem with you respecting, but I do have a problem with what I think is a dishonest approach to the whole matter.

MR. SPRINGER: And that's why I asked for a jury trial because I don't want to be tried by you as we are now.

THE COURT: Well, we'll see.

* * * * *

At 2:45 the jurors entered the courtroom as they had been taught, the rows filling up, each one standing until the last entered and stood before their seat. They sat together, orchestrated like a choir. Judge George entered and immediately called a sidebar with the attorneys. He condescended to allow one final defense witness.

MS. QUIG-TERREY: We'll call Alain Richard. Could you state your calling and your background briefly.

"Yeah," he responded with his thick choppy french accent intact.

A   I am a priest of the religious order commonly called Franceescons. I leeve in thees contry for twenty-one years. I have been involved in meeny deeferent countrees or conteenent in nonviolent action, and that what brought me in contact with Rick Springer.

As one of the founders and administrators of Pace Bene, we organize retreats and trainings workshops in nonviolence.

Q   Have you had an opportunity to train the defendant Rick Springer in these seminars?

A   Yeah, I had two deeferent opportunities. First before he started the Hundred Monkeys group he came to clarify in his mind what he wanted to do. Then after the Broadcasting convention he attended a one week retreat on the spearitual journey of nonviolence."

MR. HAM: Excuse me, Your Honor, I don't see the relevance. Civil disobedience is not a defense in this case.

THE COURT: Well, in any event the father has testified that the defendant has received instruction about nonviolence. Is there anything further?

MS. QUIG-TERREY: Do your seminars address civil resistance?

A   Oh yes, of course.

MR. HAM: Your Honor, I'll renew my objection.

THE COURT: Let's move on.

THE WITNESS: We take a very spearitual approach but at the same time veery technical. We, of course, inseest on the fact that moral law is over any kind of law, as Doctor King proclaim it very strongly from the jail of Birmingham, or Mahatma Gandhi say it very clearly when he was a member of the bar of London.

MS QUIG-TERREY: All right. Thank you, Father Richard. I have no further questions.

Mr. Ham gave a repeat performance of his closing remarks from the first trial. He concluded as if he was auditioning for the Charles Manson prosecution team. I approached the podium and laid down a few tattered scraps that had made it through the downstairs gauntlet.

MR. SPRINGER: First off, I suppose I should begin with an apology to the jury and apologies to Mr. George for my shortness here in court today. I have to confess that six months of imprisonment has already had an effect on me. I am emotionally exhausted from the experience, and it's been a great struggle being involved in the prison system and watching the inequities and injustices—

MR. HAM: Your Honor, I have to object to this type of statement.

MR. SPRINGER: The apology is completed. Thank you.

THE COURT: Go ahead. Let's move on, Mr. Springer.

MR. SPRINGER: You have a phenomenal responsibility here and you have a great challenge, and it can't be overestimated. Mr. Ham speaks, he says, for the US government. I say that you are the US government and you have the opportunity to prove that. This is not just about a failure to surrender.

International law states that "Complicity in the commission of a crime against peace, a war crime, or a crime against humanity is a crime under international law. I cannot be complicit. I know the facts, I know what's going on. I have a responsibility with that information.

In 1899 the nations of the world got together at The Hague and they signed the Hague Conventions, deciding that weapons that cause unnecessary suffering were illegal. The US was a party to that treaty. They also decided that poisonous weapons were illegal. Nuclear weapons are both poisonous and they cause unnecessary suffering. They also decided that weapons that cannot distinguish between civilians and soldiers were illegal.

MR. HAM: Your Honor, I object. It is the Court which determines the law.

MR. SPRINGER: Well, will you tell them.

THE COURT: It's evident that you have no intention to follow the instructions of the Court, or I suppose, anyone else. The jury is instructed to disregard any such discussion.

I began again, somehow unable to lay down. Instead, I willed more power to my voice. I wasn't hiding my anger anymore.

President Clinton stated, "It is outrageous for the government to have rules and regulations which take peoples money from them and spend it on things that cannot be justified." Vice President Al Gore said, `This government has grown stale, wasteful, inefficient, bureaucratic and is failing the American people." Hazel Oleary says, "It left me appalled, shocked and deeply saddened. It is apparent that informed consent could not have taken place." Former Interior Secretary Stewart Udall said of the Navaho uranium miners, "These people have been sacrificed in the name of national—"

MR. HAM: Your Honor.

THE COURT: Well, there's no evidence of any of these matters.

I was whipped but I wasn't falling down. I kept arguing though it was obvious I was on my way to the mat. Every paragraph was interrupted with another 'objection sustained.' The jury had been signalled constantly by George and Ham, in word and tone, that I was a guilty impudent upstart. And of disrespect for the judicial, the penal and the nuclear system, I was guilty.

THE COURT: Do you wish to respond, Mr. Ham?

MR. HAM: Thank you. I'm going to be very brief. Ladies and gentlemen. I think the issues are clear. The Government in this case is not afraid. Nuremburg is not the law here, Nuremburg does not supercede our democratic process.

MR. SPRINGER: I object. I object, He is talking to the law and this is not true. International law is national law, and that is an outright lie.

THE COURT: The court will instruct the jury here.

MR. SPRINGER: Well, would you instruct him that international law is national law?

THE COURT: Well, I'm telling this jury that they will follow the instructions that I give them.

MR. SPRINGER: Could you tell him not to tell things that are not true.

THE COURT: Well, international law is not involved in this case.

MR. SPRINGER: Of course it is. I am mandated by international law as I've read. It's the same as all the Native American treaties. Treaties are the supreme law of the land.

THE COURT: Fine, Mr. Springer, The jury will be instructed. Let's move on.

MR. SPRINGER: Excuse me, I thought I was in America. I'm sorry.

Mr. Ham gave his obedience rap. The court dove into jury instructions as if late for a tour of the putting greens.

THE COURT: You must follow the directions that the Court will give you.

And one of my functions is to address those issues and to tell you what issues are to be considered and determined by you.

Now with that in mind, I am going to instruct you as to the law. It is your duty to find the facts from all the evidence in the case. To those facts you must apply the law as I give it to you. You must follow the law in these instructions whether you agree with it or not. And you must not be influenced by any personal likes or dislikes, opinions, prejudices, or sympathy. That means you must decide the case solely on the evidence before you. You will recall that you took an oath promising to do so at the beginning of this case.

Another factor that is not a jury determination is punishment. The punishment provided by law for this crime is for the court to decide.

The jury retired to commence deliberations at 4:00 P.M. and were excused for the evening at 6:00, instructed to return in the morning at 9:00 A.M.

* * * * *

*"Reported confidence in the Criminal Justice System...
Over half of all groups reported very little or none."
— Sourcebook of Criminal Justice Statistics, 1993*

* * * * *

I followed Sue out the swinging courtroom doors.

"Well, it's out of our hands now. I'm gonna run over to the DOE office for the press conference."

She expressed her concern that I was supposed to be in her custody if I was not at the halfway house.

"Well, come along with me then," I encouraged.

"No, I hate the press. I'm always worried about how I look," she admitted rolling her eyes in self deprecation. "Besides I've got some important things I've got to do at the office. I have another trial on Monday that I am still not prepared for."

Brad from the Alliance of Atomic Vets drove me to the DOE and we stood around the front entrance remembering our many arrests and protests. We glanced back to see two security officers pushing through the doors. The

Wackenhut emblems sewn to their shirt pockets and the brown baseball caps made it obvious who they were.

"Mr. Springer," one began formally, "how are you doing today?"

"Well, I ain't dead yet," but I was exhausted from the trial.

"No, you don't look it either. You planning an action out here today or what?"

"Just a press conference. A few comments on Hazel OLeary and the DOE."

"UnnmmmHunmmm! Okay, well, we hope that's all. You're a celebrity now and we just thought we oughtta check."

"Well, let's hope we can stop this nuclear nonsense and move on to the real matters addressing humanity."

"Yeah, let's hope so. Looks like I'll be out of a job myself soon." The officer complained.

"Welcome to the real world."

The guards faded back into the building.

By 5:15, I was beginning to wonder. I'd never been skunked by the press before. Brad and I milled around the entrance. "I'm glad Bill Chisholm could get my press announcement out through Kinko's FAX service at lunch today, but I'm surprised no one had arrived. Must be too many house fires, auto wrecks and drug arrests today."

At 5:30 we called it a wrap. I was surprised no one showed. With all the bad DOE press about the experiments I figured my case was a shoe-in. We drove back to QT's office on 6th street .

"Let's go upstairs to the conference room where we can spread out," Sue suggested. "I have plugged into the computer and I'm not coming up with much law to support our argument," she confessed as she plopped her armload of papers on the long black formica conference table.

"Well, we're striking out, it looks like. Not one press person showed up for the conference. I know Bill got that press release FAXed out this afternoon cuz he gave me the $30.00 bill for FAXing at Kinkos and he even payed half of it."

"Well, that's strange but you know how fickle the press can be."

I sat down in a padded chair as if I were falling backward into a pool. Sue pushed her chair back to clear her feet, kicked her high heels to the floor and laid her black opaque nyloned legs on the table top. She played with a pencil, running it through her hair as we made an effort to pull together an argument that at this point represented the crux of the case.

"What is meant by 'uncontrollable circumstance?' That is the question! I cannot find a law definition of uncontrollable circumstance."

"Why didn't we get a copy of the question?"

"Because he didn't have a copy yet."

"I'll bet you John Ham has a copy." Brad interjected.

"Well, this is what we have to work with," she reminded us.

"My brain is short circuited Jello, I'm afraid. Day before yesterday I was humpin' lumber and poundin' nails," I looked at my blistered hands. "Ham mentioned earthquakes in his opening remarks relating to uncontrollable so that argument opens up the whole field into the nuke area. I told you about Professor Whiteford's studies showing that 6.0 and above earthquakes have doubled since nuclear testing began in 1945. Let's let the jury decide the meaning of uncontrollable, that's why I asked for a jury."

"Well, it's not that simple."

"Sue, can you drop me by the Clark Center on your way home?" I said goodnight to Brad, joining Sue in her car for the ride to the Clark Center.

"I think you did pretty good," Sue encouraged.

"Heck, I feel like we got butchered. I don't think I said one whole sentence."

We pulled up to the curb across from the halfway house. I sat still a moment, flashing across the course of the past two days. I thought of addressing Sue's unavailability before trial and the before trial screw-up, but what good would it do now.

"See you in the morning," I opened the door, squeezed her hand and crossed the street to enter the Clark Center lobby.

"Hey Springer, you got a call today." Phillip the Clark Center baby-sitter told me.

I got the message, "Rick, please call until 9:00." I dialed the LA number wondering if some LA press wanted some details of the trial.

"Hi, Rick Springer here."

"Mr. Springer, this is Mr. Ekert with the Van Nuys Collection Agency. We have been assigned to collect your debt with American Express. We have been notified that you are employed with Point Blank Framers in Las Vegas, I believe it is, and would like to set up a payment schedule to keep this thing out of the courts."

"Too late for that. I've been in court all day but if you hustle out to the job site you might be able to get my tools. The Skil Saw and framing bags are worth a couple hundred."

"Mr. Springer, we have to set up some payment schedule regarding this debt or litigation is about to follow."

"If you want your debt covered perhaps American Express could insert a flyer for my book in their next mailing cuz I can guarantee you that is where the money is going to come from if ever it does."

"Well, that's not likely, Mr. Springer."

"No, really! Well, send the bill to Uncle Sam federal penitentiary and I'll have them deduct it from my milk money."

"Mr. Springer, I would hate to see your credit destroyed and your wages garnished."

'What credit, what wages?' I wondered. "Thank you sir, but it's time for bed."

I heard a continuing drone as the receiver gently clicked into it's holder.

"Hey, Rick, how did court go today? I didn't see anything in the press," Big John asked but got no response. "That bad, huh?"

"I think so. The jury is in deliberation."

I entered the room, dropped the coat on the blond dresser, and took a brief glance in the mirror before falling into bed. I didn't like what I saw.

Morning came too fast and there I was pushing open the courtroom doors. I walked past the public seating, through the low, oak gates, and quietly sat at the right table. I silently mulled over yesterday's events, disappointed with my performance. How do you walk in that Gandhian light, unruffled as they lead you through the senseless arena of the courts? My effort to show the jury that I was being denied a defense had created an ugly conflict with the judge. 'Combative' was the word that came to mind and although I felt I had to stand up for my rights, it didn't feel right. Was silence the answer? 'I'm just not spiritually mature enough for this', I thought, whispering the words.

I hardly noticed Sue Quig-Terrey sit down next to me. "What's that?"

"Good morning."

The judge entered, his black pleated choir robe flowing behind, creating a sense of haste and urgency to this business. Acknowledging for the record the presence of the attorneys and defendant he began, "The law, in the judgement of the Court, is clear. Let me suggest, for your reading, an extraordinarily well written opinion by Judge Winner. It deals with civil disobedience and articulates extraordinarily well the idea that civil disobedience is a matter that some have made a choice to engage in, but it does not excuse one from the legal consequences of doing so. And this is the language of an opinion written by Judge Grunetti suggesting that 'Exercise of a moral judgement based upon individual standards does not carry with it legal justification or immunity from punishment for breach of law. Toleration of such conduct would be inevitably anarchic.'

"So it is my intention to send this response to the jury: In response to your question regarding uncontrollable circumstances, you are instructed that as a matter of law, a moral, political or religious belief, no matter how deeply held, is not an uncontrollable circumstance preventing a person from surrendering, appearing or otherwise obeying the law.'"

With that decision, my fate was sealed. The jurors had made one attempt to find an out for me and the judge promptly blocked it.

THE COURT: Mr. Springer, you should be advised, and the Court has no personal animosity towards you, but your conduct yesterday was contemptible, and an embarrassment to the supposed cause that you represent. You're put on notice, and if you want the Court to react, Mr.

Springer, you can be sure — and I'm not totally decided at this point whether or not I will not proceed. This system cannot succeed with people of your character and nature creating this kind of disruption — and I don't call for any personal respect, but as an officer of the court your insistence upon referring to Judge Pro as Mr. Pro — and frankly the character and nature of the letter, it — I simply put you on notice that any further conduct of that character will not go unnoticed. But you were an embarrassment to the system and an embarrassment to yourself. And — and I'll leave it at that."

He nodded in finality as he glared at me. I held his glare but remained expressionless, too weary and disgusted to bother with a response. I could say the same about you, I thought. 'an embarrassment to the system and yourself'.

THE COURT: "I have to say that — and I haven't read all of the media, but I was very, very pleased that at least the paper I reviewed this morning didn't succumb to the idea of providing media coverage for this. I thought that was very, very sound on their part."

A strange smile appeared on Judge George's lips as he continued his glare.

"The court will be in recess."

I held up my hand to prevent the microphone from picking up my comment to Sue, "Does he have the power to cancel a press conference?"

"Of course, he does." Sue confirmed, with a 'don't be naive' tone. "The Marshals admitted on the stand that they have informants at all the media stations, didn't they?"

*   *   *   *   *

"Robert McNamara, Defense Secretary under Kennedy and Johnson, recently retired from the board of directors of the Washington Post Co. and ex attorney general Nicholas Katzenbach currently sits on the Post board. Former cabinet rank officials also populate the boards of other major media including the New York Times, LA Times *and the* Readers Digest.*"*

— Martin Lee and Norman Solomon, <u>Unreliable Sources</u>
1990

*   *   *   *   *

"I'm gonna head back to the Clark Center."

"Okay, but stay in close contact in case the jury reaches a verdict," she advised.

I walked out of the court and decided to walk to the federal law library to do a bit of research to occupy my mind. Who is this Lloyd George?

I picked up the Hubbel and Martin federal law register and thumbed the index and pages until I found the Lloyd George page. Appointed for life by Ronald Reagan in 1984. USAF fighter pilot, Montpelier, Idaho, Mormon.

I decided I better check in with QT's office, dropped a quarter in the library phone and got her receptionist.

"Hi, this is Rick Springer. Any message from Sue?"

"Yes, they have reached a verdict and are waiting for you. You are supposed to get right over there!" She informed me.

I closed the book and put it back on the front reference counter and walked through the exit book detector. The Marshals at the front door of the court house had a more tense air about them as I passed through the metal detector in the empty marble entrance lobby. As I stood in the elevator, waiting for the door to close, I heard them talking into the hand radio, more drama in their voice, "He's in the elevator, coming up now."

I walked into the courtroom again, QT sitting nervously at our table, "Where have you been?" She asked. "George was about to sound a state wide alert for you!"

"I was at the law library doing research on George," I told her. "So, we have a verdict, huh? What do think?"

"I don't like it this soon," she confessed.

THE COURT: Please be seated. Mr. Rogers, my understanding is that you are the toreperson?

JUROR NO. 12: Yes, that's true.

THE COURT: Has the jury reached a unanimous verdict?

JUROR NO. 12: Yes sir, it has.

THE COURT: Would you give it to the Marshal, please? Thank you. Would the defendant rise and face the jury, please?

THE CLERK: We the jury in the above titled case upon our oath do say that: We find the Defendant Rick Paul Springer guilty of the offense charged in the indictment herein.

THE COURT: Please be seated. Would you poll the jurors by number.

THE CLERK: Juror number one, what's your verdict?

"Guilty" responded each of the twelve jurors, in turn.

THE COURT: "Okay, ladies and gentlemen, this has been a difficult task I'm sure. And I want you to know that the system is deeply appreciative for your assuming this burden and responsibility. Now, typically if I have the time, and I do have the time today, I meet with the jury in chambers after their service simply to express personal thanks to all of you. I'd like very much to meet with you, and it won't be more than five or ten minutes at the most, I would like very much to meet with you. Thank you very much for your service."

The jury was excused from the court and exited in the fashion to which they had been trained.

THE COURT: Mr. Ham, does the government have a position with respect to the status of the defendant at this time?

MR. HAM: Your Honor, pursuant to 3143, it is the defendant's burden now to show by clear and convincing evidence that he is not a flight risk. Given the nature of the charge and conviction, I don't believe that's possible.

THE COURT: Counsel, Mr. Springer, do you wish to address the court?

MS. QUIG-TERREY: We would urge the court to maintain the defendant's current status. He's being detained in the halfway house at Clark Center and has complied with all of the conditions of his release and we would request that status be maintained through sentencing."

THE COURT: Okay, Mr. Springer, do you wish to address the court? For the record Mr. Springer has indicated 'no,' he has nothing to say to the court. It will be the order of the court that the defendant will be remanded to the custody of the US Marshals at this time. The court will be in recess.

Judge George left his bench and the room as the Marshals descended on me.

Chapter Sixteen
AN OFFICER OF THE COURT

* * * * *

*"Then a song of power came to me and I sang it there
in the midst of that terrible place where I was.
It went like this:
A good nation I will make live
This the nation above has said
They have given me the power to make over
— Neihardt. <u>Black Elk Speaks</u> 1932*

* * * * *

I entered a fog, a pea soup of a fog, one where you don't see things, you have to bump them or feel them. I felt the Marshal grab my arm with the pointy steel fingers of a fork lift designed to pick up bomb parts. "Excuse me," I mumbled while I began to take off Bill Chisholm's sport jacket. I gently laid it on the table, quietly undid my tie, pulled the belt from the loops, and set my wallet in front of my attorney. I glanced at her eyes, but she too seemed to be in a fog and could not see me. The Marshals grabbed hold again, leading a corpse I once owned through the trick door blended into the paneling. Clink, clink, I heard my hands joined in steel bands.

Air had a different quality to it again. It was stale and dead like I was. I heard things out there moving, even people talking but they were vague and there was no need to respond.

"Cat got your tongue, Springer?" The young dapper Marshal asked. "What, have you finally decided to shut up?"

I sat on the familiar cold fiberglass bench, peed in the familiar stainless steel commode and gazed absently through the industrial strength wire mesh. The body knew what to do.

Had I died? Came the thought. Why was the body still moving? I don't want it anymore. It hurts too much! Too much pain in that thing. Let that body go back to jail. Who cares. The soul couldn't take it.

That soul had to run around amongst the Joshua Trees and the Indian Tea, what they later called Morman's tea. That soul ran off to pinch the little three-fingered, waving hands of the sage leaves and ride with that scent across the hot desert winds, drying, purifying.

He wandered off up the winter stream, the green algae growing thick in the small trickling pools. He walked across the ponds with the small bug people, pontoon feet buoying them up; he could glide on water like an ice skater. As a scent he wafted further upstream to a bank of chollas and danced among the infinite spines with the antelope squirrels as they played the ancient game of Brer Rabbit, safe from predators amongst the rigid barbs.

The hot, late-afternoon currents caught him spiraling up to the tops of a red sandstone escarpment where he became the breath of the desert Bighorn sheep, flowing in and out through the flaring nostrils of a tilted head. His scent was recognized by the animal. 'Yes, sage' the sheep thought, able to distinguish a dozen odors in a single breath. The smell of a coyote coming from the stream valley as well. The sheep's huge curving horns dipped again to munch the chamise that was clutching, determined, to a sloping crack running off the face of the ridge. He stayed with the Bighorn, meandering down the ridge into the shade of the valley.

As a Bighorn, he stood at a pool, jagged quartz and sandstone pebbles covering the bottom. As he drank deeply he heard the water talk. "I may look like water, I may taste like water, but I'm not water."

When he looked up he saw an old round faced man with short cropped hair. He was chanting, "Eh na na na ney, Eh na na na ney, Eh na na na ney, Eh na na na ney," as he held a burning sage smudge. He walked across the water like the bug people. The bighorn stayed still as the elder walked a circle, all the while chanting. He fanned the sage bundle around the four sides of the Bighorn with an eagle wing. Then as the sun dipped on the edge of the mountain tops, he began to pray in a human tongue. "There, Shundihai," he said and disappeared.

* * * * *

"Oh, he'll talk to me," he heard a soothing female voice out there.

There on the gray steel bench in the lobby of the North Las Vegas Detention Center sat another old man. The lines in his forehead were carved in deep and rough, his hair was falling out, receding, revealing a broken and ridged skull line. There was a darkness under his eyes,. He was somehow old before his time. There he sat with a vacant empty glare. He recognized the man on the bench. He used to own that retched body. But it hurt too much.

"Oh, you got nice and brown out there, Springer," the voice soothed. "Aren't you gonna talk to me?"

No, he can't talk anymore, Owen. It's just a body. But maybe he could still feel. Touch him. I know that body is cold, but perhaps if you lay down with it, tried to warm it. No, he can't talk.

They took the body into the refrigerator, grabbing an army blanket on the way. The body sat down on the linoleum floor, falling the last foot because the hands were still cuffed to the waist. Damn that body, anyway. Go ahead and shiver, piece of shit. The body laid out flat unable to wrap the blanket or curl up.

Whose neck spasms are those? I don't own those. Maybe that body should slap it's head against the wall to knock some sense into it. That body doesn't feel pain anymore. 'I'm not home, you idiot!'

"Here, Springer." The door opened and the brown dog food tray was slid into the room. He wondered how the body would eat that food. Like a dog. Sure, on your knees, then you push your face down into the slop. You have the right to remain silent. We have the right to punish you if you do.

"Grandfather, I'm ready to be a Sundancer."

"Are you sure. It requires great sacrifice to be a Sundancer. You must be willing to give up everything and to endure great hardships."

"Yes, yes, Grandfather. I am ready to go without water and food. I would be honored to dance in the hot sun all day and purify in the sweat lodge morning, noon and night. Please, help me prepare."

"I think you are not ready. I suspect you are weak. You say you would pierce your flesh and hang from the sacred cottonwood tree, but I fear you would grow weak and pale as the sticks entered your flesh. You would shame us and defecate on yourself.

"We give you this simple task. Go before the White Man's court and preserve Your Honor... Have you fulfilled this task? This simple proof that you are ready to Sundance."

"I did the best I could. They wouldn't let me talk. They kept interrupting me. They told lies!"

"But you don't need to talk to preserve Your Honor. The Judge was right, you are an embarrassment to our cause."

"Let me try again, please. I'll get better. I'll learn. Give me another body. Let me try again. I love this Earth."

"You Love this Earth?" The voice asked accusingly, "I have seen your kind before. You'll be out drinking your own piss in back of the pinon tree, hiding behind the sweat lodge. 'I was so thirsty,' you'll say. Go away. If the fate of our earth depends on you, then I *am* worried.

"You think you've suffered, but you won't even eat your oatmeal without molasses. You complain about shivering with only your one blanket in your cell, but you rarely give thanks for the blanket you do have.

"No, you are a spoiled brat American, like the rest. You will shame the Sacred Way. You have no discipline. Now, go back to that sniveling body there."

The body heard the hydraulic door bang open and knew the sounds of the rattling wheels of the meal cart before the orderly announced, "Chow Time."

The five cell combination segregation/medical unit adjoined the central, prison-control room. A wall of windows allowed the inmates to view the 9 monitor viewing screens positioned in the hallways, strategic points, and rec yard of the prison facility. The women in the central control room also kept an eye on the segregation inmates. From that central room they pushed buttons to allow doors to open or close throughout the jail.

The door of each cell opened into the small TV area, each room with one bed and a stainless tiolet/sink combo. Plastic white prefab paneling lent a ghetto hospital aura to the space. The door to each cell popped open at 6:00 AM and was locked at 10:00 PM after each inmate had entered, closing the door behind them. The broken TV received one channel. Reruns of "I Dream Of Jeannie," were the highlight of daily programming.

In the second cell, a body lay there, semi-comatose, not even interested in looking at the food, still silent two days after conviction.

"Thunder, Liiigghtening was his name." Came the incessant garbled lyrics of the old toothless black man in the next cell. His voice was like Socrates on the day he decided to improve his speech by filling his mouth full of rocks and yelling over the ocean waves. "Thuuuunder, Liiiightneeeen" came the barely discernible chorus. Pop, as the others called him, was a skittish, loose cannon; capable of a nasty bite. His tongue darted out around his lips with the speed of a fly-snatching lizard. His head and eyes bounced in syncopation like a spring-loaded, back window car toy. Pop was another mental case.

"Shut up," yelled the guard as the orderlies unloaded the breakfast. Pops hands and arms jumped up to cover his face, assuming the crouching posture of an often beaten cur.

The empty body in cell two watched the show in silence, looking through eyes no one owned. The two waterless days were beginning to have an effect. He took a deep breathe, but still felt a deep sense of suffocation. Fasting on food was nothing, the body realized. Fasting from water made the prospect of death, much more intimate and real. The stomach led the call for food, but the whole body demanded water.

Deep in an ear, he felt a vibration. No, it was a heart that felt a sound. It was a deep bass sound, 'BOOM'. A long stick, with the bark peeled and wrapped with buckskin on the tip hit on that heart, BOOM...PUMP...BOOM...PUMP. It was heartbeat, whose heartbeat? What is that? That high pitched wailing sound blending with the heartbeat.

He saw them now. The hollowed heart covered and stretched tight with the hide, the skin of an animal. Four sticks beat down in unison beating the heart. . . a drum. Pumping life into it: BOOM, BOOM, BOOM, BOOM BOOM, BOOM!

A group of young men, long black braids falling over their shoulders, stood around the drum with their mouths open, tilted to the sky, creating a body trumpet, allowing the heart to sing it's own song...straight from the heart.

The heart knew no words, too confining. Could an alphabet define an emotion. But there was the song, flowing from the heart like a river.

He felt the circle around him now, an arbor, built of the pinon, the cedar, and the juniper. Boughs of cedar covered the tops, creating a shade under them. Some of the two-leggeds, the human beings, stood in the shade. Others danced in the hot sun.

In the center of the universe stood the Tree of Life, an eighty foot Cottonwood Tree, green leaves fluttering in the freshening noon breeze, reminiscent of it's smaller, more sparkley, northern brother, the Aspen. Amongst the branches, small, walnut sized, tobacco ties were fastened, each color representing one of the six directions with a special prayer made by the tyer of the bundle. From the high branches, manila line was attached, strung down and tied at the trunk.

Forty dancers returned from the sweatlodge to the center of the arbor, the sun glistening on their sweaty skin. After two days without food and water, the glaze in their eyes told of personal journeys. They were Sundancing, seeking visions, the message, the voice and the will of the Creator.

One elder, a very solidly built native man of fifty, stood from the base of the cottonwood as the dancers entered. He and three others at the base of the tree began dancing in unison with the returning dancers.

Those elders at the trunk were connected to the tree by the manila line, the umbilical cord, high in the branches. The manila line ended and was connected to the flesh on their chests. Red stains running down their chests into the bright red loin cloths told of their commitment to this journey. The cord connecting them to the tree of life ran directly into their bodies.

Incessant, the heartbeat, the prayers, the singing of life continued. Facing the West, the Sundance leader signalled the restart of the afternoon dancing. He danced in jeans and black vest, two braids split and laying alongside the white chestpiece adorning his reddish skin.

Each one in the circle faced the cottonwood and danced in a dipping rhythm clockwise. It was a proud dance, each dancer focusing his being on the prayers of thanks, healing, and prosperity. They danced like long distance runners in for the duration, survivors in tune with the ebb and flood, the rise and fall of life.

The elder, connected to the tree, walked towards the outer circle, dancing all the while, and slowly came to the end of his line that was connected to the highest branches. He turned to face the tree, pulling the rope taut, stretching the flesh where it attached to his chest. The wounds opened, allowing his blood to trickle down over the dried, caked and cracked ribbons already on his chest and belly. His face grimaced as he layed back, dancing as the rope held his weight. He suffered, the suffering itself a prayer book of many volumes. All the while he blew on the eagle bone whistle to maintain his focus on the breath of life.

The leader gave a signal at which time a young man ran proudly to the center below the tree. Two elders stood by him, each holding one of his arms as the man's head leaned back, letting go, baring his chest to his Creator. An offering of flesh. "My body, Creator, is all I own, so I offer what I have. Hear my prayers. I am willing to suffer, to carry the burden for my people, as my own mother suffered and poured her blood to bring my life to this Earth. Thank you for these innumerable blessings. Show me the way to serve my people, the way to preserve the sacred, the way of the Pipe."

As he prayed, the leader pinched a hunk of flesh with his thumb and forefinger. With a knife he pushed the blade through piercing each side of the man's upper chest. The bright red blood flowed as he inserted a chokecherry peg into each wound and from these he attached a rope.

All the while the dancing continued, the prayers of all present focusing on support for the young man's journey. The rope was thrown over a large branch of the tree and tied to another stripped log. Four dancers were signalled forward and in unison arrived at the log. They picked it up and pushed it in front of them away from the tree. As they did, the young dancer was lifted from the ground. He held an eagle wing in each hand, fanning them to the sky.

With his soles dangling eight feet off the ground, he twirled on the rope, arms spread, flapping his wings in flight. His flesh stretched on the sticks, bright red trickling down his chest like tears on a cheek.

Finally, he began flapping so hard that he bounced on his rope until his flesh tore loose and he fell to the ground, landing on his toes and absorbing the shock with bent knees. He sprung up into the air and ran the inside circle around the arbor, empowering the entire circle as he did.

The prayers continued throughout the afternoon, the frothy bubbles in the dancers mouths void of moisture. Some pierced on the back and attached three buffalo skulls to the pegs with ropes. They dragged the skulls around the circle until finally children jumped on the skulls causing the dancer to tear loose.

In the dry, spring air many prayers went out for rain. The leader voiced the words for the people and they prayed together. Clouds began to gather like a loose tribe of white puffs touring the southwest, joining together over the Sundance. The crowd prayed more fervently as the clouds began to darken on the bottom side. The clouds were unable to resist the call of the dance, validating the prayer. Random droplets began to hit, to roll, lonely in the reddish dust of the arbor circle, gathering dust like a honey ball gathers coconut.

The dancers turned their faces upward to feel the splatter on their dusty cheeks. No one dared question the power of human prayer, they focused more. And more drops fell until they were each dancing in their own little puddle of churned red mud, unable to distinguish one blood from another. The rain poured.

"Thunder, Lightning" came the wild voice of the lunatic shaman, "Yeah, Lightening was his name."

The shaman's skin turned darker, almost charred. Words fluttered through his missing teeth as he continued to mumble the words. Soggy Frosted Flakes stuck to his chin and lips as he walked over and pounded with his fist on the glass to get the attention of the women on the other side. One of them picked up a phone receiver while Pop continued beating on the glass with an intensity that seemed powerful enough to break it.

The door slid open to reveal Officer England, with his Butchwaxed hair, protruding belly and glasses. He ran in, followed by Baby Huey, fingering his baton, drooling for an excuse to pull it from his overloaded black belt.

"All right, you're on lockdown, Pop." England yelled at him.

Pop ran to the opposite wall, laying on it like it was fly paper they could never get him off of. The officers grabbed his arms and dragged him into his cell.

Pop picked up three oranges from his cell floor and threw all three with one hand as hard as he could. They flew the six feet into his window. "Gotcha," he yelled as England ducked outside the glass. England and Huey stormed out. With Pop's cell door locked the job was completed.

In the next cell, another body lay with a dry mouth, not a cloud in the sky, just a fire sprinkler and the thunder and lightening that was radioactive. I came back to my body after three days. I drank water. It was polluted. I breathed the air. It was stale. I ate the food. It was dead. Still I lived. The Creator wouldn't let me go...I gave thanks for the Earth I love.

* * * * *

"The underlying impasse at Attica has a tragic simplicity. The inmates say, "We are people", and the authorities say, "You will obey".
— Malcolm Bell, <u>*The Turkey Shoot*</u> *1985*

* * * * *

"What the hell are you doing back here?" George asked when I walked back into the main unit at NLVDC.

"What the hell are you still doing here?"

We resumed the dodge ball circle laps as if I'd never left. We caught up on the recent past.

"The Greek consulate is afraid to make any decisions for fear of being liable themselves," George's brow furrowed with his own tale of judicial woe. "Those bastards. I've told them to just let them deport me to Greece. I'll deal with them there and be home in two weeks. Instead, I've been imprisoned for eleven months already and have yet to be charged with any crime." George's thinning hair looked thinner than ever, the twenty long strands combed across the bald top were now only five. *Readers Digest* listed imprisonment as one of the highest stress factors one could experience. It ages a person fast.

"Little Ray, any help with your teeth yet?" I asked.

"Hell, no, they ain't done sheeit." Little Ray strolled on. "Guess they still wanted yo ass, huh, Springer?"

"Hey, out of 300 trials, I was Judge Lloyd's first misdemeanor. Wanted to take me down himself. How flattering!"

Chris the Italian approached, "I'm sorree to see you back, Mr. Springer. You don't beelong here."

"I'm on special assignment from the Creator to do a story on the dysfunction of incarceration, Chris. I'll make it. How you hangin'? Stayin' outta lockdown?"

"Oh, dey lock up Crockeet and myslef again. Crockeet iss steel down."

"Lock em down, Mr. Brown, cuz you don't like just what they say."

"Yeah, Mr. Brown iss full of sheet. He say he gonna do sumping but he do nutinggg."

I excused myself to make an attorney call. I waited my turn in the line for a free phone and dialed up QT's office.

"I'm afraid she's not in, Mr. Springer." The receptionist apologized.

"Did she get my letter? I need some money on my books so I can buy stamps to write the media. Also I need the Amnesty International address in the papers I gave her. I'm surprised she hasn't been by yet."

"I have no idea, Mr. Springer, but I can leave a message."

"Yes, please do."

I explained the court railroad with Judge Lloyd as George and I kept lapping with Oprah in the background. "Four days and I haven't heard a word from her yet, George."

"I told you, she is a woman scorned and hell hath no fury."

"Really, you mean a scorned woman is worse than prison? I still don't believe she would ignore me in jail. She has my money, my addresses, my legal work, Bill Chisholm's sport coat, my medicine bag. I don't think she's that mean. I think she's probably like most Americans and got too much going on."

"Well then, quit your griping."

"When are we getting our mail, Newson?" Wade asked.

"I don't think you are getting it today!" Fresh from desert storm, Newson had a very military attitude.

Other inmates gathered around the hot water dispenser, hoping to fill the cup-o-soup packages they purchased through commissary.

"Hey, Newson, can you get us some hot water, please."

"No, you guys already had one bucket full, that's all for tonight." Newson decided to be stubborn.

The brown thermo bucket remained empty as several more inmates came to fill their soup cups and found no hot water.

"Newson, Brown agreed that we could have all the hot water we wanted just by asking the guard on duty." Wade continued.

"Well, you can take that up with him tomorrow."

At 10:45 several inmates began discussing their problems about Newson, Miller, Martine and England. The various forms of taunting and manipulation by certain guards was wearing thin.

"You can tell if there will be any fights in the unit just by which guards are on duty on any given night." I commented.

"Of course you can," Wade agreed, twisting the ends of his thin moustache. "I think we oughtta refuse to lock down until they get our mail. They got a legal duty to deliver our mail, but whenever Miller or Newson are on, we get all these power games."

"They sell us these soups but then we can't have any hot water to cook them," George added.

The word spread among the 90 inmates that we would refuse lockdown until we got our mail and hot water. Eleven o'clock came and Miller yelled, "Lock em up. Let's go".

Half of the unit sat still, not moving as Miller walked around and ordered, "Let's go, lock 'em down. Get to your cells."

"Naw, we ain't goin' anywhere till we get our mail and hot water, Miller."

"What?" Miller looked like he was ready to slap an insubordinate nine year old. "You guys are refusing to lockdown?"

"You heard it, Miller. Director Brown says we get our mail daily and hot water whenever we need it."

"Alright." Miller walked away to the desk phone connecting with the door monitor upstairs. In five minutes Sergeant Parker pimped into the room ready to kick ass. Her jaw set forward, her eyes cold, she walked into the midst of those seated.

"What the hell is going on here?"

We explained the situation. Bring our mail and hot water and we'll be off to our cells.

"Oh, no, you don't run things here. You go to your cells, then we deliver the mail to your cells."

"What's the problem with giving us our mail during the day like Ritzman or Jablonsky do. It's just these certain officers that have to power trip everybody and treat us like dogs."

"Well, if you wanta act like dogs we gonna treat you like dogs."

Parker, Miller and Newson went to the central desk, emptied logs, pens and items they deemed important. They grabbed the two desk chairs and left the room to the inmates.

"Well, it looks like the proverbial shit is about to hit the fan. Better get ready." Lewis suggested.

The doors to the empty cells were popped open to allow the inmates to reconsider. Each of the remaining thirty inmates entered their cells, returning with more clothes on and tennis shoes if they had them.

"Ever been shot by rock salt or pellets, Springer?" Big Mike asked. "It hurts. I suggest you change your shower slippers and put on all the clothes you got."

"Maybe you would like to buy me some Nikes and a line of Champion sweat clothes and a hooded sweatshirt please."

"Don't you have any socks, man?"

"What, did I miss the prison sock issue?"

Mike loaned me a pair of socks to protect my feet for what it was worth. The woman in the control booth packed up and emptied out of the building. Impending doom, an EMT term that meant you were about to die, lurked around the unit.

"Hey, Yo guys, let's remember, this is a nonviolent protest. Whatever happens. We have to be disciplined enough to not buy into their violence and power trips." I stood and announced.

The energy was buzzing. What was going to happen? We sat waiting for another half hour before viewing Director Brown through the double doors. Shortly after, a squad of police, fully donned with riot gear, came into view.

"The show is about to begin." Big Mike noticed.

"This is better than Van Damme on TV. Uh oh, that looks like a riot gun to me."

Several officers made themselves visible with pump action shotguns. The police crew milled around in a show of arms.

"Hey, George, can you believe they are going to come in here and shoot us because we have demanded our mail and hot water." I nudged George.

"A year ago, no, but now I would believe it, yes."

We were reminded of the Attica prison riot where the guards eventually shot ten of their own fellow guards in a frenzy that killed twenty-nine inmates, ten guards and wounded eighty-nine others. Sergio approached the exit doors offering to negotiate with Director Brown, who was dressed this evening in his official SWAT Team commando sweater. Sergio returned with the conditions.

"Hey, guys, listen up, these guys are not messing around. They are gonna come in here and shoot us with pellets. No conditions. We have to return to our cells for lockdown. We can talk tomorrow about the mail and hot water. No conditions," Sergio tried to impress us.

"Is this mail and hot water worth risking the loss of an eye for?" Wade asked.

"No, I don't think so." We agreed.

"I tell you these guys out there are hoping we don't lock down. They want to come in here and kick ass and they have guns, and clubs, and mace and they like using it," Sergio continued.

"Let's lock down." Wade stood, disgusted and walked to his cell door, entering ceremoniously and closed the door behind him. It was difficult to admit defeat again but at least there would be other days to try.

With the last cell closed and locked, the main doors slid open and armed police ran into the room brandishing their rifles in a display of power.

"Com'on, Mother Fuckers. Just pull one stunt. We'll crack your smart ass heads," one beer-gutted officer yelled at the upper tier inmates staring out the window slit. He raised his rifle and shook it, but in cell slot after cell slot, inmates who stared just shook their heads in disbelief at the stupidity of the scene.

The next day director Brown pulled four inmates to discuss the problem in a meeting at the intake unit.

"Ron, what's up?" Wade asked as Ron returned.

"He says he'll let us out tomorrow." Ron answered softly.

But it was four days later before the cells popped open. More practice for the prison staff in running a real lockdown facility.

* * * * *

"Since 1980 the Nuclear Resister has strived to provide comprehensive reporting on arrests of antinuclear civil resistance in the United States and Canada, with an emphasis on providing support for the women and men jailed for these actions.

"We believe that in any significant movement for social change, many committed individuals are imprisoned. Behind bars, they are physically isolated from their supporters and their own resistance activity is limited. Broader awareness is essential to the movement for a nuclear free future."

— Jack and Felice Cohen Joppa, The Nuclear Resister

* * * * *

I'll never forget the day when officer Taylor asked me to sign a paper stating that I was being refused access to the peace movement rag, *The Nuclear Resister*. It was "inciteful and inflammatory," Taylor's paper stated. The front page story was about the Plowshares action where four religious activists had beat on the nose of an F-15 fighter bomber with hammers and poured their own blood on the plane's nose cone. It was a symbolic action, mandated by Isaiah again: "And they shall beat their swords into plowshares."

That night at 9:00 the alcoholic red face of Officer Miller stood in front of our TV screen hooking up the VCR for the Friday night movie. He plugged it in while threatening not to if we didn't have all of our doors locked. The latest prison game was that we could only go in or out of our cells once each hour. If you missed the hour move, you had to hold your pee till the next hour. It was the latest twist to the on going Degradation Ceremony.

"Blood In, Blood Out" was the title of the evening flick. Some people pulled Snickers or Slim Jims out of their pockets, just like at the movies. Others without money on their accounts shared some of the white cake left over from dinner. Those confined to lockdown screamed for more KoolAid "Juuuiiice". We sat around on our backless plastic hourglass stools, eighty men jockeying to see the solitary 15" screen.

The movie was a modern day prison story of the Los Angeles Chicano gang world, a story of young men struggling to prove their manhood in a concrete and steel jungle. Graphic gang fights filled the screen. Stabbings, close range shootings, teen agers held down while others carved with switchblades, the rival gang insignia on their live flesh. The cops were chasing in highspeed pursuit through crowded alleys and neighborhoods. The little brother was found dead from shooting up a heroin overdose. And then off to prison for the film industry's obligatory rape scene where some poor chump is suckered into a corner and brutally sodomized while his face is crammed into a sack of flour to muffle his screams. The story moved along to prison riots between races, struggles for control of drugs inside prison, the visiting girl friend pulling a condom full of heroin out of her vagina as she smuggles it in to her convict boyfriend. The guards themselves smuggling drugs, abusing inmates, and being stabbed to death. But this was not inciteful or inflammatory. In fact, this family entertainment was our reward from the prison staff for good behavior.

Rather than an unusual film for prison, *Blood In, Blood Out* was a fair example of prison entertainment. The boredom of life at NLVDC, waiting in uncertainty day after day, with your life in someone elses hands, pushed everyone to accept any diversion.

One night I sat down just after the film began. Some woman was taking her laundry down the apartment stairs and the angle of the camera made you feel like someone was watching her. The name of the movie? *"Baby Doll."*

The woman began dumping her laundry into the washer when some big guy jumps on her from behind. She was so terrified, she could hardly speak. He turned her around, puts a knife to her throat and pulls her top up exposing her breasts. A couple of inmates oogle over her, exclaiming, "Yeah, bite her titties." She is begging him not to hurt her as he pulls her skirt up and rapes her. More sick comments from a couple of inmates. Some guys are obviously getting off on it.

The rapist finishes by stabbing her in the stomach, the puncture wounds dripping down her naked belly. She slumped to the floor whimpering, dying and the rapist pulls a child's doll out of his pocket and sets it in her breasts.

"Yech," I exclaimed and walked away. I walked away from the picture but the disgusting sounds were inescapable. The prison guards watch the movies from their desk.

Two days later I received a response to my kite about the *Nuclear Resister* explaining the policy against inciteful and inflammatory materials in prison.

A week later I receive the Nuclear Resister in my cell with a note from the warden. "I can see nothing inciteful or inflammatory about this paper. When are you going to write a piece for "The Inside Line?" The 'Inside Line' is a letter from an inmate that the *Resister* prints each month. I suspect Warden Brown knew I had already written a piece for "The Inside Line," but the Resister never received it. It was the same with all of my media correspondence since the first mistrial. The warden didn't deal with the mail, the guards did.

In the Nolan vs Fitzpatrick case (1971), the decision recognized the right of prisoners to communicate with newspapers unless their letters contained contraband or other objectionable material. The supreme court found that the blanket censorship of inmates mail to be unconstitutional in Procuier v. Martinez. Noting the importance of inmate communications with their attorneys and court officials, this ruling concluded that censorship was acceptable only if there was a "substantial government interest."

We poured from our cells as the door monitor flicked the panel of switches, releasing door after door on the top tier. I walked down the stairs to the cold concrete floor below. Others scrambled to be first at the bank of four phones. Someone turned on the TV, settling the dial on Oprah, as she confessed her latest food frenzy.

I turned at the end of the stair rail and stretched my legs by walking around the outside of the two stairways, cruising by the phones, careful not to get whacked by opening cell doors or cross the new red duct tape on the floor, demarking the officers desk space.

Cal Springer, my black brother, popped out and faked a bump into me as I came by his door. "Hey watch out, you old billy goat asshole," He warned me.

"You watch out, ya young asshole." I joked back while walking on. Cal reached out with his 22" inch bicep, and grabbed my arm. His chest protruded out far enough to set a pitcher of beer on. His face went cold. The white of his eyes stood in stark contrast to the deep dark chocolate brown of his skin.

"What'd you call me, Mother Fucker?" He challenged.

"I called you the same thing you called me," I explained, still joking and jiving.

"Well, what we gonna do 'bout it?" Cal asked spreading his arms to the sides as if he was about to draw his pistols. It was obvious how biceps came to be called guns. You get hit by a well pumped 22" bicep and you'll know you've been shot.

A flood of emotion washed over me as I realized Cal was playing for real. I had been sucked into a showdown by joke. As Cal stood ready to shoot I remembered Little Ray and I already knew the punch line: broken teeth.

"You want to get violent about this?" I asked, incredulous.

"Well, you dissed me, man. You callin' me an asshole." Cal continued his posturing, staring cold, playing with his quarry.

"What do you think violence is gonna do for us?" I hoped reason and dialogue would be considered before a flurry of fists. My anatomy relocated itself. I was choking on my own heart pounding in my throat.

"It's gonna make me feel gooood!" He accentuated, standing up on his toes, and quivering in the hips and shoulders, in a subtle ritual dance of violence, like a cobra about to strike.

My old standby philosophy of, "You can't kick my ass, cuz you can't catch me," was worthless in prison. Besides, the ethic of nonviolence said there was another choice to the Fight or Flight response. Still, I felt like a snared rabbit about to be clubbed.

I pulled my hands behind my back, sticking my face into Cal's, "Well, then, go for it, my man. Give it your best shot."

Cal balked for an instant, his brain struggling for the lines to a script he'd never read. He put his hands on my chest and roughly but playfully shoved me backwards, "Aw, Man, you know I'm just messin' wit' chou."

The posturing stopped altogether as a new character emerged.

"No, it didn't seem so obvious to me." I was now pissed off myself from the game of manipulation.

"Well, you racists got to get slapped down once in a while," Cal insisted, trying to turn the tables.

"Hey, if I'm a racist, you're the grand wizard."

"Com'on, now, fess up, you know you hate black people, Springer."

"No, I hate assholes and it doesn't make any difference to me what color the asshole is. You still get shit!"

"Now you callin' me an asshole again?" Cal began the posturing in jest, slapping his chest.

I put my hands over my eyes and forehead in a see no evil gesture and was rescued by George as he strolled by.

"Hey did you see the Quig-Terrey article in the Las Vegas Sun?" George flashed the paper in my face long enough to see Susan Quig-Terrey's photo in the article.

"Hey, let me check that out!" I grabbed but missed the paper as George walked on. "Catch you later, Cal." I excused myself.

"What's going on there?"

"Oh, I think Cal wanted to test me and the nonviolence rap. Boy, I sure hate being toyed with like that. It's such a phony macho thing. I can kick your ass. It's like a six-ton truck jack telling the two-ton jack, 'I can out push you. It's heavyweight Muhammed Ali fighting a feather weight, the NFL playing Pop Warner, it's the US military fighting Iraq. 'Oh, aren't they heroes!'" I mimicked a doting bimbo. "But still, I think I better go change my pants. I'm afraid I just watched my teeth flash before my eyes."

"Well, check this out first," George offered, handing me the paper. "You might wanta sit down for this one, too."

The headlines read, "Professional Women Fight Sexual Slurs".

The author was Elizabethe Holland! "Hey, this is one of QT's best friends. Not a bad shot of QT."

"Read the story."

"An attorney of five years, she is used to judges—but not the kind who judge her because she is a woman. This attorney, who asked that her name not be used, is quick, intelligent and a fighter in the courtroom. It's evident she cares about her clients and sees winning cases as more than just doing her job.

"Thing is, however, she's young, attractive and single and by God, if you've got that going for you, you had to have slept your way to success. At least that's what the guys in the courthouse say in this woman's case.

"According to the courthouse rumor mill, this attorney got a little too close to a jailed client. Not only that, her alleged illicit and not-so-legal maneuvers got her a jail cell of her own. Infuriated, she traced the absurd lie to its believed origin. She knows it isn't true but friends tell her to laugh it off.

'It's emotionally distressing' she says, 'Why should I have to worry about my looks or what I'm doing? I should just have to be the best attorney I can be and represent my client.'

Professional women fight sexual slurs

Workplace gossip, double standards wrecking reputations

ELIZABETHE HOLLAND

Quig-Terry

AN attorney of five years, she is used to judges — but not the kind who judge her because she's a woman.

This attorney, who asked that her name not be used, is quick, intelligent and a fighter in the courtroom. It's evident she cares about her clients and sees winning cases as more than just doing her job.

Thing is, however, she's young, attractive and single, and by God, if you've got that going for you, you had to have slept your way to success, or wherever. At least that's what the guys at the office have always said — or in the courthouse, in this woman's case.

According to the court-house rumor mill, this attorney recently got a little too close to a jailed client. Not only that, her alleged illicit and not-so-legal maneuvers got her a jail cell of her own.

The rumor traveled a good course, landing on the ears of some of her friends, who passed it on to her.

Infuriated, she traced the absurd lie to its believed origin. Now, she's debating the next step. Friends tell her to laugh it off. She knows it isn't true, they tell her, and so does anyone who knows her. But it's not as easy as that.

"This isn't the first such rumor about her, and it's likely it won't be the last. What should she do to make them stop?

"It's emotionally distressing," she says. "I have no clue as to why someone would start something like this. I just wonder why anyone can be so mean. That's vicious. I've never done anything to have anyone say anything about me like that. I take it as a personal, hurtful thing.

"Why should I have to worry about my looks or what I'm doing? I should just have to be the best

attorney I can be and represent my client."

It's 1994, the year after the Year of the Woman, but this woman is practicing law in the midst of cavemen wearing suits and uniforms.

"It couldn't be just that you're good," says Suzy Quig-Terry, another Las Vegas attorney, referring to a common attitude toward women lawyers and how people so often tie their legal accomplishments to rumored sexual ones.

"I think it's the showgirl mentality," she says, calling Las Vegas the worst place she's encountered in terms of sexism in the professional world. "I think the whole idea about women is so objectifying, and it works its way into the legal system. It can be real frustrating."

On a recent trip to the North Las Vegas Detention Center to visit a client, Quig-Terry was refused the visit by a jail officer. The officer said Quig-Terry couldn't be the man's attorney, that she was his girlfriend.

Quig-Terry showed the jailer a bar association card and a driver's license. They weren't convincing enough, but Suzy being an attractive woman and all.

Finally, Quig-Terry blew her top — then went to the top. She won the battle, eventually getting to see her client, but she's well aware the war is far too reaching to ever hope to claim a major victory.

"It's just really pervasive," she says of the sexism. "They really don't ever lose sight of the fact that you're a woman."

But they should, says Kathleen England, an attorney best known for her work on sexual harassment cases.

"Women are overwhelmingly competent," says England, who has long studied the Las Vegas legal scene and its slow acceptance of women.

"They can practice law in the areas men do. We can be as aggressive, clever and ethical as

they are."

And, she says, women don't have to sleep with anyone to do it.

Imagine that, cavemen.

"The basis of sexual harassment is really power and intimidation," England explains. "The abuser can think of no other way to get at the person than through her gender. She's competent, she's doing her job, so he gets at her the only way he can think of."

So the rumors spin. And there's no shortage of people to listen to them.

"As a society," she says, "we're conditioned to believe, 'Oh yeah, that happened,' when it involves a matter of sex," especially when it involves a young, attractive woman.

"A young, attractive woman is not our picture of a powerful person."

England and Quig-Terry note the age-old double standard. If a man lands someone in the sack, he's a stud with a conquest worth commending — "They get a pat on the back, and 'Isn't that great?'" Quig-Terry says; if a woman does the same, she's nothing better than a slut.

"It can be horribly damaging," England says of such rumors when attached to a woman's name. "As a lawyer, your reputation is what you have."

And for the attorney accused of sleeping with an incarcerated client, that reputation is far too valuable, the principle far too meaningful, to let this one slide.

"All I have is my law," she says. "I don't have a life other than my being a lawyer."

She's mad as hell that her reputation is undeservedly being put on the stand instead of the man who so foolishly decided to trash it.

It's not a case of being thin-skinned or not "man enough"; it's one of being appropriately reactive and angry. To laugh it off, to turn the cheek, would be a disservice to herself and others.

It is her nature and her business to believe in justice, and that is what she — and all women accused of similar falsehoods — are due.

> It's 1994, the year after the Year of the Woman, but this woman is practicing law in the midst of cavemen wearing suits and uniforms.

ELIZABETHE HOLLAND is assistant city editor of the Las Vegas SUN. Her column appears Sundays.

"It's 1994 and this woman is practicing law in the midst of cavemen wearing suits and uniforms.

'It couldn't be just that you're good,' says Suzy Quig-Terrey, another Las Vegas attorney, referring to a common attitude toward women lawyers. 'I think it's the showgirl mentality,' she says calling Las Vegas the worst place she's encountered in terms of sexism in the professional world.

"On a recent trip to the North Las Vegas Detention Center to visit a client, Quig-Terrey was refused the visit by a jail officer. The officer said Quig-Terrey couldn't be the man's attorney, that she was his girlfriend.

"Quig-Terrey showed the jailor a bar association card and a driver's license. They weren't convincing enough, Suzy being an attractive woman and all."

"Hey George, this is the story of when Sue came and Sergeant Parker wouldn't let her in to see me." I held the paper out for George to see. "When I saw her and Parker together, they looked like two cats about to go at it."

"Yeah, you told me, read on."

"QT told me that Warden Brown ordered Parker to give her a formal apology but Parker never did." I continued reading.

"Finally, Quig-Terrey blew her top—then went to the top. She won the battle, eventually getting to see her client, but she's well aware the war is far too reaching to ever hope to claim a major victory.

'It's really pervasive,' she says of the sexism.

"Kathleen England, an attorney best known for her work on sexual harassment cases says, 'Women are overwhelmingly competent. They can practice law in the areas men do. We can be as aggressive, clever, and ethical as they are.

"'And,' she says, 'women don't have to sleep with anyone to do it.'"

"Imagine that, cavemen."

"Boy this is a direct slap at the courts, George."

"The basis of sexual harassment is really power and intimidation." England explains. "The abuser can think of no other way to get at the person than through her gender. She's competent, she's doing her job, so he gets at her the only way he can think of."

"So the rumors spin. And there's no shortage of people to listen to them. . . . And for an attorney accused of sleeping with an incarcerated client, that reputation is far too valuable, the principle far too meaningful, to let this one slide.

"All I have is my law," she says, "I don't have a life other than being a lawyer."

"She's mad as hell that her reputation is undeservedly being put on the stand instead of the man who so foolishly trashed it.

"It's in her nature and her business to believe in justice, and that is what she — and all women accused of similar falsehoods—are due."

"Well, well, well," I uttered to George. "What do you think of that?"

"Well, for starters, I think the woman that asked her name not be used is your attorney, Quig-Terrey. I think the jailed client she supposedly got a little too close to is you and I think the rumor started in the courthouse is the way she was manipulated to back off from your case."

"Whoa, George, am I blind or blinded by the light."

We spent the next two hours walking in circles, dissecting the article, my conviction in the second trial, and QT's lack of availability.

Slowly the pieces fit together; the Christmas present from QT, the book, <u>A Lesson Before Dying</u>, was Sue's goodbye, 'Adios, amigo,' but I had missed it. I thought it was a strange present, but the story of a poor innocent black man maintaining his dignity while being executed for a crime he did not commit, didn't quite come through to me as Sue's swan song and her way of letting me know, "You're going down, sucker."

That explained why she was never available until the night before the retrial. She had to let me lose the second trial for fear of disbarment. The judge probably threatened her.

There was no way in hell the feds were going to allow me to be acquitted on a Failure to Surrender after smashing Reagan's trophy and then comparing the US government to Nazi Germany in a public letter. How naive could I be?...as naive as the common American citizen.

The head district judge decided to handle it himself. So what if he never tried a misdemeanor, he said it from the gitgo, "Mr. Springer, I want you to know this is going to be a very different trial."

QT knew I was convicted before she entered the courtroom. "We're screwed," she commented the first day of trial.

There was something aloof about her during the second trial. At my request, she had prepared two visuals for the defense. One, the media photo blow-up of me on the front page of the Idaho paper, holding a sign, "Please, Mr. President, No Nuclear Testing". And two, a list of the laws and conventions from the Hague to Non-proliferation Treaty showing the varieties of broken treaties and the laws clearly mandating my action. I was puzzled when at the last minute, just as I was entering the courtroom for closing arguments, she suggested that I not use our visuals. I followed her advice because I didn't have time to analyze it. Sue Quig-Terrey knew she had to let me get convicted.

That explains how the judge knew I had a motion to present and why he called me to side bar. Sue knew I wanted to present the motion in front of the jury so they could at least be reminded of Hazel O'learys press release of the radiation victims.

Besides, she didn't make any friends here at NLVDC by filing my grievance on prison conditions at the same time NLVDC was seeking federal accreditation. Sergeant Parker hated QT's guts. And then she wouldn't go to the press conference because she knew no one would be there.

The guards watched us hug and if the inmates sensed there was some attraction between us then the guards probably did too. I'll bet the rumor could have started right here, handed off to the Marshals, and delivered straightway to Judge Lloyd himself. Imagine, one of my attorneys, sleeping with a commie!

The truth is, the court did have grounds to threaten Quig-Terrey's license. At a minimum, it was illegal to bring in Sue Navy as a paralegal and then sit there while Sue and I hugged and kissed. It may well even be on film, because there are cameras in the law library. No doubt the courts could use that as a violation with which to manipulate QT.

"Now she's probably been directed by the court to stay away from me."

"And to top it all off, you never even responded to her advances," George pushed.

"George, I had Sue and Bill send her flowers and I told her she was beautiful, twice."

"Yeah, but she told you to do that."

"I'm gonna write a letter to John Smith and tell the story. See if he'll print something on it. Maybe I can get him over here for another interview."

"I think you have something big here. This could be the break you're looking for." George suggested. "Anti-Nuke protestor jailed, Attorney falls in love with convict. Courts sexually harass attorney to keep the nuke story hidden. I think you got something as big as Clarence Thomas and Anita Hill."

"I think you're right, George, but I don't see how to get it going from in here. She hasn't even responded since my trial. If what we believe is true, well." I began to read the closing lines of the article, "All I have is my law. I don't have a life other than my being a lawyer." she says.

The next day I shared a letter I'd written to QT with George:

Dear Susan,

I read Elizabeth Hollands story, several times, as a matter of fact. Things are becoming clearer every day. My personal take on the situation is that you are being slandered for doing such a good job with my case. This gossip seems to have also become successful in destroying our relationship regarding my case."

"No, no, no," George argued. "Get some romance in it. You've got to let her know that your feelings for her are something worth going to the press about. She is not going to risk her law career for some half hearted, we didn't do anything wrong. Com'on, Rick, you can get romantic, can't you?"

"Well, honestly, it's not my style, George. I'm more the `I like you. You like me? Oh, Good'."

"Good, you like her, she likes you, now tell her to come here and kiss you."

Against my better judgement I returned the next day with another draft. "Check this one out, George."

"Dear Susie,

It was strange to leave you in court the other day. As I took off my jacket and tie, left you my wallet and papers, what I wanted most to do was wrap my arms around you, breathe deeply, look into your eyes and kiss you."

"Much better."

"I'm sorry we've had so little time to share and really delve into who we are as human beings. I must confess, I am intrigued by you and your efforts to bring justice into an arena so seemingly void of that very concept."

"If there is anything I can do to alleviate the rumors or substantiate the truth, let me know.

"In the Holland story you state, "All I have is my law. I don't have a life other than being a lawyer." You have two beautiful children that are an incredible part of your life. You have the guts and brains to make it in any field, no problem... As a woman in this era, you are on the cutting edge in much the same way I am. Let's not get cut, let's do the cutting."

"Very good, Rick. That's much better.

"I just hope it gets out through this mail gauntlet. If the judge can cancel my press conference, I'm sure he can censor my mail. I realize now all my letters from her and to her have been read and copied. If I was a guard I wouldn't let some sloppy handwriting, `Attorney/client privilege' get by without checking it. Any inmate's girlfriend could write that. I'm sure they checked her letters. Heck, if they got copies of her first letters, they probably used those against her already.

"I remember, Judge George was so angry at the end of the second trial, Quig-Terrey told me, 'I'm afraid to say anything at this point besides flutter my eyelashes.'"

"Well, go ahead and try that, I agreed in a whisper behind the court mike."

To my surprise I was called for an attorney visit the very next day. Perhaps, I thought, my letters to my aunt and uncle asking them to contact QT had paid off. I grabbed my legal file and McDermott escorted me to the meeting room. As I entered the last hallway, I noticed Theresa Brown of Pre-Trial Services, the same woman who had written a slanderous and biased Pre-Sentence Report for my original sentencing.

As I entered the hallway, Ms. Brown invited me in to have a seat. I told her to forget it. "I don't have anything to say to you." To which she insisted that I sign a refusal form and I refused that, too. Officer McDermott explained to her that she couldn't make me sign anything and offered himself as a witness that I had refused.

A couple of days later my aunt and uncle wrote to me explaining that they had contacted Quig-Terrey and that she had told them she was coming to visit me this Thursday. QT never came and I learned that she was lying to all my friends that contacted her on my behalf. I suspect she knew we were going back to trial even when she was telling my friends and family she expected them to drop the charges. A week later, I received a response to my 'love letter' (if you can call it that):

"Dear Mr. Springer,

"Upon reviewing the presentence report, I notice that you refused the interview with the federal parole and probation officer, and accordingly, you were denied the points for acceptance of responsibility.

"I shall plan to meet with you on February 10, 1994 to discuss the presentence report and to review with you my proposed revisions.

"My receptionist has informed me of her recent, unpleasant conversations with you. I have also received your correspondence. I can only conclude that you have a grossly exaggerated view of your own importance as well as the complexity of your case at this time. I have advised Cheryl that she need not engage in further conversations with you. She is simply to record the fact that you called and terminate the conversation.

"Moreover, in the future please limit your correspondence to me to legal matters. You seem to have misconstrued certain anonymous comments in a recent newspaper article to have been made by me and to have been concerning you. Please rest assured that I never speak to the press anonymously. If I have something to say I speak on the record. The only relationship that has ever existed between us is that of attorney and client. I shall be appreciative if you would keep that in mind in your correspondence and conversation with me. Sincerely."

"No Love and Kisses, anymore, George. Sounds to me like the court is reading everything that goes in and out of here with my name on it."

"Yeah, this letter is designed to create a record or prove to the court that she has learned her lesson," George agreed.

"So much for going to the press with love requited. She isn't going anywhere except the judge's chambers to be instructed in proper attorney/client relations."

'An attorney is, first and foremost, an officer of the court'

'Alleged right to counsel in civil contempt proceeding was outweighed by need to preserve integrity of judicial system.'
— Fed.Rules Civ.Proc.Rule 11, 28 U.S.C.A.

'Though admonished to resolve doubts as to the bounds of the law in favor of his or her client, attorney is also an officer of the court and his or her duty to the court is paramount, even to the interests of the client.'
— Steinle v. Warren, 765 F.2d 95.

'Lawyer's duty to client cannot be permitted to override his or her duty to justice system.'
— Fed.Rules Civ.Proc. Rule 11, 28 U.S.C.A. ABA Code of Prof. Resp.

'Attorneys are expected to represent client's interests zealously but they are also expected to know when to give up.'
— D.C. Ill. 1985

"Yes, when they threaten to disbar you and spread rumors that you're sleeping with your clients, maybe it's time to give up." George added sarcastically.

11-9-93

Dear Rick,

I finally received your note this afternoon. Thanks for your kind words. They were truly a breath of fresh air after the book store guy. The First Amendment is great, but that line of business does not attract exemplary citizens.

I have really enjoyed working with you, & I value your friendship. I know sometimes you regard me as part of the system (though less often than before, I hope), but I think we worked well together.

I'll be glad it's you when all this is over, but I'll certainly miss working with you.

P.S. You're cute too! Suzy/
my hero too!

Rick,

I gathered from Sue that you were a little tired of my charming company so I'm mailing this. I'd like to file it Monday so I'll have to bother you sometime soon to get your comments.

The state schedule for trial should be firmed up on 11/4/93. It looks like it is all set, but until then it could change. I requested order suppressing heroin (enclosed). We need to discuss press on this.

Also, enclosed is a clip from the Sun. Get Sam to rest.

Love & kisses,
Suzy

Part Three

I Am Your Spy

Chapter 17
CONAIR, CONVICT AIRLINES

* * * * *

"It is not unpatriotic to criticize one's country; it is essential."
— Gerry Spence, <u>With Justice For None</u> 1989

* * * * *

The sentencing hearing came on February 18, 1994. Susan Quig-Terrey appeared and informed the court that a rift had developed between us. I suspect that the judge was the rift. She submitted her own request to be dismissed as counsel. The court denied the request but postponed the sentencing until March 10 due to the fact that I had received no counsel regarding the sentencing hearing.

During the following three weeks there was still no attorney contact whatsoever, but the March sentencing proceeded on schedule.

Judge Lloyd George entered the room in his black choir robe and scrubbed pink cheeks. After formal announcements about the proceedings, he asked if I had any comments.

I began in a calm, quiet tone. Speaking for the record meant little anymore because the record was tampered anyway. Words on paper could lie as well as words from the mouth and what was once written could be rewritten. Still, I made a short comment, "The United States, along with the nuclear powers of the world, has not tested a nuclear bomb in almost two years. I'm satisfied!"

George luxuriated in his final word: ". . . the prudent use of nuclear weapons as a deterrent has safeguarded your right to freedom of speech."

The myth of deterrence, I thought, mulling over my own stock response, Nuclear weapons are no more a deterrent to war than a gun is a deterrent to murder, cigarettes a deterrent to cancer, or fornication a deterrent to AIDS. Rather than a deterrent, they are the vehicle by which the crime is perpetrated." I asked myself, 'What about our right to freedom from radiation? What about our right to freedom from ignorance?'

George then asked for the opinion and recommendations of the probation officer, Theresa Brown. "Mr. Springer declined the PSI interview. He has chosen to blatantly disregard a court order and should be held accountable for that decision. In the case where a sentence is less than one year, supervised release is not required and in this matter is not recommended. A fine of $2,000 is suggested in addition to the mandatory penalty."

"Mr. Ham, do you have any comments" George asked.

"Yes, Your Honor. Although Mr. Springer has been found guilty in a jury trial he continues to assert his innocence despite his conviction. He claims that what he did was right and important. Mr. Springer has expressed no remorse whatsoever and exploited his illegal conduct to further his personal political beliefs. The government would recommend the maximum sentence of one year."

George went on to follow the recommendations of the Pre-sentence report and strategically sentenced me to 11 months to run consecutive to the 120 days previously imposed. He also imposed the $2,000 fine. George knew that a one year sentence would have made me eligible for good time of 54 days whereas less than one year doesn't qualify for good time. An eleven month sentence is actually 24 days longer than a twelve month sentence.

In a written statement to the court I had requested to be sent to Boron camp in southern California to be close to my sister's family. George made a formal response in court enjoying that trump as well, "although Mr. Springer has requested to be sent to Boron, I would decline to make any such recommendation."

I sat at the same table, in the same seat, as I had for both trials and several hearings, glancing at Susan Quig-Terrey occasionally. She refused eye contact. She had entered the courtroom at the last moment and on the judge's pronouncement, stood to approach the podium, her voice quivering and her body shaking. "Mr. Springer would like to file an appeal in open court in this case."

With that formality completed and the court adjourned, she turned and without a glance, departed.. It was over. The sentence pronouncement had been painless. The judge's final remarks had been stated in the trial in a hundred different ways, most often with "Objection Sustained."

The March ninth sentence produced the desired media response. "Anti-nuclear activist sentenced to prison." It read, "Springer, who built a career as a nuclear foe from the pieces of a statue he smashed after it had been given to former president Ronald Reagan, was sent to prison Tuesday."

✳ ✳ ✳ ✳ ✳

Numbers
I knew the days were numbered
As they always were
I prayed that I was ready
Though I wasn't just quite sure

I felt so alive
But knew that I was dead
And though born an Indian Guide
I was lost inside my head

I felt the hollow thud of coffee
As the Nicaraguans slaved.
They said the path was narrow
As I raced towards the grave
I cried for ten thousand openings
One for every womb and man
I saw the boy's fingers reach up
I struggled for her hand

Why did I feel so helpless
With so much left to do
The odds were overwhelming
Or was it just my point of view
So I sit here limp and impotent
Waiting for a sign
Slap me upside the head I begged
Tell me when it's time

Because I know the days are numbered
For the seeds of my existence
Unless we learn to live and act
The path of nonviolent resistance

* * * * *

With the sentence pronounced, I was now official Bureau of Prison property. Kind of like slavery, someone owned me or thought they did anyway. Since I was no longer a pre-trial inmate my days at NLVDC were numbered. The date of shipment was always kept from inmates to stop escape plans. With eight months already served, I was now looking at seven more. So often I'd heard inmates say, "Oh you can do that time standing on your head," but after eight months, I still did not accept a cage well.

Other inmates warned that the US Marshals, who hold the federal inmate shipping contract, often lost inmate's legal papers in the transport process, especially pro per defendants. 'Lost' was a kind word for 'throw away,' which was an impossible accusation to prove. The papers were mistakenly set in the circular file. There was no way to get papers out except through the prison system. "Either way I'm screwed and can't meet my appeal deadlines."

I filed a statement with the court hoping to create a paper trail. "Notice of Concern Regarding Confiscation of Legal Papers." The court either ignored the notice or ordered the Marshals to fulfill my concern.

At 4:00 AM, the cell door popped open, "Let's go Springer, Packard, you guys want a shower? Better get moving." A three-hundred pound, black guard known as Tiny, ordered us up. I grabbed my one-foot square box that contained my trial transcripts, legal research and ninth circuit appeal deadline docket, just received two days prior.

"All right, Papa gonna get a smoke today," Billy Jo Packard yelled with the enthusiasm of a tobacco junkie. After sitting for three hours in the intake lobby, the Marshals appeared, jingling the sets of chains like they were about to take the dogs for a walk.

"All right Springer, what have you got here?" US Marshal, G. Lucia questioned. Garbed in a casual Hawaiian print shirt and cotton slacks, but wearing no identification, he took my box and envelope.

"These are my legal papers. I need these to go with me to continue my appeal."

"No, your case is closed, Springer. Give me an address to ship these to."

"No, my appeal is a pending legal case. I just got the time schedule. Open up the box and look at it."

"Look Springer, I'm not going to argue with you. Give me an address to mail these to or I toss them in the garbage. It's up to you. Your case is closed."

"How can I file my appeal if you take away my legal papers?"

"In the trash, or give me an address." He insisted, getting angrier.

I took the paper Lucia was holding and wrote, "I am providing an address in protest and under threat of my legal papers being thrown away." I signed it and wrote PO Box 402, Arcata Ca. 95521.

"I don't know if anyone is picking up my mail anymore."

"Raise your arms," Lucia ordered and frisked us before wrapping the chains and cuffs.

"Billy, you're a witness to this theft of my legal papers," I told Packard, my cellmate, as he was being shackled.

"I've seen everthin'," Billy supported.

We loaded into the Marshals' blue van. Heavy wire mesh was built in around the windows and doubled steel doors separated the drivers area from the prisoners. Lucia locked us in. Seat belts were almost impossible to connect with the hand cuffs locked to our waist. Several other territorial inmates already filled the bench seats, spreading out, lounging, refusing to budge to allow us any room.

The Marshals found the closest I-15 on ramp signed LA and pushed the accelerator, 'peddle to the metal,' creating that sound of gasoline guzzling that only hot-rodders or those with someone else's gas card like to hear. Eight-thirty and on the road. Leaving Vegas behind in it's brown cloud of desert smog, we jetted off as the speedometer needle found home in the 85 to 90 mph zone. Lucia cursed the drivers daring to cruise at a mere 75 in the fast lane. The 65 mph signs were obviously not meant for US Marshals.

"Stupid shit," Lucia yelled, turning his head towards the other driver, as he swerved around on the outside shoulder to pass.

We were at the mercy of a lunatic. Fate was out of our hands if ever it was in. If the van crashed or rolled, we were stuck, burnt in the flames, the stuffy air consumed with the smoldering plastic and upholstery. You had to feel the way he swerved that van to know this was not just a pessimistic indulgence but a distinct possibility.

Being out of NLVDC was no minor joy. The discomforts were overridden by the view of Joshua Trees and Creosote.

"Jackrabbit jump, weed wave in the wind
I'm flushin crows from the shade"

I hummed a little ditty I made up as a kid wandering in the Mojave desert. I suspected from inmate rumor that we were probably off to Metropolitan Detention Center Los Angeles, MDCLA. Nine stories of criminal warehousing, overlooking Interstate 10 just before it branches off into the Harbor Freeway. Rumor was, it was a step up from NLVDC.

The American Civil Liberties Union concluded that "pretrial detainees are generally held in facilities which are in fact inferior to regular prisons, being older, more crowded and more dangerous. In fact jailed detainees are more apt to suffer abuse than are sentenced inmates. Related to overcrowding is the endemic violence and threat of violence that pervades US prisons. Both inmate on inmate violence and assaults by staff are extremely serious problems."

So much for the concept of innocent until proven guilty. Prisons after conviction seemed like a reward. As nine out of ten convictions are obtained through plea bargains, it becomes clear that life will improve with conviction. Inmates don't expect a fair trial, so they bargain in order to get out of the miserable conditions of pre-trial detention. Innocent or guilty, inmates accept bargains for lesser charges because they are unwilling to gamble on a trial and run the risk of being convicted of a greater crime.

US prosecution in 1984 was $122.2 million and by 1994 had increased to $808.1 million. Prosecution spends an average of four times as much as defense.

This results in the highest rate of incarceration in the world, with over 10 million arrested and more than a million imprisoned in 1992. The US is spending $25 billion a year on construction of prisons and management of inmates. Still, with no demonstrable results besides producing four times as many ex-convicts as it does doctors, lawyers, and PH.D.s.

Las Vegas to Los Angeles in 3 hours and 20 minutes. No ordinary citizen could get away with that kind of time. In the heart of LA, catty-corner from the tile roofs of the historic Spanish style LA train station, the van pulled into a drive at the base of a skyscraper and descended into a dark delivery area. Guards stood watch with shotguns poised, ready to prevent any escape efforts.

"Gee, I feel so important," I whispered to Billy. We unloaded into a caged area, and were herded into another holding cell by a very short, bald man, dressed in paramilitary garb with his pants tucked into his combat boots. He used his voice, a perverted PeeWee Herman squeak, like a cattle prod. In a couple of hours about twenty of us new inmates were ordered out for a line strip search. We stood, thirty naked men in a line, while every orifice was inspected as PeeWee moved down the line, staring as he ordered. Hitler almost ruled the world with men like PeeWee. Now Uncle Sam was!

We were shuffled room to room, waiting an hour or two in each. White bread and baloney sandwiches were delivered for lunch. I gave it away and ate the still-green, red apple, although my stomach was burning, the ever-present knot gnawing like a mouse stuck in a wall. With another change of clothes, an ill-fitting, one-piece, short-sleeved, tan coverall, we were loaded into an elevator for the ride upstairs.

Finally, at seven in the evening, the elevator car stopped on the top floor, Cloud 9. We were unloaded, led down a hall and into a triangular shaped unit of two tiers with a central eating area midway between them. Could have been a cafe in the center of a mini-mall. We were directed to grab a roll of bedding and find floor space in the upstairs TV room. Somehow we had missed dinner. Breakfast was at 6:00 AM tomorrow.

The 16' by 16' TV room was already full of nine hostile looking bodies covering the floor when Billy and I opened to look in. The TV was blaring a Spanish station so we backed out, hoping to find options. Inmates crowded in all the corners of the ninth floor. A pool table tucked into a lower area was a central focus. A magazine/book rack leaned against the upstairs wall, empty save some candy bar wrappers and crunched styrofoam cups.

"I'm off to bum some cigarettes, man. I need a smoke."

Billy dropped his bed roll in a corner of another TV room and disappeared out to the cage, a small walled court with a barred roof open to the sky. A Universal Gym weight machine sat in the center and an electric push button cigarette lighter was mounted on the wall. If you wanted to push weights you had to be able to endure twenty cigarettes burning around you. By the time my own tour took me to the cage, Bobby was happily sucking a stogie in the corner next to the burner coil. He smiled like a satiated addict. . . . relief!

Although, cigarettes accounted for 400,000 US deaths in 1993, although $52 billion would be saved in health care if cigarettes were gone, although $456 million is spent yearly trying to get adults and kids off of it, the Bureau of Prisons makes all types of tobacco products, from chewing tobacco to cigars, available to inmates with money. As $5 billion of the federal budget comes from the tobacco excise tax, the BOP wants it's share.

The truth is, the tobacco Mafia is in with the feds; Phillip Morris lays claim to the title, 'nations largest taxpayer', paying $3.7 billion in 1992. The tobacco corporations were also in with the advertising industry; providing $210 million in advertising revenue, and in with the nations 66,300 convenience stores which rely on tobacco for 28% of non-gasoline revenue.

Sixty percent of federal inmates were in for drug offenses in 1993; and that number is expected to rise to 70% by 1995. Although no death has ever been attributed to marijuana consumption, one in six inmates nationwide is incarcerated for marijuana. The saddest truth of the matter is that arrests and incarceration have had no demonstrable effect on drug use in our society.

Government racism reared its ugly head too clearly in the war on drugs. In 1990, the African-American population constituted 50% of the US prison population while only 12% of the overall population of the nation. In New York State, in 1989, minorities comprised 92% of those arrested for drugs. While whites accounted for only 7% of drug offenders in New York, they occupy 47% of state-funded drug treatment slots. Crack cocaine, the drug of choice for black users, brought a four year term for first offense in Minnesota, while the same quantity of powdered cocaine favored by whites, brought probation. The war on drugs focuses primarily on poor, urban, minority neighborhoods.

Another drug more powerful than Thorazine or Valium and more addictive was also provided by the prison. Three TVs eased the competition for which station to watch but constant overcrowding made finding a spot to 'zone out' difficult.

After a light weight break-in workout on the Universal gym, I staked out a piece of empty floor in the largest TV room. I rolled out my bundle amidst the smell of sweaty, farting, smoking bodies. Although smoking was allowed only in the outside rec room, smokers smoked wherever they could get away with it.

Shoulder to shoulder, we slept locked into the TV rooms after 11 PM We tried to relax and stay mellow, because the pressure of overcrowding was as thick as peanut butter. By necessity, we learned a disciplined, survival meditation.

The next morning, all the new inmates were required to hear two hours of lectures and view three films. The rules of MDCLA were laid out. The speakers were bored more than the inmates. For staff, it was a paycheck, a part of their job description that had to be done, just like room or orifice inspections. During the lecture they brought out a mattress to demonstrate bed making 1-A, usually taught by a sober mother in childhood, a luxury many inmates had missed.

According to the World Almanac, poverty rates for children are increasing. In 1993, 15.1% of Americans were classified as living at poverty level, an increase of 2% in the past four years. The poverty percentage rises to 38.7% for female head of household families but for black female households that percentage is 49.9%. Combine this with general child poverty rates of 22.7% and you have a thriving prison industry. Only 33% of prison inmates were employed full time at the time of their arrests.

After five days of crowding in the TV room, I was offered a room with a young black man of eighteen. Each room was fitted with bunks, countertops and drawers made of solid maple hardwood. Even the drawer sides and backs were solid maple. The sinks were white porcelain as well as the toilets.

"Dolomite is my name. I like to keep a clean room." The young man offered his hand with the pride and stature of a chieftain's son. The room was spotless.

My family was twenty minutes away but they might just as well have been 3000 miles. Brother John, twenty year LAPD detective, had told the Secret Service, "Rick is the most nonviolent man I've ever met." That was no special feat considering he worked in the Wilshire district of Los Angeles. My sister-in-law, a county district attorney, aspiring for judgeship, would have sent me to prison herself and then slurped her martini with Lloyd George at the country club. Fate had a cruel sense of humor, especially with families in the twentieth century... perhaps it always had.

I worked on filing an appeal extension, but the rules of the law library were set up to fulfill minimum federal requirements, while legally stifling inmate appeals. I got one hour in the first two weeks. Extra time had to be requested and was granted on an individual basis. Still, I wrote an explanation to the appeals court, hoping to have the marshals return my papers. The remainder of my inmate account, although taken in cash, was forwarded with me by check and took three weeks to clear. I didn't have the funds to do any certified mailing nor could I purchase copy tokens. The counselor could issue stamps but not $2.00 worth for certified mail. I had no way to prove I ever sent anything. For an indigent pro se appellant, an ordinary Joe with no money, appealing a conviction, it was impossible to meet the court's timelines. The smoke and mirrors were discarded by this point: creating the illusion of rights was no longer a necessity. The system now said, "We nailed your poor ass!"

The pear shaped female counselor told me in disgust, "I know what you're here for, I saw you on TV. You're designated for Allenwood Prison." She reported smugly.

"Allenwood, that's in Pennsylvania," Billy informed me.

Billy found out that he was going to St. Louis. "So much for seeing my kids for the next year and a half," he moaned. "These bastards don't care if they destroy your family." And they didn't!

"Hey, Rick, I'm in with a nig, man." Billy Jo complained standing in the dinner line behind forty other inmates, while we waited for the microwave to heat each dinner tray.

"Sooo?"

"Well, I'm about to beat his head against the wall and I don't wanna go to the hole. I hear you lose your smoking privileges."

"Well, don't beat him then."

"I hear you got a nig for a celly too. I thought maybe you might wanna switch."

I was content with Dolomite although we had little in common, but my main concern was to keep the peace and having roomed with Bobby for a month already at NLVDC, I knew we could get along.

"Well, if you can arrange it, it's fine with me," I offered.

We tried the room change through the staff channels but after three days we just made the move and lied to the guards that the counselor had approved it. That night we played Scrabble before bed.

On Friday nights, a Popcorn cart was wheeled into the unit and inmates were allowed a bag of popcorn. Some guys brought a styrofoam cup to be filled with kernels and another for the orange/yellow grease to pop it later in the microwave. That took connections with the inmate popper.

Other inmates collected fruit and sugar to make Pruno, a sickly sweet wine from fermenting oranges and fruit cocktail. The fruit and sugar were dumped into a hefty garbage bag and stashed under the bunk, way up under and behind the drawers. After the mold had taken, water was added and in about a week to ten days the pruno was ready for a drunk. Most got sick and had a terrible hangover, but they were definitely drunk. Keeping a low profile was the trick or the guards would notice and the unit would be searched until the 'makins' were found. Some inmates made a living, so to speak, by running a pruno business. They traded pruno for commissary items (soups, chips, stamps, Walkman radios, batteries, etc.)

I was amazed to see girlie movies airing on the cable TV channel. Naked women, huge, voluptuous breasts jiggling like the evening Jello, paraded across the screen, encountering the desert sheik where they performed every act dreamed of by males deprived of female contact. They were the same low budget quality as the neighborhood porno flick bachelor party, *Burnt Toast* or *Biker Babes*. A hundred and fifty horny males crammed in front of the TV, watching as the insurance salesman explains to his wife on the phone, that he won't be home for dinner. Meanwhile the naked secretary crawls out from under his desk and lifts her head from his lap, drooling and lifts a breast to insert her nipple in his mouth.

Even more surprising was the evening guard, Ms. Thompson, whose shirt and pants were packed with protruding lumpy cellulite turkey stuffing and her huge Elton John black rimmed coke bottle eyeglasses match her Jamaican coffee color skin. Her Jamaican accent was so thick no LA gang member, Crips or Bloods, could interpret it let alone some racist Honky from Louisiana. She patrolled the evening TV scene, wandering in some illusion that the little stick on her waist and bottle of mace was going to save her from being gang raped ten times before the other guards even noticed her missing. In fact, the other guard on duty didn't even like her surly attitude and would probably ignore it if she was missing. And this female prison guard is part of the reason they are kept from their own girlfriends, wives and families, or prostitutes. She has a key.

As the movie ran past the 11 o'clock lockdown, Thompson yelled, "Lockdown" and a hundred and fifty men on the ninth floor returned to their cells, pulled the door locked behind them, and lay on their bunks to long for the touch, the contact, the love that sexuality represents whether they are aware of it or not.

With a stolen plastic spoon, many inmates unscrew the cover on their light switch plate. Using pieces of foil from the cigarette packaging, they would make contact with the two electrical poles. Some inmates didn't grasp the electric current concept. Often a room's light would flicker as they shorted the circuit fuse. Sparks flew behind the narrow door window. Anything for another smoke. "Illegal, whatcha gonna do? Throw me in jail?" The guards knew why the fuse had popped, so they took their time at fixing it.

Billy Jo had the more sophisticated cigarette lighting technology. With a broken shaver, he used the razor to cut his foil packaging into long strips. In the middle of the quarter inch wide strip he would cut it narrower on each side creating a thin fuse like section. With two double AA radio batteries, he would connect the strip of foil to each end of the battery and then connect the battery ends thereby creating a complete circuit. The juice flowed through the thin spot, glowing red.

"Check the door and tell me if the guard is coming," Billy asked me to stand watch while he touched the glowing fuse to a piece of toilet paper sticking out of a drawer. Pouff, the toilet paper caught fire. Bobby set down his lighter kit to grab a smoke and light up before flushing the burning paper down the toilet.

I tried to tolerate the smoke, but my childhood haunted me. On long family trips to the desert in the 55 Ford Wagon, Mom and Dad, smoking a cigarette each, filled the car with wafting swirls of noxious smoke. I about suffocated and barfed.

The top half of the five by ten foot cell filled up with smoke, hovering around my top bunk as the vents pushed it in a swirl around my head. Sometimes Billy would need three or four cigarettes before he could fall asleep. And each night I tried to endure. It was that or listen to him toss and turn for half the night.

One night I just couldn't take it though. "Hey, could you skip the smoke tonight? I just can't deal with it."

Billy ignored the request and continued with his fire making preparations. I tried to ignore it, hoping he would make the right decision. I heard the batteries click together and leaned over to see the usual process. The toilet paper ignited but while Billy reached for his cigarette, I leaned down and snatched the burning paper, snuffing in my fist.

Billy jumped back, his face instantly turning red. "You Mother Fucker," he slurred in anger, "Don't you ever snatch my property like that." He raged. "You're outta here Mother Fucker. You're gone."

I lay in my bunk waiting for the steam to cool. I remembered that the reason for Billys' first term in prison was murder. He'd killed his girlfriends lover by beating him to death with a snow chain, till all he remembered was bloody snow. "I asked you not to smoke tonight. It is illegal in the rooms, ya know."

"Don't give me that illegal shit. This is prison, you gotta cut people some slack. You pull that on most convicts and you'd get your ass kicked," he threatened. "I'm gonna get the guard to throw you outta here."

"Please do." I suggested while laying quietly, breathing the smokeless air.

In the following days, Billy found there was no other room for me to go to. He slowly got over the encounter, and he even stopped smoking in the room.

The days passed slowly, very slowly. I paced like a caged lion at MDC. From the top tier down the catwalk, around the concrete post, back down the stairs, across the eating area down to the lower tier, around the post, by the showers, up the stairs, by the eating area, up the stairs. I knew whatever I would write would have to be given to memory since they were going to take away whatever I had when I moved. That could be two weeks or two months. We were kept in the dark.

As I walked, I thought of Mandela, imprisoned for twenty-seven years and now the president of South Africa. I remembered Mordechai Vanunu, the Israeli nuclear whistle blower that had been kidnapped and sentenced to eighteen years in solitary confinement. He was still there after nine years. And then Leonard Peltier, down for eighteen years of a double life sentence for his work with the American Indian Movement, AIM.

I asked myself, "Tell me, Mr. Einstein, Tell me how you felt, when they turned your quantum physics into nuclear hell?" More questions came in rhythm and I found myself singing, up and down the steps, around the posts, among the convicted bodies of America.

STRANGER IN A STRANGE LAND
Tell me Mr. Einstein, tell me how you felt
When they turned your quantum physics into nuclear hell
You defined the id and ego, thank you Sigmund Frued
But will the ego of technology, make us null and void
So speak up Solzhenitsyn, Alexander please
Was the gulag archipelago, the symptom or disease
And how bout you Mandela, after 27 years
Was the price of apartheid paid in blood and tears

Did you feel like a stranger in a strange land
Did you feel like a ranger in a lost land
Did you sense the danger in you homeland
And the manger and the birth that's at hand

Well, fess up Lakota, Shoshone, and Cheyenne
Have you been impressed with the supreme law of the land
In the Spirit of Crazy Horse, Mr. Leonard Peltier
Have you found any justice in the federal judiciare
Tell me Brother Eagle, Coyote, Bighorn Ram
Can you live in harmony with this greedy Uncle Sam
Still I have to ask you, Ancient Redwood Tree
Is this land still yours or mine, so sung Woody Guthrie

Chorus

What of the little ones, seems so simple Mama,
Yet still among Tibetan hills, they chase the Dalai Lama
Where are my people and where is the time
To breast feed our children on nursery rhymes
In the thousand names of Allah, I pray upon your breast
Can you teach us how to heal, our fingers to caress
Send us this Prince of Peace, keep knocking at the door
I believe we're ready, to be strangers no more

And did you refuse to, will you refuse to
Feel like a stranger in a strange land
Fear the danger, it's time for a stand
Will you be a ranger and protect the land
Prepare the manger for the birth that's at hand

* * * * *

*"Starve a herd of baby rabbits, cage them in a filthy box,
poke them with sticks through the cage and some will grow
up to attack you"*
    — Gerry Spence, <u>With Justice For None</u> 1989

"Pack it up, Springer. You're outta here tomorrow morning." After almost a month of hanging nine stories up in the LA smog, my time at MDCLA had finally passed. With only four months of prison left, the feds were shipping me across the nation to Pennsylvania, a state that had replaced a coal industry with a prison industry.

"I am your spy," I thought, remembering Vanunu, and tried to remember that I was getting an inside tour of a broad cross section of our federal prison system that no reporter could. The only way to study the dysfunction of America's prisons was from the inside, incarcerated.

Four-thirty came. I was wide awake and ready to leave this ant colony of prisoners. A process, similar to intake but reversed, unfolded as I was packaged for shipment to the next prison. As I walked into the third floor holding cell I was surprised to see Scotty Murdoch sitting on the bench.

"Scotty, I don't believe it. What happened? It's good to see you."

"Mr. Springer, fate is odd, but I went to court and the judge ruled temporary insanity. So I'm off to the mental hospital in Springfield, Missouri for six weeks of observation and then they are going to ship me home." He explained with his now endearing, clean-cutting, Scottish accent.

"Wonderful, I knew it. Congratulations!" I offered my hand.

We sat side by side on the bus journey to a private government airfield somewhere in LA. Several guards armed with shotguns stood patrol around the area and a dozen others were lined up to receive us as we were ordered off the bus by name and number. "Springer"

"Yes."

"What's your number?"

"27771-048"

I walked off the bus to the fourth search in six hours. "Open your mouth. Raise your arms. Turn around." A steep set of stairs lay out the back center of the plane like a disemboweled animal. I wobbled up each step, trying to keep my balance, my waist shackled hands unable to grab the handrail, with the ankle chains barely long enough to stretch each step.

More Marshals, male and female, directed us to our seats. Several sat idly in the center reserved rows, the preferred wider seating that was once the first class section.

Like the van ride from Vegas, life was over if there was any serious problems on this flight. Again we needed help to get buckled in. Inmates with any history of escape or violence were shackled between the wrists with the Black Box that made any hand movement impossible and comfort a forgotten concept. *Endure* was the word of the day.

We sat on the runway for two hours before finally departing, while the Marshals lounged in the first class chairs. It was a short hop to Lompoc, where Clifford Dann, the Shoshone elder had finished his time, where Leonard Peltier had escaped from, where inmates were dropped and picked up like a Greyhound bus tour. The day's stops included Sacramento, Oregon and Safford, Arizona, the destination for the day. Up and down, jet lag and re-lag.

ConAir, the US Marshals Convict Airlines, the shamed bird with the FBI tail was called the National Prisoner Transportation System, they ran a fully scheduled fleet of 727s and Sabre Liners visiting thirty-six cities per week. They recorded 152,000 prisoner movements in fiscal 1994 including over 55,000 of those in plane flights. As a successful business, the Marshals were now lobbying to secure a contract with INS, the Immigration and Naturalization Service. After all, many of the ConAir customers were already illegal aliens.

The baloney lunch was distributed. A granola bar and an apple were the highlights. I spoke in broken Spanish to my neighbors in the next chair, making friends by trading a sandwich.

I watched as several of the Marshals disappeared behind the curtain during the lunch break. When the female Marshal returned she bent over to pick up trash from the outside passenger. As her face neared mine, I couldn't help but notice the distinct smell of Vodka.

"Hhhmmmm." I questioned, sniffing the air as she left. My neighbor tilted his hand, thumb and baby finger sticking out, in that universal symbol for a bottle and drinking. He gave me a knowing nod.

As the flight continued, one of the pilots came back to get something from behind the curtain. "Are you guys drunk already?" He asked in surprise, to one of the large beer bellied male Marshals.

The Marshal laughed it off, ignoring the question. I noticed the laughter and playfulness of the Marshals increased during the flight. The curtain jumped in time to the giggling and squealing of the Marshals as they played their own version of the Las Vegas Tailhook Scandal. I suspect a full half of the Marshals enjoyed that Friday afternoon flight, complete with cocktails.

In time I noticed a group of them pointing my way. Only about eight seats forward of me stood three male Marshals and two females.

"You know who that guy is?" A dykish, medium sized woman with glasses and sandy hair asked, not waiting for an answer. "That's the jerk that jumped on stage and hit Reagan in Vegas."

I listened, sitting within easy earshot, wondering if they thought I was deaf, but more, realizing how crocked they were.

"Really," responded the taller female with half her height from a 1950's beehive hairdo. Her makeup was thick enough to rival a fifth street hooker. She moved to walk down the aisle looking directly at me. Like a baby in a basket, cuffed and helpless, I just looked back, wide eyed and curious.

"Hey there, Asshole," she dumped, her contempt well expressed as her mouth formed that very anatomical orifice.

Well, I guess there goes my frequent flyer Mileage Plus on Convict Airlines,

I thought.

The Hispanic man on my right looked at me questioningly. "Usted es un asshole importante?"

"Si, soy un asshole muy popular." I continued, "Soy un guerrero en opposicion de las bombas nucleares. Quiero el dinero para comidas y ropas para los ninos. Educacion y casas para la gente. Viva la raza. No la militaridad. Violencia no trabaja. ?Comprende?"

The man nodded and emphatically agreed. "!Si, si!"

"Tu sabes Cesar Chavez. Pues, el muerte dos semana ayer pero el son un hombre grande para la gente."

He reached awkwardly to put his hand on my forearm and nodded his approval.

Still I felt like I was about to puke from all the take offs and landings. I tried to relax but my aching kidneys and head competed for attention.

We landed, unloaded, were searched again and loaded onto a bus for the hour ride to Safford, Arizona federal prison. The last fifteen miles were covered with the Saguaro desert, that classic, tall standing desert cactus, arms outstretched to the sky. My people, I thought.

"Springer, Number?" A voice yelled.

"27771-048." Scotty and I bunked next to each other in a large room full of cots. One bathroom, no showers. A packet with toothbrush, paste and comb was deposited in the trash after one use, the small tubes still 95% full. The comb and toothpaste company must love that federal contract.

Scotty Murdoch's story was simple. He was a Scotsman working for an insurance firm in England. He was very bright, but due to a couple of bad personal and business decisions, lost his sweetheart and his fortune. Viewing himself in disgrace, he decided suicide was the best option. Guns in Britain are rare and hard to get, so Murdoch decided to travel to America (the land of shoot em up, bang-bang,) to get his own gun and perform his solo duel in the mirror. He had insulted himself and had no alternative but to shoot the offender. Arriving in America, he found it a bit more difficult to get his gun than he expected. Still, he was determined. He rented a car and finally in Texas bought a 38 revolver and a box of bullets. He drove off in a stupor realizing the deed was close at hand. Finally he arrived at a remote bay on the shores of Lake Mead in Nevada, where he parked his car and plotted his death. Simple?

But fate has a perverted sense of humor known as irony. The Shoshone say, "coyote is out there waiting and coyote is always hungry."

An older retired couple pulled into Murdoch's bay towing their modest little house trailer. So much for a nice little private suicide. In disgust, Scotty went back to his car to leave and the rest is very vague in his memory. What he did do was take his loaded revolver down to the camper's trailer and shoot them both, one in the face, the other in the neck. He left the scene and made his

ORACION DEL CAMPESINO EN LA LUCHA

Ensename el sufrimiento de los mas desafortunados;
Asi conocere el dolor de mi pueblo.

Librame a orar por las demas;
Porque estas presente in cada persona.

Ayudame a tomar responsibilidad de me propia vida;
Solo asi sere libre al fin.

Concedeme valentia para servir al projimo;
Porque en la entrega hay vida verdadera.

Concedeme honradez y paciencia;
Para que yo pueda trabajar junto con otros trabajadores.

Alumbranos con el canto y la celebracion;
Para que levantan el Espiritu entre nosotros.

Que el Espiritu florezca y crezca;
Para que no nos cansemos entre la lucha.

Nos acordamos de los que han caido la justicia;
Porque a nosotros han entregado la vida.

Ayudanos a amar aun a los que nos odlan;
Asi podremos cambiar el mundo.

Amen

Escrito por Cesar E. Chavez, Fundador de la UFW (1927-1993)

Fundacion de Cesar E. Chavez * P.O. Box 62, Keene CA 93531
805-822-5571 Ext 256 *e-mail chavezfdtn@igc.apc.org

PRAYER OF THE FARM WORKER'S STRUGGLE

Show me the suffering of the most miserable;
So I will know my people's plight.

Free me to pray for others;
for you are present in every person.

Help me take responsibility for my own life;
So that I can be free at last.

Grant me courage to serve others;
For in service there is true life.

Give me honesty and patience;
So that I can work with other workers.

Bring forth song and celebration;
So that the Spirit will be alive among us.

Let the Spirit florish and grow;
So that we will never tire of the struggle.

Let me remember those who have died for justice;
For they have given us life.

Help us love even those who hate us;
So we can change the world.

Amen

Written by Cesar E. Chavez, UFW Founder (1927-1993)
Courtesy of the Cesar Chavez Foundation

way to Barstow where after a day and a half and the torment of a recurring nightmare, turned himself in to the police. Both campers lived.

4:30 AM: Scotty was sitting on the edge of his bunk already. We were prodded off to the ritual orifice search, another clothes change and into the waiting grey dog. It was like getting the kids ready for school, but a hell of lot more expensive.

The same crew, the same plane, our flight continued on, nonstop, thank God, to El Reno, Oklahoma, the central shipping hub for the Bureau of Prisons, (BOP) and ConAir. My neighbor explained that the plane we flew was one of the old 727s. Touted as the most dangerous commercial plane ever built, the 727 had an infamous history of crashes and accidents. The feds bailed out the airlines industry by buying 727s for transporting convicts. No wonder the Marshals were sluggin down the Vodka, I realized. Society could feel better knowing that if one of them 727's did go down, at least it was just them worthless convicts on board and oh, a few Marshals.

"Welcome to El Reno," someone muttered. I felt like Cagney entering hard time. Staring at the rock walls, I wondered if old convicts had broken all those pink stacked rocks. With a kitchen spoon for a shovel, it looked like about ten years to dig out. A hundred of us were crammed into a long narrow cell, while the guards outside pulled on plastic gloves preparing for the traditional BOP pastime, checking assholes.

"Just how many assholes do you think a prison guard gets to check a year? Why, they must be asshole experts when they retire. Just what profession, I ask you, views that many assholes. Seems there's an important story here somewhere. Why they could work for Preparation H in the early detection of hemorrhoids," I rambled on like a giddy kid hardly coherent of my own talk. Scotty glanced, exhausted, without even turning his head. "No comment."

"Bend over and spread em."

With another set of pants, shirt and shoes, we followed out into the hallway to wait some more. The next obstacle was the metal detector.

"Is this the latest DOE radiation experiment?" I asked the guard.

"Yes."

"Well, you don't have my permission."

"We're not asking your permission, wise ass."

He had recognized me immediately. It's hell being popular. I heard someone humming a Talking Head's tune in my head, 'Same as it ever was, same as it ever was.' I looked at one of the female guards, 'This is not my beautiful wife. How did I get here?'

I followed the yellow painted line down a large hall, the arched ceiling and heavy, iron gates betraying the age of the building. All painted surfaces were so thickly coated that the iron was no longer necessary as the bonding agent.

After another round of names and numbers, we were led into another room that appeared to be the prison bank with little windows across a counter. After responding to a basic health questionnaire, I attempted to depart. Leaning against a counter by the door, a thirtyish woman in a black and white polka dot dress, asked me, "So, why did you hit President Reagan?"

It was so out of the blue. 'Who the hell is asking now?' I thought. I was getting kinda cranky about these stupid questions. Even the devil wanted to know. But I took a deep breath and exhaled, looking at her but not really seeing.

"I didn't hit anybody, I don't hit people." I began slowly. "The question is, why do you believe everything you read? Do you honestly believe I would have been released on my own recognizance 24 hours after the event if I had actually hit a former president?"

"Touche," she nodded as if I had just passed the exam.

Back in the hall, Scotty had another concern. "Hey, what to you think of this rash, Rick?" He asked pointing to a two inch blotch on his forearm.

"I think you just failed the tuberculosis test. That's the spot where I got poked anyway. You better get them to check it out." I thought about what things Scotty and I shared during our exciting travels together, bus rides, dinner table, neighboring cots. Although the prison system incorporated films and testing into their program, nobody ever knew, (including guards, so they said,) who might have had AIDS, TB or other potentially contagious diseases.

Society thinks you are sentenced to prison, a form of confinement, a simple loss of freedom, but there is so much more inherent in a prison sentence: the risk of rape, potential assault by guards and inmates, exposure to disease, loss of family and material world, cold exposure, malnutrition, not to mention the constant degradation. Of course, some of society are into revenge as a part of the punishment. They are ignorant of the lesson of revenge....backfire!

After returning from his exam, Scotty said goodbye and headed off to medical isolation. Yup, he was carrying the TB virus.

"Well, I hope we meet again, Scotty."

I passed the rest of the day in two more holding cells. Some inmates traded sack dinner sandwiches and the cells began filling up with poisonous gas. . . cigarette smoke.

The door was finally unlocked by a guard with fifteen huge jingling keys, much like the keys hung from a child's crib. We entered an open mall-like building with another building inside the middle. Full of little cells, side by side, it was five floors high. I called it "The Aviary" for all the pigeons sitting on the pipes. Rumors abounded about how many inmates had flown from the fourth and fifth tiers. Long since, heavy grating had been welded in to halt that pastime.

The cells were tiny, four foot by seven and cave-like. The ceilings were less than seven feet tall. No doors or fronts, only bars and a sliding gate of bars that no longer slid. The catwalk was just that, wide enough for two cats to walk by if they tilted their shoulders. There were five floors, two wings on each floor. The steep, ship-like stairwells were a constant traffic jam of bodies. The building was condemned years ago, they said. Pigeons ruled, cooing and crooning to the court of rats, cockroaches, and criminals. It was soothing to see animal life, but looking up from the lobby floor could be a mistake.

The toilet seat in each cell was so close to the inmate in the lower bunk that common courtesy forbid use of the toilet during lockdown. Peeing was tolerated if the lower bunkee was sitting up but you better not splatter.

Six-hundred to 800 transient inmates filled the hold-over facility: 130 per tier with cots filling the lower lobby on weekends, when ConAir didn't fly. Newcomers were issued a bedroll with blanket, sheets, and toiletries.

"You're a skinny guy," the squatty white guard noticed, "We'll get you a bunk on Tier Five."

I took the numbered scrap of paper and hiked the four flights up, happy for any workout but exhausted from the ordeal of travel. I found a man lying down, reading in the cell matching my numbered scrap. He spoke with a thick Colombian accent,

"Me I hilp you. No thees bunk ees fool also. Dey hab assigned you to a fool room. Yesss. I suggest you geet a cod downsteers before dey are all teeken."

It came to mind that this might be a scam to cheat me out of a bunk or to pull a switch to get buddies together, but the pain in my back and head were too much. I slumped in the stairwell landing, laying on my laundry, too tired to care about the spit and cigarette butts on the floor around me. It was 1:30 AM. The guard made his rounds and corrected the error at 2:00. He moved me down three cells, next to the door. Lots of traffic as others passed by to their cells but I just rolled into the top bunk like a pea getting back into his pod. The bed sagged as much as a pea pod. The cells doors were all left open because the mechanism that closed them all together was broken. There was no hiding. Access to the shower was on the other side and you had to walk down an unlighted cat walk to get there. Tomorrow, I decided, a shower tomorrow.

Five-thirty, the range doors opened and everybody flooded out to get in line for the dash to chow hall. It was pouring outside in the Oklahoma spring. All us new arrivals had nothing but blue polyester short sleeve work shirts. It was shivering time again. Tier five was the last in line.

I followed the herd, making mooing sounds, out the doors and across the concrete compound while guards stood along the path to prod any wanderers. Cafeteria style, omelets and real potatoes were scooped onto our plates by inmate food servers. The food was the best I'd seen all year. I watched an orderly fill up the coffee machine with a thick brown syrup and was pleased with the first reasonable facsimile of coffee in months. There were trays of milk crackers and a self-serve milk machine. Jelly packets filled another tray. I was reminded of Einstein's theory of relativity; in my home town of Arcata, Food Not Bombs wouldn't serve this slop to homeless people but compared to NLVDC or MDCLA, this food was dee-licious!

I sat down at a table and nodded to the others who ate like sharks in a tuna school. I chewed my first mouthful, about to swallow, when a guard passed by the table, "All right let's go, it's over." Fifty inmates already stood by the door ready to run the 150 yards back to the aviary. I kept eating, but began shoveling in what I could. Another guard came by yelling and waving his arm like he was shooing a flock of pigeons. I continued sitting hoping to get another few minutes but the guard stopped and stood, watching me chew.

"I just got this tray." I said gulping a mouthful.

"That's not my fault. Let's go."

As I dumped my tray in the trash, I noticed the wasted food filling it. I grabbed an orange and trotted easily across the soggy compound. At the last turn to enter the aviary, a gray cat crouched under a bush next to the building.

"Hey, Kitty," I purred, and walked over to the cat. With almost a year since any animal contact, I missed my dog Hobo and my own cat, Kahlua. I kept talking as I bent over and picked the cat up. I layed her across my chest where she immediately began purring. I stroked her back and soaked up the warm contact, surprised at how relaxed and friendly she was. Six hundred notorious criminals had just stormed by here and yet she was as calm as a Xanax downer junkie.

"Springer, let's go," an aviary guard yelled by the door. He knew my name?

The guard stood by a trash barrel full of oranges as I entered. "In the barrel," he muttered, pointing to my orange. As I set it on the full barrel I wondered, did they serve these at lunch again or chuck 'em in the dumpster? Either way, it didn't make much sense. I climbed the stairs to be in my cell for the morning count.

Books were scarce. Several religious books were on a shelf downstairs while anything really absorbing or distracting was traded around amongst the inmates. You had to ask around.

I found a title that struck me: The Cost of Discipleship, by Dietrich Bonhoeffer. I ate it like the last supper.

The story told about the man, Dietrich Bonhoeffer himself. A Christian minister in Germany during World War II, who was adamantly opposed to the war; his friends feared for his life and persuaded him to flee to England. With some reservations, he left the homeland but after a year or so was drawn back to be with his people in their struggle. He felt his place was in Germany, regardless of the perils.

"When Christ calls a man," he wrote, "he bids him come and die." So was Bonhoeffer's fate, as he was arrested and imprisoned shortly after his return. Some of his letters reached the outside, relating the struggles of those imprisoned around him. He served as a minister despite the hardships of incarceration and was eventually executed.

It was a good reminder that even in Nazi Germany there were many good Germans who refused the atrocities. Even in America, there are many good Americans.

My celly gave me a jacket, a spare he had stuffed under his mattress. Rather than being issued, jackets were passed between inmates as they came and went. The pockets had been torn out of them all to allow stashing food from the chow hall.

I learned to roll my pant cuffs to hide crackers and other snacks. Repeatedly, the aviary door search turned up nothing and I passed, waddling off up the stairs, gently stepping so as to not shake loose my contraband food. The strategy with oranges or apples took a little more chutzpah, but it always worked.

With my hands in my pockets, an orange in each, I raised my hands in the air for the frisk. I rolled my eyes and raised my eyebrows while looking at the guard. At the same time I took my hands out of my pockets, still holding the oranges and raised them over my head. The guard patted me down, underarms to the calves.

"Okay, move on," I slid my hands back in my pockets, nodding at the guard with a passive poker face. It was interesting to see how prison life could hone one's shoplifting skills. You could steal an orange in front of their face. Inmates learned how "to chump a guard."

There's a song that says, "it never rains in California, it pours." That spring in Oklahoma it did both. One day at chow hall I noticed the guys at another table were especially excited about something under them. I looked over to see a half-drowned little mouse weakly crawling around, barely avoiding the stomping feet. I grabbed a wad of napkins and stooping under the table scooped him up like a pile of dog doo. I stuffed him in my coat lining and returned to the meal, ignoring the other inmates.

"Head em up, Move em out," point guard, Gil Favor shouted through the dining hall. Everyone stuffed in their last mouthfuls as flank cowboy guard, Rowdy Yates, rolled down the walls and shooed us towards the open doors. Decent food, lots of it, but no time to eat it.

Back in the cell, I pulled out the little mouse, wondering what to do with him. Would he live, was the question. I rolled up onto my bunk, facing the wall and patted off the soggy little creature. "Are you gonna survive or give up, Little Rascal? It ain't easy, I know. And there's an old gray cat out there that wants you for dinner. But today's a good day. You'll be dry and warm and we got lots of crackers for dinner so you might as well stick around."

I tried to warm him in my damp cold hands, the days of rain having made everything soggy. I blew my warm breath on him and he wobbled from side to side. "What is it, bad breath?"

The heat from the two heaters blasting down in the lobby dissipated long before reaching tier five. This building was either a brick oven in the summer or a refrigerator in the winter.

I rolled up a wad of TP for a mouse house. A healthy mouse could leave anytime but Petey, as I decided to call him after the *Little Rascal's* dog, was in for some R & R, rest and relaxation. The critter's recovery was nothing short of miraculous. Three hots and a flop did wonders for him. In just 24 hours, he was a whisker twitching, cracker chewing, turd pooping, crawling, furry little brown... yes, a live mouse. Day two, he moved into a styrofoam cup with a book for a roof. Day three, he changed his name to Jack, hit the road and never came back.

I attempted to gain access to the law library, worried about my appeal deadlines, but holdovers were only allowed to put in orders for particular books and then that book would be brought over from the library. How was one to know which law book they wanted? The guards defended, "It's not my fault you don't know what you want. It's not my fault you broke the law and ended up in prison. You got nothin comin." And nothing came.

After two weeks in the Aviary, I began climbing the walls, literally. In the back corners of the downstairs lobby I practiced a form of rock climbing known as buildering. With the tiny fingerholds between the bricks and the mortar, I stood on the tips of my toes. Becoming a spider, I moved across the brick wall, up and down, keeping an eye for guards. Other inmates glanced up from their chess game and ignored me. An escape was a victory for all. Everyone was allowed their dreams, however unrealistic.

It was only two flights of wall to the first windows. I observed the outside bars when returning from meals. A thin man could slide up over the top but the exposure at that spot was five stories. I'd seen rock climbers in Yosemite and Joshua Tree that went up faces of granite and sandstone where mice would fear to tread. It could be done. If I had been given ten years I'd be writing an escape story right now. Some animals can survive in captivity. Some dig holes under the fence every day of their lives. Others chew off their own legs to die in freedom. I don't know if they teach it anymore, but there was once an American tradition, "Give me liberty or give me death." The people in New Hampshire agreed with that one and made it the state motto, "Live free or die!" Ironic to think that inmates make the license plates that now sport that very motto.

I only had four months left. I could make it. The overall goal of a Comprehensive Test Ban was still unreached. I could do more good without having to hide as a fugitive, at least at this point.

The morning came after 24 days of the Aviary in El Reno, Oklahoma. At 1:00 AM they called us out. Six hours later, cell after holding cell, inspection after naked inspection, we boarded the buses.

What journey lay ahead was an unknown; would it be Allenwood, my final destination or two or three other holdover jails? As the plane landed in Harrisburg, Pennsylvania, I was filled with a sense of relief.

"That's Three Mile Island right there." I heard an inmate claim as the bus departed the air field and rolled by one of the unmistakable chopped cones of a nuclear reactor.

So much for relief! I thought of the children of Chernobyl and the hospitals built since then to deal with that disaster. I remembered the nuclear accidents at the Nevada Test Site. Especially the Mighty Oak disaster which released 2000 times more radiation into the atmosphere than Three Mile Island, yet the American public never even heard of it.

A nation of spoiled brats seduced into a stupor of complacency through comfort, convenience, materialism and entertainment. We love being seduced. We get to blame someone else. Someone else did it to us.

Chapter Eighteen
ON THE ROAD TO EMMAUS

* * * * *

"In Pennsylvania criminal convictions increased 57% from 1980 to 1990, but the number of sentences involving incarceration increased 206%. During that same period, the number of violent offenders in state prison increased 125%, from 4,520 inmates to 10,192. At the same time, the number of drug offenders grew by over 1,000 %, from 268 to 3,161."
    — The Edna McConnell Clark Foundation, <u>Americans Behind Bars</u> *1993*

"Alcohol didn't cause the high crime rates of the 1920s, prohibition did. And drugs don't cause todays alarming crime rates, drug prohibition does."
    — David Boaz, <u>The Crisis in Drug Prohibition</u> *1990*

* * * * *

After a journey through a meandering river valley of ancient glacial mountains now whittled to the greenery of hills and dales, we arrived at the entrance to Allenwood, LSCI, Low Security Correctional Institute. It looked like a new age river fort set in the Indian frontier. Forests covered the hillsides of the valley created by two east/west running ridges. It was a beautiful pastoral setting with vibrant green farms covering the lowlands down by the river.

We shuffled into the front entrance, shotgun bearers always present and through a lobby that looked more like a modern library than a prison. High vaulted ceilings were juxtaposed to slate covered floors. Attractively upholstered couches lined the walls.

'So this is Club Fed. The taxpayers would be impressed,' I thought. Holding cells, fingerprints, photos, asshole check, jumpsuits, sack lunch, my gosh, wheat bread, real cheese, green lettuce, and out the door with a unit assignment, Lycoming A.

It could have been a college campus. Low attractive adobe colored block buildings with green tin roofs were surrounded huge green lawns. Dual razor wire fences contained them all. Concrete pathways zigzagged in all directions, connecting each building. I wandered slowly, soaking in the openess.

I followed a walkway north to Lycoming unit. A guard stood inside and came to unlock the door. He took my papers. "Springer, yeah, I remember you," he said, almost friendly. He wore a white shirt, slacks and a tie and after writing "Springer" in his book, led me down a hall of cubicles created by white painted concrete block walls, six-foot tall. No doors existed in the divided dormitory. It was much like a huge open office with divider walls.

I entered cell number 43 near the back of the run to be greeted by John Getsin, a fortyish, tall, white man, with his mid-back dishwater blond hair pulled back in an elastic band, and Troy, a slightly older medium sized black man. As usual I got the top bunk over John and proceeded to lay out my sheets, making the bed.

"What are you in for?" It was the standard first question. Everyone wanted to know what they were dealing with, a bank robber, drug dealer, an embezzler, or a murderer?

"I'm a political activist. They didn't appreciate my style of activism. So, three men to a cell, huh?"

"Well, we opened up the place over a year ago. They used inmate labor to build the walls in here. It's designed for two to a cell, but they're packing it already. I'm sure it will be four to a cell in a couple of years, and then they'll set up open dorms in the TV and game rooms. Prisons are a booming business, I'm sure you know. Twenty-five billion a year and growing. Nearly one third of all jails in the US are under court order to reduce crowding and improve conditions, but hey. . . "

The cost of constructing a new bed for inmates in the state system is $54,209 and $78,000 for the feds. In 1993, 113 new prisons were being constructed. The criminal justice system employs almost 2 million people, with a monthly payroll of $4.3 billion. Every life sentence costs the taxpayers nearly $1.3 million.

John Getsin was busted for marijuana distribution. He was one member of fifteen in a 30 pound pot transaction, and a DEA sting operation. The Drug Enforcement Agency had set them up for a transaction and busted them all in one evening. Since one of the fifteen had a gun in his glove box, each man was convicted of a violent felony, although only one gun was present and it was never even taken out.

John had served three of fifteen years, had exhausted his appeal and was at a loss. The thought of twelve more years was hard to swallow. John was a good, peaceful man. He sang in the prison choir, worked on the interfaith counsel, and helped Pastor Childs with the church maintenance. There were many John Getsins in Allenwood federal prison.

Troy was more tight lipped but easy to get along with. John and Troy had oak simulated formica lockers with sliding drawers underneath but the new men got flimsy sheet metal lockers without shelves. A matching desk was covered with books on health, running and spirituality. John and I had a lot in common, but it was obvious I was the odd man. My presence made their space that much smaller. Over the next few days I made a group of friends, Dusty, Bob, Joe, John, Ed, and Don. Easy going, decent guys doing their time as best they could, they were no different from my friends at home.

Dusty was a pot farmer from upstate Vermont, another of the one in six marijuana offenders wasting the taxpayers buck and diverting funds from education. He looked like one of the Smith Brothers from the cough drop box, long hair and foot long beard. You couldn't ask for a nicer guy. He faced eight years for his backwoods Vermont farming.

"Can you believe it?" Dusty asked.

"I'm sorry I can. We're throwing our money away. Instead of feeding, clothing and educating our children we are locking up individuals that grow something as harmless and useful as hemp. I'm for legalization of all drugs."

"Of course. Have you met LEB yet."

"What's LEB?"

"Lying Ed Berry. He's our unit manager and a ventriloquist liar, -- he lies through his teeth."

I had the pleasure a week later, when I met Ed Berry, the unit manager, along with Mr. Brooks, the case counselor. Giving everybody the benefit of the doubt, I attempted to create an honest relationship.

"Well, Mr. Springer, so you're the man that got Reagans goat, huh?" Mr. Berry began casually.

"He was not the focus of my action, Mr. Berry. I was there to announce a nuclear bomb test. Every judge I have been before agreed by saying, 'I'm sure you never meant to harm anyone.'"

"Can you produce the records stating that?" Berry asked, rubbing his shiny pate.

"I could, if the marshals hadn't stolen my property. I haven't recovered any of my legal papers since moving."

The meeting continued amicably enough, closing with Mr. Berrys suggestion that I be sent to the halfway house for the last six weeks of my term.

"You should know that I am fighting the sentence computation report denying me any good time. They are saying that I have two separate sentences although the court ordered that they are to run consecutively." I showed Mr. Berry and Mr. Brooks a copy from the law books. `Any sentence ordered to run consecutively shall be treated as a single aggregate.' I have one four month sentence and one eleven month sentence totalling 15 months. Anything over one year is eligible for a good time reduction of 54 days per year and so I should be released two months earlier than they claim."

"Have you talked to Mr. Taylor of Sentence Computation?" Berry asked.

"Yes, and I find him very rude. He ignores direct questions and insists that my first sentence was already completed when the second sentence was ordered, therefore, they can't run consecutive, even though I have been incarcerated nonstop since August 9th."

"Well, we can't help you with that, Springer. We'll release you when they tell us to. I've got to go to the chow hall. Why don't you come with me?" Berry grabbed his coat and we left, walking alone up the concrete walkway. "Ya know Springer, if we have an effective writ writer that is submitting torts and 5540s and helping other inmates with legal work," he stopped on the empty walk to look at me. "Now I'm not saying it's right, but they end up being shipped off for diesel therapy, if you know what I mean. They might stay on the road for a long time and it's not much fun, up and down in a plane everyday. You get the picture, Springer?"

"Mr. Berry, I have three months left at this point, half of which should be at a halfway house. Why don't you just start the paperwork and get me outta here now."

"All in good time, Springer." Berry ended with a less than satisfied expression, pulling his pants up snug to his bulging belly.

The stark contrast between the pre-trial inmate and the convicted became glaringly apparent at Allenwood. While the supposedly innocent pretrial inmate was lucky to get three hours a week access to the law library, the convicted were allowed almost 8 hours a day, whenever the library was open. Exercise and the rec yard were available just as much. Inmates could choose their activity and leave their units at will, providing it was the ten minute per hour movetime and they secured a written pass from the unit guard.

The recreation yard was a full scale county park, replete with a half-mile dirt track, two baseball diamonds, a sand filled volleyball court, handball and racket ball courts, a soccer and football field, an outdoor weight pile, and bacci ball and horseshoe pits. The indoor gymnasium housed a full scale basketball court with pull-out bleachers and an indoor weight room. Balls, horseshoes, and back supports were issued in the rec yard office. With thirteen hundred men trying to kill time, teams and leagues were plentiful. What society balked at providing for poor youth, they provided by default to fully capable men.

Men lounged on towels purchased from commissary and oiled themselves with Coppertone. T-shirts, socks, shorts, hats, sweatshirts, a dozen varieties of sport shoes (Nikes, Filo, Converse, New Balance), vitamins, protein powder, fresh fruit and vegetables, coffee, creamer, honey, peanut butter, tuna, canned chicken, cigarettes, cigars, chewing tobacco, pipes and pipe tobacco were all available for those with money in their inmate accounts. Some people refused to eat in the cafeteria and survived quite well on commissary.

The hobby center had two soundproof band rooms with electric instruments, guitars, basses, amps, drum sets, keyboards, pianos, six steel-string acoustic guitars, picks, and extra strings. They had clay and kilns, paints and easels, foosball and pool tables, but no pool and no swimming.

The $3 billion approved by congress for the new crime bill alone was equal to the entire federal budget for education. In prison, classes were mandatory for those without basic skills of reading, writing and arithmetic. College courses and credits were available, but threatened by new legislation.

Rumors spread like wild fire when the crime bill included the removal of the weight equipment from prison facilities. Strikes and riots were discussed constantly.

The "three strikes and you're out" provisions brought regular threats and promises from most inmates. "Somebody try to take me down for life and somebody goin' to hell with me. I got nothin' to lose at that point."

Racism was a constant issue throughout the prison system. Allenwood was no exception. It was explained that, "If you want to hang with the nigs then when the shit hits the fan, you will be out in the cold. You won't have any people to protect you." But I learned that there was an "independent car," composed of all races, for those that stood their ground. Those who endured the initial hazing by racists were accepted as independents.

It was an unspoken fact, the main population ignored us and we remained relatively safe from aggression. Violent inmates realized we just weren't any good for the game.

The standard issue shoe from the laundry at Allenwood was black leather, ankle high work boots, but the track was so inviting I couldn't resist. A half mile dirt track, surrounded by a forest-covered valley with the sun sparkling in the creek made the fence, razor wire and blisters insignificant.

Most inmates walked sometime during the day, lap after lap. The rec department even had a walking program, complete with a printed T-shirt and a certificate.

Canadian geese honked around the perimiter of the compound. In no short order, the geese decided that the baseball field was good eatin' grass. Most evenings a family of deer could be seen on the edge of the nearby willow thickets.

With only three months to release, I didn't have enough time to take any classes or get a program going . I was already plagued with short-timers disease, a painfully debilitating awareness of one's imminent release. It began for most at about 90 days. The clock came to a standstill. The morning of release was dreamed of so often that it became an illusory nightmare, with the short-timer waking each morning still in prison. Other inmates asked often, happy for your release, "You're a short-timer, aren't you?" You couldn't forget if you wanted. "How many days left?"

The improved diet began to have an effect. Piles of fresh spinach leaves

appeared each night at the salad bar, along with cole slaw, raw carrots, toma-
toes and a variety of other greens. I gained weight and strength, working out
three times a week with a new friend from New Hampshire, Ed Berthiaume.
We psyched each other up, joking during workouts.

Tatoos filled the arms of many inmates, -- skulls and naked women, the
inevitable death and the elusive dream, the constant suffering and occasional
pleasure, the struggle between hate and love...paradox...yin and yang!

Ed was a wild one, constantly dreaming of the babes, mostly his own, his
kids. He had three kids in New Hampshire. "It sucks," he would say about his
separation from them. He had his wall covered with their photos, two girls,
nine and thirteen, and a toddler boy. His crime was selling cocaine in New
Hampshire. He also ran a hot dog stand on Hampton Beach. He was so full of
ideas, they bubbled out of him.

His cellmates called him the slasher, because he scoured the newspapers
and magazines as he pulled them out of the trash and using a pen, scored the
articles he wanted, tearing them out like they were perforated. Try it, it works
great. Boxes of files were packed under his bunk, mostly political topics but
also business opportunities, free catalogs, and things for kids to do.

Ed was the proverbial M&M, hard on the outside and soft inside. His New
Hamsha accent added a street tough flavor, but he was dependable and well
read.

On the entrance forms, under the slot for religion, I listed Native American. My blond hair and blue eyes were not going to deter me from my beliefs.
I approached the other Native Americans on the compound to see if we had
enough in common to pray together. There were only six Native Americans at
Allenwood: Chief from Montana, Lakota; John Blackhawk from Canada,
Blackfoot; Tony, North Dakota, Lakota; Toby, Earth, he claimed; and then Art
from Northern California, Yurok, the downriver people. I made the sixth. I
was more than accepted, I was welcomed.

Father Ignacio, a five-foot two Phillipino man led the Catholic mass on
Sundays and Pastor Childs ministered to the Prostetant faction, which lumped
together the Baptist and a dozen other faiths. There was a church, newly
completed. The Jewish had the Rabbi in for special events. The Rastafarians
were given permission to use the Church for a Bob Marley Memorial and other
special feast days complete with fresh carrot juice, and delicacies from across
the world.

It is strange to see that the first people, the Indian people remained last,
even in 1994 on their own continent. Requests for the simple materials of the
sweat lodge, most of which surrounded the prison -- the willows, the rocks,
covering tarps, sage and cedar bundles, sweet grass, a drum, and a cord of
wood were major obstacles for Pastor Childs and Father Ignacio. They were
busy ministering to the Christians within the confines of a full scale church

building complete with choir robes, sacrament trays and cups, pianos, and hymnals, while offering a new bible and printed materials to each new Christian inmate.

"You white men keep your God locked up in that building. Our God is out here in the fields and lives with us in the woods and mountains." That native belief was what I felt from years of backpacking, carrying a simple home, a tent and sleeping bag, on my back.

The process of where to place a sweat lodge was a month long obstacle. We were eventually allowed to put it ten feet from the edge of the track. Finally, the willows arrived, digging bars and shovels were issued to clear the grass and dig holes for the ends of the willow to be placed in the Mother Earth.

Other inmates, ignorant of the religious significance of building the lodge would jest as they walked by, "What, ya gonna have a wienie roast here?" Or they would hoot and holler, mimicking what they thought was an Indian. We knew they were just joking in ignorance. But in spite of the Religious Freedom Act, allowing native people to perform their ceremonies, the BOP had managed to maintain the hierarchy of respect for the Christian civilization, while relegating the sweatlodge ritual to the rites of heathens using religion as a cover for escapes.

With the lodge built we had to wait for wood. In an area that had burnt wood and coal as a heating source for 300 years, they just couldn't seem to locate a cord. Tony was released to head back home. The truth remained that he had never been allowed to practice his religion in prison. The guards viewed the ritual as a curiosity, a modern day *Buffalo Bill Wild West* show.

A traveling group of young Christians managed to connect with Pastor Childs, and with the proper paperwork and channels, an entire musical play came together in the chapel in two weeks. The chapel was packed, standing room only. The cast, dressed in biblical attire, was composed of young men and women, ages 18 to 25. Some were obviously nervous, gazing out to a room full of federal convicts, but they were so well received and supported that their doubts were soon relieved. The room filled with applause after each set of script and song. The troupe left as touched by the humanity of America's incarcerated, as the inmates were by the delicious exposure to young, committed, healthy youth.

Not many weeks later, a weekend retreat was offered. It was called Emmaus, a new word to most of us. It was another Christian weekend designed to bring as many as possible to Jesus. "Jesus Loves You, Pass It On," was the theme.

We were allowed to leave the unit and remain in the chapel for the entire day if we signed up for the retreat. The guards came into the chapel at the regular morning and afternoon count to interrupt and remind that prison chapels were not a sanctuary.

A dozen women and half dozen men led the retreat, traveling across the state to communicate Jesus love to each inmate. They were an impressive and effective group, beginning with spiritually focused folk music and harmonies. It was infectious. As individuals, each one introduced themselves with personal confessions and tearfully bared their own sins. Their sins weren't criminal, but they were human, told by non-judgemental humans. Groups were formed for discussion topics, as the best of Christianity was brought forth, in example as much as in word.

They were a reminder that Christian dogma and corporate Christianity had stolen the teachings of this great leader of old. Jesus had been bastardized, and much of the modern generation was turned off to his wisdom due to the hypocrisy of organized religion. The Emmaus group understood what Jesus was teaching. They were living it.

A young woman, over eight months pregnant, barely able to reach over her belly to strum the guitar, hugged each inmate, regardless of color or crime, and gave them, "I love you, Jesus loves you, Pass it on." An energy formed -- we felt it in goosebumps and tears. If this was Jesus' Love, it was good. The prison rule of no hugging was violated the entire weekend with nothing but a positive outcome.

A pair of twins, perhaps 50 years old, which looked like the local librarian or Jane Wyman from *Father Knows Best*, were loaded all day with loving smiles and letter packets. They handed out these packets, rolled into scrolls and tied with orange and blue yarns containing letters from each of the Emmaus group. How each of them wrote a letter to the fifty participants and got them into the rolls by the end of Saturday was hard to imagine.

At the end of the weekend, inmates stood up to tell their personal stories. Dave, the softball coach for the Christian baseball team, the Redeemed, told his painful and personal story. "I was living the wild life, boozin, playin with drugs, and one day it caught up to me. I am about to walk out of here, a free man in only six days, but I will never be free from what my mistake taught me.

"I was only 24 years old, but I had a nasty temper. My wife and I were having a hard time, and one day my little four year old daughter was crying about something and I gave her a backhand." The room was still as his voice slowed, taking a breath as his tears created wet streaks across each cheek. The six foot three, well-built man breathed deeply with an open mouth. "She hit her head against the wall, sustained a concussion, and died twenty four hours later. My anger killed her." He looked at the room through bleary, tear filled eyes, holding his jaw back and licking his teeth and lips with his tongue.

"Her death almost killed me too.... But it was three years ago that this Emmaus group first came to Lewisburg where I did most of my time. And although I had known Jesus, I had never known the depth of his love for me. He forgave me for what I couldn't forgive myself. He loved me when I hated myself. His love saved me and I am walking out those gates a whole man to serve that God. They won't let me back in these prisons to lead Christian retreats because I'm a felon now, but I guarantee you that I will never be back as a criminal."

"No matter what your crime, Jesus Loves You, I Love You, Pass It On." Four people from the audience jumped up to embrace him as the tears flowed. The fervor of evangelism, in it's most positive aura, was present. Everyone was touched.

We each left with a small wooden cross placed around our necks as we passed down the line of organizers and received hugs from each one. We returned to the units still in bliss. I chanted my own version of the Jesus prayer, "Lord Jesus Christ, have mercy on me, Lord Buddha, have mercy on me, Lord Tunkashila, have mercy on me, Lord Muhammed, have mercy on me and may the thousand names of Allah have mercy on us all." Love in Hell is much sweeter than love in heaven. Hell removes the need for denial. You're there and the contrast makes definitions much easier. A little wooden cross, even with a crack in it, can give you the feeling of a free eagle soaring on the butte.

As I lay in my cell bunk, my attention was drawn across the hall, into the cell catty-corner. Tom, at about 6'4" with a butch blond head, was bent over his desk while Bill was wiping something across his shirtless back. As an EMT, I thought I'd better stick my nose in to see if help was needed.

"Hey, guys, What's up?"

"Look for yourself," Tom offered, motioning with his chin to his back.

There it was, emblazoned on his live skin, a ten inch figure of a cloaked, bearded wizard holding an eagle claw staff . The lines of the tatoo puffed out around and under the black ink, creating a raised effect. The wizard's cloak was covered with scattered stars and a moon, making the wizard and the universe one. The details of the long, straggly beard and wrinkled face were astounding. The three finger claws and opposing thumb claw of the eagle staff were complete, with the leathery palm undersides and downy fur covering the eagles ankle and toes. A floppy but dignified conical hat kept the wizard's long flowing hair in check, although a breeze moved across the universe of Tom's flesh. It was striking in its life as it seemed a hidden part of Toms character was crawling to the surface.

"Whoa, that's beautiful. When was that done?"

"About two hours ago." Tom confessed.

"How much?"

"Fifty bucks in commissary."

"I'll bet that would be three hundred on the streets. I checked into a tatoo once in Seattle when I was in the Merchant Marine. They wanted $200. for a small tattoo.

Could you connect me with the artist that did this?"

"Sure, meet me out at the weight pile tomorrow at 4:30 and I'll introduce you to Fred."

"What are you putting on it?"

"I'm supposed to smear it down with Vasoline for a week and no hot showers."

The next afternoon at the weight pile, I was introduced to a tall, muscular man covered with tattoos on his arms and chest. His long, blonde hair, and fu-man-chu moustache were unique, but most striking was the Conan style barbarian woman on his right forearm. The shading on her lips and nipples was as lifelike as flesh. It was flesh.

"Don't point to tattoos or do any motions to tip off the guards what our conversation might be about. Just describe things in words," he cautioned, aware of the patrolling guards. "I do about five tatoos a week, so I need to be real low profile, if you catch my drift. Do you have any artwork?"

I explained the vision of an eagle over the earth, the eastern and western hemispheres divided by a yin-yang symbol. The Earth as a Native American shield with eagle feathers hanging from the bottom border, six feathers for the six directions: east, south, west and north, Father Sky and Mother Earth.

"Yeah, I can draw that. Sounds like you got about thirty bucks' worth. First, I'll give you my commissary order and after you deliver on that, then we'll do the tattoo."

I spent the last of my inmate account on the ancient art of tattooing. One of the few bennies to prison was affordable tattoos. The federal prosecution called me an opportunist. They were right! I say, when opportunity knocks, at least answer the door. The commissary order of cigarettes, canned chicken, and two six packs of Pepsi was filled and delivered. The transaction was carefully passed out of the guards' view. Tattooing was illegal in prison, punishable by lockdown and confiscation of tools and inks. There was always the threat of losing good time.

But the truth was that most guards looked the other way, and unless it was flaunted in their face, they ignored it. Some were actually impressed, casually accepting that the puffy pink art was four years old. "Very nice."

After dinner I walked to the Brady unit where Fred was scheduled to perform the work in his cell. Jeff greeted me at the unit door, shuttled me through and quietly down the hall to Red's cell. Inmates were not allowed in units they didn't live in. The guard must've been off in another section of the unit.

Fred instructed me to lie on the bed after I removed my shirt. "Lay on your side. You are a hairy one, aren't you?" He commented, while he carefully dry shaved my left bicep. He strapped on a battery powered casette motor with pieces of velcro. The tattooing needle was the high E string of a folk guitar. The steel string slid in and out of a hollowed-out Bic pen.

"Don't worry, I use a new piece of guitar string on every tattoo, and I sterilize everything with hot, soapy water and then bleach. Check out this art," he said, holding up the completed piece. "Now this is Ba-Ba-Ba-Bad to the Bone."

I was pleased with the art. The earth was bounded by the sacred hoop, the circle of life. The eagle, wings spread, soared above the Earth's oceans and continents. The dividing line of the yin and yang was the medical symbol of the snake and in this case had rattles that blended into the hoop. The detailed veins and spots of each feather stood out distinctly, as did the leather thongs that lashed the feathers to the hoop.

The location on the upper left arm was wiped down with vasoline to receive the tracing paper outline. Fred positioned the art, pressed down into the vasoline, and after peeling the paper away, the bold outline remained.

"The darker the line, the deeper the needle goes into the skin, so sometimes the outline can be the most painful. Let me know if it's too much and you need a break."

Jeff stood in the doorway of the cell and kept watch for the marauding unit guard. A radio was turned up to hide the noise of the humming cassette motor. I relaxed as a prickling sensation began moving across my naked arm. I decided not to own the arm for the night. Although pain was present, somebody else owned it. Truth is, the arm is not all that sensitive.

"Here comes the guard," Jeff cautioned. I sat up and moved into the hidden corner of Fred's bed picking up a *People* magazine. To be in a unit other than your own was an out of bounds violation, but because the guards changed units often, they were not always certain who was in which unit.

"Hey what's happening?" Jeff asked the guard. "Who's gonna win tonights game? The Forty Niners are my bet."

Jeff and the guard continued to chat while Fred sipped a Pepsi, having jerked off the tatoo motor and stashed it in his locker. The guard finally departed, while Fred chewed out Jeff for keeping the guard hanging around.

" I was just trying to distract him." Jeff argued.

"Yeah, well, distract him on down the road. I only have two hours to complete this."

John Cougar Mellencamp came on the radio singing Scarecrow in the Rain. "Now that guy is one of the few people I would shoot if I ever got the chance. In fact, that might be my first mission when I get outta here. You just can't abuse power like that."

"Really, what's wrong with Mellencamp?" I asked.

"That son of a bitch goes on MTV with his nigger girlfriend. Then they're hugging and kissing. It's disgusting. What kind of example is he setting for the kids? That's abuse of power. People are supposed to stay to their own races, that's what I believe. Am I offending you?" He asked callously, with the motor whirring in his hands. He began to fill in the minute details of the eagle feathers.

"No. I disagree with you, but your opinion doesn't offend me. I just don't believe killing accomplishes anything productive. That's what this sacred hoop and this yin and yang are all about -- the interconnectedness of all life." I decided it was not a time for a philosophical debate.

With not a moment to spare, the details were completed -- the continents shaded in, the leather thongs tying the feathers to the hoop completed, and the snake's skin detailed with the diamond pattern of the rattlesnake.

"Wipe it with vasoline twice a day for a week. Stay out of the sun so the inks don't bleed. Don't get it wet or in hot water for a week, and don't let the guards see it for a couple of weeks."

"The coast is clear, my man." Jeff led the way out, watching for guards. I pulled my long sleeves down, covering the pink, puffy work."

I got back to Lycoming unit, returning to my cell in time for count. I viewed the tatoo while lying in the top bunk, facing the wall. As I checked it out, a warm glow came over me. Unlike a medicine bag, a ring, a headband or any symbolic jewelry, no prison guard or court order could remove that statement. It would be there to remind me that I was committed to create balance on Earth, that all creatures belong here and have wisdom to share, that there is power and blessings from the six directions, that with the eagle we can have vision and with the snake, the sensitivity to heal. It was bad to the bone. It was me to the bone, and the bones on this eagle were mending.

* * * * *

"He was a Buffalo Soldier   Win the war for America
Buffalo Soldier, Dreadlock Rasta.
Fighting on arrival, fighting for survival
If you know your history
Then you would know where you coming from
Then you wouldn't have to ask
Who the heck I think I am"
  — Bob Marley Confrontation

* * * * *

"Don, how are you today?"

"Most well, Brother Rick." Don McKenzie was the round-faced black min-ister of the Rastafarian faith in Allenwood. He didn't limit himself within the confines of a religion, rather he freed himself with it. He prayed to Jah, claimed glory to the Nazarene, and respected any faith that recognized the One Love. Don was a rainbow warrior, a peaceful warrior.

First cousin to Bob Marley, he had been imprisoned for flying Jamaican herb into America. We walked many laps together in that prison.

He once told me, "I remember, it was a sad day because the Jamaican government had found our marijuana fields and they had burnt many acres of the herb.

"I was with Bob the day after the burn saying how sad it was. Bob turned to me kind of chanting, saying, "Every time I plant a seed, he says, kill it before it grows." The times were hard for us then. Bob was not yet well known, but I remember one evening it was a full moon and Bob went out walking and when he came back in he said, 'I feel a change in the air. Everything is gonna be all right.'

"The next morning some white man showed up at Bob's door, barefoot, in jeans and a T-shirt and he said to Bob, 'I heard your song, I Shot The Sheriff and I was wondering if you would jam with me, teach me that song maybe.'

"Well, Bob said sure and the guy came in. They played a while and the guy was pretty good. Bob said, 'So what's your name?' To this guy and he says, "I'm Eric" and they shook hands. This guy Eric went off and recorded that song and it got famous. You see, his name was Eric Clapton, and that was the change for Bob Marley."

I shared with Don the story of nuclearism, The Hundredth Monkey, and my spiritual vision. "The key issue as I see it is the question of violence. The survival of humanity hinges on nonviolence, or as Gandhi worded it, 'Satayagraha,' soul force."

"I am certain you are right and I am also certain that there is a tremendous force working in your life. I know that your intentions are honorable. Be wary of false prophecy along the path, though, Rick."

I ran around that track every day. I made friends. We shared our lifes stories and philosophies. "Mr. King, hey Bob, how ya doin today?" I shook hands with a rugged, weathered man as Bob joined me for a few laps.

"You still in love with those niggers?" Bob pushed. "Or is it the injuns you're hangin out with this week?" He paused with a broad-grinned, Popeye smile. "What? You must be dead. I can't even get a rise outta you anymore."

"Bob, what can we do to get you over your racism? It's eatin' you up and wasting too much energy. I know you've got a good heart in there. I see it."

"I'm glad you asked. We could put every last one of em on a boat, send it out to sea and blow it to hell."

"No, really Bob." I tried to get serious. "I want to know what could realistically be done to make you hate other races less. Maybe it's all for show, to get a rise out of me, but I honestly can't grasp how someone of your intelligence can sit there in the chow hall and yell racial slurs like you do."

"Well, it's no show. I'll promise you that. You weren't a twinkle in your mama's eye when I was a successful burglar. It was an honorable profession in those days. Even the cops treated us with respect and it was reciprocated. But that was before this nation got lost and kowtowed to the coons. Look at this prison. Most of these animals are grunting some foreign language or some perverted English no one can understand. The crap these jokers pull here in Allenwood would have been a death sentence twenty years ago in Lewisburg.

"You talk about wasting time and energy. Heck, I was in prison with your gurus, Phil and Dan Berrigan. Now you tell me that Phil Berrigan is in prison again and what has he accomplished in his life? Heck, he was organizing protests in prison thirty years back and nobody gave a shit. Dan got himself in lockdown for something and Phil tried to organize a food strike. Your problem is that you think somebody gives a shit.

"All these jigaboos and tamales care about is their own mouths and keeping stoned on drugs. They're a bunch of lazy bastards. They never had it so good as here in prison. They get clean sheets, three meals a day, soccer teams, enchilada TV. Heck, they love it here. They were starvin in the old country."

"Oh Bob, get a grip. Sure some people are lazy escapists, but you can't stereotype a race because of a few. Besides, I can guarantee you that if you were born poor in Cuba, you would be one of the boat people making your way to Los EsTacos Unidos yourself."

"Careful now," Bob cautioned at the suggestion.

"Hell, you'd be that rascal that jumped up under the airplane wheels and rode exposed all the way to Miami, cuz you're a survivor. And yet you hate the Hispanics with the pioneer spirit, willing to risk it all in a country where they can't even speak the language."

Bob was shaking his head, "Don't give me that shit. Those people sold out their own. The Zulu chief was down on the beach selling his own kind when the slave boats landed. They enslaved their own people since the beginning of time."

"Perhaps so, Bob, but that doesn't make it right. All you have proven now is that some blacks are willing to enslave others, just like some whites. What I'm saying is that racism is not a color issue, it's just a simple cop-out to hate something different. You, by being a racist, join ranks with people of all colors that hate. You're in the racist club which includes blacks, whites, Latinos, Indians. There's nothing special about it. You want somebody to blame for the world dilemma, when there's nobody but you."

"Gettin a little pushy here, Rick." Bob cautioned.

"Well, fate done put us in the same cage, Bob and I shake and rattle when I'm in a cage and I see racism as a bar on that cage. 'Those who profess to favor freedom yet deprecate agitation are those who want crops without plowing the ground.'"

"Hey, that's good. I like that. Who said that?"

"Frederick Douglass, a black abolitionist."

Bob smiled, shaking his head, "Oh you got balls, man."

* * * * *

"How ya doin, Gary?" I asked as I jogged by.

"Oh, I'm not doin' so great."

"Really, what's the problem?" I stopped jogging to check in.

"Well, I told you my story. Tomorrow, I have to set up my father in the visiting room. They want me to wear a recorder and get him to say several incriminating things."

Gary had been another pot farmer from up in Northern Pennsylvania, not far from the green hills of Allenwood. He had been very successful for about ten years, even smuggling marijuana from Mexico, a deal his father, a city planner and ex-police officer, had set up for him. With a white coat, he could have passed for a lab technician, clean shaven, very short hair, receding hairline. He was a small man with bright eyes and an inquisitive mind. Amazing how a razor can turn a twenty year hippie into a respectable citizen about to sell out his father.

But Gary was still struggling with the decision. He hated himself for ratting, yet couldn't face twenty years in prison. His charges were compounded by being, what the feds call, "the king pin," which added more time to the penalty.

I had been warned several times about associating with Gary because he was suspected of being a rat. Associating with a rat is risky. If you associate with a rat then maybe you're a rat yourself. Three crimes in particular were cause for the scarlet R in prison: rape, child abuse, and implicating others. I never met or heard of a child abuser or a rapist in prison because nobody would fess up to those crimes.

Suspected rats were warned of impending doom with the traditional mattress burning. Other inmates would pile the rat's possessions on their bunk and light it all when the rat was out. They usually disappeared into segregation and were eventually transferred to the Cheese Factory, a separate prison, viewable across the dell, for government witnesses or others in need of protection.

"I have to talk about critical issues with my father without tipping him off that he's being recorded. Then they are going to use it in trial against him."

"Gary, I hope you don't talk to other people about this issue because your safety is in jeopardy if word gets out that you're a rat, and you know, it's already suspected. I've been warned about you myself."

"Well, I'll certainly understand if you feel the need to stop associating with me."

"Our friendship in Yokefellows has been sincere, and although I don't justify things, I try to refrain from judgement. You know that by now, Gary. I wouldn't want to be in your shoes but I'll pray that you and your family find The

Way."

"Thanks Rick, I appreciate that."

Two weeks later, a newspaper clipping was being passed around the units.

"This implicates *your buddy* in a major rat affair," Ed complained with a biting tone. "This asshole sold out his own father and family. He set them up right here in Allenwood."

Threats ran the gamut in Lycoming unit: "He's a marked man." "He won't make it through another day once copies of this get around." "That kind of rat gets the shank." "Burn him out." And then threats became promises.

I entered the cafeteria and saw Gary sitting at a table by himself. I carried my tray over and sat down next to him. "Gary, have you seen the article from the newspaper about your father's trial?"

"No, what's it say?" He asked holding a forkfull.

"It says you sold out your father."

"Do you have copy? You know how rumors fly around here."

"No, but by the time I get a copy you might be a hurtin man. I recommend PC and I don't mean Politically Correct." Gary knew I meant Protective Custody.

"Well, I hate to run off to segregation before I need to. I'm not looking forward to lockdown and no rec yard."

"Gary, you will hate to be gurneyed off to the hospital for facial surgery even more. You're not a bad looking guy....today!" I tried to impress Jerry.

"My recommendation is..." I felt a lot of eyes on us and interrupted my own comment. "See that guy waving his fork our direction. He doesn't like you. He's seen the press piece. He's telling others as we speak." I glanced around the room and saw two other faces looking at us. "You walk directly to your unit and submit yourself to your unit counselor for PC. Don't dally, Gary. Take care of yourself. Don't make me believe you have a death wish. You're smarter than that. It's time to go. Keep praying and looking for God, Gary."

He stood up with his half-finished tray. "I'll get your tray. Don't walk down the dishroom aisle." Gary walked out the cafeteria door and disappeared from the compound.

"I hear your Rat friend turned himself into PC this morning" Ed commented in disgust later that day.

"Good!"

Chapter Nineteen
LIFE AFTER DEATH, A GRATUITY

* * * * *

"It has become more and more difficult for researchers and journalists to gain access to prison systems."
— Selke, <u>Prisons in Crisis</u> 1993

* * * * *

I found my name on a bulletin board at the end of the hall. Adjacent to my name was the word 'TEAM.'

"Say Dusty, what is this `team?'"

"Well, really, it ought to be called 'gang,' because LEB, Brooks and Scott are gonna gang up on you and tell you just how they plan to screw you out of what you don't got comin' because you got nothin' comin'!"

"Lovely."

"Say, how is your good time Habeaus Corpus coming along?" Dusty asked.

"Oh, they're still fighting me on this bogus technicality and although the sentence computation manual is not classified, Mr. Taylor has refused to let me see a copy. How can I prove they're wrong, when they won't let me see the manual they use to compute good time?"

"Now you're figuring it out. See, the BOP is a subsidiary of Motel 6, and they want to rent every room every day. We'll leave the light on fer ya."

During my time at Allenwood, I learned that the judge in the courtroom isn't the only one to judge. Throughout the prison system I saw that every guard, every sergeant, every unit head, associate and head warden had an agenda for each inmate based on their personal beliefs.

It was apparent from the Broken Eagle Incident just what I felt about the federal system and its systemic dysfunction. For exercising that freedom of speech I deserved special attention. With1300 felons at Allenwood, I was the only misdemeanor. Yet I was refused the halfway house or home confinement. Though I enumerated valid grounds for the maximum release gratuity of $500, I was released with $100. The sentencing computation staff made efforts, through bogus technicalities, to keep me down for another two months by denying my good time. With my legal papers stolen by the marshals, I couldn't prove any of my arguments.

I found that the original district attorney charges stuck on your record and were used against you throughout the process, even if the charges had been dropped, never proven or even prosecuted. Strategically, trumped up district attorney charges were effective in further punishing inmates throughout. BOP staff accepted that you were probably guilty of all the crimes as originally charged. And many members of the prison staff take it as their personal duty to see that punishment is fulfilled.

I entered Mr. Berry's office on the day of the gang meeting.

"Have a seat, Springer," Berry instructed.

Mr. Brooks limped in, still hobbling from his government paid knee surgery, and Mr. James sat silently. With the gang together, Mr. Berry leaned over to slam the door closed.

LEB began, "Well, Springer, I'm gonna be honest with you, we have read your papers and decided that you are a flight risk and a threat to the community. So, on those grounds we are going to deny you the halfway house. You'll be released directly from here at Allenwood."

"Threat to the community? That's absurd. Perhaps you should read what the jurors said in my first trial."

"Well, you threatened a former president and resisted arrest," Berry continued.

"I never threatened anybody, and I have never been convicted of those things. They were dropped. I accepted a plea of embarrassing the Secret Service. You can't charge me with things that were dropped."

"Well, you were convicted of Failure to Surrender, so we are classifying you as a flight risk, and on that, we are denying the halfway house. You'll be released," he looked at the papers, "in November."

"No, I'll be released from here in September. I have 64 days good time coming."

"Well, that's not what the Sentence Computation says here and we just follow their instructions. You've made it clear that you will follow whatever political whim comes to you, Springer. We can't risk you running off from the halfway house for the next nuclear protest."

"Mr. Berry, if I knew that you and your family were going to be radiated from a nuclear test or another Three Mile Island, I would ignore a court order to be able to inform you and your family of the imminent threat."

"And Springer, I'd follow you into the radiated areas of Chernobyl to track you down and get you back in prison."

His statement was pathetically revealing. We all broke out in laughter.

"Mr. Brooks, you stand as my witness. That comment's gonna go in the book."

While I was willing to violate minor laws to prevent individuals and society from radiation, Mr. Berry was willing to risk radiation exposure to drag such a citizen into jail. Amazing what an individual could be trained to do for a paycheck.

I approached the associate warden, a blockish, squat character with square rim glasses, while he was attempting to hide behind the dirty dish line.

"Mr. Arnold, I have been trying to get my sentence computation adjusted to include good time, but Mr. Taylor has denied me access to unclassified documents that dictate the sentencing policy. Also, I need legal counsel to assist in that situation, as well as a US Marshal tort claim I'm working on, regarding the theft of my legal papers."

"Legal assistance is available in the law library, and you'll have to deal with Mr. Taylor on the computation manual." He responded curtly, letting me know with a quick glance that I was dismissed.

"The law says that I am entitled to professional legal counsel. The clerks in the law library have no training and are not qualified to give valid legal assistance."

That statement at least got his attention. He glared at me like a perturbed snapping turtle. "Don't try to quote me the law, Mister. I know the law and we have no obligation to provide you with an attorney."

"Well, that's not what the US code says," I insisted, but I could see I was wasting my time.

The next day I approached Associate Warden Bierly, a motherly looking woman in her early fifties. She seemed pleasant enough, sincere and willing to help. I attempted to explain my problems, but during the conversation she said "hi" to every inmate that passed. Even when I was in the middle of a sentence, she would begin talking to others. I finally walked away midsentence, blowing out my nostrils. Bierly barely noticed. It was the response she wanted.

"All sail and no anchor." Unit staff, counselors and associate wardens were mandated by BOP policy to be available to inmates during lunch hours. They dissipated the inmate's gripes, but little of consequence was achieved. Inmates learned in no short order that talking to BOP staff was a waste of time. That was the idea behind incarceration: to waste your time while over 1.7 million people worked in criminal justice nationwide, and 547,166 prison staff received over $4.3 billion in monthly payroll.

After several official complaint forms, I was finally allowed to view the sentence computation manual, while Mr. Kos observed to insure that I didn't steal pages or paperclips.

"Can I get copies of pages 1-18 to 1-27? Those are the pages pertinent to my argument."

"Well, I'll have to get approval from Mr. Taylor." He insisted on standard BOP policy, CYA (Cover Your Ass).

One month before my release, in response to court order, my legal papers, confiscated back in North Las Vegas, arrived at Allenwood. Amongst the papers was a copy of the court order stating that until the date of sentencing the 120 days had not been served.

The Court considered my time not served though in fact, I had served 150 days on the date the order was issued. The court had issued that order as a back-up to create another means to keep me incarcerated if they chose. But that very order now served to insure that Allenwood had to honor my good time. The back-up backfired.

I marched up to the sentence computation office and showed the document to Mr. Kos. "Well, if this is a valid document, then it seems you are right, Springer, but we'll have to order a copy from the court ourselves. We can't accept a copy that you provide us as valid."

I convinced Kos to correct the department's error by calling the Vegas court and ordering the document. I sat there, embarrassed for Mr. Kos as he nearly whispered in his call to Vegas. He was afraid of inciting the wrath of the department head, Mr. Taylor, who had adamantly insisted that I was not eligible for good time.

The court verified the document and said they would send a copy. I raised my finger into the air and put an imaginary mark on the cosmic chalkboard. The smell of freedom was becoming more pungent daily. It smelled like big bush sage.

$$* \; * \; * \; * \; *$$

The law states in the Statutory Index Appendix B of BOP policy that under US Code Annotated 3624. Release of a prisoner. "The Bureau of Prisons shall, to the extent practicable, assure that a prisoner serving a term of imprisonment spends a reasonable part, not to exceed six months of the term to be served, under conditions that will afford the prisoner a reasonable opportunity to adjust to and prepare for his re-entry into the community. The authority provided by this subsection may be used to place a prisoner in home confinement. The US Probation System shall, to the extent practicable, offer assistance to a prisoner during such release."

As with all BOP policy and statutes, in fact it seems with all law, the government escape clause or loophole is always present. "To the extent practicable," "a reasonable part," and "may be" were the terms granting discretion to the BOP. LEB and the staff were distinctly aware of these clauses. These clauses allowed them to do whatever they chose. The halfway house is designed to allow the inmate to blend back into society, by giving them supervised housing and provided meals while they re-enter the work force. This gives inmates a chance to save some money for release, rather than being dumped on the streets broke. Many inmates' lives have been completely destroyed by the incarceration process. Their homes, cars and possessions have been sold or repossessed. Their wives and children, families and friends, divorced or disappeared. In contrast, the Justice Department Asset Forfeiture Fund grew from $26 million in 1986 to $350.6 million in 1994.

On September 13th, thirteen months and two days after my media tour on Nagasaki day, I was hustled out at the last minute to intake and released at 6:10 am. I was issued baggy jeans, a white polo shirt and a baggy winter coat. The release officer arrived at ten to six. I was rushed out the door to a waiting taxi without even the time to count what money they dumped into my release envelope.

"Well, buddy, I hope they gave you enough money cuz you got a whopping bill already. I've been sitting here fifteen minutes. Who the hell do they think they are? Tell me to be here at 6:00 AM to sit around and wait." the moustached cabby was yelling as I climbed in.

I sized him up with squinted eyes, but only said calmly, "Take me to the airport. I have a 6:30 flight."

The grey air on this side of the fence was the same. The grey human behavior was the same. Did the fence and walls make the prison or did the people?

I remembered my prison Buddhism teacher and what Chuang Tzu said centuries before: "Free yourself from the world. Man is the author of his own suffering and bondage. All his fears spring from the web of values created by himself alone."

The cab rolled through a trough in the mountain ridge, a narrow gap dropping into the swirling fog of the next Pennsylvania valley. We wandered up the valley as I glanced across a meadow to view an airport. After driving into the town at the other end of the valley, it became apparent that the cabby was driving around to run up the bill. An old hand at scamming inmates, no doubt, he pulled into a Ramada Inn, keeping the meter running while he went in to pick up his next charge.

"I'm gonna shut the meter off now, but your bill is $40.00," he demanded after settling behind the wheel.

"I want a receipt. They only gave me $25.00 for the cab."

"Well, you aren't gonna get a receipt," he challenged.

"Well, then you aren't gonna get paid."

"Look, you convict punk. I'll drive your ass right on back to that prison and have you locked back up."

"Let's go." I called his bluff, looking him straight in the eye.

"You're the hardest con I've ever dealt with," he snorted. "All right, you'll get your receipt."

The cab was silent during the remainder of the ride to the airport. I paid the $25.00 receipt and climbed out, leaving the door open to insure that the cab wouldn't drive away until I got my boxes of legal papers out of the trunk. As I stepped in the door of the small local airport to set down the boxes, the cabby assumed I was leaving his door open on purpose.

He jumped out in a show of outrage, "They never should have let you out of prison, Mister!" He yelled, hoping to embarrass me as he reached out to slam the door.

"No, they never should have let me out," I agreed, breaking into a wild laugh as freedom began to sink in.

AFTERWORD

* * * * *

"They sell us our presidents the same way,
they sell us our clothes and our cars,
They sell us everything from youth to religion,
at the same time they sell us our wars.
I want to know who the men in the shadows are,
I want to hear somebody asking them why?
They can be counted on to tell us who our enemies are
but they're never the ones to fight or to die."
     − Jackson Browne   Lives In The Balance

* * * * *

On September 13, 1994, I was released from Allenwood federal prison in Pennsylvania. The feds flew me home on the taxpayers' dime. Contrary to my request that they fly me to DC, they insisted I go to the West Coast, back to Arcata. I thought a little congressional lobbying might be just the thing I needed after thirteen months in six different prisons.

While the sun chased and passed my plane home, I thought about the message of the Broken Eagle, a message of unmasking denial, a message of looking honestly at that which is broken.

I revisited some of the prison experiences and just what I had learned on the journey from North Las Vegas Detention Center to Allenwood, Pennsylvania. I was sucked into a vein of soundbites, which are meant to be (and sometimes are) full dissertations in themselves. The media uses soundbite after soundbite without allowing us the time to critique them or decide if they are valid. But I had time.

Sue Quig-Terrey had told Sue Navy during my trials, "I've spent more time on Rick's trial than I do on most murder cases." I worry for those charged with murder!

During the Hundredth Monkey organizing, Casey Kasem candidly told me, regarding the nuclear industry, "If ever we're ever really successful, they'll kill us." I remembered the paintings on Pre-Trial officer Theresa Brown's office wall: Gandhi, Dr. King, John Kennedy. Were they too successful?

Judge Pro's soundbite, "It's obvious to me, Mr. Springer, that you are going to spend the rest of your life in one form of community service or another, so that would not be an appropriate punishment."

Soundbites. . . . The state prosecutor: "I hear you kicked ass in federal court?" US Marshal Jim Davey: "Off the record, I'm one of your greatest supporters," and "Are you suggesting I perjured myself on the witness stand?" Lloyd George: "The prudent use of nuclear weapons has guaranteed your right to freedom of speech." Ronald Reagan: "Will America become a self-absorbed nation of couch-potatoes?" Hazel Oleary, the head of DOE: "I was shocked, appalled and deeply saddened!"

Terry Tempest Williams: "Nine women in my family have all had cancer, seven are dead." Corbin Harney: "Like I said, we got to protect what we got, all animal life, the bird lifes, our water, our air, our Mother Earth. I taught him his part, to teach his people to take care, to stand together as human people throughout the world." Franciscan Alain Richards: "Moral law is over any kind of law, as doctor King proclaim it very strongly from the jail of Birmingham."

I learned from my federal experience that in the land of the free and the home of the brave, we imprison more people than any nation on earth, a thousand people a week, 180 a day. The combined population of US prisons and jails was over 1.4 million in 1993, 455 inmates per 100,000 Americans. Our prison population has more than tripled since 1980, while research has shown that there is no demonstrable relationship between our increased incarceration and crime reduction. At the present rate of prison growth, over half the US population will be imprisoned by the year 2053.

I saw from first hand experience that inmates are far from corrected in correctional institutes. They learn from 'the degradation ceremony' to hate the system and upon release have been educated by other inmates how to 'get-over,' to be successful at crime, without getting nailed. I heard in locked cells and walking in the yard, the details of ID forgery, bank robbery, credit card scams, and the chemical components, readily available, for methamphetamine, "Crank."

Never use a gun to rob a bank: tellers are trained to give up the money upon demand. A simple note will do. If caught, possession of a weapon will increase your jail time by five years. Insist on large bills only, or the teller will fill your bags with ones. Use your own bag. Be wary of 'dye-packs,' which explode a dye all over the money, making it identifiable and worthless. Also, radio transmitters are sometimes inserted in money bundles which can allow the police to zero in on your location.

I lived, confined in cages, with drug pushers, burglars, smugglers, murderers, mercenaries, racists, and criminals of every class. Strange as it seems, even to me, I liked every one of them. Dr. King said, "True altruism is more than the capacity to pity, it is the capacity to empathize. Pity is feeling sorry for someone; empathy is feeling sorry with someone." I learned that the real issue is how to create peace, not who is right or wrong. This takes a degree of maturity, something sadly lacking in the world today. Peace Pilgrim claimed, "What people really suffer from is immaturity. Among mature people war would not be a problem—it would not be possible."

I learned in prison that each and every inmate was a human being, even the most surly, arrogant, selfish and disrespectful. What I found corroborated was my belief that, given the opportunity, everyone responds to compassion.

One in six federal inmates are incarcerated for marijuana offenses. I met lots of inmates doing time for growing or selling it. Yet conservative estimates claim that over a third of the American population over the age of eleven has smoked marijuana. Even President Clinton confessed to the "crime." We make a mockery of all law when we have laws that three million of our citizens violate daily.

Our prisons are full of people who don't belong there. Those people are being damaged by being exposed to those that do. Over 60% of the prison population is incarcerated for drug violations in a nation where we have clearly expressed that we are not concerned about drug use or abuse. It's which drugs and who you buy them from that is the concern.

The capitalist relationship between our mania to imprison and the US defense industry are evidenced in the Crime Bill proposal to convert closed military installations to federal prison facilities. The growth in US prisons has been in alarming relation to the de-escalation and supposed halt of the Cold War. As we remove small numbers of troops from a variety of locations internationally, we are building our home front militia through prison guards, police, and all forms of law enforcement. It is little known that the Department of Defense drug interdiction budget increased from $14.6 million in 1984 to $854.4 million in 1992. As rock/activist band Clan Dyken sings, "The war on drugs is a war on the people." America is economically based on war, whether abroad or at home. The spoils of capitalism require armies to protect them.

"One of the most staggering statistics to be revealed in modern times is that every year, the dollar costs of corporate crime in America, as estimated by the Bureau of National Affairs, is over ten times greater than the combined larcenies, robberies, burglaries and auto thefts committed by individuals." writes Gerry Spence. "One in five of America's top 500 corporations has been convicted of at least one major crime." Keep in mind that these same corporations employ entire law firms to prevent convictions. The bulk of our nation's judges began in corporate law firms.

Spence asks, "If the death penalty is in vogue for human felons, should it not also be used against corporate murderers? Corporate crime is the most serious social evil facing America. A justice department survey of sixty thousand citizens found that Americans viewed purposeful dumping of hazardous waste a worse act than some homicides."

On November 9, 1992, Bruce Van Voorst published in *Time* magazine a story, A Thousand Points of Blight, "From fuel spills and toxic waste to live shells and lethal landfills, the US military is the nation's No.1 polluter." While we justified the bombing of Hiroshima with the 1941 air attack of Pearl Harbor, our own military polluted that same harbor with 12,264 acres of unlined land-fills, pesticide-disposal pits, chromic acid disposal areas, heavy metal contami-nation and waste oil leakage. Although in 1978 Carter instructed the military to comply with EPA legislation, the order was never enforced. While in 1980 Congress passed the Superfund law, making private polluters responsible for cleaning up hazardous waste, the Department of Defense, (DOD) and Depart-ment of Energy (DOE) were left to regulate themselves.

Just one month before the Broken Eagle Incident in March of 92, *US News and World Report* ran a cover story on The Nuclear Epidemic. "The West's attempt to prevent the spread of nuclear weapons has failed, and a dangerous new era of nuclear proliferation has begun." The article earmarks North Korea as the latest threat in the world of nuclear wannabees. While it describes the path of uranium through the nuclear power plant to weapons grade pluto-nium, it never comes close to implicating the United States in the creation of the threat or our lead role in the continued proliferation by our own continual treaty violations. Like federal inmates, the nuclear wannabees have no respect whatsoever for this dictator Uncle Sam, who exploits every country he deals with.

In December of '92 *US News* ran a special report on A $200 Billion Scandal "Waste and fraud in the program to clean up the mess at Americas nuclear weapons plants cost taxpayers nearly 40 cents on every dollar spent." The article listed "uncontrolled costs, lax standards, excessive overhead, manage-rial incompetence, contract fraud, contractor coddling and nuclear plant fiefdoms" as the cause. It exposed major contractors from Rockwell to Dupont, showing that the DOE paid out monies they knew were stolen. They paid huge bonuses decided on by the contractors themselves. The story continued to divulge the grand jury indictment of Rockwell that ended in a backroom pay-off, but not before the jury wrote, "For forty years, DOE and corporate officials had engaged in `a continuing campaign of distraction, deception and dishon-esty' as they dumped radioactive and hazardous wastes into the nearby soil and water."

Between my first and second trials *Newsweek* published the cover story of the day, Americas Nuclear Secrets, "Human guinea pigs injected with pluto-nium, Hundreds of undisclosed atomic tests, Tons of toxic waste dumped across the US, How did it happen? What can we do now?" Judge George refused to allow any of that information into my trial. It was irrelevant.

The insidious aspects of media are hard to overestimate. While I wrote this book, *E,* touting themselves as the *Environmental* magazine, ran their tear-jerker cover story, What Killed Collette Chuda? Alongside the cover photograph of an adorable five year old clutching her scruffy pup, "Cancer is a leading cause of death in children: More than 6,000 youngsters will be diagnosed with the disease this year. Collette's parents are convinced that their daughters early death resulted from the witches brew of chemicals that pervade our environment." The lead article, Toxic Shock is a comprehensive expose on the multitude of carcinogens plagueing us. *E* goes on to critique the Environmental Protection Agency, an agency most people believe is a puppet of the very corporations they are assigned to watchdog. While *E* does a commendable job at The E EPA Index, they fail to mention in either article the effects of radiation from the nuclear industry or the military effects on the environment. They too are complicit in the cover-up of the nations number one polluter. Why?

This could be viewed as an innocent oversight. But when you see their three page interview on page 10 with Department of Energy head Hazel O'Leary, now responsible for the nation's nuclear programs, you have to wonder. She's billed as "Clinton's Energy Secretary, she plugs into alternative power and open government while trying to build partnerships with industry and keep the budget cutters at bay." The first page inset, complete with photo of this grandmotherly, silver haired atomic temptress, states "Could the Cold War truly be replaced by Ecotopia Power and Light? Why not?"

On the final page however, grandma's canines are harder to disguise. "We will continue in the design of the next generation of reactors. We will support the international marketing effort by the nuclear industry of the United States. The statistics I see indicate there is a marketplace." ...the bottom line!

I couldn't help but write to *E* and express my concern. I complained, "The concept of `open government' is meaningless rhetoric if no policy change and resulting action occurs. It was fifty years of activism that achieved the present nuclear testing moratorium despite constant lies and opposition from the DOE. Any industry willing to bamboozle the American public for fifty years is capable of seeing when a lie will no longer work. I was saddened to see the Collette Chuda story neglected ionizing radiation as a key factor in childhood deaths.

"The DOE and mainstream media have never allowed us to hear the factually supported studies of Drs. Alice Stewart, John Gofman, Rosalie Bertell, Linus Pauling, Andrei Sokarov, Ernest Sternglas and Helen Caldicott to mention just a few. These studies show conclusively that the radiation inherent in the nuclear industries is killing us all even if the wolf does dress like grandma."

A great phenonmenon exists in America. We have been spoon fed our Constitutional rights in word, while they remain constitutional illusions in reality. The message of the broken eagle is that broken word.

Freedom of Speech is touted as a gift of government rather than God. We are led to believe that speaking the truth as we best perceive it is a blessing adorned by generous rulers of old, our 'founding patriarchy.' In this light, perhaps we should be willing to kill and die for our rights to smell or hear. God gave us vocal chords. What we must have is Responsibility of Speech. We have a responsibility to speak the truth when it needs to be spoken.

The Constitution was founded by a barbarous society that enslaved the African nations while invading and murdering entire countries full of indigenous peoples. It continues around the world today! Ask those Nike employees in Indonesia that are paid $2.20 a day in a country where the livable wage is $4.25 a day.

When Gandhi was asked to join in the writing of a Bill of Human Rights, he responded that we should first write the Bill of Human Duties. The Neville Brothers say, "It's freedom of speech as long as you don't say too much." Freedom of speech in America means you have the right to complain, but freedom of speech just don't mean shit to me. I want freedom from carcinogens. I want freedom from corporate sponsored birth defects. I want the freedom to drink pure water and breathe pure air. I want All My Relations to be well fed, clothed and housed. It is not too much to ask. It is achievable!

We do not have democracy in America any more than the Soviets had communism. Both systems are perverted by governments of special interests. More accurately in America we have a 'Demockery,' a slick form of oligarchy (government by a small group or class). So disgusted is the American citizen with the government charade that over half of America doesn't even vote.

I heard Bill Clinton state during his first campaign for the presidency, "CTB, YES!" and yet three months before the moratorium was to expire he announced as president his intention to resume nuclear testing. And most recently, in his second term, he has approved the boondoggle and scam of "subcritical nuclear tests."

The Declaration of Independence, while clearly stating a citizens duty to "change, alter or abolish any government injurious to life, liberty and the pursuit of happiness," also lists the litany of reasons why the British Crown was denounced. What we never noticed in America is that even though Britain lost the war, the feudal, colonialist mindset remained.

Freedom of the press is as free as money. "For a new king dominates justice in America, a sovereign whose soul is pledged to business and whose heart is geared to profit," says 35 year attorney Gerry Spence. Advertising has become an $88 billion industry—more than the whole country spends on higher education annually.

My personal experience in the courts made a mockery of the sixth amendment. Gerry Spence supports that experience, "Today, justice is no longer tied to the ideals of ordinary people, or grounded in what ordinary people think. Instead, justice is a commodity designed by a hierarchy of judges still dedicated to the interests of power."

Terry Care, an attorney with Hunterton, Naylor Law Associates who assisted William Carrico on my case, divulged a law school story of some significance to us all. His first law school professor began immediately by explaining, "Many of you may think you have come here to study justice. If so, you are in the wrong place; you should be in a divinity school. You are here to study law, which has little to do with justice."

President Reagan appointed over half of the nation's 744 federal judges, including a new chief justice of the US Supreme Court. The profile of these judges is starkly homogeneous; 91.6% are men, 92.6% are white, and 89.6% are Republican. While 60% had between $200,000 and a million, 20% were millionaires. Most came from Ivy League or private law schools and worked for large law firms. As lawyers, they represented numerous corporate clients and many were former prosecutors.

Burt Neuborne, legal director of the ACLU, said, "Americans are less free today than they were a year ago. When the Supreme Court functions not as a vigorous guardian of the individual but as a cheerleader for the government, then individual constitutional rights mean whatever the government wants them to mean."

Spence continues, "Most judges I know are beholden to Power—by that I mean unalterably pledged to the dominant force of the system. . . . In the business of justice, the quality of the judge is the most important factor in any trial—more important even than the composition of the jury....The principal office of the law has not been to discover justice but to preserve power, to hold fast to the status quo."

"The loss of our right to a trial by jury is a classic example of a well kept secret" says Gerry Spence. What is wrong with allowing a jury to decide that an activist acted correctly in following his morals. The court claims that this would be, in essence, a referendum against government policy, which cannot be allowed.

My plane landed at the Arcata Airport in Northern California to a field of hugs ready to fulfill my every wish. The beach. . . I want a barefoot run down Clam Beach. Hobo, thirteen years old at that point, could still outrun and out swim me though I weighed 175 pounds and was in the best shape of my life after three months at a weight pile and half mile track. Hobo was alive and spunky, thanks to the care and feeding of Sue Navy and friends in Colorado and later the Willits family in Northern California. I don't know if she felt me or I felt her, but we were tapped into solar power as it beat on my skin, the sand, the ocean and the pounding waves. We were charged.

Peace Pilgrim summed it up with her statement, "This is the way of peace: Overcome evil with good, falsehood with truth, and hatred with love." Injustice can never justify in kind returned, or we relinquish our free will, succumbing as reactionaries rather than revolutionaries. Peace Pilgrim reminded, "These are laws governing human conduct, which apply as rigidly as the law of gravity."

Gandhi put it succinctly in a 1930 article titled <u>The Duty of Disloyalty</u>. He wrote, "Indeed, loyalty to a State so corrupt is a sin, disloyalty a virtue." The Truth of Orwellian doublespeak has come full circle. "It may be that in the transition state we may make mistakes; there may be avoidable suffering. These things are preferable to national emasculation. Without such suffering it is not possible to attain freedom."

History has proven that all great social changes have occurred through the insistence of small percentages of the population. They say 2% can get 10% moving, and if you have 10%, the masses will follow. The truth of this is indisputable, with less than 2% now ruling America, indeed, the world. But that rule can be changed as swiftly as the Berlin Wall fell and the Soviet Union disbanded. The Hundredth Monkey phenomenon exists. The Hundredth Monkey Project to End Nuclear Testing claimed that besides educating (The Event), walking (the Walk) and acting (The Action), we must "envision and believe in the event as an end to nuclear testing." WE must believe and then act!

It's difficult to accept one's own faults; our tough exteriors hide our soft underbelly, even from ourselves. It's difficult to accept government dysfunction and betrayal, but as Edward Abbey pointed out, "A patriot must always be ready to defend his country against his government."

It is even more difficult to accept betrayal to oneself which of course all betrayal is. It is impossible to overestimate the dysfunction of present world society. We are wandering creatures, lost from the garden. No creature on Earth is as lost from his roots and being as are human beings.

U.S. society is unique. No society in history has been exposed to the phenomenally successful media manipulation which has created a society of rampant neurotic consumers. Our exposure to violence has numbed us to our most basic compassions and respects. Nuclearism is an example of how numb we have become. The tobacco, alcohol, legal and illegal drug industries have nothing to worry about. America has become willing to accept slow suicide for immediate gratification. We are largely unaware of the joy of love, art and play. We are too busy acquiring and protecting our material possessions. As the world suffers, we desperately try to ignore it. As a people we feel whipped and depressed. More and more Americans seek relief in a myriad of drugs.

Prison guards and Nevada Test Site workers perform their jobs solely for the wage. It's good money! The money allows them to build and hide in their personal dynasties. The nuclear scientists on the other hand, are obsessed with their intellect. Like boys fascinated with salt on snails or burning leaves from a magnifying glass they now want to prove their intellectual brilliance. Combine this with a lack of social skills and you have world mayhem. Yet while I deride these professions, I know I would forgive them as cellmates.

But with all the emphasis on the fault of the governments, the corporations, scientists or the media, it is critical that we recognize that **the greatest obstacle to world peace is the 'Peace Movement' itself.** The message of the broken eagle is that we are a broken people *throughout.* While our movement is already fully empowered to succeed, it is our human immaturity that keeps us divided. We berate the US government for violating treaty after treaty, yet peace and environmental organizations violate their own agreements and charters just as often. While corporations fight to gain control of the largest military contracts, the fiefdoms of our movement keep us separated and dispirited, not on purpose but in ignorance. While dictators are installed and assassinated by the CIA, FBI, or DEA, we, in the movement, nurse lifelong grudges against other activists and assassinate their character and projects more effectively than *Time* or *Newsweek* ever could.

Whether you work in congress or Earth First, on the board of General Electric or the International Physicians for the Prevention of Nuclear War, you are a human being in the twentieth century. Betrayal, sex scandals, mud flinging, jealousy, sexism, racism, embezzlement, violence and power struggles are a part and parcel of congress and the so-called 'peace movement.' Because we have chosen a particular path is no indication of our departure, location or arrival. Most of us are still just perusing the spiritual travel literature. Because one can articulate the moral high ground in no indication of ones ability to occupy it. Presidents and activists alike, can espouse the rhetoric of our shared human ideals. . . .and then we go to war, physically, verbally, or emotionally. Racism is not under the proprietorship of a race nor sexism a sex. We are all human beings with our own styles and degrees of dysfunction.

As social change organizations, the peace, environmental and social justice movements rely heavily on volunteers. Money is not supposed to be the motivation of volunteers or even those employed for social change, be it forest, animal, human or antinuclear activism. In fact, Gandhi himself viewed tapas, self-suffering, as redemptive. What has stemmed from the focus on sacrifice rather than money is an intense yet unspoken emphasis on power, status and recognition. But we can't deal with it because it's not supposed to be there. How can you criticize someone who has done so much work for nothing? Capitalism has taught us that responsibility is linked to a paycheck. Every organizer is aware of the flake factor -- two out of three volunteers will not follow through.

Combine this with a new decision making process, consensus, which many social justice organizations attempt to embrace, and what results is struggle and dishonesty in ways that are very difficult to pinpoint and over come. Consensus, in a nutshell is a group decision-making process which attempts to achieve full agreement on issues and decisions by allowing everyone participating to have a voice and a vote. No decisions are reached until all agree. What this often accomplishes is weak and ineffectual actions because some people are not ready for bold and aggressive action.

My personal experience is that consensus is a noble process that is less functional with immature participants than is majority rules. I prefer honest hierarchy to dishonest consensus any day. Consensus does not override outgoing and aggressive human personalities. Consensus is as open to manipulation as is democracy. My experience is that individuals involved in consensus are usually poorly educated in its use. It requires study and practice, which are almost always taken for granted as new organizations assume consensus is a better model. It is better when practiced by people who have invested the time to learn it. When practiced by groups that don't grasp the inherent responsibility, it is less functional, highly time consumptive and less honest. Those that scream the most loudly about process are often the first to violate it. As individuals, raised in American society, we have absolutely no experience in group decision making.

If our successes were enough, the movement would be growing by leaps and bounds. I have seen time and again how individuals come to an organization with naive optimism and quit within a year, dispirited and not willing to waste their time.

This is the message of the Broken Eagle: humanity is broken on all fronts, as children, in intimate relationships, in families, in communities, organizations, corporations and governments. We will not heal until we see this reality. Recognition of our brokenness empowers us to focus on the healing. Like an alcoholic, the first step is to admit that we have a problem.

Family counselor and author John Bradshaw estimates that 94% of Americans are dysfunctional to some degree. This is a conservative estimate. We grew up in the most brain-washed, manipulated society on Earth, the United States of America.. Immersed in hierarchy, patriarchy and capitalism, we are at home in the land of rugged individualism,. . . ME-ism. That is why it is so difficult to organize in such a wealthy country. You do not remove this type of brainwashing as if it were an old t-shirt. It takes discipline. It is a journey -- one worth undertaking!

Nonviolence is the path whereupon real freedom exists. We must undertake to become Ph.D.'s of nonviolence. We must study and teach nonviolence in our schools and in our prisons. Nonviolence is not static, it is active. To say you are nonviolent does not make it so. It is not a place to arrive, it is a life-style. To choose nonviolence is to work so that all others have that choice.

It still is a beautiful world, but many have no chance to see that beauty and that beauty is being degraded daily. It is no longer a matter of just a positive attitude. It is a matter of positive action. In order to act we must fully grasp the present human psyche. John Trudell, one of the leading spiritual philosophers of our day, suggests that we have become a virus on Earth, immersed in a predator mindset. But we can choose to be a part of the infection or antibodies for the cure.

Three months after The Hundredth Monkey Project culminated the United States finally joined in with the world in observing a nuclear testing moratorium. Perhaps ours was The Hundredth Monkey of Events. It was the accumulation of 50 years of activism that halted the lunacy of nuclear detonations. It is critical to note that the Hundredth Monkey philosophy is not based on the importance of the hundredth monkey but on the accumulation of all hundred monkeys.

Is the threat over? Of course not. Eternal vigilance is the price of freedom! Martin Luther King Jr. claimed, "Freedom is never voluntarily given by the oppressor, it must be demanded by the oppressed."

I clearly asked the Ninth Circuit Court of Appeals for *assistance* of counsel in my appeal. They ignored my request and assigned me *representation* of counsel, the distinct difference being your ability to address the court yourself instead of having to speak through your attorney. Accepting representation of counsel is giving power of attorney. They can sign for you, speak for you and handle your money. In court, you cannot speak unless the judge or the attorney ask you to, even if you totally disagree with what your attorney is saying on your behalf. In the case of the public defender's office, you are giving great power over your life to someone you don't know, someone who is an officer of the court and receives a paycheck from the same people who are trying to convict you. In the federal arena, the judges actually appoint the head of the public defender's office themselves.

I learned first hand how the public defenders office can work hand in hand with the prosecutor and judiciary to waste your time and worse; to create Ninth Circuit case law to further disempower common citizens in their efforts to halt corrupt and immoral laws.

In the ninth circuit appeal conclusion Fernandez states, "Springer believed that nuclear bomb testing is dangerous to all humanity, including himself. There is much support for that view. Indeed there is little reason to doubt it...." But in the next paragraph he states, "While we are not insouciant (cheerfully unconcerned) about Springers concerns, we cannot agree with his definition of his obligation to obey the law." His concern, no doubt is that if he did agree with my obligation to obey the law, the nuclear industry would overturn his decision, as they did in the Karen Silkwood case.

After my release I continued my tort claim against the US Marshals, not so much for my own benefit, but as with the woman who testifies at her rape, in the hopes that the crime isn't repeated. I don't want future inmates to lose their legal papers because a US Marshal or a judge feels like it. But as with a Motion for Recusal of a federal judge, the person to decide is the judge whom you complain against. In a tort claim against the Marshals, they themselves decide if you have a valid claim. We have to chose our battles carefully. I decided to focus on a book and let you be the judge.

After prison I was promptly robbed. Somebody smashed into my newly donated VW bus and took my briefcase. Yes, there went my black bag, complete with DayRunner and federal appeal, which consisted of hundreds of pages of research and notes. My medicine bag, precious stones and knick-knacks, which had amazingly made it through the prison gauntlet, disappeared with the briefcase. I learned that your spirituality can't be kept in a bag of trinkets. It's much better kept in your heart. I had some satisfaction that my tatoo was still on my arm (see the back cover)!

The theft was always suspect but the clincher came when the Arcata Police Department called me in to receive my returned property. In excitement, I envisioned what they might have recovered, a loaned mitre saw and some tools, my medicine bag, my DayRunner? Upon arrival, I was told they had to go to their property vault somewhere else, but in an hour the young officer showed up with my anonymously returned property. He handed me one thin plastic card. I looked at it in my hand. Was this a cosmic joke or the federal government's sense of humor? There it was, my Allenwood federal prison inmate ID card, complete with convict photo and my own personal reminder of the Nazi numbering of concentration camp prisoners, Number 27771-048.

After three or four months of sitting at the laptop I realized that my correspondences were not being received and much of my mail was not coming in. Wavy Gravy told me, "It's either the feds or the Gremlins, Rick, but I haven't got anything from you." I asked him why the Gremlins would want my mail?

After a couple of months, I was robbed again of $600 cash. That theft also smacked of government involvement.

The mail tampering was so effective that I checked into the post office to see how I could halt it. My suspicion changed from mere speculation to concrete reality when an Albuquerque postmaster wrote explaining that a federal postal employee was arrested and being prosecuted for mail tampering. The letter asked,"Would you like your mail returned after prosecution?"

Two local postmasters offered no solution whatsoever. I realized that they don't want to get in between the FBI, Secret Service or the persecution of a known dissident. Postmasters like their job, the pay, the security. Three certified mail cards have yet to come back and tracers have never returned either. The one postmaster commented, "I'm sure our government is doing all sorts of things I don't want to know anything about."

Dr. Ernest Sternglas wrote "Since in our society there are so many independent magazines, newspapers, radio stations and news services there is no way to insure absolutely that a determined dissident armed with publicly available government data can be prevented from having his message eventually reach the people. Therefore, the best way to prevent wide dissemination of undesirable information is to destroy the credibility of any individual seeking to reach the public or scientific community at large. In this way the message would either not be transmitted by the wary news media or it would not be believed, especially if it was not reported in sufficient detail."

January 31, 1995

NO U.S. NUCLEAR TESTS EVER, CLINTON PLEDGES *Denver Post*

August, 1996

The City Council of Reno, Nevada unanimously passed a resolution to join the other 4,500 communities worldwide in becoming a Nuclear Free Zone.

July 8, 1996

The World Court International Court of Justice, the highest judicial body in the world, ruled that the complete elimination of nuclear weapons is a legally binding obligation. The President of the court called nuclear weapons "the ultimate evil." On September 10, 1996, by a vote of 158 to 3 the UN General Assembly adopted the text of a Comprehensive Nuclear Test Ban Treaty (CTBT). (see appendix for text)

December 2, 1996

More than 60 retired US admirals and generals issued a statement claiming that our long term policy "must be based on the declared principle of continuous, complete and irrevocable elimination of nuclear weapons." Retired US Air Force General Lee Butler argued that international security would best be served by total nuclear disarmament.

I rest content in the phenomenon that the US Marshals, the federal prosecution, the heads of the media, the Secret Service, and Sergeant Parker, in their hearts, wish us success. They don't believe we can win or change -- they've lost hope -- so they continue to collect their paycheck to slow us down. I am convinced that they want to be proven wrong.

We recognize the power of the force as much as a spoon perceives the taste of food. But unlike the spoon, we have the power to taste it. Eaknath Easwaren states in his book of sacred literature, "God makes the rivers to flow and they tire not, nor do they cease from flowing"

There is absolutely no problem addressing humankind that we can't solve if we focus on the real issues. We can't do that from place of denial. The words are broken. Look at the actions. The problem is not the solution, we have the solutions. This is the message of the Broken Eagle: that which is broken and heals is forever stronger in the broken places. In order to heal, we have to recognize that which is broken and take healing actions. Worship the real eagle, not a crystal one. It is time to unite the international nonviolent spiritual evolution.

HUNDREDTH MONKEY UPDATE *July 1997*

The Cold War is over, they say. You can go back to sleep now. . . . if ever you woke up!

But check this out in your slumber. Not including International Affairs, General Government, Justice, Science, Space and Technology, and not including Veterans' Benefits, **the military percentage of the 1998 Fiscal Budget of the United States is 50.1% or $266 billion.** This figure is $129.4 billion more than all our potential adversaries combined. Education, Training, Employment, and Social Services combined comprise a scant 8.7% or $46 billion (see appendix). But the Cold War is over. . .

America is first in weapons sales...to developing countries, to the Middle East, to areas of conflict...Indeed, **we are the #1 weapons supplier in the world.** The US supplied Somalia and Kenya with 100% of their weapons between 1991 and 1993, 91% of Israel's, 80% of Turkey's, 89% of Egypt's and 75% of the Philippines.' Yet the Cold War is over.

From a media perspective, the Cold War was largely focused on nuclear weapons. I list the party line that 'nuclear weapons are a deterrent to war' as one of the great lies of the century. Still, there are those who believe that we have not used nuclear weapons since Nagasaki. When a man robs a bank, he holds up his gun and demands the till. He didn't pull the trigger, but every court in the nation will convict him of felony use of a weapon in the commission of a crime. Carrying and holding a weapon will add years to a criminal's sentence.

Nuclear weapons are holding nations around the world hostage. The United States maintains a stockpile of over 15,000 nuclear weapons, with over 4,000 on submarines and over 2,000 on bombers. We have detonated over 900 nuclear bombs since Nagasaki, (we call them tests) each poisoning the air, water and Earth with ionizing radiation.

More important than the terror of the loaded gun is the robbery that has taken place. For much of the world, the till has been emptied. We have stolen resources and enslaved nations through the past fifty years of the Cold War. But don't worry, it's over....

On December 9, 1996, the Department of Energy unveiled a controversial plan to burn plutonium in nuclear reactors thereby increasing our potential for proliferation and terrorism, as fissile materials enter the civilian sector. The navy's nuclear waste shipments are still being crammed down Idaho's throat on the edge of a major tributary, the Snake River, thanks to a complicit governor. Lawrence Livermore Labs in California is moving full steam ahead on another government boondoggle, the National Ignition Facility (NIF). The NIF is nearly as stupid as Bush's super-collider in Texas, which we abandoned after the taxpayers were bilked of millions. DOE claims that the NIF has three missions. First on the list is "to play an essential role in accessing physics regimes of interest in nuclear weapons design." In other words, they want to continue developing nuclear weapons. Opponents of the giant laser program refer to it as 'welfare for weaponeers,' as its cost is constantly climbing. The latest estimate is $4.5 billion. To top it, off these projects take funding from clean-up programs at the labs and the Nevada Test Site.

But the most overt threat to the completion of the Comprehensive Test Ban Treaty is what the DOE euphemistically terms "subcritical" nuclear tests. In spite of the clear wording in the CTB text, (included in the appendix) which prohibits "any nuclear weapons test explosion or any other nuclear explosion," the DOE asserts that the "subcriticals" will not violate the treaty. The DOE admits that the tests will involve the use of plutonium-239 and high explosives.

On July 3rd, 1997, as countries around the world are preparing to sign the Comprehensive Test Ban Treaty the United States Department of Energy deto-nated the first nuclear bomb test in five years. Only one in a series of tests, it costs the taxpayers $20 million. It blew up 3.3 pounds of one of the most toxic substances on Earth, plutonium, with 160 pounds of chemical explosives. This test was conducted in spite of a multi-organizational law suit against the entire DOE Stockpile Stewardship Program. The judge hearing the suit declined to submit a restraining order, claiming the tests are a matter of national security. Who or where is our enemy?

It is important to remember that the Cold War is over. The term now is Numb War. It rhymes with Dumb War, if you have a hard time remembering. If it's not clear what's going on then you are indeed Numb. We have been in the Cold War for fifty years. I understand. According to the US Nuclear Weapons Cost Study Project we have been burned for over $4 trillion on nuclear weap-ons since 1940. Remember the Cold War is over -- it's now the Numb War.

A bearded, blond haired man with an old grey muzzled, fawn colored pitbull climbed out of a 1969 Volkswagen bus. "Well, we made it, Hobo." I slapped the side of the VW body like it was a good dog, too.

I looked out across the desert valley at Mercury, the Nevada Test Site. Earth First has a saying, "Nature bats last." No matter what humanity does to Mother Earth, she will recover. She has time without clocks on her side. She will survive human folly!

"Comon' Hobo," I yelled, but remembering she was mostly deaf, I slapped her on the bottom and we trotted off like two old coyotes into the desert. Sixteen-year-old Hobo, still the President of Pitbulls for Nonviolence, got slower but she wouldn't quit. She jogged for the long haul, not wasting an ounce of energy.

We jogged by the sweat lodge frames on the desert slope, site of many past actions. I could hear Corbin praying in the wind. We entered a sandy wash and brushed by the creosote bush. As the branches rubbed across my face, I inhaled deeply, becoming creosote as its essence filled my veins. I gave way in respect to the power of the jumping cholla, steering wide. We weaved between the low peaks and ridges, our hearts beating, lungs gulping. We cruised to a distant peak and began climbing. As long distance runners, we kept pumping in short choppy steps until at the end I was climbing over volcanic rocks with hands and feet.

On top of the mountain, I knelt there again at a pile of rocks, Black Woman Altar. A tortoise shell, crystals, a knife with a peace sign carved in the handle, and a wide variety of prayer offerings were tucked into the rock base and dangled from the pole.

I remembered a story that the black men I had prayed with in prison shared, the story of Shoutin John's Goat. He was the goat that fell in the dried up well. He was stuck down in that well, baa, baa, baa-ing about his problems, the injustice of being stuck down in a well. It didn't take long till those on top didn't want to hear it anymore. They decided that the best thing to do was to fill that well in and stop the noise. They started throwing shovel loads of dirt down that well on top of the goat. But that goat just shook it off and stamped it down. Every time they threw a shovel load in the well, he threw it off and stamped it down. They kept shoveling and the goat kept shakin it off and stampin it down.. And in time that well was all filled in and Shoutin John's goat walked right on out of that well..

I picked up a small doll, from among the rocks of the alter, bleached and dry from the sun. I spoke to doll as if the doll were my daughter. "So, you tell the seventh generation that our people care dearly for this Mother Earth. We are working to preserve your inheritance and we won't stop trying. We will sing the songs, dance the dances, pray the prayers, and walk the sacred path."

I faced into the westerly wind and saw all around me, Shoshone land, the Creators land and behind stood the ghost town of Mercury, Nevada. I yelled, "Excuse Me, United States of America! Stop nuclear testing!"

I heard an eagle screech overhead.

ACKNOWLEDGMENTS

When I originally thought of acknowledgments I thought, 'what a list.' The truth is there are that many people and organizations that have made this book possible. I'll never forget Carrie Dann, the Shoshone woman struggling for the land rights of indigenous people in Nevada when she spoke after a heavy defeat in the US courts. She asked in the face of defeat, "Can we forsake the breast of the Mother that feeds us?" Her answer through tear stained cheeks was a powerful, "Most definitely NOT!"

Can I forget to mention any of those who had a part in this story? They feed me when I'm broke and hand me unsolicited bags of groceries in the co-op parking lot. The homeless people hug me, "You're doing good work, I'm with you, Bro!" My dog Hobo and I are familiar with many friends couches. Other people press hundred dollar bills in my hand while a young native man passed, in the palm of a handshake, a tiny earring of an open palm, the sign of the Global Anti-Nuclear Alliance (GANA) stating, "I hold no weapons." I have to acknowledge the letters of support from Peru, the handkerchief from the hibakusha, (the radiation survivors of Hiroshima/Nagasaki), of Japan, and the VW camper donated after prison? All these things made this book possible.

So many thanks to the music makers; Clan Dyken, Francine and Nymiah, Robert Hoyt, Alice Dimicele, Peg Millet, Joann Rand, Heartbeat, Mr. Jones and the Previous, the Poisoned Squirrels, Michelle Shocked, Richie Havens, John Trudell and all, the organizations; APT, NDE, IITC, FAIR, Citizens Alert, Pace e Bene, and the Shundihai Network, individuals; Corbin and Bill, Phil and Dan Berrigan, Wavy Gravy, the Allenwood Yokefellows. Thanks to Helen Caldicott, Dan Elsberg, Casey Kasem, Oren Lyons, Dr. Frank Lucido, Terry Tempest Williams. . . thanks to all who traveled many miles to testify at my trials.

Ed Berthiaume, slashed with his pen, from prison trash barrels, comics and articles on the nuke issue and prison as well. He has been my most dependable research assistant. Thanks, Ed. Scotty Murdoch, Don McKenzie, Bob King, George Christakis, Rick Lewis, thank you for keeping me strong both in and out of prison.

I remember the people that have read and reread this work and offered constructive criticism. Among them are Sue Navy, Scott Willitts, Rick Levin, Dawn Saxon, Art Bettini, Susan Stansbury, Patsy Givens, Art Bettini, Marcie Cavanaugh, and Lesley Meriwether. Rick Levin laid the manuscript to Page Maker and Eric Brooke of Ion Graphix scanned and layed out all the photos as well as the creation of the jacket cover. Humboldt State University students, Sean Armstrong and Aaron Clegg helped with research. Aaron Clegg and Michelle Wallar impressed me with their grasp of grammar and 'sticktoitiveness' on copy editing.

Thank you to all the organizations in the appendix list because they have continued to send me newsletters in and out of prison when I rarely have a dime to send them. Thank you to Marylia Kelley of Tri-Valley CARES for updates and to all the organizations involved in the Department of Energy lawsuit.

Many thanks to the photographers who share their excellent work to bring the text to life, Caroline Dossche of Belgium, Lisa Law of New Mexico and Linda Putman of Oregon. Special thanks to Jim Laurie of the *Las Vegas Review Journal* for sharing his cover photograph of Reagan and I.

In the bibliography I have listed the many books that I researched again so that I could accurately plagiarize their excellent work. Thanks to Norman Solomon. and Bruce Lincoln. Thanks also to Jim Smith and the Las Vegas Review *Journal* as well as the *Univerisity of Chicago Magazine* for the reprints. Thanks to the Cesar Chavez Foundation for the *Prayer of the Farm Workers Struggle* and Council for a Livable World for your help.

A special thanks to those that provided the finances to see this first edition printed. And then, thank you the reader, many of whom bought this book when it was still just taps on a computer keyboard. The existence of this book represents in the broadest sense, community.

Thank you to my Mother and Father, and my Aunt and Uncle, who gave me the values I hold so dear. Thank you.

Many thanks and much love to Carol, Rose and Sarah Andersen, who lived with and loved me during much of this process. They endured the often painful healing process of the broken eagle and provided me with not just a home but a family.

Thank you to the thousands of individuals who worked on The Hundredth Monkey Project to Stop Nuclear Testing. Now on to total disarmament of which we are fully capable.

For a Healthy Life,

Rick Springer
July, 1997

About the Photographers

Caroline Dossche -- is a Belgian activist/photographer who teaches photography and works in the antinuclear movement. She believes that nonviolent civil resistance can change people, so the world.

Lisa Law -- is the photographer/cinematographer renowned for her book and film: Flashing on the Sixties. With her camera, her participation in social movements from Woodstock to The Hundredth Monkey have created a documentary history of the tribal response to war and nuclearism.

Linda Putman -- has been a peace activist, writer and photographer for 25 years. She is the mother of two sons. She is a member of Oregon Peace Works, who was influential in providing support for Oregon congressman Mike Kopetski and Senator Mark Hatfield and their introduction of the Nuclear Testing Moratorium Act.

Jim Laurie -- is the chief photographer for the Las Vegas Review Journal. Mr. Laurie won the award of excellence in the 50th annual Pictures of the Year Competition sponsored by the National Press Photographers Association for his photo of nuclear foe Rick Paul Springer and former President Ronald Reagan at the National Association of Broadcasters Convention. Of the 1,500 photographers to compete, his winning photograph was one of 25,000 submissions.

CHAPTER NOTES

Page

CHAPTER 4

54 "The highlight of the first meeting was the reading by the Soviet delegate of a statement by SOVIET PRESIDENT MIKHAIL GORBACHEV, addressed to the Conference participants: "I welcome your conference and take this opportunity to state once again the invariability of the Soviet Union's policy aimed at the speediest achievement of a comprehensive nuclear weapon tests ban as a crucial step on the path to a nuclear free world. I confirm our readiness to stop our nuclear tests at any time if the USA does likewise. We are ready to amend the 1963 Treaty so as to convert its limitations into a comprehensive test ban. We call upon other states to support this long ripened decision. I wish success to your Conference for the sake of world community and peace on Earth." - The Test Ban Treaty Conference: Summary of the Proceedings and Analysis Dr. Carolyn Cottam United Nations, New York January 7-18, 1991. Published by The United States Comprehensive Test Ban Coalition

55 All quotes from United Nations delegates and Non-Governmental Organizations taken from the written statements issued by the delegates and organizations themselves and submitted to UN records and the public in attendance. January 7-18, 1991

CHAPTER 7

101 Reagan tours GE plants touting GE as "Calvary riding to rescue." President Reagan: The Role of a Lifetime, Lou Cannon, 1991

101 G.E., as nation's second largest military contractor, builds the detonators for every nuclear bomb in America's arsenal. Unreliable Sources, Martin Lee/Norman Solomon, INFACT 1990

102-108 Remarks by President Ronald Reagan at National Association of Broadcasters' 70th Annual Convention 13 April 1992

104 Lying to press goes back to beginning of republic. thru 200,000 televised acts of violence by 16. Unreliable Sources Lee/Solomon 1990

104 You can say anything you want in a debate and 80 million people hear it. If reporters then document that a candidate spoke untruthfully so what. Maybe 200 people read it." P 127 Unreliable Sources Lee/Solomon 1990

104 "Reporters are puppets." Lyndon Johnson Unreliable Sources Lee/Solomon 1990

104 Military Budget Figures - Council for a Livable World 1997

104 Reagans spend $44 million refurbishing White House. President

Reagan: The Role of a Lifetime   Lou Cannon 1991

104 Millionaires rise during Reagan era from 4,414 in 1980 to 34,944 in 1987. Gap widens between rich and poor. President Reagan: The Role of a Lifetime Lou Cannon 1991

105 Great communicator, Amiable dunce, George Will wondered how anyone so uniformed could reach the top of the American system. President Reagan: The Role of a Lifetime Lou Cannon 1991

105 Reagan invents Star Wars and believe in Armageddon. President Reagan: The Role of a Lifetime Lou Canon 1991

Chapter 8

137-139 Interview with Rick Springer "CBS This Morning" 17 April 1992 CBS

141 In 1980, twenty corporations have over fifty percent of media industry. The Media Monopoly Ben Bagdikian 1983

141 Raytheon, ranked among the 100 largest industrial corporations, had 1991 sales of $9.3 billion with 53.7% of that total for the US government. "The company set new records for sales, earnings and earnings per share for the seventh consecutive year. – with demonstrated strong performance in Operation Desert Storm and important new contract awards, principally the pending order of Patriot fire units and missiles for the kingdom of Saudi Arabia. Additional orders for defense systems in key program areas included: Patriot, Hawk, and Standard Missile-2 surface-launched missiles; Maverick and AMRAAM air-launched missiles; AN/ALQ-184 and AN/SLQ-32 electronic countermeasures systems; naval systems and subsystems including the Seasparrow ship-launched missile system and Trident guidance electronics." Raytheon Company 141 Spring Street Lexington, Massachusetts 02173

142 The monopolistic incest between government, corporations and media was clearly exposed in a 1979 study. Exxon, the worlds largest corporation in 1983... The Media Monopoly, Ben Bagdikian 1983

142 The White House produces 15 to 20 press releases a day. Page 104 Unreliable Sources, Lee/Solomon 1990

143 Lying to the press goes back to the beginning of the republic. P126 38 The much discussed missile gap of the early 1960's turned out to be a hoax. The charge was untrue. The Times editorialized. P 105 Unreliable Sources Lee/Solomon 1990

143 The New York Times, the Washington Post and the LA Times misreported that the Soviet nuclear testing moratorium and policy shift was only a proposal. Unreliable Sources Lee/Solomon 1990

Chapter 9

154 "A long term study that compared the 1900-1949 period with the

1950-1988 period showed the average number of earthquakes of magnitude 6 or more has doubled since nuclear testing started." Gary Whiteford PHD Professor of Geography University of New Brunswick April 1989

154 Mine Blasting Blamed for German Quake East Berlin—An earthquake blamed on blasting in an East German potash mine shook both German states yesterday. ADN said the quake measured 5.5 on the Richtor scale and was triggered by a huge cave in that in turn was caused by miners blasting at the Merkeres, six miles from the borer in West Germany. Hamilton Spectator Newspaper March 1989

Chapter 10

171 "Forty percent of all state prison inmates are unable to read." Americans Behind Bars Who Goes To Prison Pg 12 Edna McConnell Clark Foundation 1993

173 Necessity Defense See Francis Anthony Boyle Defending Civil Resistance Under International Law Also Santa Clara Law Review 1986 Nuclear War, Citizen Intervention and The Necessity Defense

174 The Criminality Of Nuclear Weapons Francis Anthony Boyle Waging Peace Series Nuclear Age Peace Foundation Booklet 27 1990

174 Declaration of Independence July 4 1776

"When in the course of human events, it becomes necessary for one people to dissolve the political bands which have connected them with another and to assume, among the powers of the Earth, the separate and equal station to which the laws of nature and of natures God entitle them, a decent respect to the opinions of mankind requires that they should declare the causes which impel them to separation.

We hold these truths to be self evident: That all men are created equal; that they are endowed by their Creator with certain unalienable rights; that among these are life, liberty and the pursuit of happiness; that, to secure these rights, governments are instituted among men, deriving their just powers from the consent of the governed; that whenever any form of government becomes destructive of these ends, it is the right of the people to alter or to abolish it, and to institute new government, laying its foundations on such principles, and organizing power in such from, as to them shall seem most likely to effect their safety and happiness. Prudence indeed will dictate that governments long established should not be changed for light and transient causes; and accordingly all experience hath shown that mankind are more disposed to suffer while evils are sufferable, than to right themselves by abolishing the forms to which they are accustomed. But when a long train of abuses and usurpations, pursuing invariably the same object, evinces a design to reduce them under absolute despotism, it is their right, it is their duty, to throw off such government and so to provide for their future security.

174 The Way It Is Corbin Harney 1994

174 Chest x-ray equivalents and government exposure levels–No Immediate Danger Prognosis for a Radioactive Earth Dr. Rosalie Bertell 1985

175 Secret Fallout Low level radiation from Hiroshima to Three Mile Island. Ernest Sternglas 1981

175 Media cover-up and distortion of nuclear issues Unreliable Sources A Guide to Detecting Bias in the News Media Martin Lee/Norman Solomon 1990

176-178 All quotes are taken from court transcript, US vs Springer Docket No. CR-S-93-215-PMP(RJJ) October 7, 1993

Chapter 14

222 A $200 billion scandal...Waste and fraud in the program to clean up the mess at America's nuclear-weapons plants cost taxpayers nearly 40 cents on every dollar spent. US News and World Report December 1992

Chapter 16

276 "The McKay Report ended some of my ignorance about life at Attica before the riot. Wages for the inmates of twenty or twenty five cents a day, insufficient toilet paper, rectal searches before and after an inmate saw a visitor, correspondence only with people approved by the authorities. A guard might withhold a letter and not tell either the sender or the intended recipient. Fourteen to sixteen hours a day in a cell, boredom, little productive work.

"On orders from then Governor Rockefeller, the State Police retook the prison...on Monday the 13th , 1971. Their guns cracked and boomed more than 450 times, killing 29 inmates, ten hostages, and wounding 89 others.

"Governor Rockefeller announced that the troops had done a 'superb job.' Their shooting of all ten dead hostages was, he said, justifiable homicide." The Turkey Shoot Malcolm Bell 1985

Chapter 17

296 Prosecution spends an average of four times as much as defense. US Criminal Justice Statistics 1995

297 The US is spending $25 billion on prison construction and prison management with no demonstrable results. America Behind Bars Edna McConnell Clark Foundation 1993

298 In fact more Americans die from smoking each year than alcohol, AIDS, car accidents, murders, suicides, drugs, and fires combined. Nearly all of the 400,000 Americans who will die this year from cancer began smoking as children. Phillip Morris grossed 60.9 billion in 1993 while $5 billion was collected in federal excise taxes. USA Today What would our lives be like? By Del Jones and James Cox 6/94

298 Drugs and Racism stats Americans Behind Bars Edna McConnell Clark Foundation 1993

299   Poverty rates for children are increasing. In just four years from 1989 to 1993 poverty in America rose from 13.1% to 15.1% While 15% of American families are impoverished, 38.7% of female headed households are below poverty level with black female households reaching 49.9% 1996 World Almanac P394

Female headed households earned an average of $13,167 in 1989 compared to $26,887 for male headed households. Summary of Need Assessment prepared for St. Joseph Health System Humboldt County, California

CHAPTER 18

320 The cost of constructing a new bed for inmates is $54,209 and $78,000 for the feds. Every life sentence costs the taxpayers $1.3 million. Americans Behind Bars Edna McConnel Clark Foundation 1993

CHAPTER 19

334 In October, 1990 the criminal justice system employed 1.7 million people nationwide; 547,166 were working in corrections at a total monthly payroll of almost $4.3 billion. From 1979 to 1989 the number of corrections personnel increased by 73 percent. New York City spends $58,000 a year to keep an inmate in jail. Americans Behind Bars Edna McConnell Clark Foundation 1993

336 The Justice Department Asset Forfeiture Fund grew from $26 million in 1986 to $350.6 million in 1994. Source book of Criminal Justice Statistics Page 20 1993

Afterword

340 Only 25% of sentenced offenders have been convicted of a violent crime. Crime 'explosion' is a myth. Opinion USA Today James Austin and Marc Mauer

340 Reefer Madness Atlantic Monthly Eric Schlosser

344 The profile of federal judges is starkly homogenous.   With Justice For None Gerry Spence 1989

351 Military Budget Update Council for a Livable World 110 Maryland Ave NE. Washington, D.C. 20002   202-543-4100

351 Information on the National Ignition Facility. Citizens Watch Tri Valley CARES Citizens Against a Radioactive Environment Editor Mary Lea Kelley Oct. Nov. Dec. 1996

BIBLIOGRAPHY/SUGGESTED READING

BOOKS

Lincoln, Bruce *Authority, Construction and Corrosion* 1994 The University of Chicago Press

American Civil Liberties Union *Human Rights Violations In The United States* Human Rights Watch Dec. 93

Bagdikian, Ben H. *The Media Monopoly* Beacon Press Boston 1983

Barasch, Marc Ian *The Little Black Book of Atomic War* Dell Publishing Co. 1983

Bell, Malcolm *The Turkey Shoot* Grove Press 1985

Bertell, Rosalie *No Immediate Danger Prognosis for a Radioactive Earth* 1985

Boaz, David *The Crisis in Drug Prohibition* The Cato Institute 1990

Bollen, Peter *Nuclear Voices* Highland/Hillside Books 1986

Bonheoffer, Dietrich *The Cost of Dicipleship* MacMillan 1959

Caldicott, Helen *Nuclear Madness* Autumn Press 1978

Cannon, Lou *President Reagan: The Role of a Lifetime* Simon and Schuster 1991

DeToqueville, Alexis *Democracy in America* Charles Gosselin 1835

Easwaren, Eknath *Gandhi, The Man* 1973 Nilgiri Press

Epstein, Samuel *The Politics of Cancer* Sierra Club books 1978

Hershey, John *Hiroshima* Alfred A Knopf 1946

International Physicians for the Prevention of Nuclear War *Radioactive Heaven and Earth* A report of the IPPNW 1991 Apex Paress

Keyes, Ken *The Hundredth Monkey* Vision Books 1982

King, Coretta Scott *The Words of Martin Luther King Jr.* Newmarket Press 1983

Lee, Martin Solomon, Norman *Unrelaible Sources* Lyle Stuart 1990

Selke, William L. *Prisons In Crisis* Indiana University Press 1993

Sharp, Gene *Gandhi as a Political Strategist* 1979 Porter Sargent Publishers, Inc.

Spence, Gerry *With Justice For None* Penguin books 1989

Sternglass, Ernest J. *Secret Fallout: Low Level Radiation from Hiroshima to Three Mile Island* Copyright 1972, 1981

Wasserman, Harvey Solomon, Norman *Killing Our Own* Delta 1982

PERIODICALS AND REPORTS

The Edna McConnel Clark Foundation *Americans Behind Bars* 1993

Hanrahan, John *Testing Ground* Common Cause Magazine January/February 1989

Raytheon Annual Report 1991 141 Spring St. Lexington, Mass. 02173

Robert Aldredge and Virginia Stark *Nuclear War, Citizen Intervention and The Necessity Defense* Santa Clara Law Review 1986

Sierra *Nuclear Nightmare: The Soviet Unions Cold War Legacy* The Magazine of the Sierra Club March April 1992

United Nations Study Series 11 *Disarmament: Economic and Social Consequences of the Arms Race and of Military Expenidtures* New York 1983

Congress of the United States Office of Technology Assessment *The Containment of Underground Nuclear Expolosions* October 1989

US Department of Energy *Announced United States Nuclear Tests July 1945 to December 1990* DOE /NV-209 (Rev.11) January 1991

Arms Control Association *Do We Need Nuclear Testing?* November 1990 Arms Control Today

International Physicians for the Prevention of Nuclear War *Nuclear Weapons: A Report of* April 24, 1992

Cottam, Carolyn *The United States Test Ban Coaltion* *The Test Ban Treaty Conference Summary of the Proceedings and Analysis* United Nations, New York January 1991

Lincoln, Bruce *Upstaging Authority* The University of Chicago Magazine February 1995

American Cancer Society *Cancer: Facts and Figures* 1993

United States Department of Energy (DOE) *Frequently Asked Questions About The Nevada Test Site* June 1991

Cobb, Charles E. *Living With Radiation* National Geographic April 1989

Whiteford, Gary T. PHD. *Earthquakes and Nuclear Testing: Dangerous patterns and Trends* Presented to the United Nations Second International Conference on World Peace Seattle Wash. 14 April 1989

FILMS

Bound by The Wind 1992 Produced and directed by David Brown
Building Bombs 1989 Produced by Mark Mori, Susan Robinson
Distributed by The Video Project
The Bombs Lethal Legacy   1990 Nova Video from PBS
Produced and directed by Paula Apsell
Written by Noel Buchner and Rob Whittlesay
Deadly Deception 1988 Produced and directed by Debra Chasnoff
Written by Dana Coyle
Chernobyl, The Bitter Taste of Wormwood 1987
Produced by NHK Television Written by Films for the Humanities
Three Mile Island Revisited 1992 Produced by EnviroVideo and Green Sphere
Inc. Written by Karl Grossman
Manufacturing Consent, Noam Chomsky and the Media 1994 Necessary Illusions
The Atomic Cafe Produced and Directed by the Archives Project 1982

ADDRESSES OF ORGANIZATIONS, ALTERNATIVE MEDIA AND ACTIVIST MUSICIANS

Nuclear Resister
Jack and Felice Cohen/Joppa
POB 43383
Tucson, AZ. 85733 USA

Shundahai Network
5007 Elmhurst Lane
Las Vegas, Nevada 89108
Phone: 702-647-3095
Fax: 702-647-9385
E-mail: shundahi@radix.net

Pace e Bene
1420 Bartlett
Las Vegas, Nevada 89106
Phone: 702-648-2281

FAIR
Fairness and Accuracy in Reporting
130 West 25th Street
New York, NY 1001
Phone: 212-633-6700
FAX: 212-727-7668

Citizens Alert
POB 1681
Las Vegas, NV. 89125 USA
Phone: 702-796-5662

BAA Bay Area Action
715 Colorado Avenue # 1
Palo Alto, CA. 94303
Phone: 415-321-1994
FAX: 415-321-1995
E-Mail: baaction@igc.apc.org

International Indian Treaty Council
54 Mint St. # 400
San Francisco, Ca. 94103 USA
Phone: 415-512-1501
FAX: 415-512-1507

Survival International
11-15 Emerald Street
London, WC1N 3QL
United Kingdom
Phone: 0171-242-1441
FAX: 0171-242-1771

Alliance for a Paving Moratorium
POB 4347
Arcata, CA. 95518 USA
Phone: 707-826-7775
FAX: 707-822-7007

Alternative Energy Engineering
POB 339
Redway, CA 95560 USA
Phone: 1-800-777-6609
INTL. phone 707-923-2277
FAX: 707-923-3009
http://www.asis.com/aee

Resist:
A Call to Resist Illegitimate Authority
One summer St.
Somervill, MA. 02143
Phone: 617-623-5110

The Lawyers Committee
on Nuclear Policy, Inc.
666 Broadway, Suite 625
New York, NY 10012
Phone 212-674-7790
FAX 212-674-6199

Friends of Peace Pilgrim
43480 Cedar Avenue
Hemet, CA. 92544
Phone: 909-927-7678

FIJA
The Fully Informed
Jury Association
PO Box 59
Helmville, MT 59843

Nukewatch
The Progressive Foundation
POB 649
Luck, WI 54853 USA
Phone: 715-472-4185

National Campaign for A Peace Tax Fund
2121 Decatur Place, NW
Washington, DC 20008

Western Shoshone Defense Project
POB 211106
Crescent Valley, NV 89821
Phone: 702-468-0230
e-mail: wsdp@igc.org

MUSICIANS

A key concept of The Hundredth Monkey Project to Halt Nuclear Testing is that focused music is the most Uniting force on Earth. Indeed, music is known as a universal language. Combined with spiritually and politically focused lyrics, sung with emotional conviction, music can not only bring people together but can empower people to do what must be done. While music too can be corrupted, the bagpipes and drums used in battle for centuries are testimony to its power.

Below is a list of some of the music that makes me stand up straighter when I get tired . You may never hear it on your corporate owned radio stations. I hope it's obvious why. Please buy and check out these tapes of musicians who don't do it because the money's good, but because they are compelled to sing the Truth. I guarantee you will be rewarded.

Clan Dyken
---These eco-rockers combine reggae/rock with spirituality to create the most uplifting and empowering activist music on the west coast. These people are not only great musicians but hard core nuts and bolts, grassroots activists. My favorite albums are Family Values and Shundihai.

> Forward Productions
> POB 145
> Angels Camp, CA 95222 USA
> e-mail mdyken@goldrush.com

Robert Hoyt
---Robert Hoyt is a combination between Woody Guthrie and Leo Kotke. Buy one of his tapes and not only will you but all your children will be singing the songs. Both I'm As American As You and Dumpster Diving Across America are HOT albums.

> Folk-The-Boat
> POB 2355
> Decatur, GA 30031-2355

Mr. Jones and the Previous
For those that made the walk, or wish they could, from Las Vegas to the Nevada Test Site. "In Search of The Hundredth Monkey" written on The 1992 Walk is not only a historic statement but another excellent album to be inspired by the nonsense of nukes. Porch Music is loaded with hot numbers as well!

> The City Limits   Voice Mail 213-896-9587
> POB 7261   e-mail - previous@olywa.net
> Olympia, WA 98057

MY FAVORITE QUOTES

Mahatma Gandhi:

"The first thing you have to learn about history is that because something has not taken place in the past, that does not mean it cannot take place in the future."

"I can say without the slightest hesitation, and yet in all humility, that those who say religion has nothing to do with politics do not know the meaning of religion."

"There are many things for which I am prepared to die but nothing for which I am prepared to kill."

Martin Luther King, Jr.:

"The ultimate measure of a man is not where he stands in moments of comfort and convenience, but where he stands at times of challenge and controversy."

"It is important to see that there are times when a man-made law is out of harmony with the moral law of the universe."

"A doctrine of black supremacy is equally as evil as a doctrine of white supremacy."

" A nation that continues year after year to spend more money on military defense than on programs of social uplift is approaching spiritual death."

"I can't make myself believe that God wants me to hate. I'm tired of violence. And I'm not going to let my oppressor dictate what method I must use. We have a power, a power that can't be found in Molotov cocktails, but we do have a power. Power that can't be found in bullets or guns, but we have a power. It is as old as the insights of Jesus of Nazareth and as modern as the techniques of Mahatma Gandhi."

Dr. Helen Caldicott

"At this point in history, the US has been invested with the responsibility for saving the world. No other country has this opportunity. History has bequeathed the fate of future life on Earth to the American democracy. Will she react in time or not?"

Nelson Mandela

After his incarceration of 27 years, he was elected president of the republic of South Africa. In his inaugural address he said:

"Our deepest fear is not that we are inadequate. Our deepest fear is that we are powerful beyond measure. It is our light, not our darkness that most frightens us. We ask ourselves, "who am I to be brilliant, gorgeous, talented, fabulous?

"Actually, who are you not to be? You are a child of God. Your playing small doesn't serve the world. There's nothing enlightened about shrinking so that other people won't feel insecure around you.

"We were born to make manifest the glory of God that is within us. It's not just in some of us. It's in everyone, and, as we let our light shine, we unconsciously give other people permission to do the same. As we are liberated from our own fear, our presence automatically liberates others."

Frederick Douglass—Black Abolitionist Leader

Those who profess to favor freedom and yet deprecate agitation,
are those who want crops without plowing the ground—
They want rain without thunder or lightening—
They want the ocean without the awful roar of its waters.

This struggle may be a moral one;
or it may be a physical one;
or it may be both moral and physical
but it must be a struggle.
Power concedes nothing without a demand—
It never has and it never will.

Find out just what people will submit to,
and you have found out the exact amount
of injustice and wrong which will be imposed on them
And these will continue until they are resisted
with either words or blows or both—
The limits of tyrants are prescribed by the endurance of those
whom they oppress

Abraham Lincoln Jan 27, 1873

"At what point shall we Americans expect the approach of danger? By what means shall we fortify against it? Shall we expect some trans-Atlantic military giant to step the ocean and crush us at a blow? Never! All the armies of Europe, Asia and Africa combined, with all the treasure of the earth in their military chest with a Bonaparte for a commander, could not by force take a drink from the Ohio or make a track on the Blue Ridge in a trial of a thousand years.

"At what point then is the approach of danger to be expected? I answer, if it ever reach us it must spring up amongst us: it cannot come from abroad. If destruction be our lot, we ourselves must be its author and finisher. As a nation of free men we must live through all time or die by suicide."

Edward Abbey

"A patriot must always be ready to defend his country against his government."

Clan Dyken

Let the air I breath give me the strength
to do the work of the one great spirit
Who animates all the universe from
the smallest creature to the farthest star
Heal, heal, heal these global, heal these global wounds.

Let the water I drink give me the strength
to do the work of the one great spirit
Who animates all the universe from
the smallest creature to the farthest star
Heal, heal, heal these global, heal these global wounds.

Let the fire I make give me the warmth
to do the work of the one great spirit
who animates all the unverse from
The smallest creature to the farthest star
Heal, heal heal these global, heal these global wounds.

Let the Earth I walk give me the strength
to do the work of the onegreat spirit
Who naimates all the universe from
The smallest creature to the farthest star
Heal, heal, heal these global, heal these global wounds.

UPSTAGING AUTHORITY

By Bruce Lincoln

Courtesy of *University of Chicago Magazine* February 1995

The ceremony had gone smoothly. Ronald Reagan was given a crystal statue. His audience responded with warm applause. Then an obscure activist approached the lectern. What happened next is a modern parable of how we grant authority—and to whom.

At the annual convention of the National Association of Broadcasters in Las Vegas, Ronald Reagan was among friends.

"I want to thank you for giving this young fellow his start," he told an appreciative group of media executives, "and for all the other things you do for the country!"

No one in the audience should have been much surprised by anything in the address—a rambling affair in which jokes, flattery, and autobiographical reminisces laid the ground for predictable observations on themes dear the ex-President, his constituency, and his immediate audience: the evils of Communism and drugs, and the ways in which the Bible, the family, radio, television and the movies can help combat them.

This was not a forum for controversy and dissension, but a stage for playing out the ritual of authority—a subtle combination of the right speaker, the right speech and delivery, the right setting and props, the right time and place, and an audience whose historically and culturally conditioned expectations establish the parameters of what is judged "right" in all these instances.

When these crucial givens combine in such way as to produce attitudes of trust, respect, docility, acceptance—even reverence—in an audience, "authority" is the result. Authority depends on nothing so much as the trust of the audience—or the audience's strategic willingness to act as if it had such a trust.

When authority is operating smoothly and efficiently, its effect often obscures this process. When that authority is disrupted—as it was during Reagan's otherwise uneventful appearance at the 1992 broadcaster's convention—those interests collaborating in its support become more easily discernible. *The New York Times* reported the incident as follows:

LAS VEGAS, NEV. APRIL 13 (AP) --
Former President Ronald was jostled but was not harmed

*today when a man walked onto stage where he was speaking
and smashed an honorary crystal shrine, hitting him with its
shards.*

   *After smashing the statue, which had just been given to
Mr. Reagan by the National Association of Broadcasters, the
man tried to speak into the microphone but was grabbed by
Secret Service agents, who threw him to the ground and then
took him away.*

The man in question is one Rick Springer, who was most often identified
in the press as a 41-year-old anti-nuclear activist. Since 1987, he has committed
himself to the work of organizing, raising funds, and speaking out about the
dangers of nuclear tests, in the belief that ending tests is the first step toward
abolishing nuclear weapons altogether. The task has been difficult, and although he is convinced that most people agree with him in a general way,
complacency is widespread and few share his sense of urgency. Finding effective channels through which to spread his message has also been a problem, for
the antinuclear issue is hardly on the agenda of the major media. But in 1990,
he had an idea.

What Springer envisioned was an event mixing music and politics in the
spirit of the Woodstock and Live Aid concerts. Those attracted by the music
could be educated about the issue, and the spectacle would be so impressive as
to insure press coverage, through which the message could be further spread.
For two years, Springer devoted his efforts to realize this idea, predicting that
500,000 people would attend and that "dozens of international speakers and
world-class musical artists" would attend.

Securing such involvement and support proved difficult, however. Of the
120 performers on his original list, only one (Ritchie Havens) agreed to appear.
Established organizations would not commit themselves unless they could see
that all other aspects of the project were firmly in place. Choosing a location
also posed problems. He ultimately opted for a setting as close as possible to the
Nevada Test Site. Insurance proved expensive and permits impossible to obtain. Despite these obstacles, Springer forged ahead and laid plans for a ten-day
extravaganza in April—including the concert, a communal march to the test
site, and a mass protest of government offices in Las Vegas timed for Earth Day.

Gradually, some pieces fell together. Speakers were lined up and bands
booked, although not the top talent he had sought. Finally, 2,000 people gathered in the desert on Friday, April 10: a respectable turnout but far less than
Springer had hoped. There was no national coverage, and even the Las Vegas
paper showed little interest. Other problems were distressing. By monitoring
government radio communications, Springer and his colleagues learned that a
nuclear test was scheduled for April 14, when their own plans called for them

to be approaching the test site. A decision was made to travel to Las Vegas on April 13 to stage a protest at the offices of the U.S . Department of Energy.

Many of the group took part in this action—26 were arrested. Some 500 others, according to plan, began their march to the test site. And, on the same day, across town at the Las Vegas Hilton, the National Association of Broadcasters convened its annual meeting, with 50,000 people from the radio and television industry in attendance.

Springer had been aware of this meeting for months. Off and on, he had thought about how he might call the antinuclear issue to the attention of the NAB, a group that, in his view, "has a deathhold on the media." He made his way to the Hilton alone, holding press credentials (obtained by a friend) that would admit him to the meeting's prime event, and he pondered just what he would do.

Arriving at the Hilton's banquet room, he found a group of 3,000 top media executives listening as NAB President Eddie Fritts presented a crystal eagle and the Association's Distinguished Service Award to Mr. Reagan for his "contributions to broadcasting and the American public." Then, to warm applause, the Great Communicator himself moved to the podium. Meanwhile, off the side, Rick Springer wrestled with his conscience, prayed quietly, and worked up his courage. Finally, at what seemed to him an appropriate moment, he strode forward, slowly and resolutely.

Given his dress, manner, and general appearance, most people took him for a sound technician until he picked up the two-foot-high crystal eagle, raised it over his head, and—in what he later described as the "clearest, most meditative moment in my life"—smashed it to bits. Then he advanced to the podium, displaced Mr. Reagan from the microphone, and spoke four words—"Excuse Me, Mr. President"—before the Secret Service laid him out.

As he was dragged away, Springer was heard to shout: "Help, there's a nuclear bomb test tomorrow." Backstage, he was handcuffed and placed under arrest, then taken to a Las Vegas jail, where he was charged with state and federal offenses. (Last autumn, Springer completed a 13-month prison sentence for destroying public property, interfering with the Secret Service, and failing to surrender.) After a minute or two, President Reagan returned and finished his speech, quipping, "Is he a Democrat, by chance?"

In a subsequent series of interviews, articles, and court appearances, Rick Springer has continued to speak out, and he has had opportunities, not only to speak, but to speak in privileged settings. Among the most interesting of these was his appearance on CBS This Morning, four days after his encounter with Mr. Reagan.

This show, which is seen in two-and-a-half-million households daily, offers a mix of news, opinion, features entertainment, and pleasant chitchat among its regular hosts. Guests are presented for a number of reasons, and in styles that cue the audience on how each one is to be regarded. For example, when FDA Commissioner David Kessler, JD'78, was brought on as the show's first guest, his professional title and official position were emphasized, and co-host Paula Zahn gave him a warm welcome. Springer was treated somewhat differently.

Harry Smith (co-host): Antinuclear activist Rick Springer says he never had any intention of hurting former President Reagan earlier this week. Springer says he just wanted to make a point. Still, the incident startled Mr. Reagan and jolted the Secret Service...

In his introduction, Harry Smith gives basic information, while also signaling caution in different ways—for example, his repeated use of the phrase "Springer says" to preface his guest's characterizations of the incident, in juxtaposition to the reactions of more responsible observers. ("Still the incident startled Mr. Reagan and jolted the Secret Service.") The "activist" would be given an opportunity to speak, but the host, the show, and the network were careful not to offer anything that could be construed as an endorsement of him, his actions, or what he would say.

Smith's first question was reasonably open-ended: "What were you trying to accomplish earlier this week?" Springer seized the opportunity to explain how he hoped to use the NAB convention to alert the country to the realties of nuclear testing. At this point, Smith rapidly changed tack, and began to treat Springer himself as a curiosity or "human-interest" item. His next 11 questions focused narrowly on events at the Hilton, as he tried to steer conversation away from the issue of nuclear testing.

In his answers, Springer struggled to introduce wherever possible items he thought important: the bomb test at the Nevada Test Site, France's decision to discontinue its testing program, his lifetime commitment to nonviolence. Moving to wrap things up, Smith offered one last question, which was, in effect, a call to repent and show remorse.

Smith: Do you have any regrets about what you did this week?

Springer: Well, I certainly must offer an apology to Mr. Reagan. I am very sorry that the Secret Service jostled him in an effort to get me off the stage. I have no regrets as to the fact that I approached the—the podium, and I think that the coverage that I have received due to this act is an excellent example of what it takes to wake up and startle the media and, indeed, the American public, whose apathy is responsible for the continuation of nuclear testing to this day.

When Springer's image vanished from the screen, others joined the conversation, offering their judgments, and cueing their audience on how to regard him.

Smith: Wasn't that interesting?

Zahn: I loved that segment.

Smith: Springer.

Mark McEwen (meteorologist): He could talk. Most of the time you get people like Squeaky Fromme—remember?

Smith: Well, as it turns out, this guy is well-known—I don't know about well-known, but there is lots of tape of him leading nuclear—antinuclear demonstrations and stuff. I mean, that's what this guy is all about. That's—because he was released so quickly and everybody said, "What? Excuse me?"

McEwen: Yeah.

Smith: And so he has a —he has a real track record of pacifism, so.,..

McEwen: I thought that was great. "Do you think your going to jail?" "No I think, they're going to drop the charges," which I thought—I don't know if I would have said that> I'd say, "Oh, please—oh, please—oh, please."

Zahn: But he did apologize for hitting the former president with the shards of glass.

McEwen: Absolutely.

Smith: It's just amazing—just amazing...

Apparently, Rick Springer surprised his hosts and threw them off their script, as can be seen from the mangled syntax with which they offered their reactions. It should be noted that praise of Springer began with the member of the team who enjoys least authority, and thus has the greatest license to express unconventional opinions—the weatherman. Further, specific praises reflect a gendered division: The male host commented on Springer's principles and commitment, the female host on his courtesy, and the boyish meteorologist on his courage and powers of articulation.

In effect, after initially holding him at arm's length, the authorized spokespersons of this widely viewed show bestowed their (partial and guarded) approval of him. And this, in turn, prompted reaction from other quarters.

On April 21, the *Wall Street Journal* ran a particularly aggressive editorial that began by lamenting, "It was predictable, but a bit startling nonetheless, to find Rick Springer staring at us from our TV sets." It went on to depict him in lurid prose as "the latest entry to a special galaxy of media-produced stars—people whose aberrations, disturbances and general aggressions against society have won them fame as 'political activists,'" and to place him in the ranks of "political fanatics prepared to wreak havoc necessary to advance their notions of humanity."

So hysterical is the rhetoric, and so obvious the financial interests being defended, one is tempted to think the *Journal* felt threatened by Rick Springer. But the real target of its ire becomes clear in the editorial's closing swipe: "What would be news," the *Journal* opined, "would be if the producers of a show such as *CBS This Morning* decided that giving a character like Richard Springer a place in the media spotlight wasn't smart or healthy or in the public interests.

That wouldn't simply be news, of course. That would be a miracle."

Beyond any conflict of individuals or debate on issues of policy, plainly evident here is a conflict between stages that goes well beyond the familiar rivalry of print and electronic media. Both possess some authorizing capacity, but insofar as their backers, interests, and audiences diverge, so too do the specific principles of selectivity on which they operate.

Most often, these stages tolerate or ignore one another, but occasionally their differences lead to open conflict, as here, where the Wall Street Journal, an elite organ of and for capital, chastises *CBS This Morning*, a mildly populist middlebrow show, for what it takes to be a characteristically promiscuous and irresponsible act of authorization. The point of the struggle is not just whose speech gets authorized, but more importantly, who does the authorizing and how. In its bitching about "media-created stars," one can hear the *Journal's* displeasure with stars created by other media, and authorized speakers who speak others' interests.

Turning to the broader issue of whether authority in the modern world differs markedly from its ancient counterpart, the evidence at hand convinces me that authority itself remains very much what it always has been: an effect characteristic of strongly asymmetrical relations between speaker and audience, predisposing the latter to defer to the discourse of the former in ways that are often quite uncritical. This notwithstanding, with recent history there has emerged nothing less than a new mode of authority production, the central operation of which is no longer the production of speech, nor it authorization, but rather the production of stages with authorizing capacity.

In this we have moved from the situation of scarcity to one of abundance. The ancient world had relatively few authorized or authorizing places—the Greek Assembly or the Roman Senate, to use two examples. Consequently, each such site commanded the attention and respect of large audiences, sometimes approximating the total population, over very long periods of time. Given their obvious value, control over these sites was tightly managed, usually by an aristocratic oligarchy. Access was severely limited, and competition might be fierce, for the chief problem facing those outside the oligarchy who wished to produce an act of authoritative speech was gaining entry to these few, but extremely potent, workshops of authority production.

In contrast, we now have a large and ever increasing number of stages that are organized by entrepreneurial consortiums as instruments or factories for the mass production (and ongoing reproduction) of the authority effect. With the expansion come specialization, subdivision of markets, and competition among stages, as the controlling interests of each stage (financial, ideological, aesthetic) not only give shape and direction to its activities, but place it in rivalry with other stages that embody or advance other interests.

Success or failure in this competition—which may involve open polemic or more discreet struggles for speakers, audiences, financial backing, favorable reviews, or all of the above—produces a different, and possibly volatile, history for each stage. Some stages rise and others fall, some adapt in order to survive, and whenever one rings down its final curtain, there are others waiting to take its place.

Bruce Lincoln is professor of the history of religions in the Divinity School, with an associate appointment in the Department of Anthropology, at the University of Chicago. Among his earlier books are Discourse and the Construction of Society *(1989) and* Death, War, and Sacrifice *(1991). This article is excerpted and adapted from his latest book,* Authority: Construction and Corrosion *(The University of Chicago Press, 1994). In his book Lincoln employs examples from classical antiquity, medieval Scandinavian law, cold War scholarship, and American presidential politics to analyze the performance—and subversions—of authority.*

September 10, 1996

COMPREHENSIVE NUCLEAR TEST-BAN TREATY

PREAMBLE

The States Parties to this Treaty (hereinafter referred to as "the States Parties"),

Welcoming the international agreements and other positive measures of recent years in the field of nuclear disarmament, including reductions in arsenals of nuclear weapons, as well as in the field of the prevention of nuclear proliferation in all its aspects,

Underlining the importance of the full and prompt implementation of such agreements and measures,

Convinced that the present international situation provides an opportunity to take further effective measures towards nuclear disarmament and against the proliferation of nuclear weapons in all its aspects, and declaring their intention to take such measures,

Stressing therefore the need for continued systematic and progressive efforts to reduce nuclear weapons globally, with the ultimate goal of eliminating those weapons, and of general and complete disarmament under strict and effective international control,

Recognizing that the cessation of all nuclear weapon test explosions and all other nuclear explosions, by constraining the development and qualitative improvement of nuclear weapons and ending the development of advanced new types of nuclear weapons, constitutes an effective measure of nuclear disarmament and non-proliferation in all its aspects,

Further recognizing that an end to all such nuclear explosions will thus constitute a meaningful step in the realization of a systematic process to achieve nuclear disarmament,

Convinced that the most effective way to achieve an end to nuclear testing is through the conclusion of a universal and internationally and effectively verifiable comprehensive nuclear test-ban treaty, which has long been one of the highest priority objectives of the international community in the field of disarmament and non-proliferation,

Noting the aspirations expressed by the Parties to the 1963 Treaty Banning Nuclear Weapon Tests in the Atmosphere, in Outer Space and Under Water to seek to achieve the discontinuance of all test explosions of nuclear weapons for all time,

Noting also the views expressed that this Treaty could contribute to the protection of the environment,

Affirming the purpose of attracting the adherence of all States to this Treaty and its objective to contribute effectively to the prevention of the proliferation of nuclear weapons in all its aspects, to the process of nuclear disarmament and therefore to the enhancement of international peace and security.

Have agreed as follows:

ARTICLE I

BASIC OBLIGATIONS

1. Each State Party undertakes not to carry out any nuclear weapon test explosion or any other nuclear explosion, and to prohibit and prevent any such nuclear explosion at any place under its jurisdiction or control.

2. Each State Party undertakes, furthermore, to refrain from causing, encouraging, or in any way participating in the carrying out of any nuclear weapon test explosion or any other nuclear explosion.

☐ YES! Please send me a copy of
"Excuse Me, Mr. President"
Enclosed is a check or money order for $19.95 plus tax.

☐ Please put me on your mailing list for information about
nuclear issues.

Mail to: **Broken Eagle Press**
             P.O. Box 402
             Arcata, CA 95518

Name_____

Address_____

_____

_____

Phone_____

☐ YES! Please send me a copy of
"Excuse Me, Mr. President"
Enclosed is a check or money order for $19.95 plus tax.

☐ Please put me on your mailing list for information about
nuclear issues.

Mail to: **Broken Eagle Press**
             P.O. Box 402
             Arcata, CA 95518

Name_____

Address_____

_____

_____

Phone_____

☐ YES! Please send me a copy of
"Excuse Me, Mr. President"
Enclosed is a check or money order for $19.95 plus tax.

☐ Please put me on your mailing list for information about nuclear issues.

Mail to: **Broken Eagle Press**
P.O. Box 402
Arcata, CA 95518

Name_____

Address_____

_____

_____

Phone_____

☐ YES! Please send me a copy of
"Excuse Me, Mr. President"
Enclosed is a check or money order for $19.95 plus tax.

☐ Please put me on your mailing list for information about nuclear issues.

Mail to: **Broken Eagle Press**
P.O. Box 402
Arcata, CA 95518

Name_____

Address_____

_____

_____

Phone_____